The Illustrated dBASE III® Plus Book

Russell A. Stultz

Wordware Publishing, Inc.

Library of Congress Cataloging in Publication Data

Stultz, Russell Allen.
    The illustrated dBase III® Plus book.

    Includes index.
    1. dBase III PLUS (Computer program)   2. Data
    base management.   I. Title.
    QA76.9.D3S785   1987   005.75'65   86-29002
    ISBN 0-915381-92-3

ISBN 0-915381-92-3

10 9 8 7 6 5 4 3
8803

All inquiries for volume purchases of this book should be addressed to Wordware Publishing,
Inc., at the above address. Telephone inquiries may be made by calling:

(214) 423-0090

Recommended Learning Sequence

Contents

Contents (Cont.)

Preface

About dBASE III Plus　　This book is the third in a series of *Illustrated* dBASE books. Asthon-Tate's dBASE II, dBASE III, and dBASE III Plus database management software products have been the database standard for microcomputers for most of the 1980's. The dBASE software series is flexible, easy to learn, easy to use, yet powerful.

Although dBASE III Plus has all of the features of dBASE III, the Plus version added a number of new commands and functions. Today, dBASE III Plus is functionally competitive with many established programming languages. However, it is generally agreed that dBASE III Plus is much easier to use than conventional programming languages, because it is designed for non-programmers.

With dBASE III Plus, Ashton-Tate added a series of new menus and prompts, a "screen painter" to assist in the design of display screens, and a number of new commands and functions to make life easier for the database user and application developer.

The computer novice can create a filing system and then write procedures to store, retrieve, edit, and display on-screen menus and user-help information in a matter of a few hours. This is placing the ability to develop custom software in the hands of accountants, marketing and sales people, bankers, and many others.

The dBASE III Plus Documentation　　While the two-volume dBASE III Plus instruction manual is big, heavy, and intimidating, it is comprehensive. However, the bulk makes it hard to use. This book organizes dBASE III Plus information into easy-to-locate modules. It also contains simplified descriptions of each command and function and hundreds of working dBASE III Plus examples that are designed to clarify. You can use these examples as models from which to design your own applications.

About Illustrated Books　　As a classroom instructor of many kinds of microcomputer software applications, I find myself constantly searching for good, authoritative sources of information. This includes books that can help me learn, and that are ready-made to help me teach others. I like books that get at the "heart" of the information fast, that teach principles through practice.

That's how the *Illustrated* series got its beginning; it is designed to provide quick, easy-to-understand, well-illustrated information about an often complicated application.

The Illustrated format lets you find the area of interest quickly. A description, applications, and a step-by-step illustration are provided. This combination gets results. It provides quick answers, and it provides models that help solve real problems. You'll find the *Illustrated Book* approach goes beyond standard documentation and books that treat software theoretically or in broad, and sometimes vague, terms. I'm pleased that the series continues to gain momentum among a diverse group of users including classroom teachers, professional users, students, and "buffs" who are all using "Illustrated Books" to fulfill specific needs of their own. I hope readers continue to enjoy using this series of books as much as I've enjoyed writing it.

Russell A. Stultz

Module 1
ABOUT THIS BOOK

INTRODUCTION

This book describes Ashton-Tate's dBASE III® Plus relational database management software program. It describes how you can use dBASE III Plus in the office and home, and presents detailed information about the many dBASE III Plus commands; each command is accompanied by examples.

The book is designed for a broad range of users. It is for beginning users who wish to learn the dBASE III Plus program from scratch. It is for intermediate and advanced users as a quick reference that contains command examples that work. And finally, it is for the classroom instructor as an instructionally designed dBASE III Plus textbook.

There is one other class of reader for which this book is intended—the experienced dBASE II or dBASE III user. If you are an old hand at using dBASE II or III, you'll find dBASE III Plus to be a functional superset. Most users who have made the move from dBASE II or dBASE III to dBASE III Plus appreciate the new capabilities and speed.

The dBASE III Plus program is a sophisticated piece of software and often appears to be overwhelming to inexperienced computer users. But it's not as bad as it looks. In fact, if you're a beginning user who's not afraid to "mess around" with dBASE III Plus commands, you'll discover in a matter of minutes that dBASE III Plus is really easy to use. You can do useful things by learning only a half-dozen or so commands. The more you use dBASE III Plus, the richer it becomes. After a week or so, you'll begin to feel like a veteran computer user. That's one reason why I like dBASE III Plus. It can be as simple or as powerful as you want to make it.

To prove to yourself how easy dBASE III Plus can be, you might want to jump over to Module 2 and go through the sample session with your computer. Here, you'll actually have dBASE III Plus doing useful things. You'll see how you can have dBASE working for you in a matter of a few hours. The only limitation is imagination, and if you've got enough imagination to be using a computer, then you're exactly the right person to be using dBASE III Plus.

Beginning in Module 2, you're going to encounter many dBASE III Plus commands. At first, they may not be crystal clear, but their usefulness quickly becomes apparent with a little use and practice. They weren't clear to me for the first hour or so, but as I continued to experiment with dBASE III Plus, things began to make sense. So "not to worry," things will clear up for you too, just by using dBASE III Plus.

ORGANIZATION

To fit the broad range of users that this book addresses, the book is organized into small, easy-to-read *modules*. These modules provide descriptions, applications, and illustrations that provide insight to how dBASE III Plus can be used to solve practical, everyday problems. Literally hundreds of examples are presented in the Description, Applications, and Typical Operation sections of the modules.

These examples can be used to design applications of your own. Having working examples that let you experiment with dBASE III Plus commands takes the mystery out of what might otherwise be a technical obscurity. In addition to conducting "hands-on" experimentation, you'll probably find yourself having a lot of fun, because dBASE III Plus is a delightfully "fun" program to operate.

This module provides information about the book and briefly describes what kind of equipment is required to operate the dBASE III Plus program.

With the exception of Modules 1 through 4, most of the modules in this book contain information that pertains to specific dBASE III Plus commands, functions, or families of commands or functions.

Module 2 introduces you to dBASE III Plus. It describes the term *database*, lists dBASE III Plus capabilities and limitations, and walks you through a sample dBASE III Plus session. If you're the kind of person that likes to "dive in," you'll enjoy the sample dBASE III Plus session in Module 2. You'll discover not only how dBASE III Plus commands are used, but you can follow the sample session using your computer.

In addition to actually using some of the basic dBASE III Plus commands, you'll prepare a sample dBASE III Plus program, called *command file* and run it. By the time you've completed Module 2, the power of dBASE III Plus will be apparent because you'll have demonstrated how databases and corresponding command files are prepared and used to solve common, everyday problems.

Module 2 also contains information about dBASE III Plus' full-screen editor, which is used to create and file dBASE III Plus command files. A description of how word processors and pop-up utilties are used to create dBASE III Plus command files is also provided.

Module 3 contains a recommended sequence for learning (or teaching) dBASE III Plus commands. As you work your way through this book, you can check off the modules you've completed. They are arranged in a simple-to-complex sequence, which can be modified to fit any classroom curriculum. If you're a teacher, you may wish to use Module 3 as an aid to curriculum design.

Modules 4 through 60 describe and illustrate the many dBASE III Plus functions. The commands are arranged in alphabetical order for easy reference.

Appendices A through I contain reference information about dBASE III Plus file types, commands, operators, control keys, and a list of terms and definitions.

Appendix I is provided for both classroom and self-teaching situations. It contains dBASE III Plus exercises. If you're a classroom instructor, you may wish to include these exercises in student assignments. If you're learning dBASE III Plus on your own, the exercises are a good way to check your understanding of what you've learned about a command. If you can answer the questions, you're ready to move on to the next module in the learning sequence.

HARDWARE AND SOFTWARE REQUIREMENTS

The dBASE III Plus program operates with the PC- and MS® -DOS operating systems. It also requires an IBM® PC, XT, AT, or compatible microcomputer having 256K or more of random access memory (RAM). Your system should be equipped with two or more floppy disk drives or one floppy disk drive and a fixed disk. You'll also need a printer if you want paper copies of your database reports.

You should also have a CONFIG.SYS file on your DOS disk having the lines:

```
FILES = 20
BUFFERS = 15
```

This sets up your computer for operation with dBASE III Plus. Module 2 describes preparation of this file.

WHAT YOU SHOULD KNOW

You should be familiar with your computer, its keyboard, and the commands available on your operating system which allow you to list a directory of your diskettes (or hard disk), format a disk, and copy, rename and delete files. If you can do these things, you're ready to begin using dBASE III Plus. If you are not familiar with common DOS commands, you may wish to obtain a copy of *The Illustrated MS/PC-DOS Book* from Wordware Publishing, Inc.

Module 2
dBASE III PLUS OVERVIEW

INTRODUCTION

This module describes the term *database*, and presents information about how dBASE III Plus is used to create and apply files of information, or *databases*, to the solution of everyday problems. A description of how the dBASE III Plus program is used to create and manipulate the information within databases is presented as a basis for understanding the many dBASE III Plus commands described in this book. A table of dBASE III Plus capabilities and limitations is also presented.

This module also describes the use of the dBASE III Plus full-screen text editor, which is used to prepare dBASE III Plus procedure (or command) files. Although the dBASE editor is good for creating and editing procedure files, many dBASE users use word processing packages, such as WordStar, or "pop-up" editors, such as Sidekick, to create and modify their files.

WHAT IS A DATABASE?

A database is nothing more than a collection of information that is organized in a predictable, structured way. The structure of a database is graphically represented in Figure 2-1. This database could be an address book database because each record contains information about a different person. For example, record number 1 contains the name, address, city and state information for John Smith.

Figure 2-1   Database Structure

DATABASE			
RECORD NUMBER	FIELD 1 (NAME)	FIELD 2 (ADDRESS)	FIELD 3 (CITY_STATE)
1	JOHN SMITH	1212 MAIN STREET	TAMPA, FL
2	PAUL JONES	321 SOLAR AVENUE	DALLAS, TX
3	J.T. HOOD	PO BOX 176	CAIRO, GA
4	MARY MAXWELL	2017 CLUB DRIVE	SAN JOSE, CA
5	LOIS JACKSON	925 SYCAMORE LANE	PHOENIX, AZ

RECORDS AND FIELDS   A database may contain from 1 to 1-billion records; each record can contain from 1 to 254 fields. The example shows five records, numbered 1 through 5. Each record in the example contains three fields.

FIELD TYPES   The field types used in the example are called "character" fields, because they contain text strings consisting of characters. You can have five different types of fields. These are:

Field Type	Maximum Bytes (or Characters)
Character	254
Date	8
Logical	1
Memo	5000 (or capacity of word processor used)
Numeric	19

Character fields contain text and numbers and are commonly used for things like names, addresses, and part numbers.

Date fields contain dates in the form MM/DD/YY, where MM is the month, DD is the day of the month, and YY is the year. The correct entry for June 15, 1989 is 06/15/89.

Logical fields contain either a "true" or "false" (or "yes" or "no") value. Logical fields are often used to show the status of a record. For example, in an accounting database, you might want to know if a sales transaction record is paid. A true or false value can be used to show whether or not a customer has paid a particular bill.

Numeric fields contain numbers, which are often used in conjunction with other numeric fields to perform calculations. The following list summarizes the types of fields used in dBASE III Plus.

If you wish to enter a large amount of text into a field, you can use what dBASE III Plus calls a *memo* field.

Character	Text strings made up of alphabetical characters, alphabetical characters and numbers, or characters, spaces, and punctuation marks.
Date	The month, day, and year in the form mm/dd/yy.
Logical	.T. for true, .F. for false (Y for yes and N for no) is used.
Memo	This field type allows continuous passages of text or tabular information. During data entry, it is activated by pressing **Ctrl-Home**, and completed by pressing **Ctrl-End**.
Numeric	Numbers (numeric values) which may include decimals; alphabetical characters and internal spaces are not permitted.

dBASE III Plus CAPABILITIES AND LIMITATIONS

dBASE III Plus is quite versatile as you'll quickly see when examining Table 2-1. This table describes system capabilities and limitations.

Table 2-1   Capabilities and Limitations

Description	Capability/Limitation
Maximum fields per record	254
Maximum characters per record	
Standard database file	4,000
Database text file	512,000
Maximum records per database	1 billion
Maximum characters per database	2 billion
Maximum characters per character field	254
Accuracy of numeric fields	15.9 digits
Largest number	1×10 to the $+308$
Smallest positive number	1×10 to the -307
Maximum memory variables available	256
Maximum memory variable bytes	6,000
Maximum files open at one time	15
Maximum database files open at one time	10
(a database file = 2 if memo fields are used)	
Maximum index files per open database file	7
Maximum characters in a command line	254

Note: Values vary with computer hardware and disk capacity.

The specifications are not the whole story. dBASE III Plus' Applications Development Language (ADL), which is used in the preparation of command files written in the sample session, makes dBASE III Plus uniquely powerful. The sample procedure is only a light brush with dBASE commands. You'll learn many, many more by working your way through this book. You'll see that nearly any kind of application can be developed using dBASE. The major limitation is user imagination, and it can be expanded as you explore the power of new commands.

USING dBASE III Plus

How do you get started with the dBASE III Plus program? And how is a database created? How is it used?

The dBASE III Plus program allows database creation, updating, displaying, and printing. It also lets you write command files, which are dBASE III Plus programs (or procedures) prepared to control input, editing, mathematical computations, and screen or paper output. To familiarize yourself with how these functions are accomplished, perform the following sample session with your computer. If you're an impatient user, this activity should satisfy your eager spirit.

GETTING STARTED WITH dBASE III Plus   To use the dBASE III Plus on a two-floppy drive system, you should make a copy of SYSTEM DISK #2 and format a blank data disk for use in drive B. To prepare SYSTEM DISK #1, perform the following steps:

1.   Start your system with a DOS disk in drive A.

2.   Insert the dBASE III Plus SYSTEM DISK #1 in drive B.

3.   Type **SYS B:** and press **Return** to put DOS on the disk.

4. Type **COPY COMMAND.COM B:** and press **Return** to put the DOS command interpreter file on the disk.

You can setup your system to use drive B automatically for all new database and program files. This is accomplished by creating a file named CONFIG.DB on your program diskette. dBASE "looks" at this file when it starts. If the file contains the statement DEFAULT=B, all working files are sent to drive B. This saves you the trouble of typing **B:** in front of all filenames, or typing **SET DEFAULT TO B** after dBASE is started. Use the same creation process that was used to create the CONFIG.SYS file.

NOTE

To eliminate display of the dBASE III Plus ASSIST screen and status line, which tend to get in the way of efficient database use, eliminate the "COMMAND = ASSIST" and "STATUS = ON" lines from the CONFIG.DB file on SYSTEM DISK #2. This lets dBASE display its *dot prompt*, from which most commands are entered in this book.

To start dBASE III Plus on a two-floppy-drive system:

1. Place the SYSTEM DISK #1 in drive A.

2. Type **DBASE** and press **Return**.

3. When prompted, replace SYSTEM DISK #1 with your working copy of SYSTEM DISK #2; then press **Return**.

Hard Disk System   If you have a hard disk system, you must have a proper CONFIG.SYS file on your root menu. If you already have a CONFIG.SYS file, use EDLIN or a word processor that generates ASCII files to add the following two lines:

```
FILES = 20
BUFFERS = 15
```

If no CONFIG.SYS file exists, create one using the COPY command as follows:

1. From the DOS prompt type **COPY CON: CONFIG.SYS** and press **Return**.

2. Enter the following lines, ending each line with **Return**.

NOTE

The <cr> represents **Return**; the ^Z is produced by pressing and holding **Ctrl** while typing **Z**. This key sequence is represented by **Ctrl-Z** in text.

```
FILES = 20< cr>
BUFFERS = 15 ^ Z < cr>
```

3. Notice the "1 file(s) copied" message.

When you turn on your computer, the CONFIG.SYS file configures your system for proper operation with dBASE III Plus. The FILES = 20 command allows 20 files, including the dBASE III Plus program files and your database and command files, to be in use (or open) at the same time. This lets you take advantage of dBASE's ability to have an application work simultaneously with ten different databases in addition to program files. Command files (also called *programs* and *procedures*) contain a series of dBASE III Plus commands that are prepared and used to perform common routines automatically.

The BUFFERS = 15 line speeds up dBASE operation. Buffers are temporary storage locations in your computer's memory. During dBASE operation, data is temporarily stored in memory rather than being written to and read from disk. Memory activity is much faster than inputting and outputting data to and from your disk.

If you have a hard disk system, you can copy dBASE III Plus to your hard drive (usually drive C) with the dBASE INSTALL utility on SYSTEM DISK #1. Install dBASE III Plus on your hard disk as follows:

1. Make a dBASE directory on your hard disk by typing **MD DBASE** and pressing **Return**.

2. Log the new directory by typing **CD/DBASE** and pressing **Return**.

3. Place SYSTEM DISK #1 in drive A; then log drive A with **A: Return**.

4. Type **INSTALL C:** and press **Return**.

5. Follow the displayed prompts until the A> prompt is redisplayed.

NOTE

To eliminate display of the dBASE III Plus ASSIST screen and status line, which tend to get in the way of efficient database use, eliminate the "COMMAND = ASSIST" and "STATUS = ON" lines from the CONFIG.DB file on SYSTEM DISK #2. This lets dBASE display its *dot prompt*, from which most commands are entered in this book.

RUNNING A SAMPLE dBASE III SESSION   When the dot prompt is displayed, dBASE III Plus is ready for a command. Because dBASE is a large program, there's not enough disk space left on your floppy disk for working files. If you are using a floppy-disk PC, you'll want to use drive B as your working diskette. If you created the CONFIG.DB file described above, your files are automatically placed on drive B. If you didn't create this file, type:

    SET DEFAULT TO B:

and press **Return** to direct all commands and files to drive B. If you have a hard-disk system, you can use dBASE without having to use an alternate working disk.

Once you have dBASE in operation and have settled on your working disk, you're ready to create a database structure, or, if one already exists on the working diskette, you can bring it into use and add (called *append*), edit, or delete records.

In the following sample session, you create a database called PHONE. In the following examples, the dot prompt is supplied by dBASE III, so don't type a period. Remember to press **Return** to enter each dBASE command. Where considered helpful, explanatory remarks are provided after command lines.

As with DOS commands, dBASE commands and field names are typed in either lower or upper case. However, if you're trying to match a string within a database field, the exact upper case and lower case is required.

NOTE

dBASE commands are abbreviated by typing the first four characters of the command. For example, DISPLAY can be typed DISP.

1. Create a database called PHONE as follows (don't type the Remarks):

NOTE

Entries are typed and then accepted by pressing **Return**. The field type (Character) is accepted by pressing **Return**. Other types are displayed with the **Spacebar**. Pressing **Return** after typing the width moves you to the next line. If you make a typo, back space and correct it. Pressing **Return** in a blank field name area ends the CREATE function.

NOTE

The period in front of commands represents the dBASE dot prompt and is not typed.

```
                                              Remarks
  . CREATE                                    Creates a new database


    Enter the name of the new file: PHONE     Names database "phone"
    field name        type      width   dec
    ________________________________________

  1  PARTY            Character   30           Field name party, type Character, width 30.
  2  NUMBER           Character   14           Field name number, type Character, width 14.
  3  <cr>             Character                Pressing <cr> in blank field ends creation.


    Input data records now? (Y/N)
```

2. The option to enter information is offered. Typing **Y** lets you enter database information immediately; typing **N** takes you back to the dBASE prompt. For our sample session, let's enter a few records now. To do this, respond to the prompt by typing **Y**. The following display is presented:

```
                                                         Remarks
Record No       1                    First blank record of the database
PARTY      [                       ] Blank field named party; 30 characters long
NUMBER     [              ]           Blank field named number; 14 characters long
```

3. Enter the following information into the party and number fields for five records. Typing the last character of the NUMBER field causes the following record to be displayed. Pressing **Return** when blank Record No. 6 is displayed ends the data entry session and returns you to the dBASE III prompt.

```
        Record No       1
        PARTY      [Smith, John                ]
        NUMBER     [(408) 232-1210]
        -----------------------------------------------
        Record No       2
        PARTY      [Jones, Paul                ]
        NUMBER     [(813) 267-9500]
        -----------------------------------------------
        Record No       3
        PARTY      [Hood, J.T.                 ]
        NUMBER     [(405) 343-1090]
        -----------------------------------------------
        Record No       4
        PARTY      [Maxwell, Mary              ]
        NUMBER     [(214) 232-4545]
        -----------------------------------------------
        Record No       5
        PARTY      [Jackson, Lois              ]
        NUMBER     [(201) 599-6111]
        -----------------------------------------------
        Record No       6
        PARTY      [<cr>                       ] Pressing <cr> ends data entry session.
        NUMBER     [              ]
```

4. Now that you have a database with five records, you can use it to look up phone numbers. dBASE "knows" that you just created the phone database and that it is in use. If you had just started dBASE, you would have to type:

```
. USE PHONE
```

Because it is already in use, you can ignore this step for now.

5. Before you list the database to the screen, you may wish to clear the screen of unnecessary text. This is done with the CLEAR command.

    ```
    . CLEAR
    ```

6. List the database on the screen by typing **LIST** and pressing **Return**.

    ```
    . LIST
    Record#  PARTY                         NUMBER
          1  Smith, John                   (408) 232-1210
          2  Jones, Paul                   (813) 267-9500
          3  Hood, J.T.                    (405) 343-1090
          4  Maxwell, Mary                 (214) 232-4545
          5  Jackson, Lois                 (201) 599-6111
    ```

    If you wish to omit the record numbers from the display, you can use the command:

    ```
    . LIST OFF

    PARTY                         NUMBER
    Smith, John                   (408) 232-1210
    Jones, Paul                   (813) 267-9500
    Hood, J.T.                    (405) 343-1090
    Maxwell, Mary                 (214) 232-4545
    Jackson, Lois                 (201) 599-6111
    ```

7. It may be handy to sort your phone list alphabetically. To do this, we'll sort on the party field to a new database that we'll name ALPHA. Then we'll use this new database and display it to see our list in alphabetical order. Enter the following SORT command:

    ```
                                            Remarks
    . SORT ON PARTY TO ALPHA                Alphabetically sorts the records on the party field
                                            to a new database named "alpha."

      00% Sorted
     100% Sorted            5 Records sorted
    ```

    Notice the message "5 Records sorted." This is dBASE's automatic dialog which tells you what's happening. You may want to suppress the dialog with the command:

    ```
    . SET TALK OFF
    ```

    To turn the dialog back on, use the command:

    ```
    . SET TALK ON
    ```

8. To print our sorted phone list, we can put the alpha database in use and turn on the printer with the SET PRINT ON command. Once on, everything that is displayed on the screen is listed to the printer. To turn off the printer, the SET PRINT OFF command is used. Use the alpha database, turn on your printer, and list the sorted phone list as follows:

```
                                        Remarks
. USE ALPHA                             Puts the alpha database in use.
. SET PRINT ON                          Directs displayed text to the printer.
. LIST OFF                              Lists the database without record numbers.


PARTY                    NUMBER
Hood, J.T.               (405) 343-1090
Jackson, Lois            (201) 599-6111
Jones, Paul              (813) 267-9500
Maxwell, Mary            (214) 232-4545
Smith, John              (408) 232-1210


. SET PRINT OFF                         Turns printing off.
. CLEAR                                 Clears the display screen.
```

9. To conserve disk space, you may wish to return to the original phone database and delete the alpha database. By doing this, you can use the phone database to add new parties and numbers to your phone list. If you need a sorted list, simply repeat the procedure in steps 6 and 7 above. To delete the alpha database, it must not be in use. Therefore, you may clear the in-use condition with the USE command before issuing the ERASE command. Proceed as follows:

```
                             Remarks
. USE                        Closes the active database file.
. ERASE ALPHA.DBF            Erases the alpha database file from your disk.


File has been deleted        dBASE dialog.
```

10. All of the steps described above can be consolidated into a procedure, or *command file*, which is simply a list of the commands used to exercise your database. Procedures eliminate the time required to enter each command individually. They are also good for inexperienced dBASE users, who only need to type a simple command to put a complex procedure to work.

    The MODIFY COMMAND instruction followed by a filename puts dBASE into the file editing mode. In the file editing mode, you can type in your command lines. You may wish to refer to the end of this module to read about dBASE III's full-screen editor, and how word processors, like WordStar, can be used to create database command files. At this point, you can enter the command file editing mode by typing the following command.

<pre>
                                           Remarks
  . MODIFY COMMAND PHONELST   Opens a file named "phonelst"; you're now ready to
                                 begin typing the command file.
</pre>

11. Before creating the procedure, you should be familiar with a few of dBASE's editing keys. These are presented in Appendix D. For now, you can get by with the following keys:

> **NOTE**
>
> Some systems allow use of built-in cursor control keys. However, if they don't work, use the ones shown here. The expression **Ctrl-Key** means that the **Ctrl** key is pressed and held while the designated **Key** is typed. This is like pressing and holding the **Shift** key to type a capital letter.

Arrows	Move cursor in the direction of the arrow.
Ins	Turn the insert function on or off to insert text at the cursor position. When off, text struck over; when on, text is displaced to the right as new text is typed.
Ctrl-N	Insert a line at the cursor position.
Del	Delete the character at the cursor position.
Back Space	Delete word to left of cursor position.
Ctrl-T	Delete the next word.
Ctrl-Y	Delete the line at the cursor position.
Ctrl-W	Write (or save) the command file and end the editing session.
Ctrl-Q	Quit the editing session without saving.

12. In our sample session, we'll combine the commands we used above into a command file that uses our phone database, alphabetically sorts it into the alpha database, lists the alphabetized contents to the printer, clears database use, and then deletes the alpha database.

<pre>
                                           Remarks
  * TELEPHONE LIST PROGRAM   && A line beginning with an asterisk is a remark line;
  * PHONELST   it does not affect command file operation.
  SET TALK OFF   && Turns off dBASE' built-in message dialog.
  CLEAR   && Clears the screen.
  USE PHONE   && Puts the phone database in use.
  SORT ON PARTY TO ALPHA   && Alphabetically sorts on the party field to a database
  *   named alpha.
  USE ALPHA   && Puts the alpha database in use.
  SET PRINT ON   && Activates printer during listing operations.
  LIST OFF   && Lists database to screen and printer; "off" eliminates
  *   record numbers.
  SET PRINT OFF   && Turns printing off.
</pre>

```
USE                       && Closes database in use.
ERASE ALPHA.DBF           && Deletes alpha database that was used for sorting.
SET TALK ON               && Turns dialog back on.
RETURN                    && Closes this command file and returns to dBASE dot prompt.
```

Press **Ctrl-W** to save, or "write," the command file to disk.

13. Run the command file by typing **DO PHONELST** and press **Return**.

14. Once a database is created, it must be maintained. You can edit, add, and delete records. In this portion of our sample session, we'll edit record number 3 by changing the phone number. We'll also add a new record to our database, and we'll delete one.

   a. Edit record number 3 as follows:

```
                                          Remarks
. USE PHONE                           Places the phone database in use.
. EDIT 3                              Displays record number 3 at the top
------------------------------------------- of the screen for editing.

Record No      3
PARTY    [Hood, J.T.                 ]
NUMBER    [(405) 343-1090]
```

Move the cursor down to the number field (press **Dn Arrow** once), and type **(408) 221-3454**. The next record is automatically displayed. Press **Ctrl-W** to save the change and return to the dBASE prompt.

   b. Add a new record as follows:

```
                                          Remarks
. APPEND                              This command displays the next record
------------------------------------------- number, which is 6.
Record No        6
PARTY    [Acme Brick Company    ] Enter the text as shown after the number is
NUMBER    [(512) 960-1415]          typed, record 7 is automatically displayed;
                                    press <cr> to exit the append mode.
```

   c. Delete a record as follows:

```
                               Remarks
. DELETE RECORD 2    Marks record 2 for deletion.
  1  record deleted  dBASE dialog indicates one record marked for deletion.
. PACK               Deletes marked record and resequences following record numbers.
  5  records copied           dBASE dialog indicates the number of records
                              that remain.
```

15. You can quit dBASE by typing **QUIT** and pressing **Return**. If you want to experiment with the full-screen editor commands described in the next paragraph, use the QUIT command later.

USING A WORD PROCESSOR TO CREATE AND TEST COMMAND FILES

Although the dBASE full-screen editor is quite satisfactory for creating most command files, its file size is limited. There are also times when a series of statements are repeated several times within the same command file. At times like this, it's handy to have a word processor's block copy function.

To start the dBASE editor, begin at the dot prompt. Type

. MODIFY COMMAND *myfile.txt*

(or use the short form "MODI COMM *myfile.txt*") and press **Return**. The file *myfile.txt* can be any legitimate one- to eight-character filename with a one- to three-character optional extension. If you don't type an extension, dBASE assumes that the file being edited is a command file and assigns the extension .PRG.

An editing screen is displayed.

```
 Edit: myfile.txt

 ┌──────────────────────────────────────────────────────────────────┐
 │ CURSOR    <-- -->            UP  DOWN    DELETE      Insert Mode    Ins │
 │ Char        ← →      Line    ↑   ↓     Char   Del   Insert line     ^N  │
 │ Word    Home End     Page  PgUp PgDn   Word   ^T    Save ^W Abort Esc   │
 │ Line      ^←  ^→     Find   ^KF        Line   ^Y    Read file       ^KR │
 │ Reformat  ^KB        Refind ^KL                     Write file      ^KW │
 └──────────────────────────────────────────────────────────────────┘
```

You can suppress and redisplay the editing key help information at the top of the screen by pressing **F1**.

Think of the blank screen as a blank sheet of paper—just waiting for you to start typing text. So start typing. If you make a typographical error, back space and retype your text.

If you type beyond the 66th character on a line, an automatic word wrap occurs. If you want to move the cursor, insert or delete characters, words, or lines, or perform other word processing functions, use the control keys on the following page.

To delete a character, you can space over it with the **Spacebar** or press **Del**, which deletes the character at the cursor and closes up text to the right. You can delete an entire line by pressing **Ctrl-Y**. To replace a character, simply move the cursor to it and type the correct character. In word processing, this is called *strikeover*. To insert characters, press **Ins** to go from the strikeover mode to the insert mode. As you type new characters in the insert mode, following text is displaced from left to right. To return to the strikeover mode, simply press **Esc** again.

Operation	Key Sequence(s)
Cursor left	Left arrow/Ctrl-S
Cursor right	Right arrow/Ctrl-D
Cursor up	Up arrow/Ctrl-E
Cursor down	Down arrow/Ctrl-X
Cursor to beginning of previous word	Home/Ctrl-A
Cursor to beginning of next word	End/Ctrl-F
Tab cursor 5 characters to the right	Tab/Ctrl-I
Move screen up	PgUp/Ctrl-C
Move screen down	PgDn/Ctrl-R
End current line; move cursor to beginning of next line	Enter
Turn insert mode on/off	Ins/Ctrl-V
Insert a blank line	Ctrl-N
Delete character at cursor position	Del/Ctrl-G
Delete character to left of cursor	Back Space
Delete next word	Ctrl-T
Delete current line	Ctrl-Y
Saves file and ends editing mode	Ctrl-End/Ctrl-W
Quits without saving file	Esc/Ctrl-Q
Read an entire file into the current file	Ctrl-KR *filename*
Write an entire file to another file	Ctrl-KW *filename*

Once you're through preparing your text file, press **Ctrl-W** (or **Ctrl-End**) and the file is saved under the filename and extension that you assigned. If you decide to throw away the text because it was only a practice session, press **Esc** (or **Ctrl-Q**) to quit without saving. dBASE asks you if you really want to "Abort Editing? (Y/N)." Type **Y** for yes and the dBASE dot prompt is displayed. If you type **N** for no, you can continue editing your file.

USING A WORD PROCESSOR TO CREATE AND TEST COMMAND FILES

Although the dBASE full-screen editor is quite satisfactory for creating most command files, it's file size is limited. There are also times when a series of statements are repeated several times within the same command file. At times like this, it's handy to have a word processor's block copy function.

There are also times when new command files are similar to existing ones. When this is the case, you can make a copy of the existing command file under a new filename and edit the changes with either the dBASE full-screen editor or a word processor, such as WordStar or Sidekick's notepad. Only those word processors that create pure ASCII files are useful. If your word processor creates a binary file, don't use it.

"Pop-up" notepads, like the one in Borland International's Sidekick, are convenient, because you do not have to leave the dBASE III Plus operating environment. You can pop up the editor, make changes to a command file, write the file back to disk, escape from the editor, and run the program.

Module 3
RECOMMENDED LEARNING SEQUENCE

INTRODUCTION

This module provides a checklist of the modules within this book. The checklist is arranged in a simple-to-complex learning sequence. The checklist provides a road map, suggesting where to begin and how to progress through the dBASE commands. You'll start with the fundamental, easy-to-use, and easy-to-understand commands. As your personal knowledge of the fundamental dBASE commands increases, you'll find the advanced commands easier to understand. Within a matter of hours, you'll be using dBASE to solve real problems of your own. You'll find that one of the attractive features of dBASE is that you can do useful things with only a half-dozen or so commands.

If you wish you can study the use and form of dBASE commands by simply reading this book. However, learning by doing is strongly recommended. There's simply no substitute for actually trying out commands on your computer as you read about them. You'll get immediate feedback about how they work and, more importantly, how you can apply them to your own needs.

THE LEARNING SEQUENCE

If you follow the sequence contained in Table 3-1, you'll begin by building a real database of information. You'll start with commands that let you create and use databases. You'll then learn how to add, edit, insert, and delete records, move around within the database, list the database to the screen or printer, and display selected information.

Next you'll learn how to create, store, and use memory variables, which are like temporary "storage bins" in memory. Then you'll learn how to incorporate these commands into command files, which let you save a command sequence in a file for automatic operation. You'll also learn how to design reports for either screen display or hardcopy.

You'll get "sneak previews" of dBASE commands as you work your way through the early modules. In other words, you'll use new commands in conjunction with ones you're learning so that things work properly. When used in command files, the commands are explained so you'll understand their purpose. If you're curious about some of these new commands, you may want to find out more about them by looking them up in the "modules" within this book or in your dBASE manual. You can also review commands by using the built-in dBASE III Plus HELP utility.

By the time you finish this book, you'll have built databases, edited them, written procedures to display menus and prompts, entered data, retrieved information, and designed and produced reports. So if you follow the recommended sequence, you'll have models for dBASE applications that really work.

Once you're finished, you can use these models as a basis for applications of your own. In fact, you may even want to copy some of the practice files, make slight modifications, and then enter and process your own information.

HOW TO GET STARTED

You should recall how you started in the sample dBASE session in Module 2. If you don't, turn back to Module 2 and review it. Use the operating and startup information for the kind of system you have (two-floppy drives or a hard disk system).

Table 3-1   Recommended Learning Sequence Checklist

	Sequence	Command(s)	Module	Page
☐	1	About This Book	1	1
☐	2	dBASE III Plus Overview	2	4
☐	3	Recommended Learning Sequence	3	17
☐	4	QUIT	54	237
☐	5	DIR	27	124
☐	6	RENAME	55	239
☐	7	HELP	39	165
☐	8	CREATE	18	75
☐	9	DISPLAY, LIST, CLEAR	28	126
☐	10	MODIFY STRUCTURE	47	208
☐	11	USE	69	307
☐	12	CLOSE	15	64
☐	13	CLEAR ALL, CLEAR TYPEAHEAD	14	61
☐	14	TYPE	67	301
☐	15	ERASE, ZAP	34	150
☐	16	ASSIST	7	33
☐	17	APPEND	5	23
☐	18	EDIT	32	144
☐	19	BROWSE	10	47
☐	20	EJECT	33	147
☐	21	Interactive Mode (?), RECNO( )	43	185
☐	22	GO, GOTO, GO BOTTOM, GO TOP, SKIP	38	162
☐	23	INSERT, INSERT BEFORE, INSERT BLANK	42	182
☐	24	DELETE, RECALL, PACK	26	119
☐	25	CHANGE	13	59
☐	26	REPLACE	56	241

Table 3-1   Recommended Learning Sequence Checklist (Continued)

	Sequence	Command(s)	Module	Page
☐	27	COPY	16	67
☐	28	CREATE FROM	19	81
☐	29	EXPORT/IMPORT	35	153
☐	30	SORT	61	277
☐	31	INDEX, REINDEX	41	177
☐	32	LOCATE, CONTINUE	45	195
☐	33	FIND, SEEK	36	154
☐	34	STORE, RELEASE, SAVE, RESTORE	62	280
☐	35	SUM (was SUM, TOTAL)	63	287
☐	36	AVERAGE	9	45
☐	37	ACCEPT, INPUT	4	20
☐	38	PRIVATE/PUBLIC	52	230
☐	39	COUNT	17	72
☐	40	MODIFY COMMAND, Developing Command Files	46	199
☐	41	DO	29	132
☐	42	RUN	57	244
☐	43	CANCEL, RETURN	12	54
☐	44	WAIT	70	309
☐	45	SUSPEND/RESUME	64	292
☐	46	PARAMETERS	50	220
☐	47	PROCEDURE	53	234
☐	48	NOTE or *, &&	48	211
☐	49	TEXT, ENDTEXT	65	294
☐	50	Print Statement (?)	51	222
☐	51	AT (@ROW,COL), Positioning Text and Data	8	39
☐	52	SAY, SAY GET, SAY PICTURE, CLEAR GETS, READ	58	246
☐	53	GET, GET PICTURE, CLEAR GETS, READ	37	157
☐	54	DO CASE, OTHERWISE, ENDCASE	30	134
☐	55	IF, ELSE, ENDIF	40	170
☐	56	DO WHILE, EXIT, LOOP, ENDDO EOF( )	31	134
☐	57	SELECT, SET RELATION	59	252
☐	58	JOIN	44	190
☐	59	TOTAL	66	297
☐	60	UPDATE	68	302
☐	61	ASC( ), CHR( )	6	30
☐	62	DATE( ), TIME( )	25	117
☐	63	SET Functions	60	261
☐	64	ON ERROR/ESCAPE/KEY, INKEY( )	49	213
☐	65	CREATE/MODIFY REPORT, REPORT FORM	22	96
☐	66	CREATE/MODIFY LABEL, LABEL FORM	20	84
☐	67	CREATE/MODIFY QUERY	21	90
☐	68	CREATE/MODIFY SCREEN	23	104
☐	69	CREATE/MODIFY VIEW	24	111
☐	70	CALL/LOAD	11	52

Module 4
ACCEPT, INPUT

DESCRIPTION

The ACCEPT and INPUT commands are used in command files. Both are used to display prompts and to pass text or numbers directly from your keyboard to a memory variable. Once text or numbers are typed, pressing **Return** completes the entry.

There's one important distinction between the two commands. The ACCEPT command accepts only character-type variables, while the INPUT command lets you input numeric-type variables.

The form for these commands is:

    ACCEPT 'Type the member ID number ' TO MID

    INPUT 'Enter the membership fee ' TO MFEE

The text within quotes is displayed as a user prompt. The TO MID and TO MFEE statements transfer your typed response to memory variables named MID and MFEE.

If you wish to use an apostrophe (or "single quote") within the user prompt text, use double quotes around the prompt. If you want to use a double quote within the prompt text, enclose the prompt in single quotes. You can also use brackets around prompt text. This is necessary when both single and double quotes are used within the prompt text. Look at the following examples to see how quotes and brackets are used.

    ACCEPT "Type the member's initials " TO MINIT

    INPUT 'Enter the fee or type "0" (zero) and RETURN to Quit ' TO MFEE

    ACCEPT [Type member's name or "X" to exit.] TO MNAME

The space between the last character of the prompt text and the trailing quote is optional, and only used to ensure adequate separation between the text of the displayed prompt and the cursor position.

Using the above lines in a command file results in a display similar to the following.

```
    Type the member's initials _

    Enter the fee or type "0" (zero) and RETURN to Quit _

    Type member's name or "X" to exit. _
```

The typed response to the ACCEPT and INPUT commands is always completed by pressing **Return**. When **Return** is pressed, the typed value is stored to the named memory variable.

APPLICATIONS

The ACCEPT and INPUT statements are excellent ways to allow a user to enter either a character- or numeric-type value to a memory variable. Typed values are used in many ways. A common use is to search for records containing a "match." For example, if you want to find a record containing the name Jones in the NAME field of the active database, you could use the ACCEPT command to store the name to a memory variable. The command might read:

```
ACCEPT 'Enter the name to look up ' TO MNAME
```

There's nothing magic about what you call a memory variable, but it's advisable to use a meaningful "handle." In the preceding example, the memory variable name is the same as the field name preceded by the letter "M" (for "memory"). This is an easy way to remember that the memory variable MNAME is associated with the NAME field. As you work your way through the development of a command file, you can remember what you called the memory variable containing the name value. An ADDRESS field might be associated with MADDRESS, AMOUNT with MAMOUNT, and so on.

TYPICAL OPERATION

In this illustration the ACCEPT and INPUT commands are used in a command file to display prompts and store keyboard inputs to memory variables. Begin at the dBASE dot prompt.

1. Type **MODIFY COMMAND PEOPLE** and press **Return** to use the dBASE editor.

2. Type the following command file. (Don't type explanatory remarks.)

```
                                           Remarks
* PEOPLE.PRG -- Prints information about people.
CLEAR                           && Clears the screen.
SET TALK OFF                    && Turns off dBASE dialog.
?
?                               && Question marks enter three blank lines.
?
? '          ENTER YOUR NAME'   && Displays text within single quotes.
ACCEPT '          AND PRESS RETURN ' TO MNAME  && Stores entry to MNAME.
CLEAR                           && Clears screen.
?
?                               && Enters three blank lines.
?
? '          TYPE YOUR AGE'     && Displays text within single quotes.
INPUT '          AND PRESS RETURN ' TO MAGE  && Stores entry to MAGE.
CLEAR                           && Clears screen.
?
```

```
?                                      && Enters three blank lines.
?
? '          YOUR NAME IS ',MNAME      && Displays text and contents of MNAME.
?                                      && Enters a blank line.
? '          YOUR AGE IS ',MAGE        && Displays text and contents of MAGE.
?                                      && Enters a blank line.
WAIT                                   && Pauses operation until a key is pressed.
CLEAR                                  && Clears screen.
SET TALK ON                            && Turns dBASE dialog back on.
CANCEL                                 && Returns control to dBASE dot prompt.
```

3. Press **Ctrl-W** to write the command file to disk.

4. Run the command file by typing **DO PEOPLE** and press **Return**.

5. Respond to the following screen prompt by typing your name and pressing **Return**.

```
        ENTER YOUR NAME
        AND PRESS RETURN :_
```

6. Respond to the next screen prompt by typing your age and pressing **Return**.

```
        ENTER YOUR AGE
        AND PRESS RETURN :_
```

7. Notice the following display.

```
        YOUR NAME IS ____________

        YOUR AGE IS __
```

   Press any key to continue...

8. Press any key to return to the dBASE dot prompt.

9. When you are finished experimenting, erase the practice file by typing **ERASE PEOPLE.PRG** and pressing **Return**.

10. Turn to Module 52 to continue the learning sequence.

Module 5
APPEND

DESCRIPTION

The APPEND commands are used to add records to the database in use. The command is either issued from the dBASE dot prompt or used as a statement in a command file. The general form of the command is:

APPEND FROM *filename* FOR *expression* TYPE *file type*

A "DELIMITED WITH delimiter/BLANK" clause is also available.

Some forms of the APPEND command include:

APPEND BLANK   Appends a blank record to the bottom of the database

APPEND FROM *filename*   Appends records from another database file. If the filename does not have an extension, place a period at the end of the *from*

APPEND FROM *filename* FOR *expression*   Appends selected records from another database file that matches the expression.

APPEND FROM *filename* TYPE WKS   Appends from a Lotus 1-2-3 worksheet file.

APPEND FROM *filename* DELIMITED   Appends records from a matching text file using comma and quotation delimiters (separation marks) between each character type field. The resulting record might look like this:

"James Sanders", "1201 Lakeview", "Tampa", "FL", "34656"

APPEND   When APPEND is used alone, a screen is displayed that includes the record number, field names, and record lengths, similar to the one shown in the following screen illustration. The record lengths are indicated by a highlighted, or *reverse video*, block which shows you the field boundaries.

```
. APPEND

Record No.      29
NAME       [Phillips, Sara T.      ]
EMPL_ID    [P-1467  ]
EMP_DATE   [04/16/84]
CLASS      [56 ]
```

You can also type **SET DELIMITER ON** which places colons as field boundaries on the display screen. If you like brackets, you can follow the SET DELIMITER ON command with **SET DELIMITER TO "[ ]"**.

If you type **SET CARRY ON** prior to entering the APPEND command, the contents of the last record in the database are "carried" into the present record. The intent of the SET CARRY ON mode is to save the time required to type repetitive information. You can make any necessary changes to field contents and append another record by pressing **Return** or the **Down Arrow** key when the cursor is at the last field of the current record. The **PgDn** and **PgUp** lets you move to the next and previous records. If you want to exit the carry mode, type **SET CARRY OFF** when you return to the dBASE dot prompt.

To enter text into a Memo field, position the cursor to the Memo field and press **Ctrl-Home**. This puts you in dBASE's full-screen editor. Once you type the text, press **Ctrl-End** to move back to the APPEND data entry mask.

To exit the APPEND process, press **Ctrl-W** to write the added records, including the one that is currently displayed. Press **Ctrl-Q** or **Esc** to quit without saving the present record. In the APPEND mode, you can move between fields by using the cursor control keys (see Appendix D).

APPEND BLANK   The APPEND BLANK command adds a blank record to the end of the database in use and positions the record pointer to the new blank record. You can edit the blank record at a later time with EDIT, BROWSE, REPLACE, or from within a command file. Often, the APPEND BLANK command is used within command files; data entry is guided by a set of explanatory prompts. The form for the APPEND BLANK command is:

```
. APPEND BLANK
```

APPEND FROM   The APPEND FROM *filename* command is used to add data from the named database to the one in use. You can create the structure of a new database, using the CREATE command, and fill it from an existing one. The form for the APPEND FROM command is:

```
. APPEND FROM filename
```

If you want to add only a certain class of records, say ones that have Zip codes in the range of 70000 to 79999, use:

```
. APPEND FROM filename FOR ZIP >= 70000 .AND. ZIP <= 79999
```

Each record in the named database is checked. Those records with 70000 to 79999 in the ZIP field are appended to the database in use.

The APPEND FROM command is also used in conjunction with the SDF (System Data Format) clause. This tells dBASE that the FROM file is a standard ASCII (text) format file. It is read into a database as long as the appended fields are equal to or smaller in size than those in the target database. An example of this command looks like the following:

```
. APPEND FROM filename SDF
```

When the records are copied into the database in use, the SDF clause copies the delimiters into the database file. Following are nine records from a database file.

```
1  N-1040       NUT, 1/4 X 1       4.500      12.00
2  B-1040       Bolt, 1/4 SS       0.012       0.29
3  W-1125       Washer, 1/4 SS     0.002       0.05
4  "N-1040","NU T, 1/4 X 1",       4.500      12.00
5  "B-1040","Bo lt, 1/4 SS",       0.012       0.29
6  "W-1125","Wa sher, 1/4 SS",     0.002       0.05
7  N-1040       NUT, 1/4 X 1       4.500      12.00
8  B-1040       Bolt, 1/4 SS       0.012       0.29
9  W-1125       Washer, 1/4 SS     0.002       0.05
```

The above database originally contained records 1 through 3. These three records were copied to a temporary file using:

. COPY TO *filename* DELIMITED WITH "

Records 4 through 6 were then appended to the database using:

. APPEND FROM *filename* SDF

When field lengths of a FROM file are shorter than those of the database being appended, they are "padded" with trailing blanks. If the fields lengths are longer, the characters that won't fit are discarded.

The APPEND FROM command can also be used with the DELIMITED clause. This adds a delimited text file (with the extension .TXT) to the database in use. This type of file is created with an ordinary word processor that produces standard ASCII files. Records 7 through 9 of the above example were appended to the database using

. APPEND FROM *filename* DELIMITED

This tells dBASE that the FROM file is a delimited text file.

THE TYPE CLAUSE   You can append data from several spreadsheet programs. The rows are converted to records, the columns to fields within each record. The TYPE clause specifies the spreadsheet program used.

SDF—Standard Data Format (ASCII) text files

DIF—VisiCalc and SuperCalc spreadsheet files

SYLK—MultiPlan spreadsheet files

WKS—Lotus 1-2-3 spreadsheet files

A series of examples are provided for your examination.

```
. APPEND FROM sales.wks TYPE WKS
. APPEND FROM sales.mp TYPE SYLK
. APPEND FROM sales.sc TYPE DIF
. APPEND FROM sales. SDF
```

APPLICATIONS

There are a number of uses for the APPEND commands. The APPEND command used alone allows the addition of records directly from the keyboard of your computer. The APPEND BLANK command is used to enter an empty record to the bottom of the active database for field entry with the EDIT, BROWSE, or REPLACE commands. The APPEND BLANK command is also used in command files to add new records in conjunction with programmed user prompts. This process is described with the SAY GET commands in Module 58.

The APPEND FROM command is a powerful tool that is often used to build new databases from existing ones. Selected information is added by either using a certain number of fields, or by using the FOR statement as illustrated in the Description section of this module. Finally, the APPEND FROM command is often used to enter ASCII format data files that are appropriately structured into a database. This means that a data file prepared with a word processor, spreadsheet, or even from AutoCAD can be added to a dBASE file.

For example, you can use your word processor to prepare a data file in which fields are separated by commas. The data file should have a .TXT file extension. Be sure your fields are organized in the proper sequence, and their widths are compatible with the field widths of the dBASE database file. If you're using WordStar, use the non-document mode to create a "clean" ASCII file. By clean, we mean one that is void of any special format control characters which are often produced by word processors. Once the data file is created and saved, start dBASE, put your database file in use, and type the command

```
. APPEND FROM filename DELIMITED
```

This adds the records from the word processed data file to the bottom of your database file.

If you are using AutoCAD, be sure you've included all the necessary fields to match the "tags" created with AutoCAD's ATTDEF command. Then create your control file and output the attributes with the ATTEXT command. Once the .TXT file is created, open your matching database file and use

```
APPEND FROM filename.txt SDF
```

TYPICAL OPERATION

In this operation you use the APPEND and APPEND FROM commands in the interactive mode, and the APPEND BLANK command in a command file that requests data entry by displaying prompts. Although you have not encountered the command file design process yet, following along in this exercise provides a brief introduction. Begin at the dBASE dot prompt.

1. Type **CREATE XYZ** and press **Return**. A database-create structure screen is displayed.

2. Type the name, type, and width information as shown; then type **Y** in response to the data entry prompt to input fields as shown.

```
      field name  type       width  dec          Remarks

   1  NAME        Character    20
   2  EXTN        Character     4
   3  MAIL        Character     4
   4  <cr>                                  -Press <cr> to end CREATE.


Record No.        1
NAME        Sergio, Vincent
EXTN        3596
MAIL        84
----------------------------------
Record No.        2
NAME        Bishop, Sam
EXTN        2234
MAIL        430
----------------------------------
Record No.        3
NAME        Collins, Arthur
EXTN        4554
MAIL        323
----------------------------------
Record No.        4
NAME        Harris, Robert
EXTN        3353
MAIL        2230
----------------------------------
Record No.        5
NAME        <cr>
EXTN
MAIL
----------------------------------
```

Press **Return** twice; then type **N** in response to the "Input" prompt.

3. Type **APPEND** and press **Return**; then enter the following record contents.

```
Record No.      5
NAME       Alexander, T.G.
EXTN       1104
MAIL       84

---------------------------------

Record No.      6
NAME       <cr>
EXTN
MAIL

---------------------------------
```

4. Create a new database by typing **CREATE ABC** and press **Return**. A database create-structure screen is displayed.

5. Type the field contents as shown; then type **N** in response to the "input records" prompt.

```
    field name  type      width  dec          Remarks
    ===================================

1   NAME        Character   20
2   EXTN        Character    4
3   <cr>                               -Press <cr> to end CREATE.
```

6. Type **APPEND FROM XYZ** and press **Return**. Notice dBASE dialog indicates "5 records added."

7. Type **LIST** and press **Return** to verify that the name and extension fields have been transferred.

NOTE

In the following steps, a command file is prepared that uses the APPEND BLANK command. The && notation lets you place comments on a command line without being interpreted as part of the command. However, do not type the remarks.

8. Enter the dBASE full-screen editor by typing **MODIFY COMMAND PBX** and press **Return**.

9. Type the following command file. (Don't type the explanatory remarks.)

<u>Remarks</u>

```
* PBX.PRG               && Used to add names and extensions to ABC database.
CLEAR                   && Clears the screen.
SET TALK OFF            && Turns off dBASE III dialog.
USE ABC                 && Puts ABC database in use.
APPEND BLANK            && Adds blank record to bottom of database.
@ 7,20 SAY ' Enter the directory name ' GET NAME   && Displays NAME field data entry prompt.
@ 9,20 SAY 'Enter the phone extension ' GET EXTN   && Displays EXTN field data entry prompt.
READ                    && Reads typed field contents into blank record.
?
?                       && Question marks enter three blank lines.
?
WAIT                    && Pauses operation and displays prompt until a key is pressed.
CLEAR                   && Clears the screen.
CANCEL                  && Returns control to dBASE III dot prompt.
```

10. When the command file is complete, save it by pressing **Ctrl-W**.

11. Run the command file by typing **DO PBX** and press **Return**.

12. Respond to the following screen prompts by entering a name, a four-digit telephone extension, and press any key to return to the dBASE dot prompt.

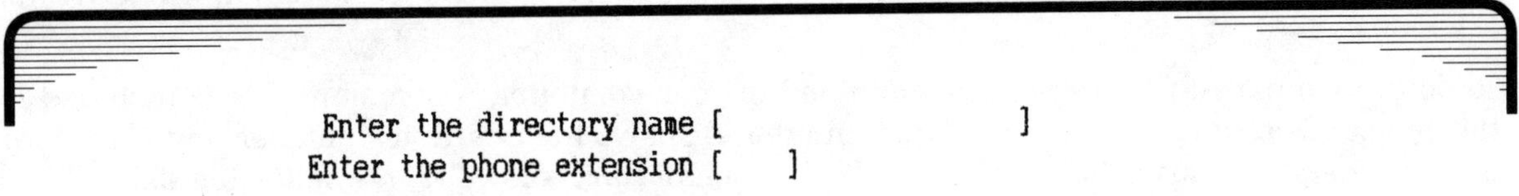

Press any key to continue..._

13. Verify that the name and extension you typed were added to the database by typing **LIST** and pressing **Return**.

14. Type **CLEAR ALL** to close all files. This concludes the APPEND operation.

15. Turn to Module 32 to continue the learning sequence.

Module 6
ASC( ), CHR( )

DESCRIPTION

The ASC( ) function returns the ASCII equivalent of a character within the parentheses. For example, the command:

    . ? ASC('A')

returns the number 65, which is the ASCII code for capital A. The CHR( ) function returns the character equivalent to the ASCII code typed within the parentheses. For example, the command:

    . ? CHR(65)

returns the character A. Let's take a closer look at these handy functions.

CHR( )   If you've ever played with the BASIC programming language, you probably know about the CHR$( ) function, which displays the ASCII character equivalent to the number within parentheses. dBASE's CHR( ) function is similar. On your computer you should find that a CHR(7) outputs a "beep" on the speaker. The standard for a carriage return is CHR(13); a line feed is CHR(10). Special graphic symbols are also displayed using the CHR( ) function. You may want to use these functions in command files to display special symbols or to shade areas within a window.

To determine the ASCII characters contained in your computer, a command file is included in the Typical Operation section of this module that displays the character number and character in your computer. Some forms of the CHR( ) command are shown in the following list.

```
. ? CHR(64)         && Displays the character equivalent to an ASCII
@                      64, which is an at sign.

. ? CHR(75)         && Displays the character K.
K

. STORE 64 TO X     && Stores 64 to the memory variable X.
  64

. STORE 75 TO Y     && Stores 75 to the memory variable Y.
  75
```

```
. ? CHR(X),CHR(Y)        && Displays the character equivalent to an ASCII 64
@ K                         and 75, where memory variables X and Y are used
                            in place of 64 and 75.


. STORE CHR(61)+CHR(61)+CHR(61) TO A       && Stores three ASCII 61
===                         characters to the memory variable A.


. ? A                    && Displays the contents of memory variable A.
===


. STORE CHR(42)+CHR(42)+CHR(42) TO B       && Stores three ASCII 42
***                         characters to the memory variable B.


. ? B                    && Displays the contents of memory variable B.
***


. ? A+B+A+B+A            && Displays the contents of memory variables A and
===***===***===             B in a series. This type of command series can be
                            used in the design of display screens.
```

ASC( ) If you want to check the ASCII code for a certain character, you can use a statement similar to the first example in this module. If several characters are used in the string within parentheses, only the value of the first character is returned. Look at the following command line.

```
. ? ASC('Hello')
72
```

This is the same as using . ? ASC('H').

APPLICATIONS

You can use the CHR( ) function to add special effects to menu screens. You can also use the CHR(7) to cause your speaker to "beep" during data entry or to get attention during command file operation. As shown in the preceding list of examples, the CHR( ) function is also used to store values to memory variables for later use.

There are times when you want to underline printed text. The CHR(13), which is a carriage return (without a line feed), is often used to move the print head back to the beginning of the printed line without causing a line feed. Next, you can space over and print the underline character at the desired location. A simple way to demonstrate this function is to type the following command file and run it.

```
                                         Remarks
    * PRINT.PRG -- Prints a line of text with underlines.
    SET PRINT ON                    && Sends displayed text to printer.
    ? ' Every other word is underlined.',CHR(13),;  && Text within quotes is displayed;
       '____       ___    ________'            CHR(13) is a <cr> without a line feed.
    ?
    SET PRINT OFF                   && Turns simultaneous printing off.
    CANCEL                          && Returns control to the dBASE dot prompt.
```

TYPICAL OPERATION

In this illustration the CHR( ) function is used in a command file that displays all ASCII characters between 1 and 254. Begin at the dBASE dot prompt.

1. Type **MODIFY COMMAND CHR** and press **Return** to use the dBASE editor.

2. Type the following command file. (Don't type the explanatory remarks.)

```
                                      Remarks
    * CHR.PRG -- Displays character set and corresponding numbers.
    CLEAR                    && Clears the screen.
    ? '           CHR  VALUE' && Displays heading.
    X = 1                    && Stores the value 1 to memory variable X.
    DO WHILE X < 255         && Causes continuous operation until X = 255.
    ? X,'    ',CHR(X)         && Displays the value of X and the ASCII character.
    X = X + 1                && Adds 1 to X (increments X by 1).
    ENDDO                    && Ends DO WHILE loop; passes control to the next statement.
    CANCEL                   && Returns control to dBASE dot prompt.
```

3. Press **Ctrl-W** to write the command file to disk.

4. Type **DO CHR** and press **Return** to run the command file.

5. You can pause the display action by pressing **Ctrl-S**. Press any key to resume the display.

6. When you are through with the command file, you may wish to save it for future reference. However, it is not used again in this book.

7. Turn to Module 25 to continue the learning sequence.

Module 7
ASSIST

DESCRIPTION

The ASSIST command provides a system of dBASE III Plus menus and prompts to help the beginning user create, modify, use, and display database files and the information within them. The following screens show the ASSIST menu bar and corresponding selections.

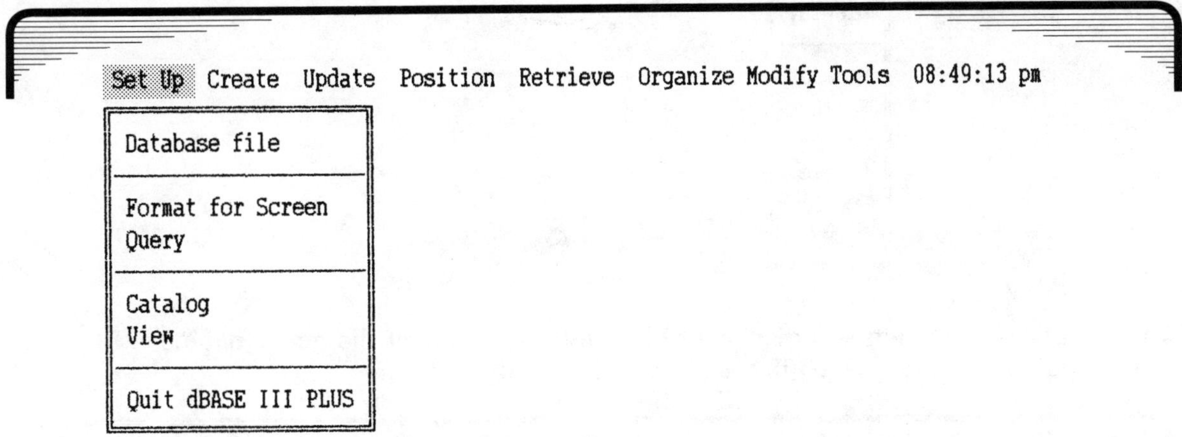

The Set Up menu lets you select the disk drive and database file. You can also select other types of files from this menu, including Query, Catalog, and View files. Finally, it lets you Quit dBASE III Plus.

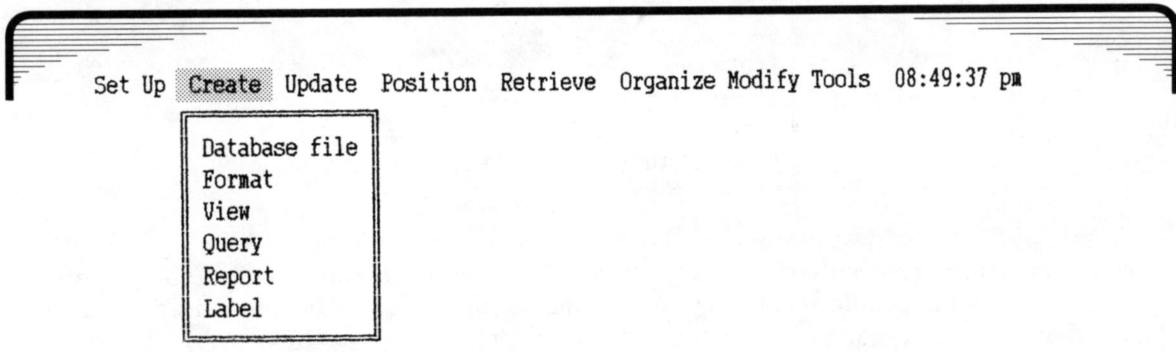

The Create window lets you create a new database file. You can also create format, view, query, report, and label control files. The creation process for each of these file types is described in

Modules 65 through 69. The file creation menus are accessed through ASSIST or by typing the appropriate CREATE command from the dot prompt. For example, CREATE REPORT lets you create a report control file with the extension .FRM. You must place a database file in use before you can create any of these file types.

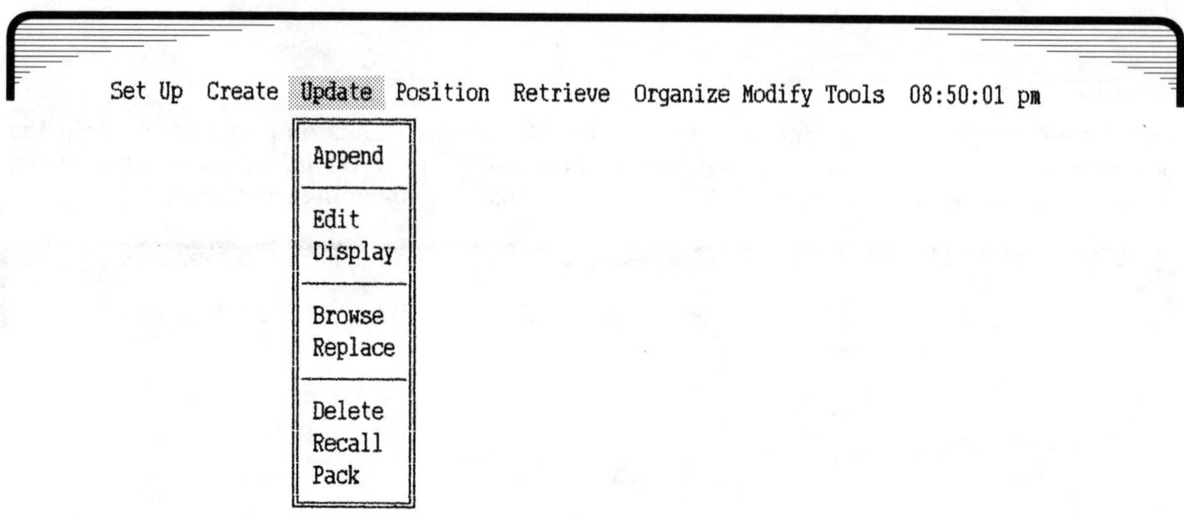

The Update selection lets you display or change the contents of the active database file. Each of the activities are described in their respective modules of this book.

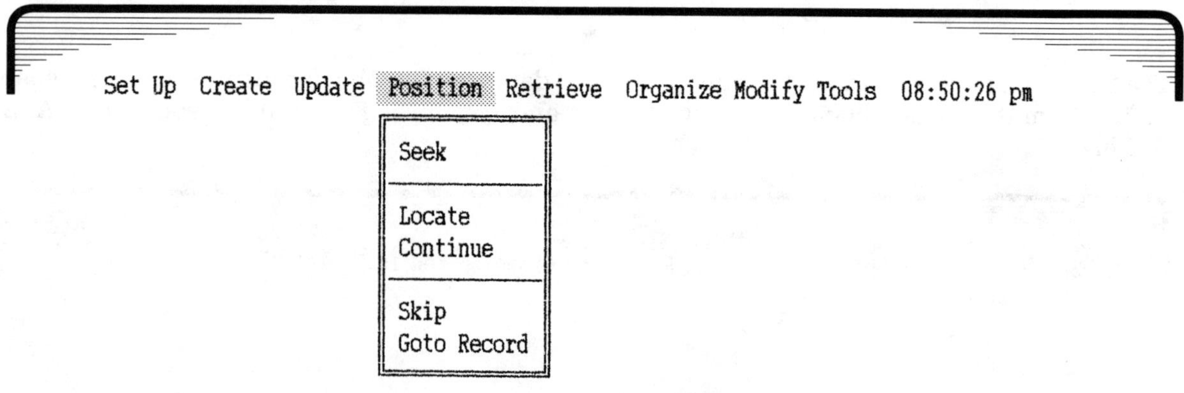

The Position option lets you control the position of the dBASE record pointer. As you can see, you can search out specific records by their contents (using Seek, Locate, and Continue), skip forward or backward a specified number of records, or Goto a specified record number.

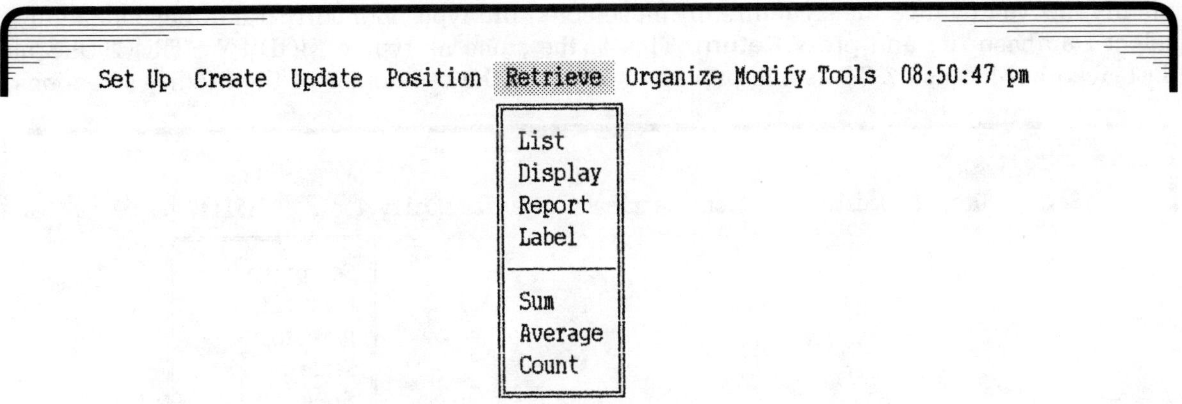

The Retrieve option is used to display certain information. Use of the Report and Label options requires that a report and label file (with the extensions .RPT and .LBL) be present. The creation process for these file types is described in Modules 65 and 66). The Sum and Average options are used to find the arithmetic sum or average of designated numeric fields. The Count function counts the number of records in a database. You can also count the number of records that match a selected parameter.

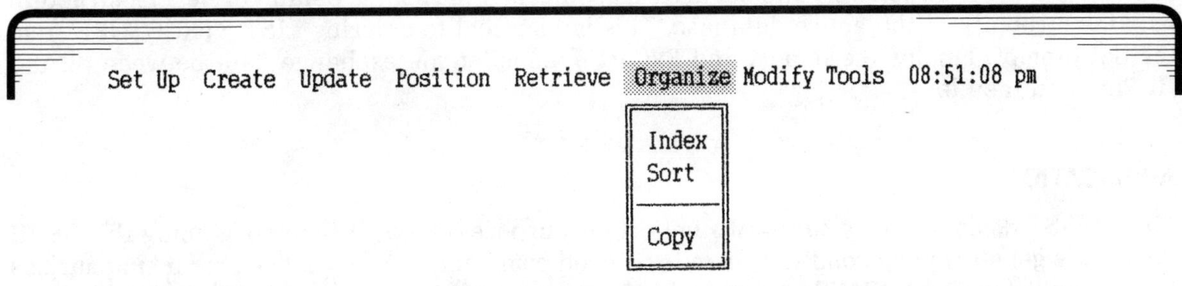

The Organize option lets you perform an alphabetical Sort or Index operation on one or more fields within the database. The Copy operation lets you copy the database file to a new database. The SORT, INDEX, and COPY commands are described in Modules 61, 41, and 16.

Modify lets you change the structure of the selected file type. To modify a database structure, select Database file and press **Return**. This is the same as typing MODIFY STRUCTURE as described in Module 47. The same process is true for the remainder of the Modify selections.

```
  Set Up  Create  Update  Position  Retrieve  Organize  Modify  Tools  08:51:47 pm

                                                    ┌──────────────────┐
                                                    │ Set drive        │
                                                    │ Copy file        │
                                                    │ Directory        │
                                                    │ Rename           │
                                                    │ Erase            │
                                                    │ List structure   │
                                                    ├──────────────────┤
                                                    │ Import           │
                                                    │ Export           │
                                                    └──────────────────┘
```

The Tools option lets you perform a number of DOS-like functions. You can copy, rename, and erase files and list directories. The Set drive selection lets you set the default drive. List structure lists the structure of the active database. This is identical to entering LIST STRUCTURE from the dot prompt. Finally, the Import and Export options let you exchange data between dBASE III Plus and pfs:file.

APPLICATIONS

The ASSIST command may serve two important purposes. First, it helps beginning dBASE III Plus users get started. Secondly, it provides a good command reference, because it summarizes the purpose of many of dBASE's commands. However, as you begin to use dBASE and learn what each command does, you will find that you can perform database operations much more quickly by typing the desired commands directly from the dBASE dot prompt.

TYPICAL OPERATION

In this illustration the ASSIST command is used to select the **MEMBERS** database, last modified in Module 10. Next, the names and addresses for those members with a paid status (Paid = .T.) is listed. Begin at the dot prompt.

1.   Press **F1** and notice that the following screen is displayed.

Set Up Create Update Position Retrieve Organize Modify Tools   08:52:37 pm

```
Database file

Format for Screen
Query

Catalog
View

Quit dBASE III PLUS
```

2.   Use the following keystrokes to place the MEMBERS database in use.

Keystrokes	Result
< cr >	Selects Database file; displays disk drives.
< cr >	Selects active disk drive; displays database files.
Point to MEMBERS.DBF	Selects database to use.
< cr >	Puts MEMBERS.DBF in use.
N	Database not indexed; Set Up window redisplayed.
Right Arrow to Retrieve	Displays Retrieve menu window.
< cr >	Selects List option.
Point to Build a search	Displays field name list.condition < cr >
Point to PAID field	Selects Modify function for use.
< cr >	Selects PAID as a condition for display.
< cr > Point to Construct	Ready to select fields to list.a field list
< cr >	Displays field name list.
< cr > < cr > < cr >	Selects NAME, ADR, and CSZ fields.
Right Arrow, Down Arrow	Selects Execute the command.
< cr >	Displays the selected fields for all PAID records.
< cr > Esc	Takes you back to the dBASE dot prompt.

The results of the above activity is the following display.

```
Record#  NAME                        ADR                     CSZ
      1  Williams, David             3456 Fresno Circle      Tampa, FL 32656

      2  Phillips, George W.         11205 Dawn Drive        Lago Vista, TX 78641
```

The same result is accomplished by typing the following commands from the dot prompt.

```
. use members
. display name,adr,csz for paid
```

As you can see, it is generally much simpler to learn and use commands from the dot prompt than to go through the ASSIST command process.

3.   Turn to Module 5 to continue the learning sequence.

Module 8
AT (@ ROW,COL)
POSITIONING TEXT AND DATA

DESCRIPTION

The @ symbol followed by a row and column position is used to position text or variable values at a specific row and column location on your screen. You can think of @ row,col as "at row number, column number" say something, get a value, or both. The SAY and GET statements, individually or in combination, are used with @ row,col. Some examples of how the @ row,col statement is used follow. The line numbers are for reference only and are not used as part of the command lines.

```
1        @ 7,10 SAY "WHAT'S YOUR NAME? "
2        @ 7,40 GET NAME
3        @ 9,10 SAY "    PHONE NUMBER? "
4        @ 9,40 GET PHONE PICTURE '(999) 999-9999'
5        READ
or

6        @ 7,10 SAY "WHAT'S YOUR NAME? " GET NAME
7        @ 9,10 SAY "    PHONE NUMBER? " GET PHONE PICTURE '(999) 999-9999'
8        READ
```

Line 1 displays the question (or "prompt"), "WHAT'S YOUR NAME?" beginning at row 7, column 10 of the display screen.

Line 2 allows data entry from the keyboard into the NAME field of the database in use beginning at row 7 column 40.

Lines 3 and 4 are similar to lines 1 and 2, except that line 4 makes use of the PICTURE clause, which controls the format of typed information.

Line 5 contains the READ command. This command reads your typed response to the GET statement into the specified field of a corresponding database. For example, GET NAME lets you type a name; READ reads the typed name into the NAME field of the open database file. Of course, the database must be in use for these operations to work.

Lines 6 and 7 are alternate forms of lines 1 through 4, except the exact position of data entry is not controlled. Data entry takes place to the right of the prompts. You can add leading or trailing spaces within the quotation marks following the SAY statement to control horizontal text placement.

Another command, CLEAR GETS, is used in place of READ to prevent data entry. What this command says is, "Keep the GET statements clear." The following example shows how the NAME field is displayed, but protected from data entry, while the PHONE field accepts input.

```
6        @ 7,10 SAY "WHAT'S YOUR NAME? " GET NAME
6a       CLEAR GETS
7        @ 9,10 SAY "    PHONE NUMBER? " GET PHONE PICTURE '(999) 999-9999'
8        READ
```

ROW-COLUMN NOTATION   The row-column notation starts at 0,0, which is the first row and first column. Therefore, rows are 0 to 24 for a 25-line screen, and columns are 0 to 79, which provides for 80-column coverage.

THE PICTURE CLAUSE   The PICTURE clause is used with @ row,col SAY to control the format of displayed and printed information. Look at the following example:

> @ 11,38 SAY AMOUNT PICTURE '$9999.99'

In the balance of this discussion, row and column notation is treated literally; that is, @ 10,20 specifies row 10, column 20. Just remember that they are actually offset by one row and column.

In the previous example, the contents of the AMOUNT field of the active database begins at row 11 column 38. The display includes a dollar sign, four number places (which are controlled by the 9's), a decimal point, and two number places. The value 125.76 is displayed as:

> $ 125.76.

Other forms of the PICTURE clause are described in Modules 37 and 58.

The GET-PICTURE clause is used to control information as it is typed into a database record. Look at the following example.

> @ 12,60 GET FRACTION PICTURE '999/999'

OTHER STATEMENTS   Besides positioning text and fields, there are a number of other uses for the @ row,col statement. Some are described in the remaining paragraphs of this section.

The @ Row,Col SAY CHR(7) Statement   You can use the @ SAY statement with CHR(7) to cause a "beep" on your computer's speaker. For example, the statement:

> @ 12,1 SAY CHR(7)

is used to cause a beep (or "bell") when encountered during command file operation.

The @ Row,Col Statement using @ 10,0 by itself clears row 10 beginning at column 0. This is often used to clear a single line on your screen.

Positioning Memory Variables   You can also control the position of memory variables with the
@ row,col statement. The following command file lines show a memory variable GW being created
and then displayed.

```
STORE 'GEE WHIZZ!' TO GW
CLEAR
@ 12,24 SAY 'The little kid said '+GW
```

This sequence prints "The little kid said GEE WHIZZ!" beginning at row 12 column 24.

Clearing the Screen   You can use the CLEAR command with @ row,col to clear a specific area
of the screen. Some forms of this combination are provided in the following list.

1.   @ row,col CLEAR   This statement clears the screen to the right and below the specified
     row-column coordinates.

```
@ 12,0 CLEAR
```

2.   @ row1,col1 clear to row2,col2   This statement clears a window from row1,col1 (upper-left)
     through row2,col2 (lower-right).

```
@ 3,10 CLEAR TO 12,68
```

Drawing Lines and Boxes   There are three forms of the @ row,col statement used to draw lines
and boxes. These are:

1.   @ row,col SAY REPLICATE(CHR(n),no.)   Repeats (or *replicates*) the specified character (CHR)
     a specified number of times across the screen.

```
@ 5,5 SAY REPLICATE(CHR(196),69)
```

2.   @ row1,col1 TO row2,col2   Draws a box from row1,col1 (upper-left) to row2,col2 (lower-right).
     A single rule is used.

```
@ 9,10 TO 19,69
```

3.   @ row1,col1 TO row2,col2 DOUBLE   Identical to number 2 except a double rule is used for
     the outline of the box.

```
@ 9,10 TO 19,69 DOUBLE
```

SET Statements Used with @ Row,Col   There are several SET statements that are commonly
used with @ row,col. These are summarized in the following list.

SET BELL ON/OFF   To turn off the "beep" when you reach the end of a field, use
                                         SET BELL OFF.

SET DEVICE TO SCREEN/PRINT   Formatted text is routed to your choice of the screen or printer. The default is SCREEN.

SET FORMAT TO *filename*   This command uses a format file with the extension .FMT. When APPEND, CHANGE, EDIT, or INSERT are used, the .FMT file, which contains @ row,col statements, is used to control the prompts and position of data entry. A .FMT file is created with an editor or with the CREATE SCREEN command (See Module 23). An example of a format file follows.

```
* SAMPLE.FMT - Used to enter records into the ABC database.
@  8,20 SAY 'Enter employee name      ' GET NAME
@  9,20 SAY 'Enter employee extension ' GET EXTN
@ 10,20 SAY 'Enter mail station       ' GET MAIL
@ 11,20 SAY 'Enter employment date    ' GET DATE
@ 12,20 SAY 'Enter employee age       ' GET AGE
READ
```

To use this format file, the command SET FORMAT TO SAMPLE is issued. When APPEND, CHANGE, EDIT, or INSERT are used, the active format file controls the data entry mask on the screen.

SET INTENSITY ON/OFF   The system default (normal condition) is ON. This displays half-intensity (or reverse video) text. To eliminate half-intensity, simply enter the command line SET INTENSITY OFF. This works only on computers supporting half-intensity display.

SET SCOREBOARD OFF/ON   Line 22 of your dBASE screen displays file information. You can suppress this line with SET SCOREBOARD OFF.

SET STATUS OFF/ON   Line 0 of your dBASE screen displays dBASE status information. You can suppress this line with SET STATUS OFF.

Storing Row-Column Positions to Memory Variables   You can store screen position numbers to memory variables and use them in place of numbers. For example, you might store 5 to Y as the vertical line position, and 15 to X as the horizontal column position. Then you can use "@ Y,X" instead of "@ 5,15."

You can use a continuous loop in which the row value (Y) is incremented (or increased) by 1 each time a line is displayed or printed. This is accomplished by storing Y + 1 to the present value of Y. In other words, if Y starts out being 5, then 5 + 1 changes the value of Y to 6. By using a DO WHILE loop, this process can continue until the value of Y reaches some predetermined number, like 55. At this point, you can cause a page eject (form feed), reset the value of Y back to 5, and start over on the next page. An example of such a procedure exists in the Typical Operation section of this module.

Field values are displayed in "reverse video" (black on a white background) when @ GET is used. If you wish to eliminate this effect, you can add SET INTENSITY OFF to your command file or type it at the dBASE dot prompt.

APPLICATIONS

As you can see from the examples, @ SAY is a powerful formatting tool. It is used to position text on either the screen or printer. The SET FORMAT TO PRINT routes data to the printer; SET FORMAT TO SCREEN routes the same data to the screen. You can use @ row,col SAY to format lists, mailing labels, reports, or any other information from database fields or memory variables.

TYPICAL OPERATION

In the following illustration @ row,col SAY is used in a command file that uses the ABC database created in Module 10 and modified in Module 56. Begin at the dBASE prompt.

1. Type **MODIFY COMMAND PHDIR** and press **Return** to use the dBASE editor.
2. Type the following command file. (Don't type the explanatory remarks.)

```
                                  Remarks
* PHDIR.PRG -- Lists all records in the ABC database.
CLEAR                   && Clears screen.
SET TALK OFF            && Turns off dBASE dialog.
*                       && The following five lines display the text in quotes at the
                           indicated row and column numbers.
*
@  7,20 SAY 'THIS PROGRAM PRINTS A TELEPHONE LIST.'
@  9,20 SAY 'BE SURE YOUR PRINTER IS READY.'
@ 11,20 SAY 'PRESS P TO PRINT THE LIST, OR'
@ 13,20 SAY 'PRESS Q TO QUIT.'
WAIT ' ' TO CHOICE      && Pauses operation; stores keystroke to memory variable CHOICE.
CLEAR                   && Clears screen.
IF UPPER(CHOICE)='Q'    && Looks for Q; the UPPER(CHOICE) converts lower case to upper case.
   CANCEL               && If CHOICE = 'Q', returns to dBASE prompt.
ENDIF                   && Passes control to next command line.
*
SET DEVICE TO PRINT     && Directs @ row,col output to printer and causes form feed.
Y = 5                   && Stores 5 to memory variable Y.
X = 15                  && Stores 15 to memory variable X.
USE ABC                 && Puts ABC database in use.
*
DO WHILE .NOT. EOF()    && Continues operation until end-of-file condition exists.
   IF Y >= 55           && Looks for condition where Y is greater than or equal to 55.
      EJECT             && If Y >= 55, performs a form feed.
      STORE 5 TO Y      && If Y >= 55, stores 5 to Y.
   ENDIF                && Passes control to next command line.
   *
```

```
@ Y,X SAY NAME              && Positions NAME field contents at row Y column X.
@ Y+X,X SAY PHONE           && Position PHONE field contents at row Y+1 column X.
Y = Y+3                     && Adds 3 to current value of Y to skip 3 lines.
SKIP                        && Positions record pointer to next record.
*
IF EOF()                    && Checks for end-of-file condition.
  EJECT
  SET DEVICE TO SCREEN      && Directs @ row,col output to screen.
  WAIT                      && Pauses operation; displays Press any key... prompt.
  CLEAR                     && Clears screen.
  CANCEL                    && Returns control to dBASE prompt.
ENDIF                       && Passes control to next command line.
ENDDO                       && Ends DO WHILE statement.
```

NOTE

If you would rather print the phone list to your
screen, change the SET DEVICE TO PRINT to
SET DEVICE TO SCREEN and place an asterisk
at the right margin in front of EJECT (two places).

3. Press **Ctrl-W** to save the command file.

4. Run the command file by typing **DO PHDIR** and pressing **Return**.

5. Respond to the following screen prompt by typing **P** to continue or **Q** to quit.

```
THIS PROGRAM PRINTS A TELEPHONE LIST.

BE SURE YOUR PRINTER IS READY.

PRESS P TO PRINT THE LIST, OR

PRESS Q TO QUIT.

_
```

6. Notice that the command file prints names and telephone extensions.

7. When you finish experimenting with this command file, delete it from your disk by typing
   ERASE PHDIR.PRG and pressing **Return**.

8. Turn to Module 58 to continue the learning sequence.

Module 9
AVERAGE

DESCRIPTION

The AVERAGE command is similar to the SUM command, except instead of summing the values of one or more numeric fields within a database, it finds the average (or *arithmetic mean*). The result is either displayed or stored to a memory variable. Forms of the AVERAGE command and corresponding examples are shown in the following list.

AVERAGE *field name*   Averages the contents of the specified field name and displays the following result (with SET TALK ON).

```
. AVERAGE QTY
     12 records averaged
   qty
   168
```

AVERAGE *field1,field2* . . . Averages specified field names and displays the following results.

```
. AVERAGE QTY,COST,PRICE*1.05
      105 records summed
qty  cost      price
2309 34523.48 74560.86
```

AVERAGE *fieldname(s)* TO *memory variable(s)*   Averages specified field name to the named memory variable.

```
. AVERAGE QTY TO MQTY
. AVERAGE QTY,COST TO MQTY,MCOST
```

AVERAGE *fieldname* TO *memory variable* FOR *expression* Averages specified field name to named memory variable for those records that match the specified expression.

```
. AVERAGE QTY TO MQTY FOR COST > .99
```

> AVERAGE *fieldname* TO *memory variable* WHILE *expression* Averages field name to named memory variable while expression is valid. If expression becomes invalid, averaging ceases.

```
. AVERAGE QTY TO MQTY WHILE COST <= 100.00
```

APPLICATIONS

The AVERAGE command is used to store the arithmetic mean of one or more fields within a database file to one or more memory variables for later use, or to display an arithmetic mean in response to a direct user inquiry. The AVERAGE command is used both in command files and in the interactive mode.

TYPICAL OPERATION

In this illustration the AVERAGE command is used with the PICNIC database created in Module 63. Begin at the dBASE dot prompt.

1. Type **USE PICNIC** and press **Return**.

2. Type **AVERAGE GUESTS,AMOUNT TO GU,AM** and press **Return**. Notice the following:

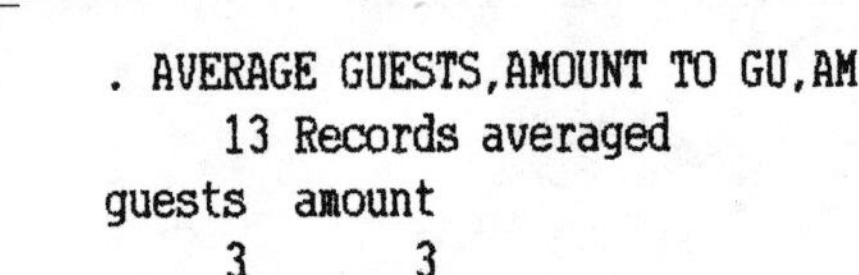

3. Type **? GU,AM** to check the values of the memory variables.

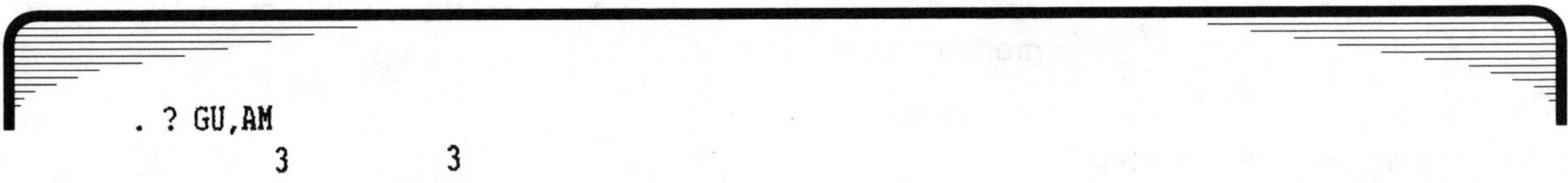

4. Type **CLEAR ALL** to close all files and to release all memory variables.

5. Turn to Module 4 to continue the learning sequence.

Module 10
BROWSE

DESCRIPTION

The BROWSE command is a powerful function, that lets you browse through the contents of the active database file. You can examine records, edit them, mark or unmark records for deletion, and even add new records.

Typing BROWSE from the dBASE dot prompt displays the database and an editing help window similar to the one in the following screen illustration.

```
 Bottom        Top         Lock        Record No.          Freeze  01:11:14 pm

 CURSOR   <-- -->              UP   DOWN       DELETE        Insert Mode:  Ins
 Char:        ← →     Record:  ↑    ↓        Char:    Del    Exit:        ^End
 Field: Home End     Page:  PgUp PgDn        Field:   ^Y     Abort:        Esc
 Pan:       ^← ^→     Help:    F1            Record:  ^U     Set Options: ^Home

 NUMBER NAME---------------------------- ORD_DATE CUST_PO-------- INVOICE INV_DATE
     11 U.S. NAVAL BASE                  05/20/86 USN-A001-3      8601101 05/20/86
      3 MICRO SOFTWARE OF AMERICA        05/20/86 X-0900          8601102 05/20/86
      4 WORDMITE SYSTEMS                 05/20/86 VERBAL          8601103 05/20/86
```

You can suppress the editing help window with **F1**. You can display a menu bar at the top of the screen with **Ctrl-Home** or **F10**. Each menu bar option shown is described in the following list.

```
 Bottom        Top         Lock        Record No.          Freeze  08:55:37 pm
```

Top   Takes you to the first record (top) of the displayed database file.

Bottom   Takes you to the last record (bottom) of the displayed database file.

Lock   Locks the left-most fields on the display for reference purposes. You are prompted to "Change number of columns to lock to."

Record No.   Jumps the cursor to the selected record number. You are prompted to "Enter new record number."

Freeze   Restricts editing to a selected field. You are prompted to "Enter field name to freeze."

Find   Finds the record containing a specified expression within the key field. Find is only displayed when the database is indexed. You are prompted to "Enter search string."

You can enter the BROWSE command with a number of useful options. An example of each is listed with a brief description.

BROWSE NOMENU	Displays the browse editing screen without displaying the editing help menu.
BROWSE NOAPPEND	Prevents the addition of new records to the browsed database. Suppresses the prompt ===> Add new records? (Y/N)
BROWSE FIELDS NAME,ADDRESS	Displays only the named fields.
BROWSE LOCK 2	Locks the display of the first two fields on the screen even when scrolled from right to left.
BROWSE FREEZE ADDRESS	Restricts editing to the named field.
BROWSE WIDTH 5	Sets the display width of all fields to 5 characters. Field contents are scrolled with the Left and Right Arrow, Home, and End keys.
BROWSE NOFOLLOW	Used with indexed files; when the key field is edited, it is resequenced according to the index parameters. Nofollow moves the next indexed record into position. Without nofollow, the cursor remains in the current (edited) record.

You can move around in a browsed database by using the cursor control keys. Editing is accomplished using **Del** and **Ins** keys. The following list contains those control keys that are active in the BROWSE mode.

Up Arrow or Ctrl-E	Cursor up one line
PgUp or Ctrl-R	Cursor to top record
Dn Arrow or Ctrl-X	Cursor down one line
PgDn or Ctrl-C	Cursor down one record
Left Arrow or Ctrl-S	Cursor left one character
Ctrl-H or Backspace	Deletes character to the left
Rt Arrow or Ctrl-D	Cursor right one character
Home or Ctrl-A	Cursor left one field
End or Ctrl-F	Cursor right one field
Ins or Ctrl-V	Turns insert/strikeover mode on/off
Del or Ctrl-G	Deletes character under cursor position
Ctrl-Y	Deletes field contents
Ctrl-T	Deletes next word
Ctrl-U	Marks/unmarks record for deletion
Ctrl-B or Ctrl- ←	Scroll records to the left
Ctrl-Z or Ctrl- →	Scroll records to the right
Ctrl-Q or Esc	Quit the BROWSE mode without saving changes

Ctrl-W or Ctrl-End   Write (save) changes to the database and return to the dBASE dot prompt

Ctrl-Home or F10   Turns menu bar off and on

If you try to move below the last record in the database, the prompt:

```
===>Add new records? (Y/N)
```

appears. Typing **Y** for "yes" lets you enter a new record from your keyboard.

As you can see, the BROWSE mode uses a large number of control keys to allow moving from field to field or from record to record within a database. The available editing keys make changing the information within a database easy.

The BROWSE mode displays each record on a single line. If the record has more than 80 characters, characters 81 and greater are hidden from view. To scroll the hidden fields to the left, press **Ctrl-Left Arrow** (or **Ctrl-B**). To scroll back to the right, press **Ctrl-Right Arrow** (or **Ctrl-Z**).

You can alter the contents of a record by simply moving the cursor to the field to be changed and typing in the new information. You can use **Del** (or **Ctrl-G**) to delete characters and **Ctrl-Y** to delete from the cursor position to the end of the field. **Ctrl-T** deletes the word to the right of the cursor. You can insert text by pressing **Ins** (or **Ctrl-V**). When the insert mode is active, the word INSERT is displayed at the top of the screen. When text is typed, following text is displaced to the right.

Once you've finished modifying a database using BROWSE, you can save your changes by pressing **Ctrl-End** (or **Ctrl-W**) which "writes" the changed records to disk. If you decide to leave the database as it was before you made changes, press **Ctrl-Q** or **Esc** to quit without saving the changes. Both the **Ctrl-W** (write changes) and **Ctrl-Q** (quit without saving) commands take you back to the dBASE dot prompt.

APPLICATIONS

The BROWSE command is used to view and update the contents of a database. It is perhaps the most "direct" way to view and edit. The EDIT and LIST commands provide an alternative to the BROWSE command. However, there are several advantages to the use of the BROWSE command.

First, several records are viewed simultaneously using BROWSE, while only one record is displayed at a time when EDIT is used. When using the LIST command to view a database, records wrap at the 80th column. This often clutters the appearance of the displayed data, making it difficult to distinguish one field from another. BROWSE displays the information in a structured manner. Records are on a single, continuous line. Fields are aligned in columns beneath their field names, which are displayed at the top of each column.

TYPICAL OPERATION

In this operation the BROWSE command is used to display the contents of a new database named ABC. Begin at the dBASE dot prompt.

1.   Type **CREATE ABC** and press **Return**.

2.   Prepare the following database structure.

```
    field name   type        width  dec
    ==================================
1   NAME         Character   20
2   PHONE        Character    4
3   MAIL         Character    4
```

3.   Press **Return** twice to save; then type **Y** in response to the "Input data records now? (Y/N)" prompt, and type the following records.

```
Record No.      1              Record No.       4
NAME        Sergio, Vincent    NAME         Harris, Robert
PHONE       3596               PHONE        3353
MAIL        84                 MAIL         2230


Record No.      2              Record No.       5
NAME        Bishop, Sam        NAME         Alexander, T.G.
PHONE       2234               PHONE        1104
MAIL        430                MAIL         84


Record No.      3              Record No.       6
NAME        Collins, Arthur    NAME         <cr>          (End data entry.)
PHONE       4554               PHONE
MAIL        323                MAIL
```

4.   Type **BROWSE** and press **Return**.

5.   Move around in the database with the **PgUp**, **PgDn**, and the cursor control keys.

6. Move to record 5 and press **Ctrl-U** to mark the record for deletion. Notice that the word "DEL" indicates that the record is marked for deletion.

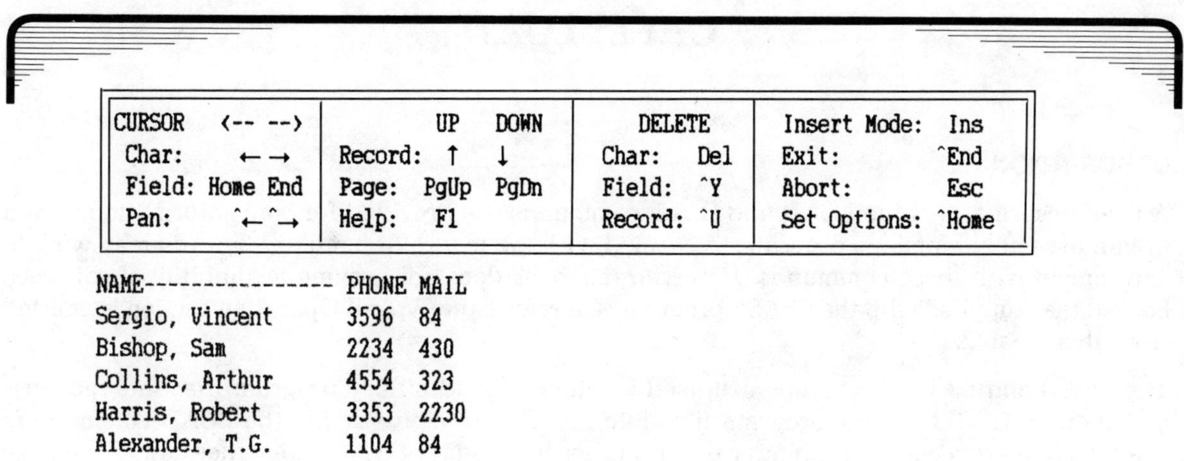


```
NAME---------------- PHONE MAIL
Sergio, Vincent      3596  84
Bishop, Sam          2234  430
Collins, Arthur      4554  323
Harris, Robert       3353  2230
Alexander, T.G.      1104  84
```

7. Exit to the dBASE dot prompt by pressing **Ctrl-W**.

8. Type **LIST** and press **Return**; notice that record 5 includes an asterisk. This verifies that the record is marked for deletion.

9. Type **PACK** then press **Return** and notice that 4 records are copied. Record 5 is deleted.

10. Turn to Module 33 to continue the learning sequence.

Module 11

CALL, LOAD

DESCRIPTION

A brief description of the LOAD and CALL commands are provided for your information. If you are an assembly language programmer armed with the macro assembler, then you may wish to experiment with these commands. However, this book does not assume availability of software beyond that supplied with the dBASE program. Therefore, the Typical Operation section is omitted from this module.

The LOAD and CALL commands are used together to load binary program files into memory, and then to call the binary program files into use. Before using CALL, the LOAD command is used to place from one to five binary program files into memory. The binary files can be as large as 32,000 bytes. The default file extension for a binary file is .BIN.

Once loaded, the CALL command is used to call the binary file (or memory resident program module) into use, as you would use the DO command to run a dBASE command file.

The form of the LOAD command is:

LOAD *binary filename*

The named binary filename is placed into memory where it is accessed with the CALL command. The called file is treated as a subroutine, or *module*, rather than as an external program.

The general form of the CALL command is:

CALL *binary filename* WITH *character expression* or *memory variable*

Omit the filename extension when using the CALL command. In addition, you should always use unique filenames. The following command file uses the LOAD and CALL commands, and assumes that CLOCK.BIN is loaded into memory as a callable module.

```
LOAD CLOCK
CALL CLOCK
MX=0
DO WHILE MX < 100
    MX = MX + 1
ENDDO
RELEASE MODULE CLOCK
CLEAR
RETURN
```

If you have .BIN files loaded into memory, you can use DISPLAY or LIST STATUS to review their names. Because dBASE doesn't check the integrity of the loaded modules, they must be of binary type and operate properly.

Some assembly language programming notes supplied by Ashton-Tate are listed here for your convenience.

- An offset of zero is required at origination (ORG) for the first executable instruction.
- The LOAD command uses the file size to allocate memory; therefore, the program must not allocate memory beyond its actual size.
- The length of memory variables must not be changed by the assembly language program.
- The Code Segment (CS) and Stack Segment (SS) registers must be restored by the module before returning to dBASE.
- A RET FAR is required rather than the more common exit call to return dBASE control.

You must use the macro assembler or an equivalent assembler to assemble the source program. This operation is beyond the scope of this book, which is restricted to dBASE III Plus commands and functions.

APPLICATIONS

The ability to load and then call memory-resident program modules increases the speed of program operation. In addition to increasing speed, you can address certain DOS interrupts and perform other operations that are normally unavailable through standard dBASE commands.

Module 12
CANCEL, RETURN

DESCRIPTION

The CANCEL and RETURN commands are used to end command file operation. Both commands close the active command file and transfer control. Each of these commands is described in the following paragraphs.

CANCEL   The form for the CANCEL command is:

    CANCEL

When the command is encountered in a command file, command file execution ceases and the dBASE dot prompt is displayed. Once it displays, you can enter commands directly from your keyboard.

RETURN   RETURN always takes you back to the point of command file origin. The general form for the RETURN command is:

    RETURN

If the active command file was called from the dBASE dot prompt with the DO *filename* command, then RETURN operates like CANCEL. It stops command file operation, closes the active command file, and redisplays the dBASE dot prompt. If the command file was called by another command file, then RETURN passes control back to the calling command file.

RETURN is often found as the last line in a called command file. If RETURN or CANCEL is not used as the last line of a command file, operation passes through the last line of a called command file and returns to the command file from which it was called automatically. However, files remain open until either the CLEAR ALL or QUIT command is used. Open files can be damaged if a computer reset, like a power failure, is encountered, causing your computer to "hang." Therefore, it's best to terminate command files with either RETURN or CANCEL.

RETURN TO MASTER   The TO MASTER clause is sometimes used with the RETURN command to return operation to the top-level (or master) command file. Look at the following diagram.

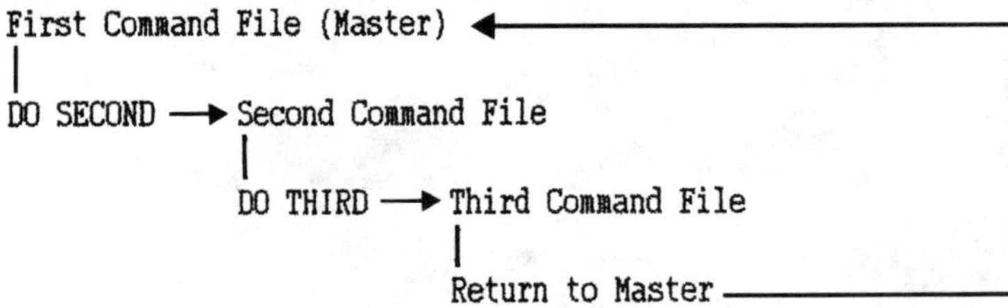

The RETURN TO MASTER command in the Third Command File transfers operation back to the First Command File. Without the TO MASTER clause, operation is transferred back to the Second Command File.

APPLICATIONS

The CANCEL command is frequently used in command files to give you the opportunity to stop command file operation. For example, you might use a series of command lines similar to these to provide an "exit" option.

```
WAIT 'Type X to exit, any other key to continue...' TO EXIT
IF UPPER(EXIT)='X'
    CANCEL
ENDIF
```

If an X is typed, the CANCEL command displays the dBASE dot prompt, and control is returned to your keyboard. Pressing any other key bypasses the IF statement and command file operation continues. Use of the UPPER() function accepts either an upper or lowercase X.

The RETURN command is used inside a command file in the same way as the CANCEL command. In fact, you can substitute RETURN for CANCEL in the previous example if you want to return to a calling command file. As previously mentioned, if the current command file was called from the dBASE dot prompt, control returns to the dot prompt.

TYPICAL OPERATION

In this illustration the CANCEL and RETURN commands are used in three small command files called DEMO1, DEMO2, and DEMO3. These command files pass control back and forth to demonstrate the use of CANCEL and RETURN. Begin at the dBASE dot prompt.

1. Type **MODIFY COMMAND DEMO1** and press **Return** to access the full-screen editor.

2. Type the following command file. (Don't type the explanatory remarks.)

```
                                              Remarks
* DEMO1.PRG -- Uses DEMO2 and DEMO3 to demonstrate CANCEL and RETURN.
SET TALK OFF            && Turns off dBASE dialog.
DO WHILE .T.            && Continues operation while true.
CLEAR                   && Clears the screen.
?                       && ? lines display following text.
? 'This is the DEMO1 command file.'
? '   Press 2 to run the DEMO2 command file,'
? '   Press 3 to run the DEMO3 command file,'
WAIT 'or Press X to eXit.' TO WHAT  && Pauses operation; stores keyed character to
*                                 memory variable WHAT.
```

```
DO CASE                    && Begins CASE statement to check for value of WHAT.
   CASE UPPER(WHAT)='X'    && Checks value of WHAT for uppercase X.
      SET TALK ON          && Turns dBASE dialog back on.
      CANCEL               && Cancels command file operation if WHAT = X.
   CASE WHAT='2'           && Checks value of WHAT for 2.
      DO DEMO2             && Runs DEMO2 command file if WHAT=2.
   CASE WHAT='3'           && Checks value of WHAT for 3.
      DO DEMO3             && Runs DEMO3 command file if WHAT=3.
ENDCASE                    && Passes control to following command line.
ENDDO                      && Completes DO WHILE statement.
```

3. Press **Ctrl-W** to write the command file to disk.

4. Type **MODIFY COMMAND DEMO2** and press **Return** to type the following command file.

Remarks

```
* DEMO2.PRG -- Uses DEMO1 and DEMO3 to demonstrate CANCEL and RETURN.
CLEAR                      && Clears the screen.
DO WHILE .T.               && Continues operation while true.
?                          && REMARK lines display following text.
? 'This is the DEMO2 command file.'
? '   Press 1 to RETURN to the DEMO1 command file,'
? '   Press 3 to run the DEMO3 command file,'
WAIT 'or Press X to eXit. ' to WHAT  && Pauses and stores keyed character to
*                                       memory variable WHAT.
DO CASE                    && Begins CASE statement to check for value of WHAT.
   CASE UPPER(WHAT)='X'    && Checks value of WHAT for uppercase X.
      SET TALK ON          && Turns dBASE dialog back on.
      CANCEL               && Cancels command file operation if WHAT=X.
   CASE WHAT='1'           && Checks value of WHAT for 1.
      RETURN               && Runs DEMO2 command file if WHAT=1.
   CASE WHAT='3'           && Checks value of WHAT for 3.
      DO DEMO3             && Runs DEMO3 command file if WHAT=3.
ENDCASE                    && Passes control to following command line.
ENDDO                      && Completes DO WHILE statement.
```

5. Press **Ctrl-W** to write the command file to disk.

6. Type **MODIFY COMMAND DEMO3** and press **Return** to type the following command file.

```
                                                    Remarks
* DEMO3.PRG -- Uses DEMO1 and DEMO2 to demonstrate CANCEL and RETURN.
CLEAR                           && Clears the screen.
?                              && ? lines display following text.
? 'This is the DEMO3 command file.'
? '   Press Spacebar to return to the previous command file,'
WAIT 'or Press X to eXit. ' TO WHAT  && Pauses operation; keyed character is
*                                      stored to memory variable WHAT.
DO CASE                         && Begins CASE statement to check for value of WHAT.
   CASE UPPER(WHAT)='X'         && Checks value of WHAT for uppercase X.
      SET TALK ON              && Turns dBASE dialog back on.
      CANCEL                   && Cancels command file operation if WHAT=X.
      CLEAR                    && Clears the screen for the next display.
   CASE WHAT=' '
      RETURN
ENDCASE                        && Ends CASE statement. control passes back to next line.
ENDDO                          && Completes DO WHILE statement; control passes back to
*                                 calling command file.
```

7. Press **Ctrl-W** to write the command file to disk.

8. Now type **DO DEMO1** and press **Return**. Notice the following displays and respond to the prompts by typing the numbers shown.

```
. DO DEMO1

   This is the DEMO1 command file.
      Press 2 to run the DEMO2 command file,
      Press 3 to run the DEMO3 command file,
   or Press X to eXit. _                    -Type 2

   This is the DEMO2 command file.
      Press 1 to RETURN to the DEMO1 command file,
      Press 3 to run the DEMO3 command file,
   or Press X to eXit.                      -Type 3
```

```
This is the DEMO3 command file.
    Press RETURN to return to the previous command file,
or Press X to eXit.                       -Press Spacebar

This is the DEMO2 command file.
    Press 1 to RETURN to the DEMO1 command file,
    Press 3 to run the DEMO3 command file,
or Press X to eXit.                       -Type 1

This is the DEMO1 command file.
    Press 2 to run the DEMO2 command file,
    Press 3 to run the DEMO3 command file,
or Press X to eXit.                       -Type X
```

9. Experiment with command file operation until you understand how it works. Then exit to dBASE's dot prompt and erase the practice files with:

    ERASE DEMO1.PRG
    ERASE DEMO2.PRG
    ERASE DEMO3.PRG

10. Turn to Module 70 to continue the learning sequence.

Module 13
CHANGE

DESCRIPTION

The CHANGE command is used to exchange the contents of a specified field within the current record with whatever you type. You can also use the EDIT or BROWSE commands to achieve the same results. However, CHANGE is sometimes the quickest way to achieve a single field change.

When the CHANGE command is issued, dBASE displays the current record number and the contents of the named field(s). The display is similar to the following.

```
                              Remarks
CHANGE FIELD PHONE

Record No.      1       Record number is displayed.
PHONE        3596       Field name and contents are displayed.
```

You can change the contents by typing in the new information. When you're done, the next record is displayed. Press **Esc** or **Ctrl-Q** to quit. Some forms of the CHANGE command are shown in the following list.

1. CHANGE FIELD *field name*   Displays current record number, field name, and contents. Example:

   . CHANGE FIELD PARTY

2. CHANGE FIELD *field1, field2, . . .*   Displays current record number, and each named field, and the field contents. Example:

   . CHANGE FIELD NAME, GUESTS

3. CHANGE FIELD *fieldname* FOR *expression*   Displays every record number matching the expression, each named field within the matching records, and the field contents. This process continues until the last matching record is presented for change or you press the **Esc** key. Example:

   . CHANGE FIELD PHONE FOR PHONE ='(201)'

You may wish to display the file with the LIST command so you can see which records require changing. You can move the record pointer to the desired record by typing the record number and pressing **Return**. Then type the CHANGE command to make the changes. If every record requiring change has a common expression, you can use the "FOR expression" in one CHANGE command to fix all records. For example, if you wish to change all records containing "Orlando" in the CITY field, you can use:

```
CHANGE FIELD CITY FOR CITY='Orlando'
```

APPLICATIONS

The CHANGE command is a fast way to change a field within a specific record or a group of records containing a common expression. This situation eliminates the need to search every record for the target expression. The preceding example demonstrates this approach, where the expression is "FOR CITY='Orlando'." The CHANGE command is generally used in dBASE's interactive mode, although you can also use it in a command file.

TYPICAL OPERATION

In this illustration the CHANGE command is used in conjunction with the ABC database created in Module 10. All phone numbers beginning with "3" are changed to begin with "4." Begin at the dBASE dot prompt.

1. Type **USE ABC** and press **Return**.
2. Type **LIST** and press **Return**. Notice the following display.

```
. LIST
Record#  NAME              PHONE MAIL
      1  Sergio, Vincent   3596  84
      2  Bishop, Sam       2234  430
      3  Collins, Arthur   4554  323
      4  Harris, Robert    3353  2230
```

3. Type **CHANGE FIELD PHONE FOR PHONE = '3'** and press **Return**.
4. Type **4** in place of the 3 and press **Return**. Notice that Record 4 is displayed because it is the next record starting with "3."
5. Type **4** in place of the 3 and press **Return**.
6. Type **LIST** and press **Return** to verify the changes. Check your screen:

```
. LIST
Record#  NAME              PHONE MAIL
      1  Sergio, Vincent   4596  84
      2  Bishop, Sam       2234  430
      3  Collins, Arthur   4554  323
      4  Harris, Robert    4353  2230
```

7. Turn to Module 56 to continue the learning sequence.

Module 14
CLEAR ALL, CLEAR TYPEAHEAD

DESCRIPTION

This module describes the CLEAR ALL and CLEAR TYPEAHEAD commands. Although both commands perform a clearing process, they are not directly related.

CLEAR ALL   The CLEAR ALL command is used to reset dBASE to a "CLEAR" state. All database files are closed and all active memory variables are released from memory, as if the RELEASE ALL command (described in Module 62) were given. The command form is:

    . CLEAR ALL

The CLEAR command used alone (without "ALL") is used to clear the display screen, like the DOS CLS command, and is not related to CLEAR ALL. One other use of the CLEAR statement is CLEAR GETS, which is described in Modules 37 and 58. Here again, CLEAR GETS is not related to CLEAR ALL, which is the subject of this module.

CLEAR TYPEAHEAD   The CLEAR TYPEAHEAD command clears the type-ahead buffer of any stored keystrokes. Keystrokes can reside in the type-ahead buffer while your computer performs an operation. Clearing the type-ahead buffer ensures that program operation responds to keyboard input in a predictable way. Otherwise, the program may respond to a previously stored keystroke.

To clear the type-ahead buffer, use CLEAR TYPEAHEAD either from the dot prompt or within a command file. The command is entered by typing:

    . CLEAR TYPEAHEAD

You can also control the size of the type-ahead buffer, i.e., the number of stored keystrokes, with the SET TYPEAHEAD TO command. The form of this command is:

    . SET TYPEAHEAD TO n

where n is a number from 0 to 32,000. The default value is 20. You can disable the type-ahead buffer with SET TYPEAHEAD TO 0. The CLEAR TYPEAHEAD command works only when the SET ESCAPE ON command is in effect. If you type beyond the type-ahead buffer capacity, your computer's speaker (or *bell*) sounds.

APPLICATIONS

There are three situations where you may wish to use the CLEAR ALL command. First, you can issue it at the dBASE prompt to close all files and release all memory variables, giving you a "clean slate" in which to work.

You can use CLEAR ALL at the beginning or end of a command file. Used at the beginning of a command file, it releases any memory variables that may exist and closes all files. This makes all 256 memory variables available for use. It also assures you that only those files needed are open, eliminating unwanted surprises during operation.

Used at the end of a file, it eliminates all memory variables and closes all files so that following activity is predictable. If you call one command file from another, and the first command file requires a memory variable for operation, you can issue the CLEAR ALL command, then STORE the value you need as a public memory variable (Module 52) before you RETURN to the previous command file. An example of this could be:

```
CLEAR ALL
PUBLIC CHOICE
STORE ' ' TO CHOICE
RETURN
```

Setting the TYPEAHEAD BUFFER to zero disables the ON KEY command and the INKEY( ) function. This is especially useful if you use a command file that includes the ON ERROR command. More about this in Module 49.

TYPICAL OPERATION

In this illustration the CLEAR ALL command is used to demonstrate its effect on an open database file and memory variables. The MEMBERS database, created in Module 18 and modified in Module 10 is used in the following procedure, but any database file can be used. Begin at the dBASE dot prompt.

1. Type **USE MEMBERS** and press **Return**.

2. Type **LIST NAME OFF** and press **Return**. Compare your screen to the following:

```
. list name off
name
Williams, David
Phillips, George W.
Galvin, Theodore A.
```

3. Type **STORE 45 TO MVAR1** and press **Return**.

4. Type **STORE 'Hello' TO MVAR2** and press **Return**.

5. Type **STORE .T. TO MVAR3** and press **Return**

6. Type **LIST MEMO** and press **Return**. Notice the following:

```
. list memo
MVAR1        pub  N          45  (         45.00000000)
MVAR2        pub  C  "Hello"
MVAR3        pub  L  .T.
       3 variables defined,      18 bytes used
     253 variables available,   5982 bytes available
```

7. Type **CLEAR ALL** and press **Return**.

8. Verify that **CLEAR ALL** deleted all memory variables by typing **LIST MEMO** and pressing
    Return. Check your screen for the following:

```
. list memo
       0 variables defined,       0 bytes used
     256 variables available,   6000 bytes available
```

9. Verify that CLEAR ALL closed the database file by typing **LIST NAME OFF** and pressing
    Return. Notice the following:

```
. list name off
No database file in USE, enter filename:
```

10. Press **Return** to redisplay the dBASE prompt.

11. Turn to Module 67 to continue the learning sequence.

Module 15
CLOSE

DESCRIPTION

The CLOSE command is used to close specific file types. It is important for you to understand the command forms for closing files. These include:

1.	CLOSE ALL	Closes all open files.
2.	CLOSE DATABASES	Closes database (.DBF) files.
3.	CLOSE INDEX	Closes index (.NDX) files.
4.	CLOSE FORMAT	Closes format (.FMT) files.
5.	CLOSE PROCEDURE	Closes procedure, or command, (.PRG) files. Opened with SET PROCEDURE TO *filename*.
6.	CLOSE ALTERNATE	Closes active "alternate" (.TXT) files. Opened with:

```
SET ALTERNATE TO filename
SET ALTERNATE ON
```

Other commands used to close files include CLEAR ALL and QUIT. Typing **USE** and pressing **Return** closes the active database file.

APPLICATIONS

The CLOSE command is used to close specific file types during dBASE operation. It may be issued from dBASE dot prompt or included in a command file. This command gives you the ability to close selected file types while leaving others open. Without the ability to close specific files, you would have to use the CLOSE ALL command and then selectively reopen the ones needed.

TYPICAL OPERATION

In this illustration the MEMBERS database, created in Module 18 and modified in Module 47, is used. Next, two index files are created. Finally, the CLOSE command is used to close the index files while the database file stays open. Begin at the dBASE dot prompt.

> **NOTE**
> Index files are created with the INDEX command
> described in Module 41. Although you may not
> be familiar with index files yet, just follow the
> procedure to see how CLOSE works.

1. Type **USE MEMBERS** and press **Return**.

2. Create an index file called NAMELIST by typing **INDEX ON NAME TO NAMELIST** and pressing **Return**.

3. Display the status of open files by typing **DISPLAY STATUS** and pressing **Return**. Notice the display:

```
. use members
. index on name to namelist
  100% indexed              3 Records indexed
. display status

Currently Selected Database:
Select area: 1, Database in Use: C:members.dbf    Alias: MEMBERS
     Master index file:  C:namelist.ndx  Key: name
            Memo file:   C:members.dbt


File search path:
Default disk drive: C:
Print destination:  PRN:
Margin =     0
Current work area =    1


Press any key to continue...
```

4. Press **Esc** to return to the dot prompt.

5. Type **CLOSE INDEX** and press **Return** to close the index file.

6. Verify that the index file is closed by typing **DISPLAY STATUS**. Note that the index file is no longer displayed on the status screen.

```
. close index
. display status

Currently Selected Database:
Select area: 1, Database in Use: C:members.dbf    Alias: MEMBERS
            Memo file:   C:members.dbt


File search path:
Default disk drive: C:
Print destination:  PRN:
```

```
Margin =      0
Current work area =    1

Press any key to continue...
```

7. Press **Esc** to return to the dot prompt.

8. Now type **CLOSE DATABASES** and press **Return**.

9. Verify that the database is closed by typing **DISPLAY STATUS** and pressing **Return**. Notice that no database name is displayed.

```
. close database
. display status

File search path:
Default disk drive: C:
Print destination:  PRN:
Margin =      0
Current work area =    1

Press any key to continue...

ALTERNATE  - OFF   DELETED    - OFF   FIXED      - OFF   SAFETY      - ON
BELL       - ON    DELIMITERS - OFF   HEADING    - ON    SCOREBOARD  - ON
CARRY      - OFF   DEVICE     - SCRN  HELP       - ON    STATUS      - OFF
CATALOG    - OFF   DOHISTORY  - OFF   HISTORY    - ON    STEP        - OFF
CENTURY    - OFF   ECHO       - OFF   INTENSITY  - ON    TALK        - ON
CONFIRM    - OFF   ESCAPE     - ON    MENU       - ON    TITLE       - ON
CONSOLE    - ON    EXACT      - OFF   PRINT      - OFF   UNIQUE      - OFF
DEBUG      - OFF   FIELDS     - OFF

Programmable function keys:
F2  - assist;
F3  - list;
F4  - dir;
F5  - display structure;
F6  - display status;
F7  - display memory;
F8  - display;
F9  - append;
F10 - edit;
```

10. Turn to Module 14 to continue the learning sequence.

Module 16
COPY

DESCRIPTION

The COPY command lets you copy either an entire database file or selected records within the active database to a new database file. You can assign a filename of your choice to the copied file. A number of clauses are available with the COPY command. These include:

- STRUCTURE
- DELIMITED
- SDF
- TYPE
- STRUCTURE EXTENDED

All of these let you control the format of the newly created (copied) file.

The STRUCTURE clause lets you copy a database structure without the contents.

The DELIMITED clause formats the copied file with a field separator (delimiter), such as a comma.

The SDF clause lets you copy the database in standard data format, which produces an ASCII text file that is readable by most word processing programs.

The TYPE clause lets you copy the database in a number of popular program formats. The types are:

    DIF—VisiCalc format
    SDF—System data format (ASCII)
    SYLK—Multiplan spreadsheet format
    WKS—Lotus 1-2-3 spreadsheet format

The DIF, SYLK, and WKS type formats convert records to rows and fields to columns.

The STRUCTURE EXTENDED clause copies the structure of a database into fields.

The following list shows forms of the COPY command accompanied by explanations and an example of each.

1. COPY TO *filename* Copies database structure and contents to the named file.

    . COPY TO NEWFILE

2. COPY NEXT n TO *filename* Copies database structure and contents of next n records to the named file.

    . COPY NEXT 10 TO NEWFILE

3. COPY TO *filename* FOR *expression*   Copies database structure and contents to the named file for those records meeting the requirements of the expression.

   . COPY TO NEWFILE FOR AGE >= 18

4. COPY FIELD *name1,name2, . . .* TO *filename*   Copies structure and contents of specified fields to the named file.

   . COPY FIELD NAME,ADR,CSZ TO NEWFILE

5. COPY FIELD *name1,name2* TO *filename* FOR *expression*
   Copies structure and contents of specified fields to the named file for those records matching the expression.

   . COPY FIELD NAME TO NEWFILE FOR AGE >= 18

6. COPY STRUCTURE TO *filename*   Copies database structure (without contents) to the named file.

   . COPY STRUCTURE TO NEWFILE

7. COPY TO *filename* DELIMITED   Copies database contents with each character type field enclosed in quotes and separated by a comma. The file is copied in standard data format (ASCII). The filename is assigned the extension .TXT, unless you assign an extension of your own choosing. Trailing blanks are trimmed (eliminated) from character-type fields.

   . COPY TO NEWFILE DELIMITED

8. COPY TO *filename* DELIMITED WITH #   Copies database contents to the named file. Each character field is enclosed in specified delimiters, such as #. The file is copied in standard data format (ASCII). Trailing blanks are trimmed.

   . COPY TO NEWFILE.LST DELIMITED WITH #

9. COPY TO *filename* DELIMINTED WITH BLANK   Copies the database contents to the named file. The fields are separated by one blank space.

   . COPY TO NEWFILE DELIMITED WITH BLANK

10. COPY TO *filename* SDF   Copies database contents as a standard data format file (ASCII), without delimiters. Trailing blanks are left intact.

    . COPY TO NEWFILE SDF

11. COPY FIELD *name1,name2. . .* FOR *expression* TO *filename* DELIMITED
    Copies field contents of those records meeting a specified expression to the named file. The copied file is a delimited text file.

    . COPY FIELD NAME FOR AGE >= 18 TO NEWFILE DELIMITED

12. COPY TO *filename* TYPE WKS   Copies database contents in Lotus 1-2-3 spreadsheet (or worksheet) format. Records convert to rows and columns convert to fields.

```
. COPY TO NEWFILE TYPE WKS
```

13. COPY TO *filename* STRUCTURE EXTENDED   Creates a new database having four fields that correspond to the field name, field type, field width, and number of decimals. Once the extended structure file is created, the CREATE FROM command is used to create a new database structure from the extended file.

```
. COPY TO NEWONE STRUCTURE EXTENDED        && Creates extended structure file.
. CREATE NEWTWO FROM NEWONE                && Creates new database structure from
                                              extended structure file.
```

14. COPY *filename* TO *newfile*   Like the DOS COPY command, makes a copy of the named file.

```
. COPY DATA1.DBF TO DATA2.DBF
```

ADDITIONAL INFORMATION   The DELIMITED and SDF clauses are also used with the APPEND command to add standard ASCII data files to a dBASE database. This application is described in Module 5. The EXPORT and IMPORT commands, described in Module 35, are used to transfer data between PFS:file program data and dBASE III Plus.

The STRUCTURE EXTENDED clause creates a new database with four fields that correspond to the field name, field type, field length, and number of decimal places. The fields within the four-field database contain field names, field types, field lengths, and the number of decimal places in numeric fields. The structure has been "extended" across the fields of this new database.

APPLICATIONS

The ability to COPY an entire database, selected records, or selected fields of only certain records makes the COPY command extremely flexible. But even more, the ability to copy a database with a delimiter of your choice, as an ASCII file, or in another program format, gives dBASE the ability to prepare the contents of a database for use with other programs. As described, you can tranfer the contents of database files into Multiplan, Lotus, and VisiCalc. The EXPORT command formats data for PFS:file. The result of copying a file with the DELIMITED clause prepares data for direct use with MicroPro International's MailMerge program.

You can also COPY specific fields and records with the SDF clause putting them in standard data format. The resulting file can be used by a conventional word processing program. This means you can prepare word processed reports from database files. This is an extremely valuable capability for several reasons.

First, you can output selected fields and records using FIELD and FOR *expression* as described in the preceding list. This provides a file that is automatically "preprocessed" to save manual editing of unwanted records and fields. Second, you can use dBASE's SORT command (Module 61) to alphabetize the output using a field of your choice as the object of the sort.

If you wish to view, or view and "touch up," a file that's been copied with DELIMITED or SDF, you can use dBASE's full-screen editor by typing **MODIFY COMMAND** *filename*.TXT and pressing **Return**. The copied file is displayed. If it's alright the way it is, press **Ctrl-Q** to quit. If editing is necessary, make your changes and press **Ctrl-W**, which saves the changed file. Both **Ctrl-Q** and **Ctrl-W** take you back to the dBASE dot prompt.

TYPICAL OPERATION

In this illustration the COPY command is used to transfer data from a sample database in several file formats. The copied files are displayed using the TYPE command. Begin at the dBASE dot prompt.

1. Type **CREATE STOCK** and press **Return**.

2. Prepare the following file structure and enter the data as shown.

```
Field   Field Name  Type        Width   Dec
   1    PART_NO     Character     15
   2    DESCRIP     Character     20
   3    COST        Numeric        7     2
   4    PRICE       Numeric        7     2
   5    QTY_IN      Numeric        7
   6    QTY_OUT     Numeric        7
```

```
Record#  PART_NO       DESCRIP               COST   PRICE  QTY_IN QTY_OUT
     1   TX-345-02     BOOT, TIRE            2.76    4.95     20      11
     2   GG-4544-15    TUBE, INNER          6.55   11.95     48      23
     3   BR-78R-14     TIRE, RADIAL        33.45   56.55     24      14
     4   FS-3455-120W  BATTERY, MAINT. FREE 22.47  34.95     12       7
```

3. Type **COPY FIELD PART_NO, DESCRIP, PRICE TO TEMP** and press **Return**.

4. Type **USE TEMP** and press **Return**.

5. Type **LIST OFF** and press **Return** and examine the contents.

```
Record#  PART_NO       DESCRIP             PRICE
     1   TX-345-02     BOOT, TIRE           4.95
     2   GG-4544-15    TUBE, INNER         11.95
     3   BR-78R-14     TIRE, RADIAL        56.55
     4   FS-3455-120W  BATTERY, MAINT. FREE 34.95
```

6. Type **USE STOCK** and press **Return**.

7. Type **ERASE TEMP.DBF** and press **Return**; the TEMP.DBF file is deleted.

8. Type **COPY FIELD PARTNO, DESCRIP, COST FOR COST > 10 TO TEMP SDF** and press **Return**.

9. Type **TYPE TEMP.TXT** and press **Return**; notice the records in this file.

```
BR-78R-14        TIRE, RADIAL          33.45
FS-3455-120W     BATTERY, MAINT. FREE  22.47
```

10. Type **ERASE TEMP.TXT** and press **Return**; the TEMP.DBF file is deleted.

11. Type **COPY FIELD PARTNO, DESCRIP, COST TO TEMP DELIMITED** and press **Return**.

12. Type **TYPE TEMP.TXT** and press **Return**; notice the records in this file.

```
"TX-345-02","BOOT, TIRE",2.76
"GG-4544-15","TUBE, INNER",6.55
"BR-78R-14","TIRE, RADIAL",33.45
"FS-3455-120W","BATTERY, MAINT. FREE",22.47
```

13. Type **ERASE TEMP.TXT** and press **Return**; the TEMP.DBF file is deleted.

14. Type **COPY FIELD PARTNO, DESCRIP, COST TO TEMP DELIMITED WITH #** and press **Return**.

15. Type **TYPE TEMP.TXT** and press **Return**; notice the field separation in this file.

```
#TX-345-02#,#BOOT, TIRE#,2.76
#GG-4544-15#,#TUBE, INNER#,6.55
#BR-78R-14#,#TIRE, RADIAL#,33.45
#FS-3455-120W#,#BATTERY, MAINT. FREE#,22.47
```

16. Type **ERASE TEMP.TXT** and press **Return**; the TEMP.TXT file is deleted.

17. Type **CLEAR ALL** to close all files.

18. Turn to Module 19 to continue the learning sequence.

Module 17
COUNT

DESCRIPTION

The COUNT command is used to return the number of records in a database file. Used alone, the COUNT command returns a numeric value equal to the number of records in a database. If the FOR expression is used, then it returns a number equal to the number of records meeting the expression. The COUNT value, which is an integer (whole number), can also be saved to a designated memory variable. Some forms of the COUNT command are shown in the following list.

COUNT   Counts the number of records in the database in use and displays the number (if SET TALK is ON).

```
. COUNT
    13 records
```

COUNT FOR *expression*   Counts the number of records in the database meeting the expression.

```
. COUNT FOR AMOUNT > 2
    8 records
```

COUNT TO *memory variable*   Stores the number of records in the database to the designated memory variable.

```
. COUNT TO MVCT
    13 records
```

COUNT FOR *expression* TO *memory variable*   Stores the number of records in the database meeting the expression to the designated memory variable.

```
. COUNT FOR AMOUNT = 3 TO MVCT
    3 records
```

APPLICATIONS

The COUNT command is convenient for determining the number of records that contain a certain value. The value returned by the COUNT command is useful in computations that require the number of records as part of an arithmetic expression. The COUNT command is often used in the interactive mode, and is also used in command files. It is often used to return the last record number in the active database.

TYPICAL OPERATION

In this illustration the COUNT command is used in a command file. You use it to display statistical
information about the PICNIC database file created in Module 63. Begin at the dBASE dot prompt.

1. Type **MODIFY COMMAND COUNT** and press **Return** to use the dBASE editor.

2. Type the COUNT command file. (Don't type the explanatory remarks.)

```
                                              Remarks
* COUNT.PRG - Uses COUNT to produce statistical information.
CLEAR                          && Clears the screen.
SET TALK OFF                   && Turns off dBASE dialog.
USE PICNIC                     && Puts PICNIC database in use.
COUNT TO MRECS                 && Counts number of records to memory variable MRECS.
SUM GUESTS TO MGST             && Sums contents of GUESTS field to memory variable MGST.
COUNT FOR GUESTS = 0 TO M0     && Stores record count for Guests = 0 to memory variable M0.
COUNT FOR GUESTS = 1 TO M1     && Stores record count for Guests = 1 to memory variable M1.
COUNT FOR GUESTS = 2 TO M2     && Stores record count for Guests = 2 to memory variable M2.
COUNT FOR GUESTS = 3 TO M3     && Stores record count for Guests = 3 to memory variable M3.
COUNT FOR GUESTS = 4 TO M4     && Stores record count for Guests = 4 to memory variable M4.
COUNT FOR GUESTS = 5 TO M5     && Stores record count for Guests = 5 to memory variable M5.
COUNT FOR GUESTS = 6 TO M6     && Stores record count for Guests = 6 to memory variable M6.
? '       DESCRIPTION                      NUMBER'   && Lines beginning with ? print text in
? '                                              '   && quotes followed by designated memory
? ' MEMBERS WITH 0 GUESTS          ', M0            && variables.
? ' MEMBERS WITH 1 GUEST           ', M1
? ' MEMBERS WITH 2 GUESTS          ', M2
? ' MEMBERS WITH 3 GUESTS          ', M3
? ' MEMBERS WITH 4 GUESTS          ', M4
? ' MEMBERS WITH 5 GUESTS          ', M5
? ' MEMBERS WITH 6 GUESTS          ', M6
? ' AVERAGE GUESTS PER MEMBER ', 1.0000*(MGST/MRECS)   && 1.0000 used to obtain four
?                                                      && decimal places.
? ' TOTAL MEMBERS              ', MRECS
? ' TOTAL GUESTS              ', MGST
? '                                      '
? '       TOTAL ATTENDANCE    : ', MGST + MRECS
? '                              '
?
WAIT                           && Pauses operation until key is pressed.
CLEAR                          && Clears the screen.
CLEAR ALL                      && Closes database in use and clears memory variables.
SET TALK ON                    && Turns dBASE dialog back on.
CANCEL                         && Returns control to dBASE dot prompt.
```

3. Press **Ctrl-W** to write the command file to disk.

4. Run the command file by typing **DO COUNT** and pressing **Return**. Notice the information displayed by the command file.

```
. DO COUNT

        DESCRIPTION                        NUMBER


MEMBERS WITH 0 GUESTS                         0
MEMBERS WITH 1 GUEST                          0
MEMBERS WITH 2 GUESTS                         2
MEMBERS WITH 3 GUESTS                         6
MEMBERS WITH 4 GUESTS                         5
MEMBERS WITH 5 GUESTS                         0
MEMBERS WITH 6 GUESTS                         0
AVERAGE GUESTS PER MEMBER                  3.2307


TOTAL MEMBERS                                13
TOTAL GUESTS                                 42
                                          ______

    TOTAL ATTENDANCE                         55
                                          ======


Press any key to continue...
```

5. When you are through experimenting with the command file, type **ERASE COUNT.PRG** and press **Return** to conserve disk space.

6. Turn to Module 46 to continue the learning sequence.

Module 18
CREATE

DESCRIPTION

The CREATE command is used to build a database from scratch. If you followed the sample session in Module 2, you used the CREATE command to create the PHONE database file. To create a new database, type:

```
. CREATE
```

and press **Return** at the dBASE dot prompt. dBASE displays the prompt:

```
    Enter the name of the new file:
```

Type any filename ranging from one to eight characters in length and press **Return**. If you wish, you can type CREATE followed by a filename to omit the "Enter the name . . ." prompt. Once the filename is entered and you press **Return**, dBASE displays:

```
      Field Name  Type      Width  Dec      Field Name  Type      Width   Dec
      ──────────────────────────────        ──────────────────────────────
  1               Character
```

At this point, dBASE is waiting for you to assign field names, field types, field widths, and the number of decimal places if the field is a numeric type. The following list provides information about names, types, widths, and decimal places.

Field Name—A field name can be up to ten characters in length, must start with an alphabetical character, and may contain numbers or undersores, but no spaces are permitted within a field name. Your field name should identify the contents as clearly as possible to make it easy to remember.

Type—The type may be C for character, D for date, L for logical, M for memo, or N for numeric. Character type fields can contain alphabetical, numeric, punctuation marks, or spaces and can contain as many as 254 characters. Date type fields have the form MM/DD/YY. Logical type fields may contain a true (T) or false (F), yes (Y) or no (N), or a blank. Memo type fields contain running text up to 5,000 characters, or more depending on the word processor used. The database file contains only 10 bytes of information if it is a Memo type. A special .DBT file, where DBT stands for *database text*, is created to store the text. This file has a 512,000-byte capacity. Numeric type fields can contain only numbers and a decimal point.

Width—The widths of fields are:

Character - 254 characters (or bytes)
Date - 8
Logical - 1
Memo - 5,000 (the database file indicates only 10 bytes)
Number - 19 (including the decimal point if one is used)

Dec—During creation or database structure modification (see Module 47), you may specify the number of decimal places contained in a numeric type field. If you type 2 for a dollars and cents value, you should remember to provide for two number spaces and a decimal point space in your record length.

A database record can have up to 128 fields and 4,000 characters. No single character field can exceed 254 bytes. A sample database structure follows. Notice that the field parameters, which you type when you create your database structure, are displayed directly beneath the appropriate headings. You can delete an unwanted field by putting the cursor on the desired line and pressing **Ctrl-U**. To insert a field line, position the cursor and press **Ctrl-N**.

A sample database structure follows:

NOTE
An edit menu is displayed at the top of the screen.
This menu is suppressed and redisplayed with
the **F1** key.

```
    Field Name  Type       Width  Dec           Remarks
    ==========================================================
  1 PRODUCT     Character    20          Type PRODUCT<cr> C<cr> 20<cr>
  2 PRICE       Numeric       6     2    Type PRICE<cr> N<cr> 6<cr> 2<cr>
  3 IN_STOCK    Logical       1          Type IN_STOCK<cr> L<cr>
  4 <cr>        Character               Press <cr> to end CREATE.
```

Pressing **Return** displays the prompt:

```
        Enter to confirm.  Any other key to resume.
```

Pressing any key other than **Return** lets you resume CREATE. Pressing **Return** displays the prompt:

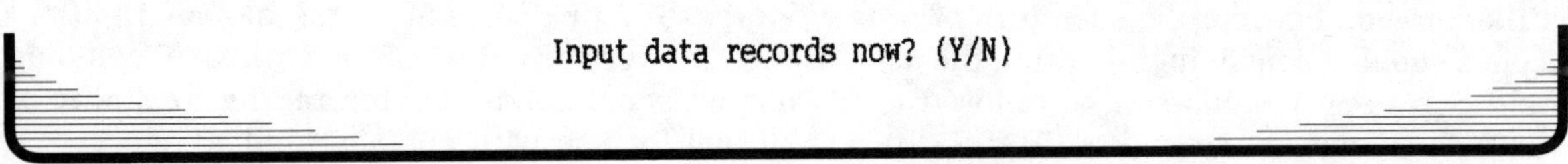

Typing **N** returns you to dBASE's dot prompt; **Y** lets you begin data entry by displaying the following entry mask:

```
    Record No.       1
    PRODUCT
    PRICE
    IN_STOCK      ?
```

You may now type the contents of the fields of your sample database. If you make a typographical error, backspace to it with the **Backspace** or cursor key and retype. Once you enter the INSTOCK value, the next record is displayed automatically for data entry. This process continues until you press **Return** in the first field of a blank record. Pressing **Return** takes you back to the dBASE dot prompt.

To enter data into a Memo field, move the cursor to the Memo field and press **Ctrl-Home**. This puts you in dBASE's full-screen editor, which is like a word processor. Type your text (up to 5,000 characters). When you are through, press **Ctrl-End** to save the text and to return to the data entry mask.

The structure of your database can be changed using the MODIFY STRUCTURE command described in Module 47. The contents of a record is edited using the EDIT, BROWSE, CHANGE, or REPLACE commands (Modules 32, 10, 13, or 56).

There are other CREATE commands used for creating reports, labels, and format control and filter files, called query, view, and screen files. These commands are described in the following modules:

Create Command	Module
CREATE LABEL	20
CREATE REPORT	21
CREATE QUERY	22
CREATE SCRREN	23
CREATE VIEW	24

APPLICATIONS

The CREATE command is the first command used by most dBASE users. With it you can assign a filename and design the structure of a new database. Your choice of both filename and field names should be meaningful to you, the user. In fact, the very structure of the database including field types and lengths can be tailored to fit your personal needs. Therefore, the flexibility of the CREATE command makes dBASE a powerful tool for use with custom applications.

TYPICAL OPERATION

In this illustration the CREATE command is used to design a database that contains information about each member in a professional organization. The information includes name, address, professional affiliation, member's birth date, member's age, dues status, and general information. Go ahead and CREATE this database, because it is used later with other commands. Unless you have a hard disk system, SET DEFAULT TO B should be active. Begin at the dBASE dot prompt.

1. Type **CREATE MEMBERS** and press **Return**. dBASE displays the following:

```
                                        Bytes remaining:    4000


    Field Name  Type       Width  Dec     Field Name  Type       Width   Dec
    =========================================     =========================================
1               Character
```

2. Create the database structure by typing the following:

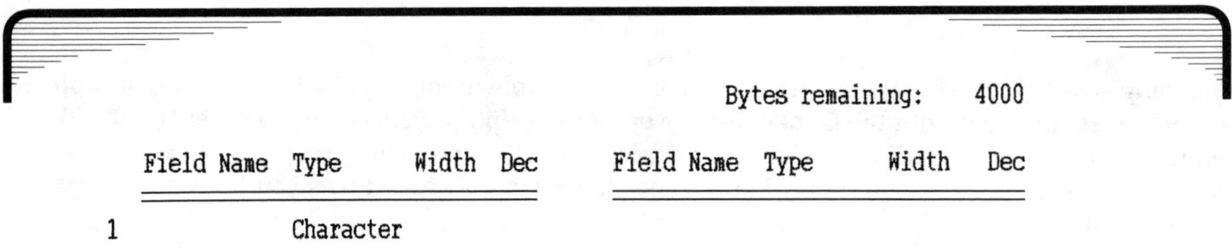

```
    field name   type      width  dec            Remarks
                                                 =======
1   NAME         Character   25            Type NAME<cr> <cr> 25<cr>
2   ST_ADR       Character   25            Type ST_ADR<cr> <cr> 25<cr>
3   C_S_Z        Character   25            Type C_S_Z<cr> <cr> 25<cr>
4   AFFIL        Character   25            Type AFFIL<cr> <cr> 25<cr>
5   JOINED       Date         8            Type JOINED<cr> D<cr>
6   AGE          Numeric      2    0       Type AGE<cr> N<cr> 2<cr> <cr>
7   PAID_UP      Logical      1            Type PAID_UP<cr> L
8   INFO         Memo        10            Type INFO<cr> M
9   <cr>                                   Press <cr> to end CREATE.
```

3. Press **Return** once more to confirm your entries.

4. Type **Y** in response to the "Input data records now?" prompt, notice the following data entry mask, and enter the data as shown. To enter text into a memo field, position the cursor, press **Ctrl-Home**, type the text, and press **Ctrl-W** to redisplay the entry mask.

```
Record No.      1                                    Remarks
NAME       Williams, David
ST_ADR     3456 Fresno Circle
C_S_Z      Tampa, FL 32656
AFFIL      U.S. Air Force (Ret)
JOINED     11/15/80
AGE        56
PAID_UP    Y
INFO       Attended last meeting.    (Press Ctrl-Home, type text, then Ctrl-End.)
           ________________________

Record No.      2
NAME       Phillips, George W.
ST_ADR     11205 Dawn Drive
C_S_Z      Lago Vista, TX 78641
AFFIL      Austin Medical Center
JOINED     06/01/81
AGE        39
PAID_UP    Y
INFO       Wants active role in organization.
           ________________________

Record No.      3
NAME       Galvin, Theodore A.
ST_ADR     5545 Gulch Road
C_S_Z      Culver City, CA 96750
AFFIL      Miracle Micro Shop
JOINED     02/15/83
AGE        42
PAID_UP    N
INFO       May cancel membership.
           ________________________

Record No.      4
NAME       <cr>                     -<cr> in first blank field ends entry.

C_S_Z
AFFIL
JOINED
AGE
PAID_UP
INFO
           ________________________
```

5. The database structure is created, three records are present, and you are back at the dot prompt. CREATE automatically puts the new database in use. However, if you are just entering dBASE, it is necessary to place an existing database in use with the USE command, described in Module 69.

6. Close the database file by typing **CLOSE ALL** and pressing **Return**.

7. Turn to Module 28 to continue the learning sequence.

Module 19
CREATE FROM

DESCRIPTION

The CREATE FROM command is used in conjunction with the COPY TO *filename* STRUCTURE EXTENDED command to establish a standard database file structure. The COPY command and its variations, including STRUCTURE EXTENDED, is described in Module 16.

The general form of the CREATE FROM command is:

    CREATE *file2* FROM *file1*

where the file1 is an extended structure database. The result of this command is a new database that uses the field contents of the extended database as field names.

It is necessary to illustrate the entire process for a clear understanding of what happens when the COPY TO *filename* EXTENDED STRUCTURE and CREATE FROM commands are used. You can examine the results of these commands by performing the step-by-step procedure in the Typical Operation section of this module.

APPLICATIONS

An extended structure database contains four fields that correspond to the field name, field type, field length, and number of decimal places. The database contains a record for each field in the source database file. The records within this four-field database contain field names, field types, field lengths, and the number of decimal places in numeric fields. The structure has been "extended" across the records of this new database.

There are programs that use control files that have the same or similar structure as an extended structure database. For example, the AutoCAD computer-aided drafting program from Autodesk uses an extended structure file to output drawing attributes into an ASCII file that is readable by dBASE by using the COPY TO SDF command (See Module 16). This lets AutoCAD users transfer drawing information to a database that can be used as a bill of material, or perform other types of data analysis.

TYPICAL OPERATION

In this illustration you create a small database, COPY it to an extended structure database file, and then use the CREATE FROM command to create a new database file based on the extended structure. Begin at the dBASE dot prompt.

1. Type **CREATE ADDRESS** and press **Return** to create the following database structure. Respond with **N** to the "Input data..." prompt.

```
Field   Field Name  Type        Width   Dec
    1   NAME        Character     20
    2   ADDRESS     Character     20
    3   CITY        Character     15
    4   STATE       Character      2
    5   ZIP         Character      5
** Total **                      63
```

2. Type **COPY TO TEMP1 STRUCTURE EXTENDED** and press **Return**.

3. Type **USE TEMP1** and press **Return**.

4. Type **LIST STRUCTURE** and press **Return**. Notice the extended structure.

```
. list structure
Structure for database: C:temp1.dbf
Number of data records:        5
Date of last update   : 06/17/88
Field   Field Name  Type        Width   Dec
    1   FIELD_NAME  Character     10
    2   FIELD_TYPE  Character      1
    3   FIELD_LEN   Numeric        3
    4   FIELD_DEC   Numeric        3
** Total **                      18
```

5. Type **LIST** and press **Return** to view the database contents. Notice how each record corresponds to a field in the source (ADDRESS) database.

```
. list
Record#  FIELD_NAME FIELD_TYPE FIELD_LEN FIELD_DEC
     1   NAME       C                20         0
     2   ADDRESS    C                20         0
     3   CITY       C                15         0
     4   STATE      C                 2         0
     5   ZIP        C                 5         0
```

6. Create a new database from the extended structure database file by typing **CREATE NEWADR FROM TEMP1** and pressing **Return**.

7. Type **USE NEWADR** and press **Return**; then type **LIST** and press **Return** to list the contents of the resulting database file. Check the following screen.

```
. create newadr from temp1
. list structure
Structure for database: C:newadr.dbf
Number of data records:        0
Date of last update   : 06/17/88
Field  Field Name  Type       Width    Dec
    1  NAME        Character     20
    2  ADDRESS     Character     20
    3  CITY        Character     15
    4  STATE       Character      2
    5  ZIP         Character      5
** Total **                      63
```

8. Notice that the NEWADR database file structure is identical to the original source file, ADDRESS.DBF created in step 1.

9. Type **CLOSE ALL** and press **Return** to close all database files.

10. Erase the practice files by typing the following command lines and pressing **Return** after each:

    ERASE NEWADR.DBF
    ERASE TEMP1.DBF
    ERASE ADDRESS.DBF

11. Turn to Module 35 to continue the learning sequence.

Module 20
CREATE/MODIFY LABEL, LABEL FORM

DESCRIPTION

The CREATE/MODIFY LABEL command is used to create or modify a label format file. A label format file has the extension .LBL and is used to print labels from a database file. Once a label format file is created, the LABEL FORM command is used to display and print labels.

CREATE/MODIFY LABEL   The common form of the CREATE LABEL or MODIFY LABEL command is:

> . CREATE LABEL *filename*

> or

> . MODIFY LABEL *filename*

The CREATE LABEL command is used to prepare the label file from scratch, while MODIFY LABEL is used to edit an existing label file. The filename is given the extension .LBL unless you provide an extension of your own.

There are two main label screens to help guide you through the creation and modification of a label control file. The first is shown in the following illustration.

```
 Options                      Contents                  Exit  09:05:16 pm
 ┌───────────────────────────────────────────────────────────┐
 │ Predefined size:       3 1/2 x 15/16 by 1                  │
 ├───────────────────────────────────────────────────────────┤
 │ Label width:           35                                  │
 │ Label height:          5                                   │
 │ Left margin:           0                                   │
 │ Lines between labels:  1                                   │
 │ Spaces between labels: 0                                   │
 │ Labels across page:    1                                   │
 └───────────────────────────────────────────────────────────┘
```

Standard label size selections, in inches, are:

Wide	High	No. Across
3 1/2	15/16	1
3 1/2	15/16	2
3 1/2	15/16	3
4	1 7/16	1
3 2/10	11/12	3

Some label range settings follow:

Width	1 to 120 characters
Height	1 to 16 lines
Left margin	0 to 250 characters
Lines between labels	0 to 16 lines
Spaces between labels	0 to 120 characters
Labels across the page	1 to 15 labels

The Contents menu bar selection displays the following screen.

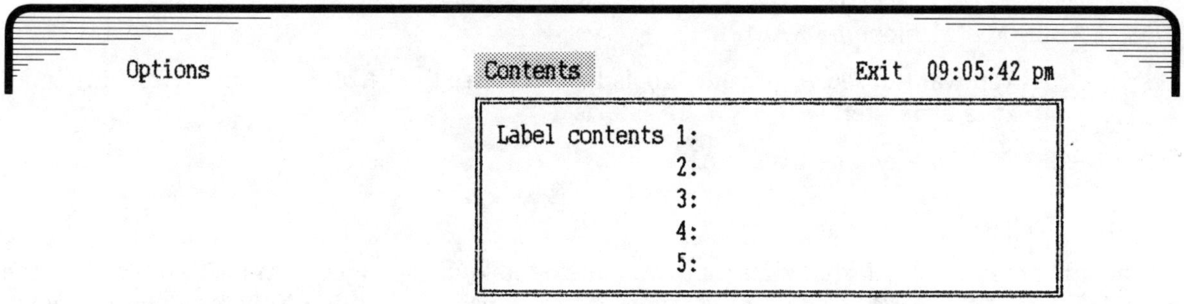

This screen lets you select fields from within the active database. Pressing **F10** displays a window containing the field names. The Typical Operation section of this module lets you use the screens to see how they operate.

LABEL FORM   The LABEL FORM command is used to print your labels. To use the label file, type **LABEL FORM** *filename* from the dBASE dot prompt. If you just type **LABEL**, dBASE displays the prompt "Enter label file name:." Enter the filename and press **Return**.

There are a number of options available with the LABEL command. These are briefly described in the following list:

1. LABEL FORM *filename* TO PRINT

    This form of the LABEL command sends the information to your printer.

2. LABEL FORM *filename* TO FILE *filename*

    This form of the LABEL command writes the information to a disk file having the specified filename.

3. LABEL FORM *filename* WHILE *condition*

    This form of the LABEL command outputs information as long as some established condition exists.

    LABEL FORM ADDRESS WHILE ZIP < = '96000'

4. LABEL FORM *filename* FOR *expression*

    This form only outputs records matching the expression.

    LABEL FORM ADDRESS WHILE ZIP = '75080'

5. LABEL FORM *filename* SAMPLE

    If you want to see what your labels look like, use the SAMPLE clause. Here, the label text is simulated with rows of asterisks.

6. LABEL FORM *filename* SUMMARY

APPLICATIONS

Although labels can be designed using print statements and @ row,col SAY-GET statements, the CREATE/MODIFY LABEL command is much easier to use. In addition to being able to quickly and easily design printed labels, you can also edit them with MODIFY LABEL.

Forms of the LABEL command let you select your label output (printer or disk file), select specific records, and display a graphic presentation of your label format. The SAMPLE clause is quite helpful, because you can see the number of lines, label width, and spacing between labels.

TYPICAL OPERATION

In this illustration a label form is created and used with the CREATE LABEL and LABEL FORM commands. The ADDRESS database file created in Module 49 is used. Begin at the dBASE dot prompt.

1. Type **USE ADDRESS** to open the address database file.

2. Type **CREATE LABEL ADR** to create a new label format file named ADR.LBL.

3. Notice the opening entry mask and prompts.

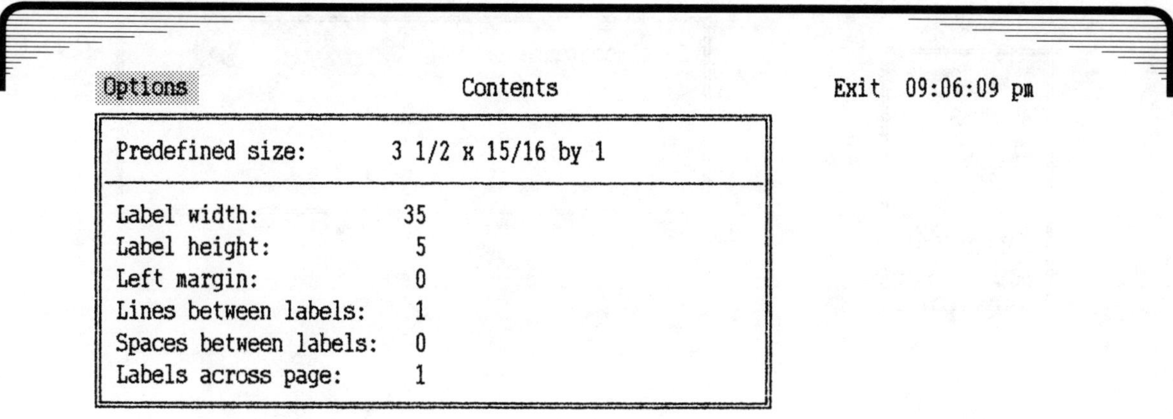

4. For a single column label, accept the default values and press the **Right Arrow** to highlight the Contents selection on the menu bar.

5. Notice the display and prompt associated with Contents.

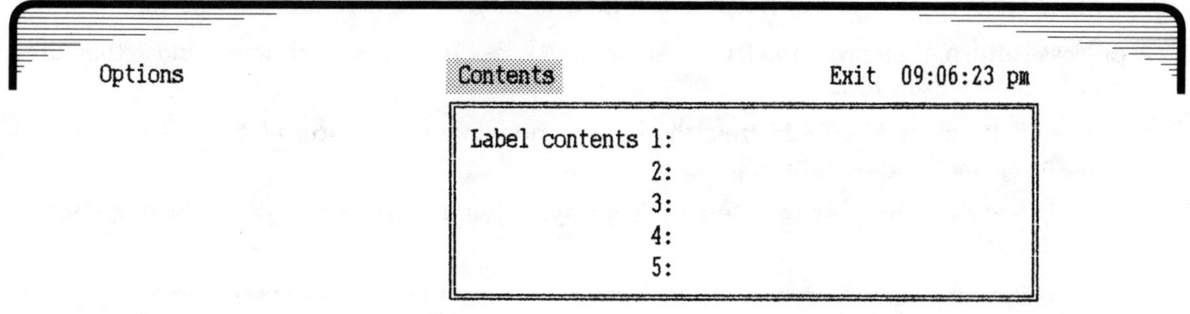

6. Press **Return**. Then press **F10** to display the field names within a window.

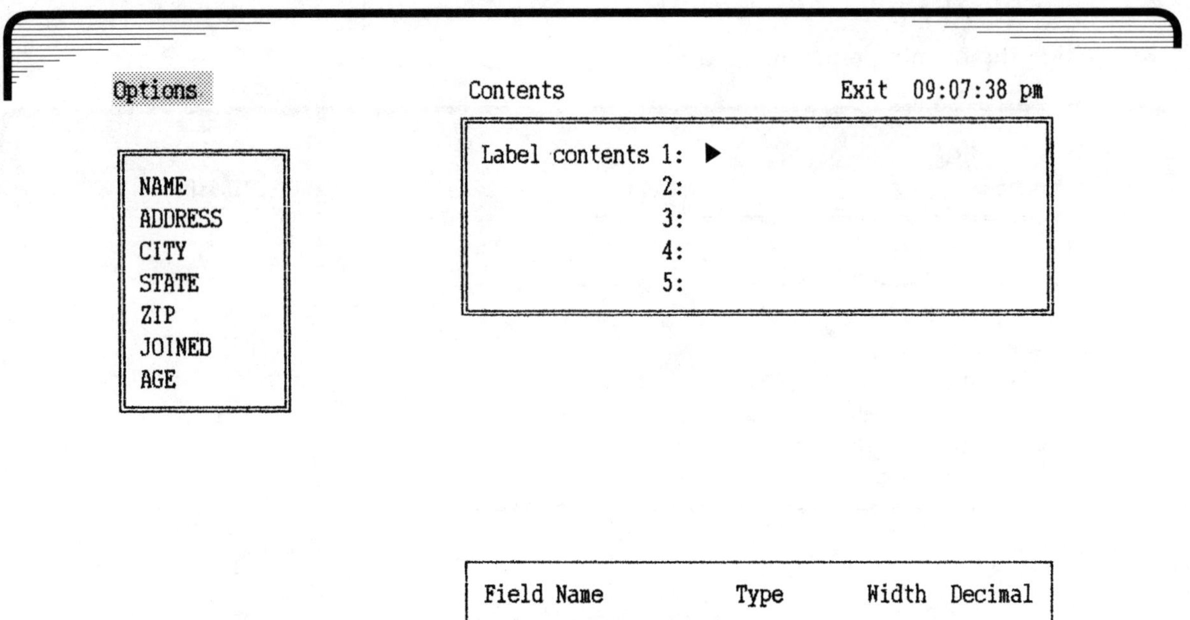

7. Press **Return** to move the hightlighted field to line 1 of the contents window.

8. Press **Return**, then press the **Down Arrow**, and press **Return** a final time to move the cursor to the entry area of line 2.

9. Press **F10**, select ADDRESS from the field name window, and press **Return** a final time to move the field name to line 2.

10. Press **Return**, **Down Arrow**, **Return**. Then type line 3 as shown in the following contents window.

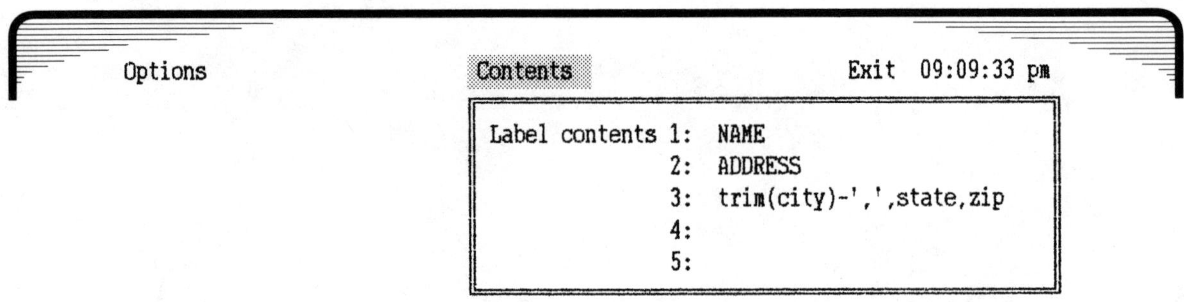

11. Press **Return** to leave the entry area; then move the cursor to Exit on the menu bar and press **Return** to Save the label file.

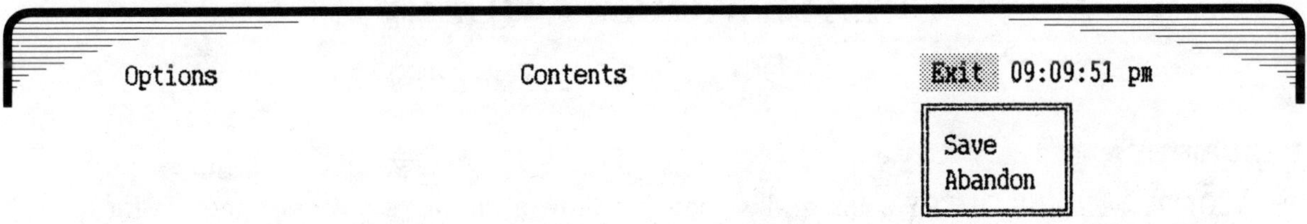

You are now ready to print labels that use the contents of the ADDRESS database.

12. Type **LABEL FORM ADR** and press **Return** to view your labels on the screen.

13. Type **LABEL FORM ADR TO PRINT** to route the labels to your printer. The labels produced by ADR.LBL resemble the following ones.

```
John Billings
2320 Hawthorne Ave.
Trenton, NJ 03565
```

```
Mary Tremore
56 Park Lane
Culver City, CA 95065
```

```
Fred Franklin
3900 Brookside Road
Hobbs, NM 85676
```

```
Chuck Williams
56 Walmart Plaza
Jasper, TX 75611
```

14. Experiment with the label generator by trying different values for two- and three-up (column) format labels.

15. Turn to Module 21 to continue the learning sequence.

Module 21

CREATE/MODIFY QUERY

DESCRIPTION

The CREATE/MODIFY QUERY command is used to create or change a database inquiry (or query) file that selects specific fields or records matching a set of established rules. This process is often referred to as a filter, because it "filters out" unwanted information and "passes" information meeting the criteria that you establish.

When CREATE QUERY *filename* is used, a query file with the extension .QRY is created. More precisely, CREATE QUERY is used to originate the query file; MODIFY QUERY is used to alter the contents of the query file. When used, the dBASE query generation utility is used for data entry screen design in the same way that the report or label generation utilities are used to design report and label form (.FRM and .LBL) files. The database file containing the query contents must be open for the CREATE/MODIFY QUERY command to work.

When you type **CREATE QUERY** *filename*, the following screen is displayed.

```
   Set Filter              Nest            Display           Exit  09:10:40 pm

  | Field Name                                        |
  | Operator                                          |
  | Constant/Expression                               |
  | Connect                                           |
  |---------------------------------------------------|
  | Line Number           1                           |
```

Line	Field	Operator	Constant/Expression	Connect
1				
2				
3				
4				
5				
6				
7				

The menu bar across the top of the screen displays four options, each of which displays a menu window. To understand the use of each, you may wish to move to the Typical Operation section of this module to experiment with query file generation.

APPLICATIONS

You can use query files to control the way database information is displayed. After creating and saving a query file, you can call the query file into action using SET FILTER TO *query filename*. Commands that control data output, like LIST and DISPLAY, are controlled, or filtered, by the query file.

TYPICAL OPERATION

In the following illustration you use the CREATE QUERY command to produce a query file that is used with the ADDRESS database file created in Module 49. Begin at the dBASE dot prompt.

1. Type **USE ADDRESS** and press **Return** to open the address database file.

2. Type **CREATE QUERY ADR1** and press **Return** to create a query file with the filename ADR1.QRY.

3. Press **Return** and notice that a field name window is displayed.

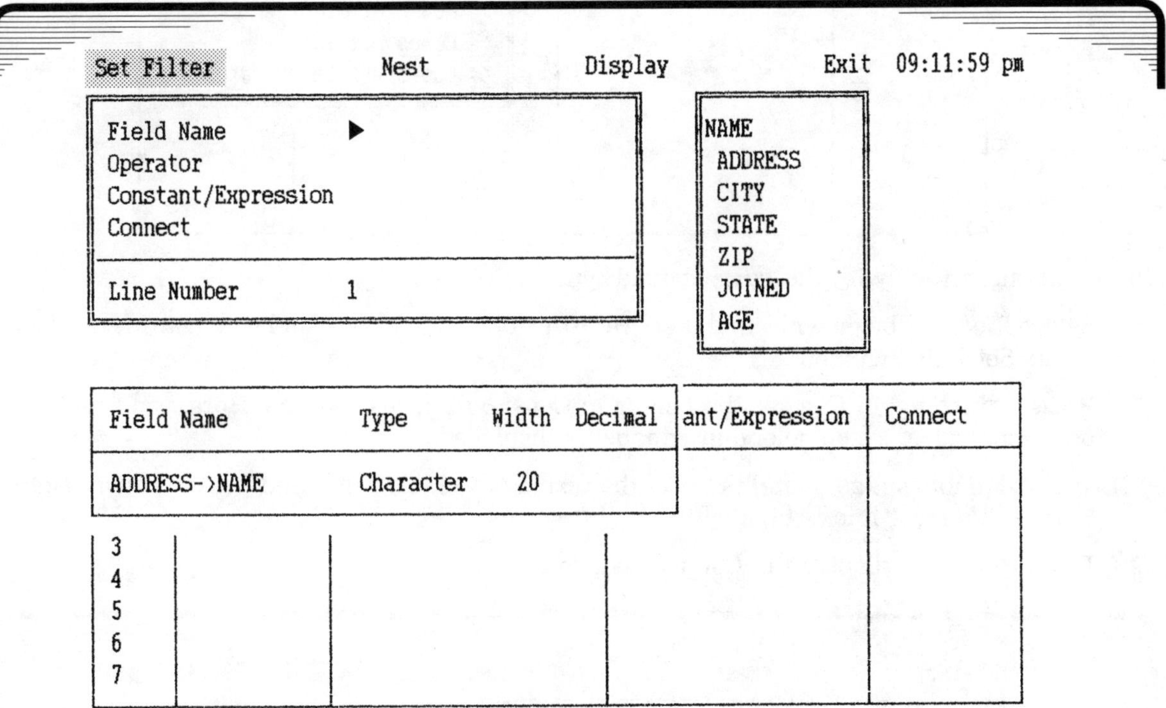

The first field (NAME) is highlighted.

4. Press **Return** again and notice that NAME is selected as the first Field Name in the Set Filter window. It is also entered as Line 1 in the table, and the Operator field is highlighted.

5.   Press **Return** to display an Operator choice Window.

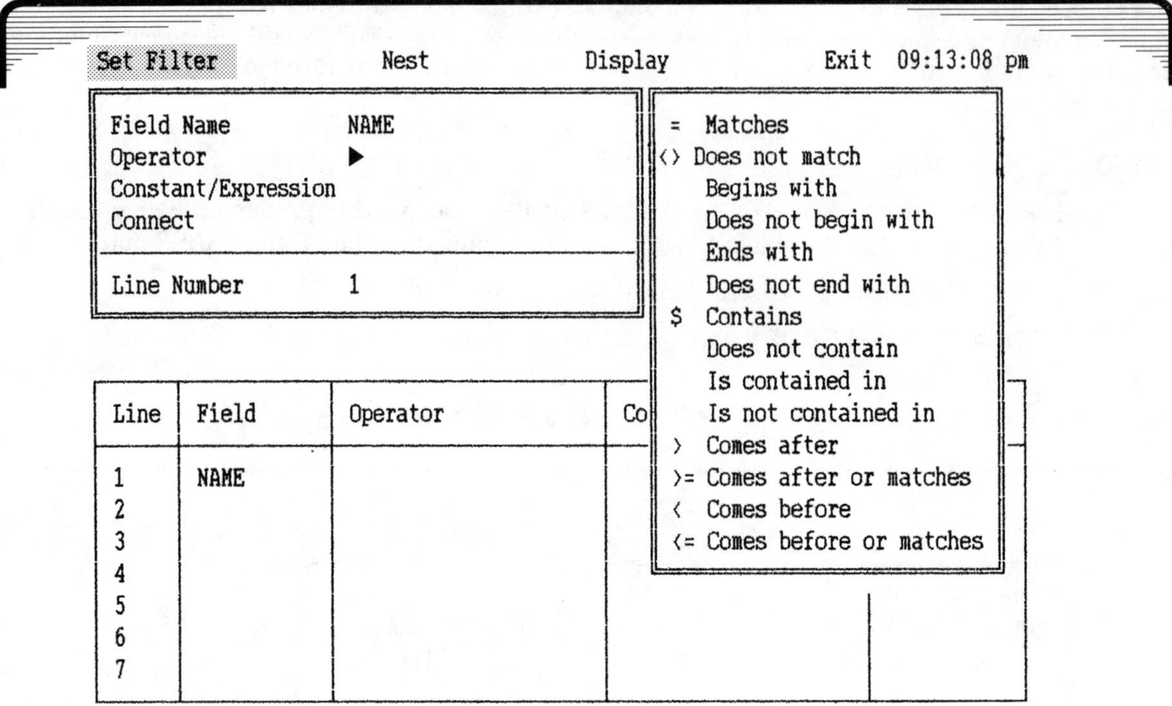

These operators vary with the current field type.

6.   Select "Does not begin with" and press **Return**; notice that "Does not begin with" is displayed in the Set Filter window.

7.   Press **Return** again to move the cursor to Constant/Expression line. Here, you input your own expression, as no selection window is displayed.

8.   Type ' ' (quote space quote) to avoid the display of blank fields and press **Return**. Notice that the Connect line is highlighted.

9.   Press **Return** to display the Connect window.

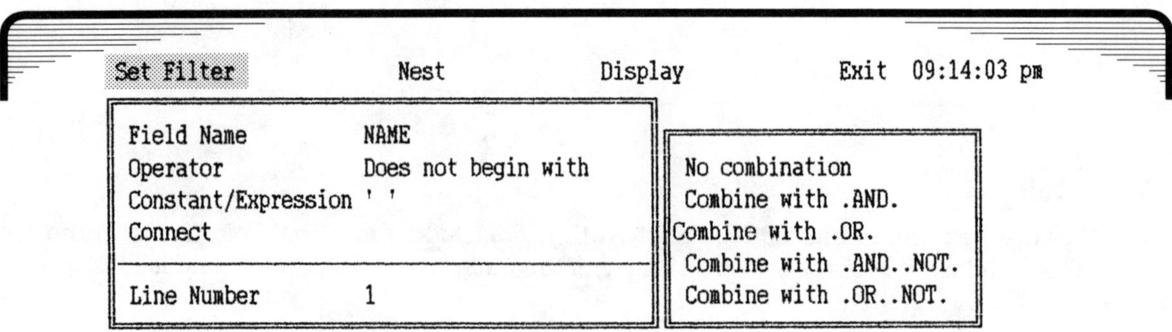

10. Select "Combine with .AND. .NOT." and press **Return**. Notice that Line 1 of the query file contains the following information.

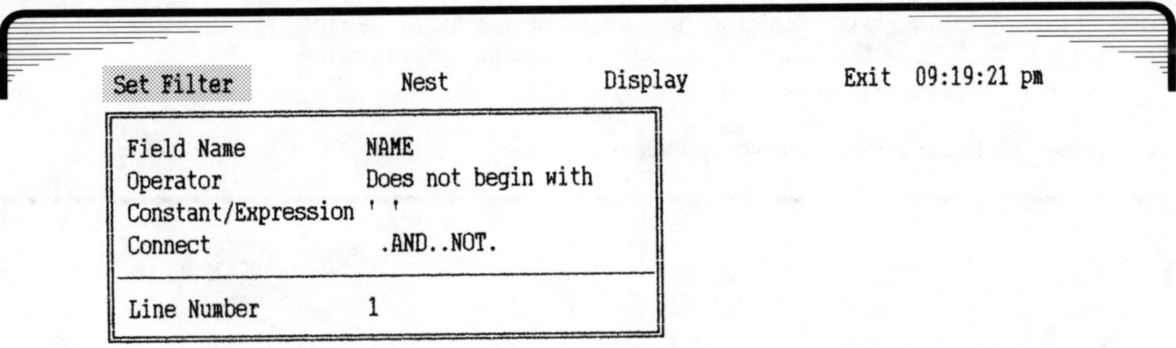

11. Press **Return** again to accept the information for Line 1, and prepare Line Number 2 in the Set Filter mask so that it contains the following information.

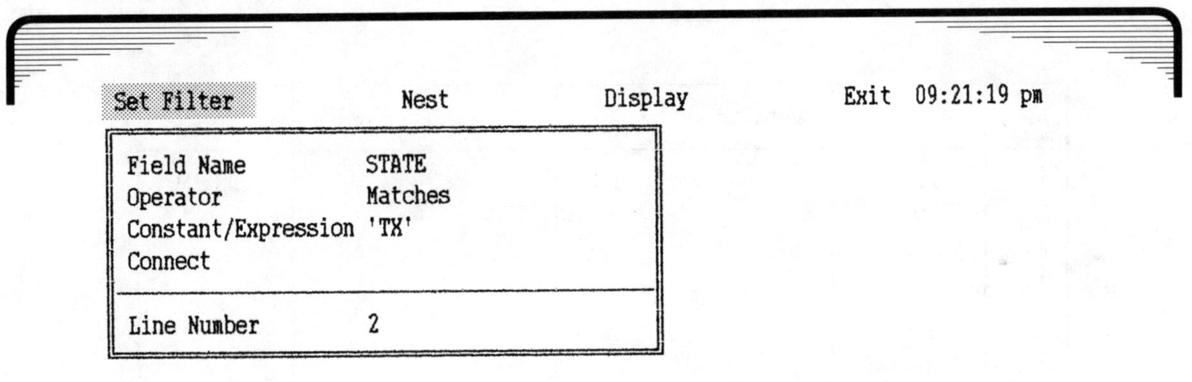

Line	Field	Operator	Constant/Expression	Connect
1	NAME	Does not begin with	' '	.AND..NOT.
2	STATE	Matches	'TX'	
3				
4				
5				
6				
7				

NOTE

If you have several expressions that require nesting, that is, one series of filter instructions is combined within parentheses, you can use the **Right Arrow** to move to the Nest option on the menu bar.

12. Press the **Right Arrow** to display a nest window.

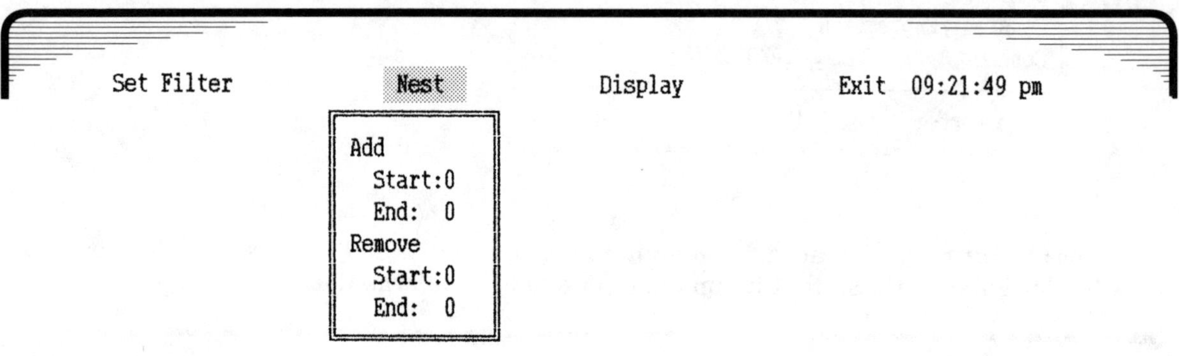

Line	Field	Operator	Constant/Expression	Connect
1	NAME	Does not begin with	' '	.AND..NOT.
2	STATE	Matches	'TX'	
3				
4				
5				
6				
7				

NOTE

The Add Start: option lets you place an open parenthesis at the beginning of line number 1 through 7. Add End: places a close parenthesis on the selected line number. The Remove Start:/End: options are for editing parentheses placement. Nesting is not required in this example, so move on to the Display option on the menu bar.

13. Use the **Right Arrow** to move the cursor to the Display option on the menu bar and press **Return**. Notice that the first field of the address database file is displayed.

14. Use **PgDn** and **PgUp** to test your filter. If everything is right, no records containing a blank space at the beginning of the NAME field or TX in the STATE field are displayed.

15. Move to the Exit option on the menu bar and press **Return** to save your query file (ADR1.QRY).

NOTE

Saving the query file activates the command SET FILTER TO file adr1.qry automatically. To deactivate the query file, type **SET FILTER TO** and press **Return**.

16. Type **list** and press **Return**. Notice that the filter is on.

```
. list
Record#  NAME                 ADDRESS              CITY         STATE ZIP
      1  John Billings        2320 Hawthorne Ave.  Trenton      NJ    03565
      2  Mary Tremore         56 Park Lane         Culver City  CA    95065
      3  Fred Franklin        3900 Brookside Road  Hobbs        NM    85676
```

17. Type **SET FILTER TO** and press **Return**. Notice that record number 4 is no longer filtered from the display.

```
. list
Record#  NAME                 ADDRESS              CITY         STATE ZIP
      1  John Billings        2320 Hawthorne Ave.  Trenton      NJ    03565
      2  Mary Tremore         56 Park Lane         Culver City  CA    95065
      3  Fred Franklin        3900 Brookside Road  Hobbs        NM    85676
      4  Chuck Williams       56 Walmart Plaza     Jasper       TX    75611
```

18. Turn to Module 23 to continue the learning sequence.

Module 22

CREATE/MODIFY REPORT, REPORT FORM

DESCRIPTION

Report form files are created and modified with the CREATE or MODIFY REPORT command. Before the command is used, a database file must be in use. The field characteristics within the selected database file are used to help you design your report form.

Both .DBF and .VUE files are used with the CREATE or MODIFY REPORT command. Once designed, the REPORT FORM *filename* command is used to reproduce the report on your screen. If you add the TO PRINT clause to the REPORT FORM command, the report is printed as it is displayed on your screen.

The default extension given a report form file is .FRM. However, you can assign a different extension upon creation, or you can use the RENAME command to rename the file extension.

Typing **CREATE FORM** *filename* and pressing **Return** displays the following screen.

```
  Options          Groups        Columns        Locate      Exit  09:22:58 pm
 ┌─────────────────────────────────────┐
 │ Page title                          │
 │ Page width (positions)     80       │
 │ Left margin                 8       │
 │ Right margin                0       │
 │ Lines per page             58       │
 │ Double space report        No       │
 │ Page eject before printing Yes      │
 │ Page eject after printing  No       │
 │ Plain page                 No       │
 └─────────────────────────────────────┘
```

During creation and modification of a report form, the following keys are used.

Description	*Key(s)*
Editing menu/form width toggle	F1
Begin/finish an entry	Return
Move to another menu bar selection	Right or Left Arrow → ←
Erase a delimiter	Backspace

Select a field name	Up or Down Arrow ↑ ↓
Choose a field name	Return
Display field name list upon entry	F10

The selections across the top of the screen is called the *menu bar*. Each selection on the menu bar has a corresponding menu window. These windows are used in the Typical Operation section of this module.

Selecting Groups displays the following menu window.

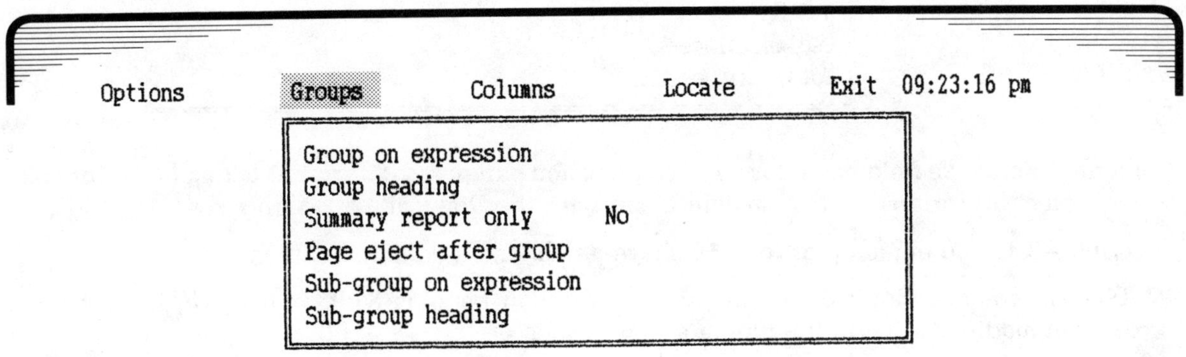

You can enter dates in character form by placing them within parentheses and quotes, in the form ('03/03/93'). When entered this way, the date-to-character function (DTOC) is applied automatically.

The prompts on this screen are described in the following list.

Group on expression—Groups records having a common value in a key field. New groups are started when a new value is encountered. The key field is selected in the Columns menu selection.

Group heading—Lets you enter a report heading that is displayed as each new group is encountered and displayed.

Summary report only—No includes all records in the report. Yes eliminates detail information, and only provides subtotals.

Page eject after group—Yes causes a form feed after each group is printed. No prints the groups together.

Sub-group on expression—Lets you specify a secondary level of grouping for sub-groups within groups. Like the main group, sub-groups should also be indexed or sorted.

Sub-group heading—Lets you enter a report heading that is displayed as each new sub-group is encountered and displayed.

The Column selection displays the following menu window:

```
Options          Groups         Columns         Locate        Exit  09:23:43 pm
                              +------------------------------------------+
                              | Contents                                 |
                              | Heading                                  |
                              | Width                                    |
                              | Decimal places                           |
                              | Total this column                        |
                              +------------------------------------------+
```

Contents—Enter the field name for each column. You can press Return F10 to display a field list. Select and return to the Column menu with the Right or Left Arrow key.

Heading—Lets you enter up to four 59-character lines as column headings.

Width—The column widths default to the field width or heading width, whichever is larger. You can modify the width by typing a new value.

Decimal places—Uses the file structure value. If you enter a smaller number, the displayed result is rounded. Only applies to numeric fields.

Total this column—The default is to print the total at the bottom of the report. Type No to suppress printing.

The Locate selection lists the selections that you made using the Columns menu window. Exit lets you Save or Abandon your form work.

The Typical Operation section of this module uses the CREATE REPORT command to guide you through the creation of a report form.

REPORT FORM   The REPORT FORM command is used to print information from the active database. It uses a report form file created with the CREATE REPORT or modified with the MODIFY REPORT commands. The form of the command is:

    . REPORT FORM *filename*

  1.   REPORT FORM *filename* TO PRINT

        This form of the command outputs the report directly to your printer.

where the filename is a report form file. Report files normally have the extension .FRM.

A number of options are available with the REPORT FORM command. You can direct report output to a file, to the printer, suppress headings, suppress form feeds, add a unique heading, and include only those records containing a specific expression. Forms of the command are included in the following list:

2. REPORT FORM *filename* TO PRINT NO EJECT

    The NO EJECT clause suppresses the first form feed. This lets you use the first sheet of paper in your printer.

3. REPORT FORM *filename* TO FILE *filename*

    This command outputs the report to a disk file having the specified filename.

4. REPORT FORM *filename* FOR *expression*

    Here, only those records matching the expression are contained in the report.

    . REPORT FORM INVOICE FOR .NOT. PAID

    In this example all records containing a false condition in the PAID field are included in the report.

5. REPORT FORM *filename* WHILE *expression*

    The records are displayed in the report while an expression is true.

    . REPORT FORM INVOICE WHILE INV_NO < '8607'

    Displays reports while the INV_NO field contains a value of less than "8607."

6. REPORT FORM *filename* PLAIN

    The PLAIN clause suppresses printing of the date and time and prints only the heading on the first page to the report.

7. REPORT FORM *filename* HEADING *'heading text'*

    The report is printed with the extra heading line. The heading text is always enclosed in single or double quotes or brackets.

8. REPORT FORM *filename* SUMMARY

    The SUMMARY clause suppresses the printing of detail, and only lists subtotals and totals.

APPLICATIONS

The MODIFY REPORT command is a fast way to create standard reports. The displays that show you how many characters are used in a column or how many remain on the page are helpful during report design. The alternative to using the MODIFY REPORT command is to use print statements and @ row,col SAY-GET statements.

The ability to print summaries and subtotal values quickly and easily is also a valuable byproduct of the dBASE report generator.

The REPORT FORM command is used to access report form files. The optional forms of the command let you add information to your heading, print selective records, or output the report to either the printer or a file on demand.

TYPICAL OPERATION

In the following illustration, the ADDRESS database created and used in Module 49 is used as the basis for report design. Once the report is designed, the REPORT FORM command is used to display the report on your screen. Begin at the dBASE dot prompt.

1. Type **USE ADDRESS** and press **Return**.

2. Type **CREATE REPORT MEMBERS** and press **Return**; Notice the following screen.

```
Options          Groups        Columns        Locate        Exit  09:25:19 pm

   Page title
   Page width (positions)     80
   Left margin                 8
   Right margin                0
   Lines per page             58
   Double space report        No
   Page eject before printing Yes
   Page eject after printing  No
   Plain page                 No
```

3. Press **Return** to enter a heading, type **Membership Report**, and press **Ctrl-End** to complete the entry.

4. Accept the rest of the Options values as they exist, and press the **Right Arrow** to select Groups. Notice the selections in the Groups window.

```
Options          Groups        Columns        Locate        Exit  09:26:00 pm

       Group on expression
       Group heading
       Summary report only      No
       Page eject after group
       Sub-group on expression
       Sub-group heading
```

NOTE

The Groups selection is optional. You can use this selection to group selected fields that comply with an expression or value. You may sort or index a database if you wish to use a key field, i.e., a field that is the basis of a sort or index.

5. Notice that the bottom line of your screen provides information about each choice in the Groups window. Use the **Down** and **Up Arrows** to see the different prompt lines.

6. Press the **Right Arrow** to select Columns on the menu bar. Notice the following screen. The editing keys window now presents a view of an empty report form. This changes as you enter field names.

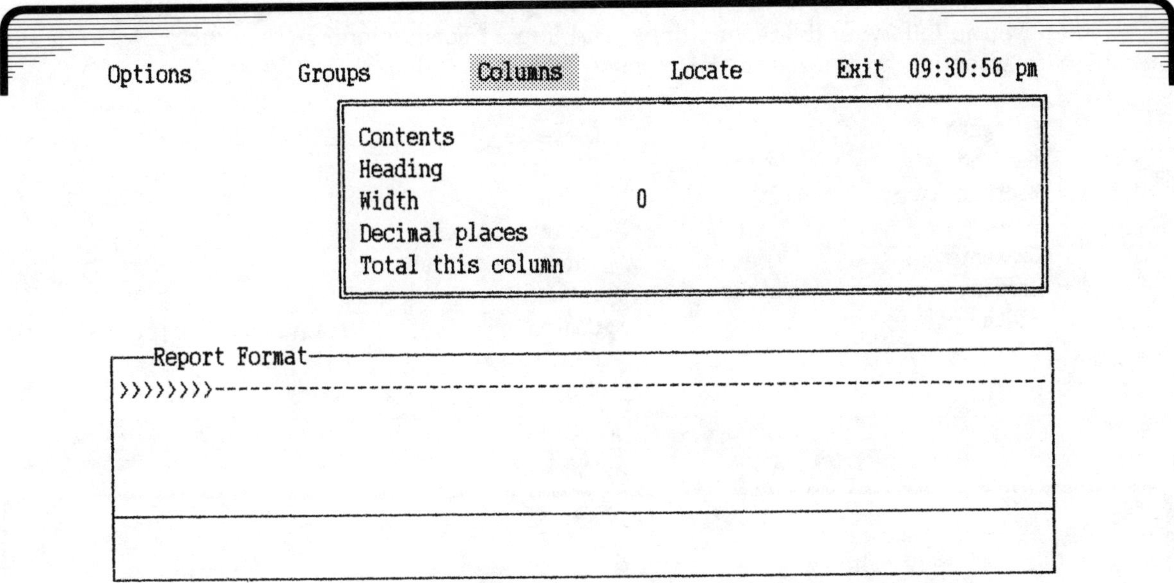

7. With "Contents" highlighted, press **Return** to move the cursor to the entry area. Then press **F10** for field name selection. Notice that "NAME" is highlighted.

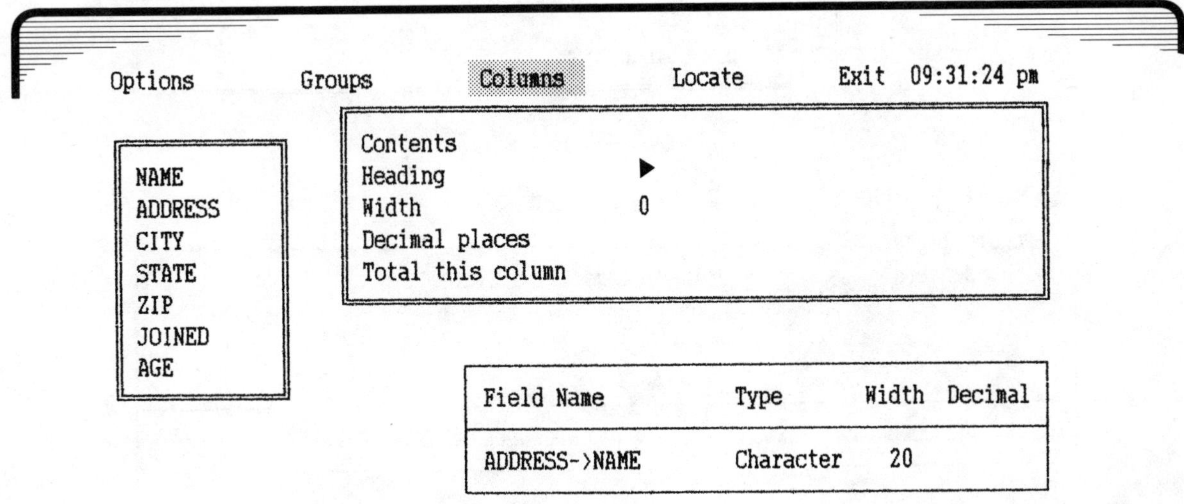

8. Press **Return** twice to accept NAME as the field. Notice that the field width is represented by X's in the Report Format window.

9. Press the **Down Arrow** to move the Heading selection and press **Return**. A window is displayed in which to type a column heading. Respond by typing **Member** and press **Ctrl-End** to end the heading entry.

10. Press **PgDn** to select the next field. Repeat the process described in steps 6 through 8 until you have the following fields, headings, and Report Form window. (Use **PgUp**, **PgDn** or the Locate selection on the menu bar to move between fields.)

```
Contents        NAME           Contents          AGE
Heading         Member         Heading           Age
Width           20             Width             3
                               Decimal places    0
Contents        JOINED         Total this column No
Heading         Joined
Width           8              Contents          trim(city)-', '+state+' '+zip
                               Heading           City, State, Zip
                               Width             35
```

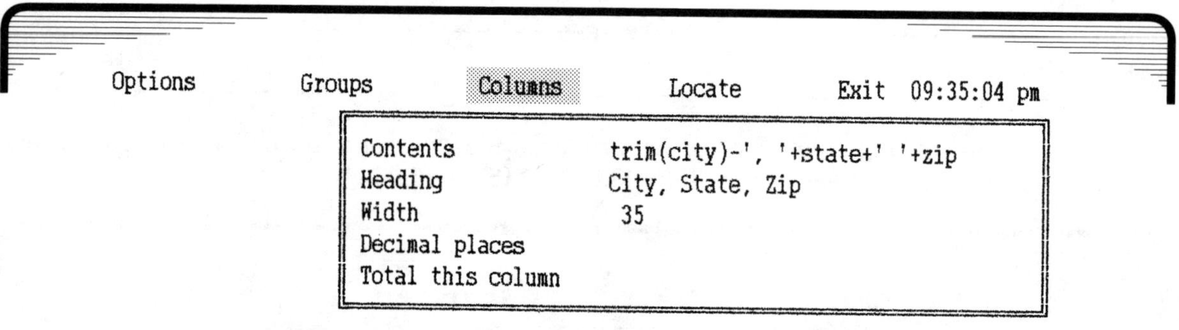

11. When your form resembles the one shown, you can use Exit-Save on the menu bar to save your report format file.

12. View the report by typing **REPORT FORM MEMBERS** and pressing **Return**.

The Report Format window displays symbols that represent the type of information contained in columns. The following list describes each symbol.

Symbol	Meaning
)))))	Left margin
(((((	Right margin
XXXXX	Character field
99999	Number field
mm/dd/yy	Date field (SET CENTURY ON displays mm/dd/yyyy)
.L.	Logical field
?	Memo field

13. Turn to Module 20 to continue the learning sequence.

Module 23
CREATE/MODIFY SCREEN

DESCRIPTION

The CREATE SCREEN and MODIFY SCREEN commands give you access to the dBASE screen painter. A series of menu windows and prompts are displayed to guide you through the generation of a data input or a report display screen.

A screen (.SCR) file, which contains the names of one or more database files, and a corresponding format (.FMT) file are produced. The .FMT file contains a series of @ row,col-GET and @ row,col-SAY command lines. The .FMT file may be used as part of a standard program (or command) file, as well as being used with SET FORMAT TO *.fmt filename*. This SET command links the database file to the .FMT file to control the display of database information and input screens when using EDIT, APPEND, and INSERT.

The CREATE SCREEN command is sometimes used to create a database file structure. If you have forgotten the name of screen files that correspond to an open database file, you can type **MODIFY SCREEN ?** to list a catalog of .SCR files associated with the open database file.

You are guided through the use of the CREATE SCREEN command in the Typical Operation section of this module. There, you see the menus and prompts associated with this powerful utility.

APPLICATIONS

The CREATE/MODIFY SCREEN command is versatile, and you should take some time to experiment with this command. It can save you hours of programming time when @ row,col-GET and SAY lines are required. The alternative is to write your programs by selecting row and column positions by trial and error.

To use the screen painter (blackboard) as a program generator, you can use a dummy database filename with one field. Once the screen is designed, change the file extension from .FMT to .PRG and integrate it into a standard dBASE command file.

TYPICAL OPERATION

In the following illustration, the ADDRESS database file, created in Module 49, is used and a data entry mask is created using the CREATE SCREEN command. The corresponding .FMT file is shown following the entry instructions. Try it out to see how easy this convenient dBASE utility makes screen design. Check Module 49 for the ADDRESS.DBF file structure and contents. Begin at the dBASE dot prompt.

1. Type **USE ADDRESS** and press **Return** to open the ADDRESS.DBF file.

2. Type **CREATE SCREEN ADR1** and press **Return**. The following screen is displayed.

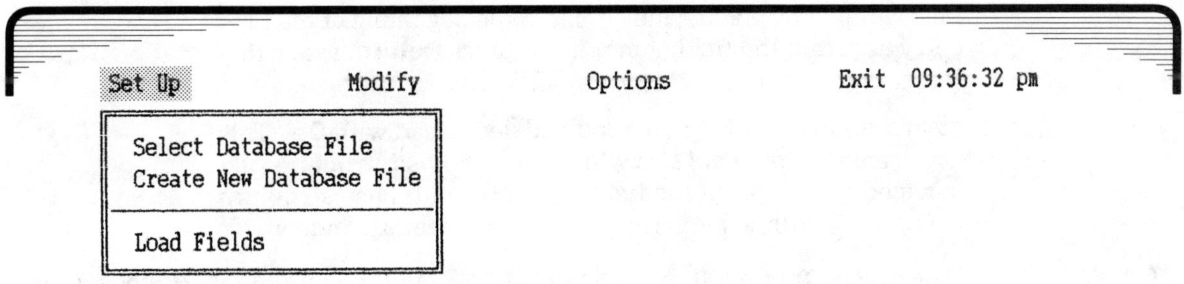

3. Press the **Down Arrow** key to highlight the Load Fields selection in the Set Up window and press **Return**. Notice that the database field names are displayed in a window.

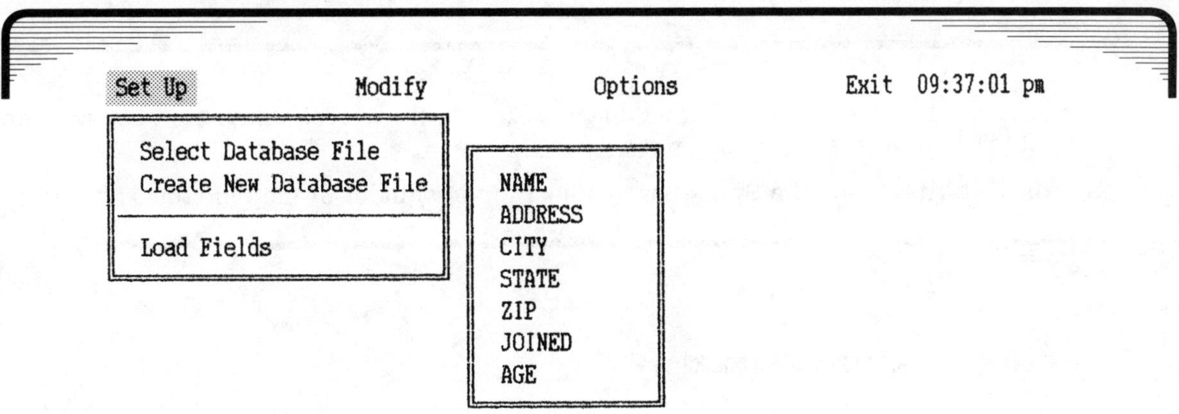

4. Press **Return** and **Down Arrow** until a triangular marker is displayed at the beginning of each field name. The marker designates that these fields are selected.

5. Press either the **Left** or **Right Arrow** and notice the screen painter's "blackboard" is displayed, and includes all marked fields.

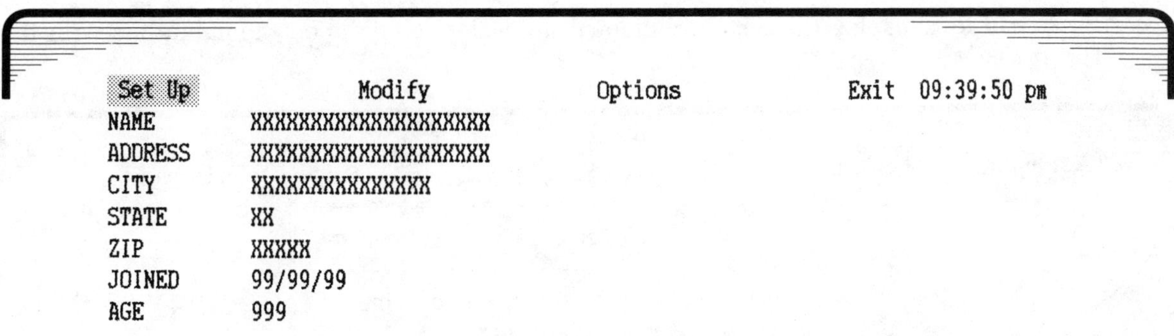

NOTE

When using the screen painter's blackboard, you can move fields around by placing the cursor at the beginning of the field entry area (not the field name). Then press **Return**, reposition the cursor, and press **Return** again.

Field sizes are enlarged with **Ins** and decreased with **Del**. This doesn't modify the field size within the database structure. You can modify the size of the field within the database structure using the Width selection in the Options menu window.

6. With the cursor at Row 00 Col 00, press **Ins** (or **Ctrl-V**) to turn on the insert mode. Check the CREATE SCREEN bar for "Ins."

7. Press **Return** to move the NAME field down to Row 01; then press **Spacebar** once to move the NAME field to the right one space.

8. Use the **Return** key and the **Spacebar** to adjust the remainder of the field lines as shown.

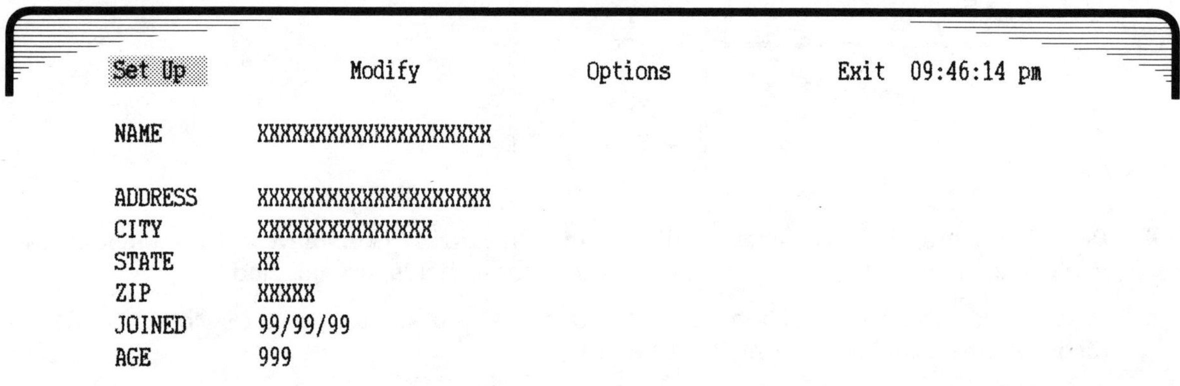

9. Press **F10** to redisplay the Set Up window; then select Options on the menu bar with the **Right Arrow**.

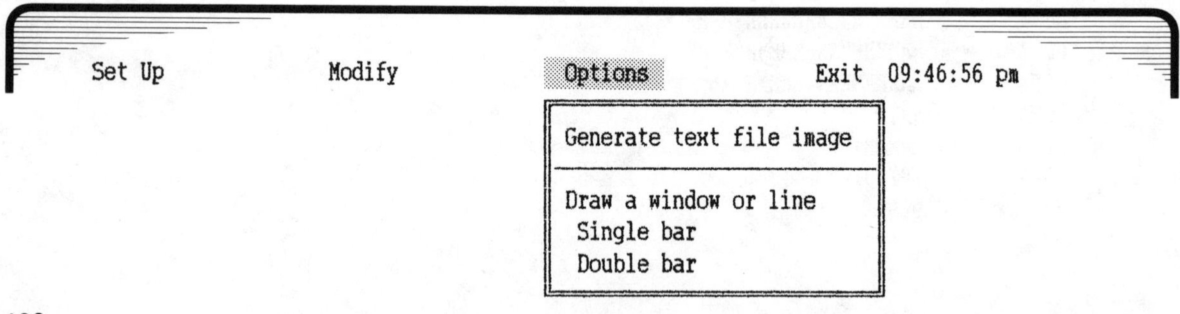

10. Select Double Bar with the **Down Arrow** and press **Return**.

11. Move the cursor to Row 00 Col 00 and press **Return**.

12. Move the cursor to Row 09 Col 34 and press **Return**. Notice the double bar frame.

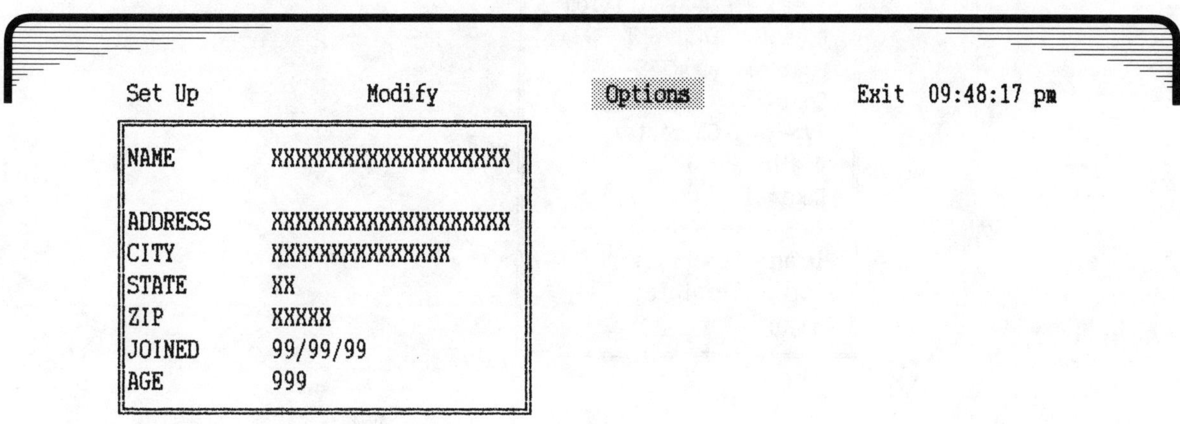

13. Press **F10** and redisplay the Options menu.

14. Select the Single bar and press **Return**.·

15. Move the cursor to Row 02 Col 01 and press **Return**; then move the cursor to Row 02 Col 33 and press **Return**. Your display should now resemble the following one.

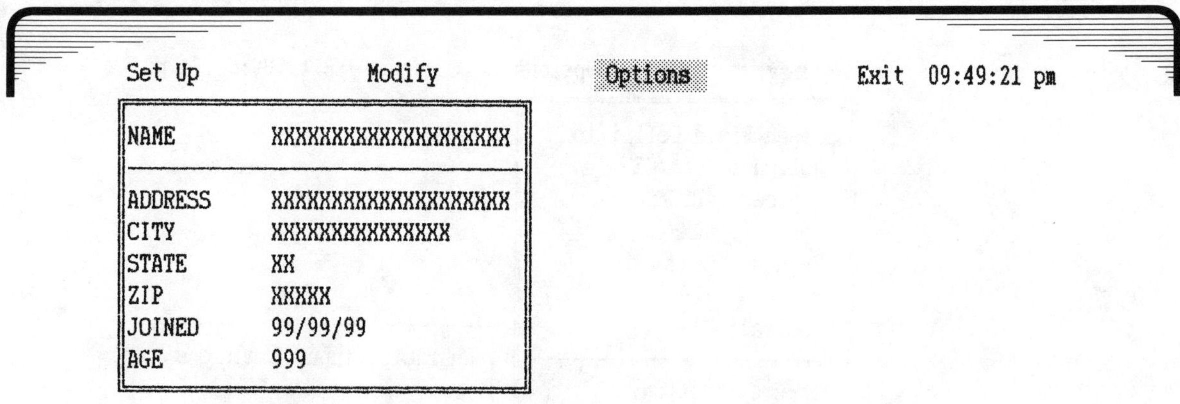

16. You now have a data entry mask for the ADDRESS database file. The default setting is @ row,col Edit/GET *fieldname*. You can change Edit/GET to Display/SAY using the Modify window. Check the Modify menu window by pressing **F10**.

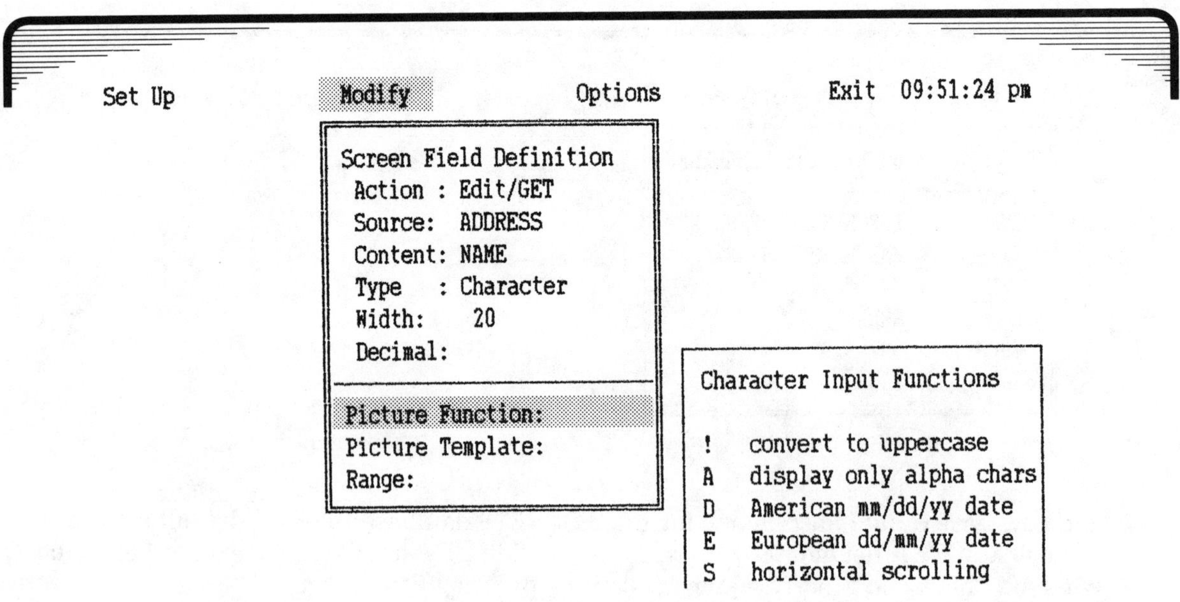

17. Move to the Content selection and press **Return** to display a field list. This lets you select one or more fields. To see how it works, select NAME and check the display as follows.

   a. Select Content and press **Return**; then select NAME and press **Return**. Notice that the field characteristics are displayed.

   b. Select Picture Function and press **Return**. Notice that the display shows you picture options and prompts you to make a picture selection.

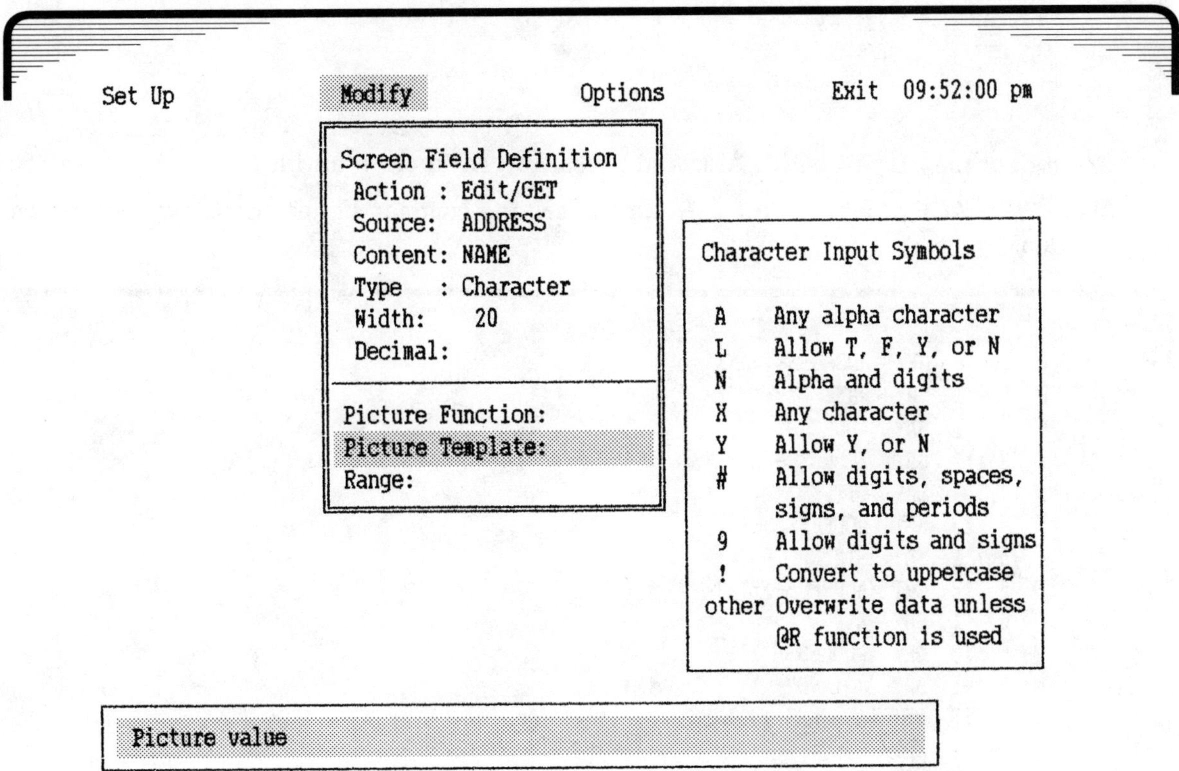

c. Press **Esc** and use the **Down Arrow** to select Picture Template. Press **Return** and notice the Picture Template Character Input Functions.

d. Pick other field types and notice that the Picture Function and Template choices vary. Use **Esc** to back out of selections.

18. Select Exit Save on the menu bar to save your original setup.

19. Type **SET FORMAT TO ADR1** and press **Return**.

20. Type **EDIT** and press **Return**; notice how the .fmt file controls the database entry mask.

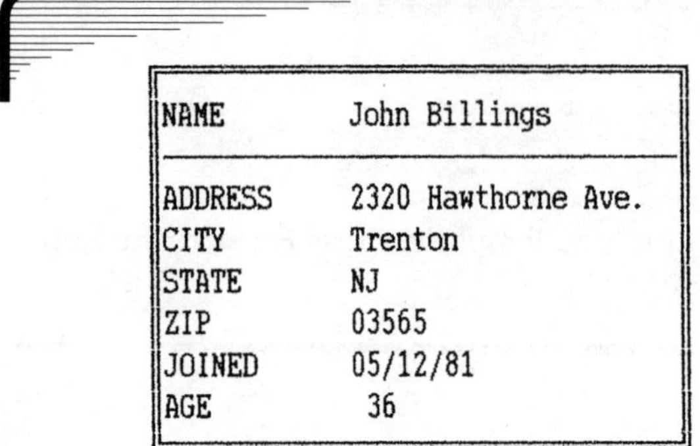

21. Press **Esc**; then type **CLOSE ALL** and press **Return** to close all files.

22. Type **TYPE ADR1.FMT** and press **Return** to see the command lines created by the screen painter.

```
@ 0,  0  GET  ADDRESS->NAME
@ 1,  1  SAY  "NAME"
@ 3,  1  SAY  "ADDRESS"
@ 3, 13  GET  ADDRESS->ADDRESS
@ 4,  1  SAY  "CITY"
@ 4, 13  GET  ADDRESS->CITY
@ 5,  1  SAY  "STATE"
@ 5, 13  GET  ADDRESS->STATE
@ 6,  1  SAY  "ZIP"
@ 6, 13  GET  ADDRESS->ZIP
@ 7,  1  SAY  "JOINED"
@ 7, 13  GET  ADDRESS->JOINED
@ 8,  1  SAY  "AGE"
@ 8, 13  GET  ADDRESS->AGE
@ 0,  0  TO  9, 34    DOUBLE
@ 2,  1  TO  2, 33
```

23. Experiment with the screen painter until you are satisfied you understand its operation.

24. Turn to Module 24 to continue the learning sequence.

Module 24
CREATE/MODIFY VIEW

DESCRIPTION

A view file is used to link several fields from a number of related database and corresponding index files. View files also let you use one format file (with the extension .FMT) and one filter condition.

A view file is created using CREATE VIEW *filename*, and modified using MODIFY VIEW *filename*. The resulting file is assigned the extension .VUE. Like FORMAT, LABEL, and SCREEN files, dBASE provides a menu-driven, full-screen editor to create and modify view files.

To view a list of available .VUE files, you can type **MODIFY VIEW ?**. A catalog of .VUE files is displayed. (.VUE filenames are added to the catalog when created, unless you have entered **SET CATALOG OFF**, where ON is the default condition.)

To call a .VUE file into use, use SET VIEW TO *filename*. When a .VUE file is created and saved, the SET VIEW TO *filename* condition is assumed by dBASE.

The FROM ENVIRONMENT clause is a fast way to create a .VUE file from the current open database, index, and format (.FMT) files and active SET RELATION commands. To create a .VUE file from the current operating environment, type:

    CREATE VIEW *filename* FROM ENVIRONMENT

and press **Return**.

For a look at the CREATE VIEW command and its editor, perform the steps contained in the Typical Operation section of this module.

APPLICATIONS

A .VUE file lets you display and edit information contained in several related database and index files. It also lets you operate with one format and filter file. If you have a number of files that are commonly used together, you can set up the relationships automatically using the view file instead of having to use a series of SELECT and USE statements every time the files are called.

The CREATE VIEW *filename* FROM ENVIRONMENT command form lets you establish the database relationships from the dot prompt (or from within a command file) and then capture this relationship in a view file for later use. Needless to say, once the relationship is known and established, the view file becomes a convenient tool.

TYPICAL OPERATION

In this illustration the CREATE VIEW command is used with the ADDRESS database file created in Module 49. Begin at the dBASE dot prompt.

1. Type **USE ADDRESS** and press **Return**.

2. Create 2 new database files named AD1.DBF and AD2.DBF as follows:

   a. Type **COPY FIELDS NAME,ADDRESS,CITY,STATE,ZIP TO AD1** and press **Return**.

   b. Type **COPY FIELDS NAME,JOINED,AGE TO AD2** and press **Return**.

3. Index both new databases on the NAME field as follows:

   a. Type **USE AD1** and press **Return**; then type **INDEX ON NAME TO NAME1** and press **Return**.

   b. Type **USE AD2** and press **Return**; then type **INDEX ON NAME TO NAME2** and press **Return**.

4. Close the database files with **CLOSE ALL** and press **Return**.

5. Type **CREATE VIEW MBR** and press **Return** to enter the VIEW file editor.

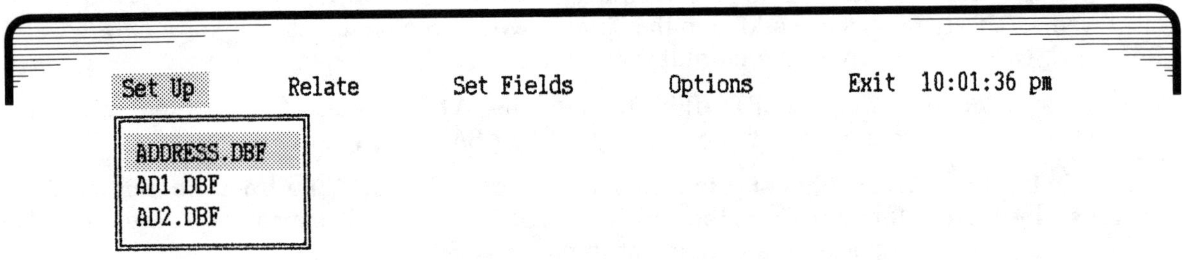

6. Select AD1.DBF with the **Down Arrow** and press **Return**. Notice that a triangle marks the AD1.DBF file, and that the following window is displayed.

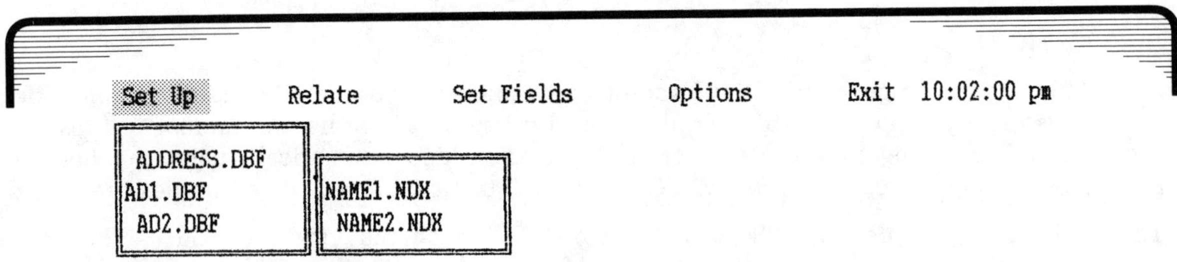

7. Press **Return** to select the NAME1.NDX file, and press the **Left Arrow** to move back to the Set Up selection window.

8. Now highlight AD2.DBF and press **Return**; then select NAME2.NDX as above, and press the **Left Arrow** to close the index file window.

9. Use the **Right Arrow** to select Relate on the menu bar and press **Return**. Notice the following selection window.

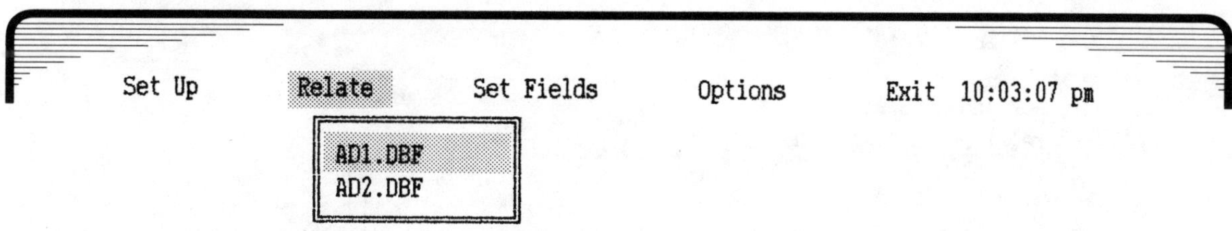

10. Press **Return** to select AD1.DBF; then press **Return** again to accept ADR2 as the "set relation to" database.

11. Now press **F10** to display the field name list. Your display should resemble the following.

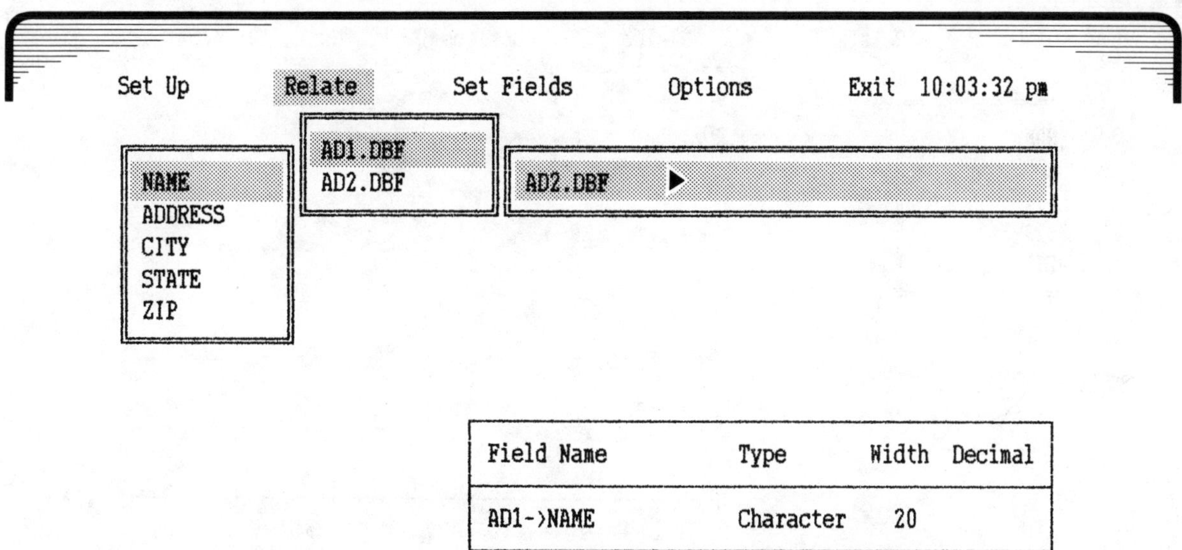

Field Name	Type	Width	Decimal
AD1->NAME	Character	20	

12. Press **Return** to select the NAME field. Notice that NAME is displayed in the relation window to the right of AD2.DBF. This uses the NAME field to establish the relation between the AD1 and AD2 databases.

TIP: If you had additional indexed database files, you could establish additional relationships. The database relationships "cascade," or "link" from first to last. The following diagram illustrates the relationships.

```
file1->fieldname_
            \_file2->fieldname_
                         \_file3->fieldname_
                                      \_...
```

In the example, only one link and two files are used. The view file establishes the same relation as:

```
select 1
use ad1 index name1
select 2
use ad2 index name2
set relation to name into 1
```

13. Press **Return** again to complete the selection and then press **Left Arrow** to close the window.

14. Press **Right Arrow** to select Set Fields on the menu bar and press **Return**. Notice that the AD1.DBF field names are displayed. The triangular "ticks" designate that the fields are all selected.

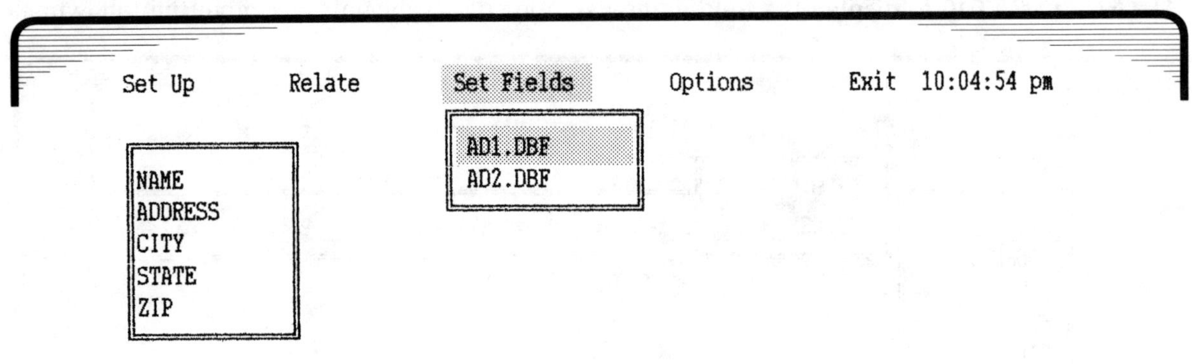

Field Name	Type	Width	Decimal
AD1->NAME	Character	20	

15. Press the **Right Arrow** and then the **Down Arrow** to select AD2.DBF and press **Return** to display the AD2 field names. All fields are ticked.

16. Press the **Right Arrow** twice to close the window and to move to the Options selection on the menu bar.

17. Notice that Filter is highlighted. Press **Return** to select Filter. Then press **F10** to display a window of field names. Check your display for the following:

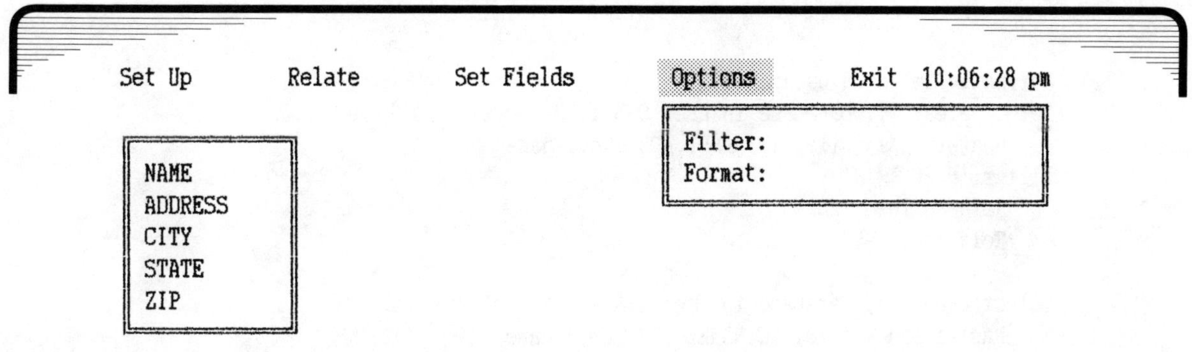

18. Press **Return** to select the NAME field. Now you can enter a "filter" expression. To pass all names that begin with a letter lower than H, the Filter line should read:

     Filter: NAME < 'H'

19. Press **Return** after typing the preceding expression to accept it.

> **NOTE**
> The Format option makes use of established format (.FMT) files to control the display of database information. If you select Format: and press **Return**, a list of corresponding format files are displayed for your selection. This example excludes the use of Format files, but you may create one and select for additional experience.

20. Press the **Right Arrow** to select Exit on the menu bar. Then press **Return** to save your MBR.VUE file. When you save and exit, the SET VIEW TO MBR.VUE command is issued automatically.

21. Type **DISPLAY STAT** and notice how the CREATE VIEW command has set the current operating environment.

```
        Currently Selected Database:
        Select area:  1, Database in Use: C:AD1.DBF   Alias: AD1
            Master index file:  C:NAME1.NDX  Key: name
        Filter: NAME < 'H'
            Related into: AD2
            Relation: NAME

        Select area:  2, Database in Use: C:AD2.DBF   Alias: AD2
            Master index file:  C:NAME2.NDX  Key: name
```

22. Type **LIST** and press **Return**. Notice how the view file filters out the records containing the names "John " and "Mary ."

```
    . list
    Record#  NAME                 ADDRESS            CITY        STATE ZIP
         4  Chuck Williams       56 Walmart Plaza   Jasper      TX    75611
         3  Fred Franklin        3900 Brookside Road Hobbs      NM    85676
```

23. Type **CLOSE ALL** and press **Return** to close all files.

24. Use the ERASE command to remove the AD1 and AD2 databases and the MBR .VUE files from your disk.

25. Turn to Module 11 to complete the learning sequence.

Module 25
DATE( ), TIME( )

DESCRIPTION

The DATE and TIME functions are used to return the system date and time. For example, if you wish to view the current date or time from the dBASE dot prompt, you can type:

```
. ? DATE()
MM/DD/YY
. ? TIME()
HH:MM:SS
```

You can store the date or time to a memory variable using:

```
X = DATE()
```

or

```
STORE DATE() TO X
```

In either case, the date is ready for use. You can also print the date and time on a report using a command like:

```
? 'Report Date: ',DATE()
? 'Report Time: ',TIME()
```

You can display a date in European notation with:

```
X = DATE()
@ 05,10 say 'DATE' GET X PICTURE '@E'
```

The date is displayed in the form DD/MM/YY.

There are numerous date and time functions available for converting the way the date and time appear, or converting a date to a character string. These functions are described in Appendix F.

APPLICATIONS

The most common application of the DATE( ) and TIME( ) function is to display or print the current date and time on reports. This makes the DATE( ) and TIME( ) functions important, and you should familiarize yourself with them as well as with the other functions described in Appendix F.

You may wish to store the date or time to a memory variable, as shown in the previous examples, and then display the contents of the memory variable each time the date is needed. The alternative is to use the DATE( ) and TIME( ) functions directly. An example of a command file using both of these approaches is contained in the Typical Operation section of this module.

TYPICAL OPERATION

In this illustration the DATE( ) function is used in a command file. Begin at the dBASE dot prompt.

1. Type **MODIFY COMMAND DATE** and press **Return** to use the dBASE editor.

2. Type the following command file. (Don't type the explanatory remarks.)

```
                                    Remarks
* DATE.PRG -- Shows uses of the DATE() function.
SET TALK OFF              && Turns dBASE dialog off.
CLEAR                     && Clears the screen.
? " TODAY'S DATE IS",DATE() && Displays text in quotes followed by system date.
? " THE TIME IS",TIME()    && Displays text in quotes followed by system time.
STORE DATE() TO MDATE      && Stores system date to memory variable MDATE.
?                          && Displays blank line.
? ' USE',MDATE,'ON ALL REPORTS.'  && Displays text in quotes and memory variable MDATE.
?                          && Displays blank line.
SET TALK ON                && Turns dBASE dialog back on.
CANCEL                     && Returns control to dBASE dot prompt.
```

3. Press **Ctrl-W** to write the command file to disk.

4. Type **DO DATE** and press **Return** to run the command file; notice the following display.

```
. DO DATE


TODAY'S DATE IS 12/26/86
THE TIME IS 19:02:19


USE 12/26/86 ON ALL REPORTS.


Do cancelled
```

5. Erase the DATE.PRG file by typing **ERASE DATE.PRG** and pressing **Return**.

6. Turn to Module 60 to continue the learning sequence.

Module 26
DELETE, RECALL, PACK

DESCRIPTION

This module describes commands used to mark and unmark records for deletion and the command that actually removes marked records from the active database. The deletion process begins with marking one or more records for deletion with the DELETE command. The RECALL command unmarks records; the PACK command eliminates marked records from the active database. Each of these commands is described in following paragraphs.

The DELETE FILE command is used to delete files from your disk, rather than marking records for deletion. The ERASE command, described in Module 34, is also used to delete files.

DELETE   The delete command is entered in several ways. These are summarized in the following list.

1.	. DELETE	Marks the current record for deletion.
2.	. DELETE RECORD n	Marks record n for deletion.
3.	. DELETE NEXT n	Marks next n records for deletion.
4.	. DELETE ALL	Marks all records within a database for deletion.
5.	. DELETE FOR *expression*	Marks all records for deletion that match a specified expression.
6.	. DELETE FILE XYZ.FRM	Deletes file XYZ.FRM on logged disk.
7.	. DELETE FILE B:XYZ.FRM	Deletes file XYZ.FRM on disk drive B:.
8.	. DELETE WHILE *expression*	Marks records for deletion, beginning at the current record, while the expression is true. Unlike the DELETE FOR command form, the deletion process stops when a record is encountered that does not match the expression.

When a database is listed using either the LIST or DISPLAY ALL command (Module 28), an asterisk appearing next to a record number indicates that record is marked for deletion. You can also mark a record for deletion when a database is displayed using the BROWSE command (Module 10). When using BROWSE, pressing **Ctrl-U** marks and unmarks (or recalls) the current record.

When records are marked for deletion, they are not transferred during APPEND FROM (Module 5), COPY (Module 16), and SORT (Module 61) operations, if SET DELETE ON is in effect. However, they are transferred during INDEX (Module 41) operations.

Entry 5 in the preceding command list shows the DELETE command used to mark those records that contain certain field contents. For example, if you want to delete all records that contain a number less than 50, you can use the following command.

    . DELETE FOR AGE < 50

This command tells dBASE to mark all records for deletion that have an entry in the AGE field of 0 through 49.

If you wish to delete records containing a date prior to January 31st, you can use a command like:

    . DELETE FOR DTOC(DATE) > '01/31'

The DTOC (date-to-character function) converts the date notation into a character string. Once in text form, you can use the SUBSTR (substring function) to focus on the year, then month and day-of-month. For example, if you wish to delete all records containing a date prior to 12/31/87 in the DATE field, you can use the command:

    . DELETE FOR SUBSTR(DTOC(DATE),7,2) <= '87' .AND. SUBSTR(DTOC(DATE),1,5) <= '12/31'

This says, "Mark all records for deletion where the 7th and 8th characters of the DATE field are less than or equal to (<=) '87' *and* where the first 5 characters of the DATE field are less than or equal to '12/31'."

The DELETED( ) function is a handy tool for checking the status of deleted files. If you have several files marked for deletion, you can display them with a command like:

    . DISPLAY FOR DELETED( )

If you want to check a file for its deletion status, you can use:

    . ? DELETED( )

The notation .T. is returned if it is marked; a .F. is returned if not.

Entries 6 and 7 in the preceding examples demonstrate how the DELETE command is used to delete files. If you wish to delete a backup file with the filename INSRECD.BAK from the diskette in drive B:, the command is:

    . DELETE FILE B:INSRECD.BAK

You can also use:

    . ERASE B:INSRECD.BAK

to delete a file. ERASE is covered in more detail in Module 34.

RECALL   The RECALL command is used to unmark those records that were marked for deletion with the DELETE command. As with DELETE, RECALL has several forms. These are shown in the following list.

1.   . RECALL   Unmarks the current record for deletion.

2.   . RECALL RECORD n   Unmarks record n for deletion.

3.   . RECALL NEXT n   Unmarks the next n records for deletion.

4. . RECALL ALL   Unmarks all records within the database for deletion.

5. . RECALL FOR *expression*   Unmarks all records within the database that match a specified expression.

6. . RECALL WHILE *expression*   Unmarks records while the expression is true.

Entry number 5 in the above list is similar to entry 5 in the DELETE command list. Using the RECALL FOR *expression* example, you can unmark all records containing February dates using the following command.

```
. RECALL FOR SUBSTR(DTOC(DATE),1,5) >= '02/01' .AND. SUBSTR(DTOC(DATE),1,5) <= '02/28'
```

PACK   The PACK command deletes the marked records from the database in use and resequences (closes up or "packs") the record numbers. For example, if you have three records in a 10-record database marked for deletion, issuing the PACK command eliminates the marked records and renumbers the remaining records from 1 to 7. When the PACK command is issued, the marked records are gone forever, so don't pack a database unless you intend to eliminate the marked records.

If you PACK an indexed file (Module 41), the marked records in the database and index file are deleted simultaneously. If the database is large, the pack process may take quite a bit of time. Therefore, it may be faster to PACK the database and then reindex it.

APPLICATIONS

One of the obvious applications for the DELETE and PACK command is to eliminate unwanted records. The DELETE FILE and ERASE commands are also convenient "housekeeping tools" for eliminating unwanted files from your diskette. For example, when you modify a command file, a backup file with the extension .BAK is created automatically. If you wish to recover the disk space occupied by a backup file, you can use the DELETE FILE or ERASE command to eliminate it.

One convenient application of the DELETE command is to mark records for deletion, and then enter SET DELETE ON prior to using a command like COPY or LIST. When file operations are performed, marked records are ignored. For example, if you wish to copy all records having Tampa in the CITY field from a CUSTOMER database to a temporary database named TEMP1, you can use the series:

```
. USE CUSTOMER                && Puts database in use.
. DELETE FOR CITY <> 'Tampa'  && The symbol <> means "not equal to."
. SET DELETE ON               && Sets delete function on.
. COPY TO TEMP1               && Copies all records not marked for deletion.
. SET DELETE OFF              && Sets delete function off.
. RECALL ALL                  && Unmarks all records for deletion.
```

All of these commands are used in the interactive mode or as statements within a command file. Frequently, they are used in conjunction with the LOCATE (Module 45) or FIND (Module 36) commands to delete records containing specified information.

The DELETE FILE or ERASE commands are also used in command files to remove temporary files created for the express purpose of sorting and displaying information. Deleting temporary sorting and "scratch pad" files restores valuable disk space once the temporary file has served its purpose.

TYPICAL OPERATION

In this illustration a command file is prepared that deletes records from the MEMBERS database, modified in Module 47. The command file makes use of the DELETE and PACK commands. Begin at the dBASE dot prompt.

1.   Type **MODIFY COMMAND DELREC** and press **Return**. You are in dBASE's full-screen editor.

2.   Type the **DELREC.PRG** command file. (Don't type the explanatory remarks.)

<u>Remarks</u>

```
* DELREC.PRG                && Deletes all unpaid member records from MEMBERS database.
CLEAR                       && Clears screen.
SET TALK OFF                && Turns off dBASE dialog.
? '        CHECK TO SEE IF ANY MEMBERS ARE UNPAID.'  && Displays user prompt.
? '        (UNPAID RECORDS ARE TAGGED ".F.")'
WAIT                        && Pauses operation until a key is pressed.
CLEAR                       && Clears screen.
USE MEMBERS                 && Puts MEMBERS database in use.
DISPLAY ALL NAME, PAID      && Displays NAME and PAID fields of MEMBERS database.
?                           && Question mark commands display lines and user prompt.
?
? '        TO DELETE UNPAID MEMBER RECORDS, PRESS "D"'
? '        OR PRESS ANY OTHER KEY TO QUIT'
?
WAIT ' ' TO OPTION          && Pauses operation; stores keystroke to memory variable OPTION.
CLEAR                       && Clears screen.
IF UPPER(OPTION) = 'D'      && If OPTION = upper or lower case D, executes following commands.
   DELETE FOR .NOT. PAID    && Marks all records with a logical False (or "No") in
                               the PAID field.
   PACK                     && Deletes all marked records.
ENDIF                       && Passes control to the following command line.
SET TALK ON                 && Turns dBASE dialog back on.
CANCEL                      && Returns control to the dBASE prompt.
```

3.   Press **Ctrl-W** to write the command file to disk.

4.   When ready, type **DO DELREC** and press **Return**.

5. The following prompt is displayed; respond by pressing **Return**.

```
    CHECK TO SEE IF ANY MEMBERS ARE UNPAID.
    (UNPAID RECORDS ARE TAGGED ".F.")
Press any key to continue...
```

6. The following information is displayed on the screen.

```
Record#  name                  paid_up
      1  Thompson, Bill G.      .T.
      2  Williams, David        .F.
      3  Phillips, George W.    .T.
      4  Galvin, Theodore A.    .F.

    TO DELETE UNPAID MEMBER RECORDS, PRESS "D"'
OR PRESS ANY OTHER KEY TO QUIT'
```

7. Type **D** to delete the unpaid records; Williams' and Galvin's records are marked for deletion, packed, and the dBASE prompt is redisplayed.

8. Turn to Module 13 to continue the learning sequence.

Module 27
DIR

DESCRIPTION

The DIR command is similar to the DOS DIR command. It is used to list a directory of files on the screen. Typing **DIR** by itself and then pressing **Return** lists database files having the file extension DBF. A typical listing might resemble the following:

```
. DIR
  Database files      # records      last update      size
  EMPL.DBF                   24      10/21/88         1827
  PHONEBK.DBF                 5      09/15/88         2706
  TEMPOR.DBF                  6      09/21/88          369

     4902 bytes in       3 files.
   248128 bytes remaining on drive.
```

You can also use the DOS wild card (*) to list selected files. For example, if you want to list all files having the extension .PRG, you can use the command form:

```
. DIR *.PRG
```

Every filename having the extension .PRG is listed. To list all files on the logged disk drive, type:

```
. DIR *.*
```

Notice that the last two command forms are identical to those used by DOS.

APPLICATIONS

The DIR command is used to review filenames on the logged disk drive and to check their sizes. The number of records in a database file, file sizes, and disk space information is often valuable for planning purposes. Having the DIR command available in dBASE eliminates the need to return to DOS to check file information.

TYPICAL OPERATION

In this illustration the DIR command is used to check all programs having the extension .PRG. Start at the dBASE dot prompt.

1. Type **DIR *.PRG** and press **Return**.

2. Notice the display.

```
. DIR
MENU.PRG          PHONELST.PRG          TEST.PRG

   19264 bytes in     3 files.
   122128 bytes remaining on drive.
```

3. Turn to Module 55 to continue the learning sequence.

Module 28
DISPLAY, LIST, CLEAR

DESCRIPTION

This module describes the DISPLAY and LIST commands, which are used to display the contents of a database. It also describes the CLEAR command, used to clear the screen. The RECNO( ) function (where RECNO stands for *record number*) is also introduced. The RECNO( ) function is used to display or store database record numbers. The term *current record* represents the current location of the dBASE record pointer. BROWSE is another command used to display the contents of a database. However, BROWSE gives you the ability to edit the contents of a database. The BROWSE command is described in Module 10.

Before the DISPLAY or LIST commands or the RECNO( ) function are used, a database must be opened with the USE command. Once the database is open, you can position the record pointer to records within the database using the GO and SKIP commands, which are described in detail in Module 38.

DISPLAY   The DISPLAY command is used to perform a number of tasks. These include:

- Display the contents of a database.
- Display the status of open files and set commands.
- Display the active memory variables and their contents.
- Display a record of the last several commands used.
- Display and print database information simultaneously.

A number of DISPLAY command forms are included in the following list.

1.	DISPLAY	Displays record number and contents of current record.
2.	DISPLAY OFF	Displays contents of current record; omits record number display.
3.	DISPLAY RECORD n	Displays record number and contents of record number n.
4.	DISPLAY NEXT n	Displays record number and contents of next n records.
5.	DISPLAY ALL	Displays all records (similar to LIST, except DISPLAY ALL pauses every 15 records and waits for you to press a key before displaying is continued).
6.	DISPLAY ALL TO PRINT	Displays all records to the screen and printer.
7.	DISPLAY RECNO( )	Displays current record number.
8.	DISPLAY *field1, field2, . . .*	Displays contents of specified fields.

9.	DISPLAY FOR *expression(s)*	Displays records matching expression(s).
10.	DISPLAY *fieldname(s)* FOR *expression(s)* (OFF)	Combines 7 and 8 above.
11.	DISPLAY *'expression'* $ *fieldname*	Displays record numbers that have strings within the specified field that match the string in the expression.
12.	DISPLAY WHILE *expression*	Displays records while the expression is true.
13.	DISPLAY STRUCTURE	Displays database structure.
14.	DISPLAY HISTORY	Displays last ten commands in the order entered.
15.	DISPLAY MEMORY	Displays active memory variables.
16.	DISPLAY FILES	Displays all database files on the logged disk drive.
17.	DISPLAY FILES ON B: LIKE *.PRG	Displays all files on disk drive B: having the extension .PRG. (The * is a wild card, which can be substituted to represent all filenames and/or extensions.)
18.	DISPLAY FILES ON B: LIKE *.*	Displays all files on disk drive B:
19.	DISPLAY STATUS	Displays active database filename(s), the status of the SET commands, and the commands issued by your computer's function keys (later versions only).

NOTE

The SET HEADING OFF command is used to suppress the display of field name above the field columns. Adding the TO PRINT clause causes simultaneous display and printing.

Most of the entries in the above list are self explanatory; however, a few can use some examples for clarification. In entries 1 through 3, *current record* means the record at which the record pointer is located. A variation to entry 7 is to use:

    . ? RECNO( )

In entry 8, *field1, field2*. . . is one or more field names in the form:

    . DISPLAY NAME, ST_ADR, PAID_UP

Assuming the open database contains the indicated fields, this command displays the record number followed by the contents of the NAME, ST_ADR, and PAID_UP fields for the current record. If you want to display this information for all records, you can use:

    . DISPLAY ALL NAME, ST_ADR, PAID_UP

The same command followed by the OFF clause suppresses the display of the record numbers.

In entry 9 an expression is one or more values that match one or more fields within a record. For example, you could use:

. DISPLAY FOR SUBSTR(DTOC(JOINED),7,2) >= '83'.AND. .NOT. PAID_UP

This command displays the record numbers that match those fields containing:

> a year value greater than or equal to '83' in the JOINED field, and
> a false value (logical .F.) in the logical field PAID_UP.

The substring function (SUBSTR) tells dBASE to look at the 7th and 8th character in the JOINED field. The date-to-character function (DTOC) converts date-type fields into character data types.

You can combine entries 8 and 9 in an expression like the one shown in entry 10 to display certain information. Let's say you want to display the NAME, ST_ADR, and C_S_Z (city, state, zip) fields for all records that contain a logical true (.T.) in the PAID_UP field. You also want to suppress the record number display. The command

. DISPLAY NAME, ST_ADR, C_S_Z FOR PAID_UP OFF

displays the contents of the named fields that have a logical true (.T.) in the PAID_UP field for all records within the active database.

Entry 11 is a powerful command form that can find all records having the specified expression in the specified string. If you wish to display all records having a partial match, the expression followed by a $ and the field name is used in the form:

. DISPLAY ALL '(201)' $ PH_NBR

The above command displays all record numbers followed by .T. or .F. (for true or false), where .T. indicates that the record contains the expression (201) in the PH_NBR field. The expression can be located at any position within the PH_NBR field. When the DISPLAY ALL command is used, the display pauses for each screen of information. You are prompted to press a key to see the next screen.

Here's another example. Suppose you wish to find all records having a 'Jo' in the name field with this command form. You can also display other fields within the records by including their field names in the statement. The expression:

. DISPLAY NAME, AGE FOR 'Jo' $ NAME

where NAME and AGE are field names. This finds records containing names like Joe, Johnson, Joel, Jones, and Joseph. The display includes the contents of both the name and age fields.

Item 14 introduces the DISPLAY HISTORY command. This form of the DISPLAY command lists all the commands that have been executed and stored in dBASE III Plus' history file. You can add the TO PRINT clause to list the command lines to your printer, in the form:

. DISPLAY HISTORY TO PRINT

If you want to see the last six commands, use

. DISPLAY HISTORY LAST 6

As you might guess, this command form is printed by adding the TO PRINT clause. Displaying command lines is ofted used as a debugging tool.

LIST   The LIST command is almost the same as DISPLAY ALL. You can use LIST in place of DISPLAY in LIST FILES, LIST STRUCTURE, and LIST MEMORY. You can also use the TO PRINT and OFF clauses.

The primary advantage of the LIST command is that it is shorter to type. If you simply type LIST, the contents of the database are displayed on the screen. Where DISPLAY automatically pauses and displays "Press any key to continue. . .," LIST displays the entire file without pausing. However, you can pause the listing by pressing **Ctrl-S**; press any other key to resume.

CLEAR   The CLEAR command clears your display screen. It also clears previous formatting commands from your computer's memory when displayed text is being routed to your printer. It's like erasing a chalkboard for a clean slate. If you want to erase the bottom of your screen and leave information at the top, you can specify where the CLEAR command is to take effect. For example, the command

```
. @ 12,0 CLEAR
```

clears everything from row 12 column 0 (the left-most column number) to the bottom of the screen.

Another form of the CLEAR command is CLEAR ALL. This command form closes files and clears any active memory variables. It is described in more detail in Module 14.

APPLICATIONS

The DISPLAY and LIST commands are used in a number of ways. First, they are used to simply "dump" the contents of a database to the screen. You can simultaneously route displayed data to your printer if you type SET PRINT ON before using the DISPLAY or LIST commands. You can achieve the same result by adding the TO PRINT clause to your command line. If you use SET PRINT ON, be sure to enter SET PRINT OFF when printing finishes.

Being able to display information selectively begins to show the real power of dBASE. With the DISPLAY and LIST commands, you can limit the display of certain fields, and specify that only those records that match certain parameters are displayed.

The DISPLAY HISTORY command is extremely useful for debugging. You can review the last series of commands to search for errors. The SET DOHISTORY ON function is available to capture lines in command files. This lets you see what the last lines looked like prior to a "bug." Under normal operating conditioins, DOHISTORY should be off, as it slows down command file execution.

The CLEAR command is essential to the legible display of new information. Without the ability to clear your screen, previously displayed information would clutter your screen reports. If you wish to leave a portion of the screen displayed, use the form @ row,col clear, where row,col are the line and column numbers of your screen, beginning with 0,0 at the upper left.

The RECNO( ) function is more than just a way to determine the current position of the record pointer. You can use RECNO( ) to store the integer (whole number) value of the current record number to a memory variable for future use. The command:

```
. STORE RECNO( ) TO RN
```

stores an integer equal to the current record number to the memory variable RN. This little trick is used to save the number of a record that contains some needed information for later use. Memory variables are described in detail in Module 62.

All of the commands described in this module can be entered at the dBASE dot prompt or placed in command files. The CLEAR command is often one of the first commands used in a command file, as it erases previous prompts and menus and prepares the screen for the display of new information.

TYPICAL OPERATION

In this illustration the CLEAR and DISPLAY commands are used to view certain records in the MEMBERS database created in Module 18. Begin at the dBASE prompt.

1. Type **USE MEMBERS** and press **Return**.

2. Type **LIST NAME, C_S_Z, PAID_UP** and press **Return**. Compare your screen to the following:

```
. LIST NAME, C_S_Z, PAID_UP
Record#  name                 c_s_z                 paid_up
      1  Williams, David      Tampa, FL 32656       .F.
      2  Phillips, George W.  Lago Vista, TX 78641  .T.
      3  Galvin, Theodore A.  Culver City, CA 96750 .F.
```

3. Type **DISPLAY RECORD 1** and press **Return**; notice the following:

```
. DISPLAY RECORD 1
Record#  NAME                 ST_ADR                C_S_Z
         AFFIL                JOINED   AGE PAID_UP INFO
      1  Williams, David      3456 Fresno Circle    Tampa, FL 32656
         U.S. Air Force (Ret) 11/15/80  56 .F.      Memo
```

4. Type **DISPLAY STRUCTURE** and press **Return**. Check the display:

```
. DISPLAY STRUCTURE

Structure for database : B:members.dbf
Number of data records :        3
```

```
Date of last update    : 10/21/89
Field  Field name   Type       Width    Dec
    1  NAME         Character    25
    2  ST_ADR       Character    25
    3  C_S_Z        Character    25
    4  AFFIL        Character    25
    5  JOINED       Date          8
    6  AGE          Numeric       2
    7  PAID_UP      Logical       1
    8  INFO         Memo         10
** Total **                     122
```

5. Type **DISPLAY NAME, JOINED FOR .NOT. PAIDUP OFF** and press **Return**. Compare your screen to the following illustration.

```
. DISPLAY NAME, JOINED FOR .NOT. PAID_UP OFF


NAME                     JOINED
Williams, David          11/15/80
Galvin, Theodore A.      02/15/83
```

6. Type **STORE RECNO( ) TO REC** and press **Return**; then type **DISPLAY MEMORY** and press **Return**. Notice the following:

```
. STORE RECNO() TO REC


        4
. DISPLAY MEMORY

REC         pub  N        4 (           4.00000000)
    1 variables defined,        9 bytes used
  255 variables available,   5991 bytes available
```

7. Type **CLEAR ALL** to close all files and to clear all memory variables.

8. Turn to Module 47 to continue the learning sequence.

Module 29
DO

DESCRIPTION

The DO command is used to start the operation of a dBASE command (or program) file. The DO command is used either from the dBASE dot prompt or as a statement within a command file. The form of the DO command is:

> DO *filename*

where filename is the name of a command file. The DO *filename* command is also used as a statement in a command file. When used as a statement within a command file, the DO command causes the named command file to begin operation. The named command file operates until:

1. The end of the file is reached, which passes control back to the dBASE dot prompt.

2. A CANCEL command is encountered, which passes control back to the dBASE dot prompt.

3. A RETURN command is encountered, which returns control to the command file from which the present command file was called. If the DO command was made from the dBASE dot prompt, RETURN passes control back to the dBASE dot prompt.

4. The **Esc** key is pressed, which interrupts program operation and displays a "Cancel, Resume, Ignore" prompt.

5. A command file error is encountered, such as not closing an IF with an ENDIF or a DO WHILE with an ENDDO.

6. An error message is displayed.

You can also start operation of a dBASE command file directly from the DOS prompt by typing

> DBASE *filename*

where the *filename* is the name of a command file.

You can also place a command statement in the CONFIG.DB file to automatically run a command file any time dBASE is started. For example, the CONFIG.DB file can contain the line:

> COMMAND = DO *filename*

where the *filename* is the name of a command file.

APPLICATIONS

There are many applications for the DO statements. The initial DO *filename* command is applied every time you start a command file from the dBASE III prompt. It is also used from within command files to cause subsequent command files to run. An example of this use of the DO command is illustrated in Module 38.

TYPICAL OPERATION

In this illustration a small command file is prepared and the DO command is used to run it. Begin at the dBASE dot prompt.

1. Type **MODI COMM SHORT** and press **Return** to use the dBASE editor.

2. Type the following command file. (Don't type the explanatory remarks.)

```
                                              Remarks
    * SHORT.PRG -- A short command file.
    CLEAR                            && Clears the screen.
    ?                                && Displays a blank line.
    ? 'This is a short command file' && Displays the text within quotes.
    WAIT                             && Pauses operation.
    RETURN                           && Returns control to dBASE dot prompt.
```

3. Press **Ctrl-W** to write the command file to disk.

4. Type **DO SHORT** and press **Return**. Notice the following:

```
    This is a short command file.
    Press any key to continue..._
```

5. Type **ERASE SHORT.PRG** and press **Return**.

6. Turn to Module 57 to continue the learning sequence.

Module 30
DO CASE, CASE, OTHERWISE, ENDCASE

DESCRIPTION

The family of CASE commands is used to check for a specified condition. If the condition is detected, i.e., "in case it's true," the appropriate CASE statement is used. The following paragraphs describe each element of the CASE statement, beginning with DO CASE.

DO CASE   The DO CASE command is the first statement used. This statement tells dBASE that one or more CASE statements follow.

```
DO CASE
  CASE X = 1
    command line(s)
  CASE X = 2
    command line(s)
  CASE ...
     |
ENDCASE
```

CASE   Each CASE statement is followed by one or more command lines. If a CASE expression is true, the command lines associated with that CASE statement are used. Once operation is complete, control passes to the command line following the ENDCASE statement. All remaining CASE statements are ignored once a case statement is satisfied.

The CASE statements are evaluated one at a time, from top to bottom. If a CASE statement is false, associated command lines are ignored and control passes to the next CASE statement. This process continues until either a true CASE is found, or the ENDCASE statement is reached.

ENDCASE   As you've probably noticed, the CASE statement starts with DO CASE and ends with ENDCASE. ENDCASE is necessary to complete the CASE statement. When ENDCASE is encountered in the command file, control passes to the command line following the ENDCASE statement.

OTHERWISE   OTHERWISE is an optional statement that is used as an alternative case. If none of the CASE expressions are true, the OTHERWISE statement comes into play, and the command lines associated with the OTHERWISE statement are used. Look at the following example:

```
DO CASE
  CASE X = 1
    command line(s)
  CASE X = 2
    command line(s)
         |
  OTHERWISE
    command line(s)
ENDCASE
```

The DO CASE, CASE, OTHERWISE, and ENDCASE commands are diagrammed in the following illustration.

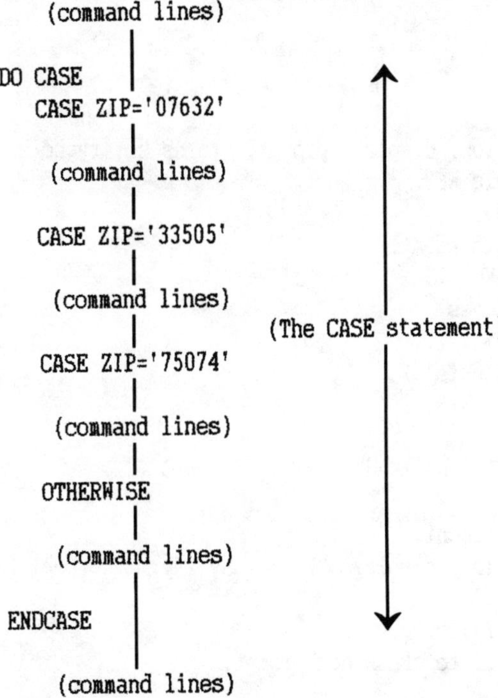

APPLICATIONS

You can apply the DO CASE series of commands any time you're confronted with a multiple choice situation. You can test as many alternatives (or CASES) as you like, since there is no limit to the number of CASE expressions within the CASE statement. For example, if you're checking property descriptions in a real estate database or options and colors in an automobile dealership database, you can use CASE after CASE to find those records that match your customer's needs.

TYPICAL OPERATION

In this illustration the CASE statement is used in a command file to check for a keyboard entry. Begin at the dBASE dot prompt.

1. Type **MODI COMM TRYCASE** and press **Return** to use the dBASE editor.

2. Type the following command file. (Don't type the explanatory remarks.)

```
                                          Remarks
* TRYCASE.PRG -- Uses the CASE commands.
CLEAR                          && Clears screen.
SET TALK OFF                   && Turns off dBASE dialog.
TEXT                           && Displays text until ENDTEXT is encountered.
        Type 1 to display fruit.
        Type 2 to display sports.
        Type 3 to display colors.
ENDTEXT
WAIT 'Type 1, 2, or 3' to KEY && Pauses operation, displays prompt, stores key typed key to
*                                 memory variable KEY.
CLEAR                          && Clears screen.
DO CASE                        && Begins CASE statement.
   CASE KEY='1'                && Checks for KEY = 1.
     ? 'Apples, Bananas, Cherries, Oranges, Peaches'
   CASE KEY='2'                && Checks for KEY = 2.
     ? 'Baseball, Basketball, Football, Golf, Tennis'
   CASE KEY='3'                && Checks for KEY = 3.
     ? 'Blue, Green, Orange, Red, Yellow'
   OTHERWISE                   && Operates if KEY isn't equal to 1, 2, or 3.
     ? "You didn't type 1 through 3."
ENDCASE                        && Ends CASE statement.
WAIT                           && Pauses operation; displays "Press any key..." prompt.
CLEAR                          && Clears screen.
SET TALK ON                    && Turns dBASE dialog back on.
RETURN                         && Returns control to dBASE dot prompt.
```

3. Press **Ctrl-W** to write the command file to disk.

4. Type **DO TRYCASE** and press **Return**.

5. Try selections 1,2,3, and any other key to see how the CASE commands work.

6. When you are finished experimenting with the CASE commands, type **ERASE TRYCASE.PRG** and press **Return** to delete the file from your disk.

7. Turn to Module 40 to continue the learning sequence.

Module 31
DO WHILE, EXIT, LOOP, ENDDO, EOF( )

DESCRIPTION

The DO WHILE command is a *looping* command that sustains operation "while" some condition is true. The first line of the DO WHILE statement has the form:

```
DO WHILE expression
```

Continuous operation is sustained as long as the *expression* is true, or until an ENDDO or EXIT command is encountered. The complete DO WHILE statement has the form:

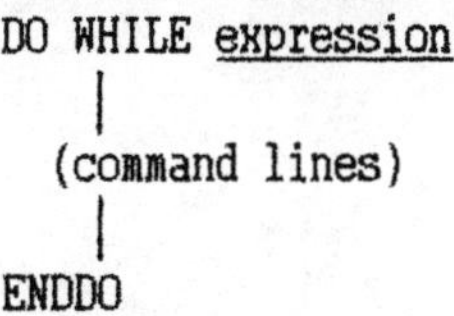

The EXIT command transfers control from within the DO WHILE loop to the command line following the ENDDO statement, which is always the last line in a DO WHILE statement.

The LOOP command is also available to "loop" control back to the command line following the DO WHILE command line. The series of commands beginning with DO WHILE *expression* and ending with ENDDO is considered the complete statement. You can think of DO WHILE and ENDDO as bookends with the books in between representing command statements. So for every DO WHILE there is always a corresponding ENDDO.

You can "nest" interior DO WHILE's and ENDDO's as well as IF's and ENDIF's and DO CASE's and ENDCASE's within a DO WHILE statement. An example containing IF's and ENDIF's follows. Notice how each DO WHILE and IF has a corresponding ENDDO and ENDIF. Interior (nested) DO WHILE-ENDDO pairs (and IF-ENDIF pairs) must reside within the statement.

If an ENDDO or ENDIF statement is missing or misplaced, command file operation stops. When this happens, carefully check your ENDIF and ENDDO statements. Some examples of DO WHILE statements are contained in the following list.

DO WHILE .T.	&& Continues operation until an EXIT, CANCEL, RETURN, or QUIT command is encountered.
STORE .T. TO RUN	&& Stores a true value to the memory variable RUN.
DO WHILE RUN	&& Continues operation until an ENDDO or the command STORE .F. to RUN is encountered.
STORE ' ' TO OKAY	&& Stores a blank space to the memory variable OKAY.

DO WHILE .NOT. OKAY = 'X'   && Continues operation until an ENDDO or the value of OKAY is changed to X. This value is changed by one of the following command lines.
    STORE 'X' TO OKAY
    WAIT 'Type a key' TO OKAY   && Displays "Type a key" prompt and stores keyboard entry to the memory variable OKAY.
DO WHILE .NOT. EOF( )   && Continues operation until an ENDDO or an end of file is encountered. A common use of this form is:
    DO WHILE .NOT. EOF( )   && Operate until end of file is reached.
      DISPLAY   && Displays current record of database in use.
      SKIP   && Position record pointer to next record.
    ENDDO   && Passes control to next statement when end-of-file condition is reached.

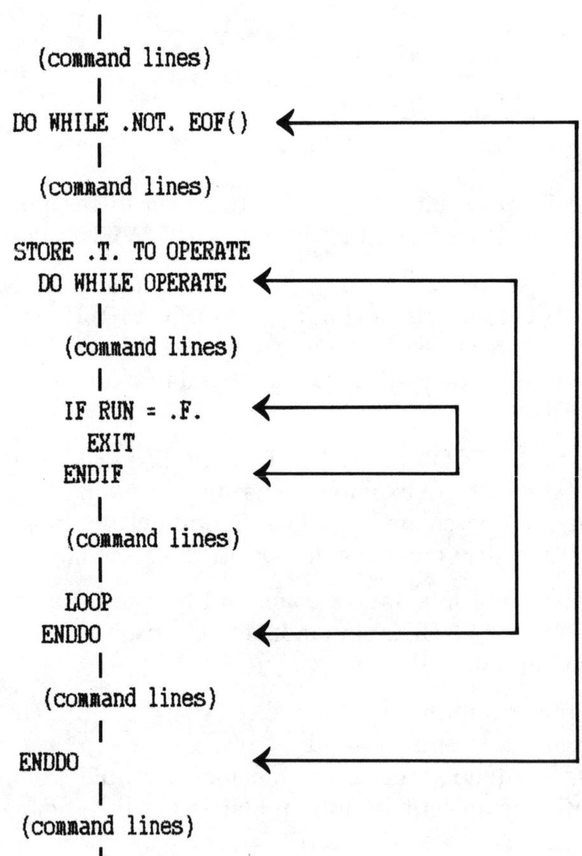

LOOP   When the LOOP command is encountered, control passes back to the command line following DO WHILE. The LOOP command is used when a condition is encountered within a command file that makes it necessary to start over. The DO WHILE statement continues operation and loops back automatically unless the DO WHILE condition becomes false or the EXIT, CANCEL, RETURN, or QUIT command is encountered.

EXIT   The EXIT statement is a convenient way to get out of a DO WHILE loop. The alternative is to set the DO WHILE condition to false. You can put a routine similar to the following one in your command file to escape from a DO WHILE loop. Notice that the UPPER( ) function is used to interpret either an upper or lowercase input.

```
WAIT 'Press "X" to exit, any other key to continue... ' TO MVAR
IF UPPER(MVAR) = 'X'
  EXIT
ENDIF
```

EOF( )   The EOF( ) statement, which stands for *end of file*, is used with several commands including DO WHILE, DO CASE, and IF. When an end-of-file condition exists, EOF( ) returns a true value. Going to the bottom of a file with GO BOTTOM doesn't position the record pointer to the end of file, it positions the record pointer to the last record in the file. There's a distinct difference. To prove this to yourself, try the following commands from the dBASE dot prompt.

```
                            Remarks
. USE MEMBERS        && Put the MEMBERS database file in use.
. GO BOTTOM          && Go to the last record in the file.
. ? EOF()            && Check for end-of-file status.
.F.                  && dBASE says False.
. SKIP               && Move record pointer down (hits end of file).
. ? EOF()            && Check for end-of-file status.
.T.                  && dBASE says True, you've reached end of file.
```

You can also go to the end of file with the COUNT command. If COUNT had been used in place of GO BOTTOM in the last example, the first ? EOF( ) check would have returned a True value.

APPLICATIONS

You can apply the DO WHILE command any time sustained operation is required. A delay loop was illustrated in the DO WHILE and LOOP description early in this module. But the DO WHILE command is also useful for repetitive operation, such as displaying every record in a database until the end of file is reached (DO WHILE .NOT. EOF( )). You can also use DO WHILE, STORE, and LOOP as an incrementor or decrementor, as shown in the following delay loop example. You can apply this principle to count displayed lines and cause a line feed (EJECT) when the bottom of a page is reached. The command file in Module 33 illustrates this application.

As mentioned, a practical use for the DO WHILE statement is to install time delays. For example, you may wish to display a message for several seconds, and then move on to another activity. The following illustration demonstrates this process. First, the message is displayed. Then a time delay is established using a DO WHILE loop. Once the delay loop is exhausted, the screen is erased and following commands are processed.

```
                                        Remarks
* DELAY.PRG -- Displays a message for approximately 10 seconds.
CLEAR                    && Clears the screen.
SET TALK OFF            && Turns off dBASE dialog.
? '     THIS MESSAGE WILL DISAPPEAR IN A FEW SECONDS'
X = 0                   && Store 0 to the memory variable X.
DO WHILE .NOT. X=370    && Continue operation until X equals 370.
   X = X+1              && Increments X by one for every pass of the loop.
ENDDO                   && When the DO WHILE expression becomes false (X = 370),
*                          control passes to the next command line.
CLEAR                   && Clears the screen.
SET TALK ON             && Turns dBASE dialog back on.
RETURN                  && Returns control to dBASE dot prompt.
```

NOTE

In this example, the DO WHILE .NOT. X = 370 statement sustains operation while X isn't equal to 370. STORE X + 1 TO X adds 1 to the value of X each time control is looped by the LOOP command. When the value of X reaches 370, the DO WHILE loop terminates.

Finally, the EOF( ) function is one that's often used when you want to display or print a series of records. The ability to return a True condition when the end of file is reached makes the EOF( ) function a useful tool.

TYPICAL OPERATION

In this illustration DO WHILE, DO CASE, and EOF( ) are used in a command file to demonstrate their use. The PICNIC database created in Module 63 is used by the command file. Begin at the dBASE dot prompt.

1. Type **MODIFY COMMAND DOCMDS** and press **Return** to use the dBASE editor.

2. Type the following command file. (Don't type the explanatory remarks.)

<u>Remarks</u>

```
* DOCMDS.PRG -- Illustrates the use of various DO commands.
SET TALK OFF             && Turns off dBASE dialog.
USE PICNIC               && Puts PICNIC database in use.
DO WHILE .T.             && Continues operation while true.
   CLEAR                 && Clears the screen.
   TEXT                  && Displays text until ENDTEXT is encountered.
           TYPE A NUMBER TO DISPLAY WHAT'S BEING BROUGHT
                                              Press
                    POTATO CHIPS                1
                    DIP                         2
                    HOT DOGS                    3
                    BUNS                        4
                    BEANS                       5
                    MUSTARD                     6
                    RELISH                      7
                    PICKLES                     8
                    EVERYTHING                  9
                    EXIT TO dBASE III           X
   ENDTEXT
   WAIT 'Enter selection' TO CHOICE  && Pauses operation; keyed input stored to CHOICE.
   CLEAR                 && Clears the screen.
   DO CASE               && Starts DO CASE statement; looks for CHOICE = expression.
      CASE CHOICE='1'                && Checks for CHOICE equal to 1.
         DISPLAY FOR BRING='Chips'   && Displays records with Potato Chips in BRING field.
   CASE CHOICE='2'
         DISPLAY FOR BRING='Dip'     && Displays records with Dip in BRING field.
      CASE CHOICE='3'
         DISPLAY FOR BRING='Hot Dogs' && Displays records with Hot Dogs in BRING field.
   CASE CHOICE='4'
     DISPLAY FOR BRING='Buns'        && Displays records with Buns in BRING field.
   CASE CHOICE='5'
     DISPLAY FOR BRING='Beans'       && Displays records with Beans in BRING field.
   CASE CHOICE='6'
     DISPLAY FOR BRING='Mustard'     && Displays records with Mustard in BRING field.
   CASE CHOICE='7'
     DISPLAY FOR BRING='Relish'      && Displays records with Relish in BRING field.
   CASE CHOICE='8'
     DISPLAY FOR BRING='Pickles'     && Displays records with Pickles in BRING field.
   CASE CHOICE='9'                   && Checks for CHOICE equal to 9.
     DISPLAY ALL                     && Displays all records in database.
   CASE UPPER(CHOICE)='X'            && Checks for CHOICE equal to X.
     EXIT               && Exits DO WHILE loop.
```

```
    OTHERWISE                && If CASE is not satisfied, executes following command lines.
        LOOP                 && Returns control to command line after DO WHILE statement.
    ENDCASE                  && Completes DO CASE statement.
    WAIT                     && Pauses operation, and displays "Press any key..." prompt.
ENDDO                        && Completes DO WHILE statement.
USE                          && Closes database file.
CLEAR                        && Clears the screen.
SET TALK ON                  && Turns dBASE dialog back on.
CANCEL                       && Returns control to dBASE dot prompt.
```

3. Press **Ctrl-W** to write the command file to disk.

4. Run the command file by typing **DO DOCMDS** and pressing **Return**. Compare your screen to the following:

```
    TYPE A NUMBER TO DISPLAY WHAT'S BEING BROUGHT
                                    Press
            CHIPS                     1
            DIP                       2
            HOT DOGS                  3
            BUNS                      4
            BEANS                     5
            MUSTARD                   6
            RELISH                    7
            PICKLES                   8
            EVERYTHING                9
            EXIT TO dBASE             X
    Enter selection _
```

5. Type **2** and notice the following information.

```
    Record#  NAME             GUESTS BRING      AMOUNT MEASURE
          2  Collins, Ric        4 Dip             3 Cartons
         13  Jasper, Dave        2 Dip             2 Cartons
    Press any key to continue... _
```

6. Press any key to redisplay the menu. Try other selections and when you've completed testing the program, type **X** to exit.

7. Delete the file from your disk by typing **ERASE DOCMDS.PRG** and pressing **Return**.

8. Turn to Module 59 to continue the learning sequence.

Module 32
EDIT

DESCRIPTION

The EDIT command is used to change the contents of one or more records in a database. The BROWSE command is also used for editing. BROWSE is described in Module 10. Before the EDIT command is used, a database must be opened with the USE command. Forms of the EDIT command are presented in the following list. As with all commands, you must press **Return** at the end of the command line.

1.	. EDIT	Displays the contents of the current record in an "editing mask." Editing is achieved by typing in new information, deleting old information, or both. When a record is displayed, you can delete the entire record by pressing **Ctrl-U** and **Return**. When you are back at the dot prompt, typing **PACK** and pressing **Return** eliminates the record from the database.
2.	. EDIT n	Edits the specified record number, where n is the number.
3.	. EDIT *field1,field2*	Restricts editing to the named fields.
4.	. EDIT FOR ZIP > = '90000'	Restricts editing to records having a value equal to or greater than 90000 in the ZIP field.
5.	. EDIT WHILE STATE = 'FL'	Edits records while the state field contains FL. You may wish to sort (or index) your database and then use the LOCATE or FIND command to position the record pointer to the first record containing the sought expression.

To edit record number 2 of the MEMBERS database modified in Module 10, type the following command lines.

```
. USE MEMBERS
. EDIT 2
```

Record number 2 is displayed in an editing mask.

```
Record No.       2
NAME       Phillips, George W.
ADR        11205 Dawn Drive
CSZ        Lago Vista, TX 78641
AFFIL      Austin Medical Center
JOINED     06/01/81
PAID       Y
INFO       Memo
```

The cursor is positioned at the beginning of the NAME field, ready for use. You can move the cursor within the record with the cursor control keys to make changes. You can strikeover text or blank text with the **Spacebar**. You can delete and insert text using **Del** (or **Ctrl-G**) and **Ins** (or **Ctrl-V**). You can jump to the previous record with **PgUp** (or **Ctrl-R**) and jump to the following record with **PgDn** (or **Ctrl-C**). Attempting to move beyond the last record within the database takes you back to the dBASE dot prompt.

If you want to enter text into a Memo field, press **Ctrl-Home**. This puts you in dBASE's full-screen editor. When you finish typing the Memo field text, press **Ctrl-End** to return to the data entry mask. Memo fields are generally limited to 5,000 characters when using the dBASE editor.

Once you've made your changes, you can save them and return to the dBASE dot prompt by pressing **Ctrl-W** (for "write"). If you decide not to save a change in the current record, you can press **Ctrl-Q** (for "quit"). This abandons the displayed record without saving changes and takes you back to the dBASE dot prompt. However, you should know that if you edit the contents of a record and move to another record, the edited record is automatically saved when you move to the next record.

APPLICATIONS

The EDIT command lets you update or correct the contents of a database. It is also used to display the contents of a record for review purposes. Once you review the record contents, you can return to the dot prompt with **Ctrl-Q** or by pressing **Esc**. The EDIT FOR *expression* form of the command lets you restrict editing to those records that contain a specific value or phrase. This is a powerful time saver. The alternative to this command is to manually search through every record in a database to find the desired expression.

TYPICAL OPERATION

In this illustration the EDIT command is used to change the PAID status in record number 1 of the MEMBERS database last modified in Module 47. Begin at the dBASE dot prompt.

1.   Type **USE MEMBERS** and press **Return**.

2. Type **EDIT 1**, press **Return**, and notice the following display:

```
        Record No.       1
        NAME       Williams, David
        ADR        2345 Fresno Circle
        CSZ        Tampa, FL 32656
        AFFIL      U.S. Air Force (Ret)
        JOINED     11/15/80
        PAID       T
        INFO       Memo
```

3. Move the cursor down to the PAID field with the **Down Arrow** key and type **F**.

4. Press the **Down Arrow** once more and notice that record number 2 is displayed.

```
        Record No.       2
        NAME       Phillips, George W.
        ADR        11205 Dawn Drive
        CSZ        Lago Vista, TX 78641
        AFFIL      Austin Medical Center
        JOINED     06/01/81
        PAID       T
        INFO       Memo
```

5. Press **Ctrl-W** to save your changes and to return to the dBASE dot prompt.

6. Turn to Module 10 to continue the learning sequence.

Module 33
EJECT

DESCRIPTION

The EJECT command causes a printer form feed. Most computer printers use continuous-form paper, although some are sheet fed. If the printer uses a form tractor or a cut-sheet feeder, EJECT causes the printer to advance the present sheet up and out of the way and the next sheet is rolled into position, ready for printing. The EJECT command operates independently of the SET PRINT ON command, which echos, or simultaneously prints, displayed text.

The form of the EJECT command is:

    . EJECT

The EJECT command is entered from either the dot prompt or from a line within a command file.

DEBUGGING A COMMAND FILE CONTAINING THE EJECT COMMAND   To suppress form feeds caused by the EJECT command, you can place an asterisk in front of the line that contains the EJECT command. This converts the line into a comment, which is ignored during command file opertion.

It is often desirable to suppress feeds during trial runs of a new command file to prevent your printer from unnecessarily feeding paper.

THE FORM FEED FUNCTION   The standard number of line feeds per inch is six, which means that an eleven-inch-long sheet of paper is 66 lines long. Most printers count the number of line feeds received. When turned on, the printer marks the top-of-form position as the zero reference point. So it's important to have your paper properly aligned when you turn on your printer.

EJECT causes an advance of 66 lines or 66 lines less the number of line feed codes already used. Therefore, the printer is automatically indexed to the top of the next sheet of paper. For example, if your printer has received 30 line feed codes and then receives an EJECT command, it will issue 36 additional line feed codes (30 + 36 = 66) to advance to the top of the next sheet of paper. In summary, your printer counts the number of line feed codes received to "know" how many additional line feeds are required to reach the top of the next sheet of paper.

APPLICATIONS

The EJECT command is applied in a number of ways. First, it is often placed at the beginning of a print run to ensure that a clean sheet of paper is in position before printing begins. It is sometimes used to cause a form feed after each full page is printed to start the next report at the top of a clean sheet.

The EJECT command is often used in command files designed to print custom reports. The following command lines, or ones like them, are used to contol form feeds when the page reaches a certain number of lines. You may wish to adopt this technique in command files of your own.

```
                                        Remarks
  * EJECT.PRG              && Demonstrates use of the EJECT command.
  CLEAR                    && Clears the screen.
  SET HEADING OFF          && Turns off display of field names.
  SET TALK OFF             && Turns off dBASE dialog.
  SET PRINT ON             && Causes displayed text to be printed.
  EJECT                    && Causes a form feed to the top of the next sheet.
  USE PICNIC               && Puts PICNIC database in use.
  X = 0                    && Store 0 to the memory variable X.
  ? '-------------------------------------------------' && Draws a line.
  DO WHILE .NOT. EOF()     && Causes continuous operation until end of file is en
     IF X = 50             && Checks for a condition where X equals 50.
       ? '-------------------------------------------------' && Draws a line.
       EJECT               && Causes a form feed (if X = 50).
       ? '-------------------------------------------------' && Draws a line.
       X = 0               && Resets memory variable X to 0 (if X = 50).
     ENDIF                 && Passes control to next command line.
     DISPLAY NAME, GUESTS  && Displays the NAME and GUESTS fields.
     X = X + 1             && Adds 1 to the present value of X (increments X by 1
     SKIP                  && Positions record pointer to the next record in line
  ENDDO
  ? '-------------------------------------------------' && Draws a line.
  EJECT                    && Causes form feed (if end of file).
  SET HEADING ON           && Turns field name display back on.
  SET PRINT OFF            && Turns off printing (if end of file).
  SET TALK ON              && Turns dBASE dialog back on (if end of file).
  CLEAR                    && Clears screen (if end of file).
  CANCEL                   && Returns control to dot prompt (if end of file).
```

TYPICAL OPERATION

In this illustration the EJECT command is used in conjunction with the MEMBERS database modified in Module 47. Selected fields are listed to your printer and then the EJECT command is used to feed the next clean sheet into position. Begin at the dBASE dot prompt. Be sure your printer is ready to print.

1. Type **USE MEMBERS** and press **Return**.

2. Type **LIST NAME, CSZ** and press **Return**.

3. Type **EJECT** and press **Return**; notice that a printer form feed occurs.

4. Type **USE** and press **Return** to close the database.

5. Turn to Module 43 to continue the learning sequence.

Module 34
ERASE, ZAP

DESCRIPTION

The ERASE command is used to erase files from your disk. The ZAP command is used to remove all records from a database file. Each of these commands is described in this module.

ERASE   When a file is erased, it is removed from your disk. The form of the ERASE command is:

    . ERASE *filename.ext*

For example, if you wish to erase a command file named TEST1.PRG, type:

    . ERASE test1.prg

The message "File has been deleted" is displayed to verify that it has been erased.

DELETE FILE command is also used to achieve the same result. For example:

    . DELETE FILE test1.prg

yields the same result.

Open files cannot be erased. If you attempt to erase an open file, the message, "File is already open" is displayed. Therefore, it's necessary to close the file before it is erased with the CLEAR ALL, CLOSE ALL, or the appropriate CLOSE *filetype* command.

ZAP   When the records are "zapped" from the database, all that remains is the database structure.

To empty a database, type **ZAP** and press **Return**. The message:

```
    Zap B:filename.dbf? (Y/N)
```

is displayed to give you a chance to change your mind. Typing **Y** for *yes* does the deed. Typing **N** for *no* (or any other key) returns you to the dot prompt without zapping the records.

APPLICATIONS

The ERASE (or DELETE FILE) command deletes an entire file from your disk. Like most commands, ERASE is used from either the dot prompt or embedded within a command file. Very often, command files create temporary indexes and sorting files. To avoid the consumption of unnecessary disk space, you can use the ERASE command to eliminate temporary files.

The ZAP command, on the other hand, is handy for quickly deleting all records from within a database file without destroying the database structure. For example, if you are using someone else's database in which you intend to place your own information, the ZAP command becomes a useful tool. However, you should be sure to use ZAP cautiously. If you ZAP a database containing important information, it is lost forever.

TYPICAL OPERATION

In this illustration a small database file called SHORT is created, a few records are entered, and then ZAP is used to demonstrate its effect. After emptying the database, you'll ERASE the file from disk using the ERASE command. Start at the dBASE dot prompt.

1. Type **CREATE SHORT** and press **Return**.

2. Use CREATE SHORT to create a 2-field file having the following fields:

```
    field name  type      width  dec

  1 Name        Character    10           -Type Name<cr> <cr> 10<cr>
  2 Grade       Numeric       2    0       -Type Grade<cr> N<cr> 2<cr> <cr>
  3 <cr>                                   -Press <cr>
```

3. Respond with **Y** to the data entry prompt and type the following information into the database:

```
Record No.    1
Name       John
Grade       8
-------------------------
Record No.    2
Name       Mary
Grade       9
-------------------------
Record No.    3
Name       Sue
Grade       8
-------------------------
Record No.    4
Name       <cr>              -Press <cr> to end data entry.
Grade
```

4. Type **LIST** and press **Return**. Compare your screen to the following:

5. Delete the contents of the new database by typing **ZAP** and pressing **Return**. Then type **Y** in response to the (Y/N) prompt.

6. Type **LIST** and press **Return** again; note that nothing is displayed as the contents have been zapped from the database.

7. Close the database by typing **USE** and pressing **Return**.

8. Delete the database from your disk by typing **ERASE SHORT.DBF** and pressing **Return**.

9. Verify that the SHORT database is gone by typing **DIR** and pressing **Return**. Notice that SHORT.DBF is not displayed in the list of database files.

10. Turn to Module 7 to continue the learning sequence.

Module 35

EXPORT, IMPORT

DESCRIPTION

The EXPORT and IMPORT commands are used to exchange data between PFS:FILE program files and dBASE III Plus database files. To convert (or *export*) a database file in PFS:FILE format, place the database file in use and type:

. EXPORT TO *filename* TYPE PFS

The exported file retains its original structure. You can use a format (.FMT) file (with SET FORMAT TO *filename*) to control the structure of the resulting file. If you specify an existing filename, it is overwritten automatically. You can prevent overwriting a file accidentally by using SET SAFETY ON. This displays an "overwrite file" message, which tells you that the filename you selected already exists, and gives you the opportunity to halt the process and select another filename.

Similarly, you can convert (or *import*) a file from a PFS:FILE program file to a dBASE III Plus database file with the command:

. IMPORT FROM *filename* TYPE PFS

The imported file retains the original filename with the .DBF extension.

APPLICATIONS

Because the PFS:FILE program has been in use for a number of years, there are many users and existing databases in the PFS:FILE format. Provisions for transferring data between the two programs lets users of both dBASE and PFS:FILE share information. This powerful transfer process prevents the need to retype information to achieve data exchange.

TYPICAL OPERATION

In this illustration you use the ABC database last modified in Module 56 to create a PFS:FILE database. Begin at the dBASE prompt.

1. Type **USE ABC** and press **Return**.

2. Type **EXPORT TO XYZ TYPE PFS** and press **Return**. Notice the "4 Records copied" display, which verifies the creation of the PFS:FILE data file.

3. Type **USE** and press **Return** to close the database.

4. Type **ERASE XYZ** and press **Return** to erase the exported file.

5. Turn to Module 61 to continue the learning sequence.

Module 36
FIND, SEEK

DESCRIPTION

The FIND and SEEK commands let you find the first record within an indexed database that matches a predetermined expression. FIND operates with character strings, while SEEK operates with either character strings or numeric values. However, if SEEK is used with a character string, the string must be enclosed in single or double quotes or square brackets. The following FIND and SEEK commands achieve the same result.

```
                               Remarks
. USE PNFILE              && Puts database in use.
. INDEX ON PN TO PNDEX    && Indexes database on ZIP field.
. FIND AF234-6            && Locates first record containing AF234-6 in PN field.
        or
. SEEK 'AF234-6'
        or
. SEEK "AF234-6"
        or
. SEEK [AF234-6]
```

Remember, SEEK character strings must be enclosed in *delimiters* when searched. However, memory variables and numbers are entered without delimiters. The following command lines demonstrate SEEK with a number and memory variable. The memory variable takes advantage of dBASE's *macro substitution* function.

```
. INDEX ON AGE TO AGEDEX  && Indexes database on AGE field.
. SEEK 35                 && Locates first record containing 35 in AGE field.
    or
. STORE 35 TO MAGE        && Stores 35 to memory variable MAGE.
. SEEK &MAGE              && Locates first record containing 35 in AGE field.
```

The ampersand (&) placed in front of the memory variable MAGE (&MAGE) is referred to as a *macro substitution* expression. When used, the contents of the memory variable MAGE are substituted for the expression &MAGE.

As you can see, the FIND and SEEK commands are similar to LOCATE. However, these commands only operate with key fields, which are fields used during the indexing process (see Module 41). Remember, FIND and SEEK find only the first match within a database. Also, the "FOR expression," as in LOCATE FOR AGE > = 35 is unavailable with these commands. On the other hand, LOCATE and CONTINUE search through records within a database until a matching record is found or the end of the database is reached. LOCATE is also used with logical values (.T. or .F.), while FIND and SEEK cannot locate logical values.

Some forms of the FIND and SEEK commands are shown in the following list.

1. FIND *expression* — Positions the record pointer to the first record containing the expression in a key field.

    . FIND Jo — Finds the first record containing "Jo" as the first two characters of a key field. Jo matches strings such as Jones or Johnson. Note that an exact upper and lowercase match is required.

    . DISPLAY NAME, — ZIP Displays NAME and ZIP fields.

2. FIND &MNAME — Finds the first record containing the contents of the memory variable MNAME in a key field. The macro substitution function (&) substitutes the memory variable contents for its name.

    . STORE 'Joh' TO MNAME — Stores string Joh to MNAME.
    . FIND &MNAME — Finds the first record containing Joh as the starting string of the key field.

3. SEEK 'Jones' — Finds the first record containing the name "Jones."

4. SEEK 112 — Finds the first record containing 112.

5. SEEK MVAL — Finds the first record containing the contents of the memory variable MVAL in a key field.

If you want to FIND an exact match for the FIND or SEEK string, you can enter the statement SET EXACT ON. When on, the statement "FIND Smith" ignores Smithe, Smithville, or Smithsonian. However, trailing blanks are ignored when SET EXACT ON is active.

APPLICATIONS

FIND and SEEK are fast and simple to use. Once a file is indexed, it's easy to find the first matching record. The major advantage to FIND and SEEK is that they are extremely fast (practically instantaneous), while LOCATE may take a while to find a matching record in a large database. Disadvantages include the fact that only the first record is found, and a "FOR expression" clause can't be used, as in LOCATE FOR AGE > = 35. FIND and SEEK are both used in either the interactive mode (from the dBASE dot prompt) or in command files.

TYPICAL OPERATION

In this illustration the FIND and SEEK commands are used to locate selected records within the ABC database last modified in Module 56. Begin at the dBASE dot prompt.

1. Type **USE ABC** and press **Return**.

2. Index the ABC database file by typing **INDEX ON NAME TO NABC** and pressing **Return**.

3. Find the record containing "Bishop" by typing **FIND Bish** and pressing **Return**.

4. Check the position of the record pointer by typing **DISPLAY** and pressing **Return**. Notice that the record containing Bishop was found.

5. Store the string "Ser" to the memory variable MNAME by typing **STORE 'Ser' to MNAME** and pressing **Return**.

6. Find the record containing Sergio by typing **SEEK MNAME** and pressing **Return**.

7. Check the position of the record pointer by typing **DISPLAY** and pressing **Return**. Notice that the record containing Sergio was found.

8. Find the record again by typing **FIND &MNAME** and pressing **Return**.

9. Check again using the DISPLAY command.

10. Type **CLEAR ALL** to close all files and remove all memory variables.

11. Delete the index file by typing **ERASE NABC.NDX** and pressing **Return**.

12. Turn to Module 62 to continue the learning sequence.

Module 37

GET, GET PICTURE, CLEAR GETS, READ

DESCRIPTION

This module deals with a set of dBASE statements used to display and change the contents of database fields and memory variables. The GET, CLEAR GETS, and READ statement were briefly introduced in Module 58 with the SAY statement.

The information in this module is directed at forms of the GET statement. However, because the GET statement is often used in combination with @ row,col and SAY, these statements are also presented to show the roles they play with forms of the GET statement. For more information about @ row,col and SAY, see Modules 8 and 58.

Some forms of GET are presented in the following list.

1. @ row,col GET *fieldname*   The statement specifies the row and column coordinates and the effected field name of the database in use. Information is either displayed, or can be entered into the field from the keyboard, depending upon following READ or CLEAR GETS command. READ and CLEAR GETS are described later in this module.

     @ 12,10 GET NAME

     This command displays the NAME field of the active database at row 12 column 10.

2. @ row,col SAY "*text*" GET *fieldname*   Here, the GET statement is preceded with a SAY statement to display a user prompt on the screen. This form of the statement lets you guide a user through the data entry process by displaying helpful information.

3. @ row,col GET *fieldname* PICTURE *expression*   The PICTURE clause allows you to control the format of displayed or printed field contents. Function and template characters used within the PICTURE clause are contained in Module 58, Table 58-1.

4. @ row,col GET *fieldname* RANGE *expression*   The RANGE clause is used with numeric and date variables to specify the minimum and maximum values allowable in the GET statement. The character-to-date CTOD function is used with dates. Look at the examples.

     @ 10,12 GET AGE RANGE 21,65
     @ 08,20 GET DATE RANGE CTOD('01/01/87'),CTOD('12/31/87')

     The first example allows entry of values from 21 to 65. The second example restricts date entry to 1987.

ORGANIZING GET STATEMENTS   When the GET statement is used, it's best to have row and column positions organized sequentially. That is, row numbers should start at the top and move down. Likewise, column positions should begin at the left and move to the right. This is essential when information is printed, because the printer operates from left to right, top to bottom, and can't back up if a row-column position is out of order.

CLEAR GETS and READ   If one or more GET statements are followed by a command line containing the CLEAR GETS command, the field contents are restricted to display only. CLEAR GETS prevents the displayed field information from being modified, because you cannot place the cursor in the field to make alterations. However, if followed by READ instead of CLEAR GETS, you can move the cursor to the field, and you can enter changes from the keyboard. Therefore, the READ statement lets you enter information that is read into the database. An example of the GET statement used with CLEAR GETS and READ follows for clarification.

```
USE INVTORY
@ 10,55 GET DES
@ 11,55 GET PN
CLEAR GETS
@ 12,55 GET QTY
@ 13,55 GET COST
READ
```

COMBINING GET WITH SAY   When the SAY-GET combination is used, as in example 2, the field contents are displayed immediately to the right of the SAY text. An example of this form of the GET statement follows.

```
USE MEMBERS
@ 5,15 SAY "                    Member's Name " GET NAME
@ 6,15 SAY '                   Street Address ' GET ADR
@ 7,15 SAY '         City, State, and Zip Code' GET CSZ
CLEAR GETS
@ 8,15 SAY "Is this member's dues paid (Y/N)?" GET PAID
READ
```

The NAME, ADR, and CSZ fields are restricted to display in rows 5, 6, and 7; the CLEAR GETS command prevents field contents from being modified. However, the cursor is positioned at the PAID field to allow modification. This is accomplished with the READ command on the line following the last GET statement.

USING GET WITH MEMORY VARIABLES   You can also get memory variables with the GET statement. Here's a small command file that demonstrates the use of the GET statement with memory variables. You may wish to type it and try it out on your computer.

```
* GETEST.PRG
SET TALK OFF
X = 0
Y = 0
C = 5
CLEAR
@ 5,5 SAY 'Enter a new value for X ' GET X
@ ROW()+1,C SAY 'Enter a new value for Y ' GET Y
READ
SET INTENSITY OFF
CLEAR
@ 5,C SAY 'The value of X and Y are ' GET X PICTURE '@B'
@ ROW(),C+1 SAY 'and' GET Y PICTURE '@B'
CLEAR GETS
WAIT
SET TALK ON
SET INTENSITY ON
CLEAR
CANCEL
```

APPLICATIONS

The GET statement has many applications. With @ row,col, GET is used to display and modify the contents of fields and memory variables at specific screen positions. The ability to use SAY with GET lets you display or print field contents at any row and column position with corresponding text. The contents are displayed only if the GET statement is followed by the CLEAR GETS command. They can be altered if followed by the READ command.

Finally, the PICTURE clause is used to format field contents with dollar signs, commas, slash signs or other desired characters or symbols. It controls the format of data entry. For example, you can force uppercase entry by using a statement like:

```
@ 12,15 GET NAME PICTURE '!!!!!!!!!!'
```

TYPICAL OPERATION

In this illustration several variations of GET are used in a command file named GET.PRG. The command file uses the MEMBERS database last used in Module 58. Begin at the dBASE dot prompt.

1.   Type **MODIFY COMMAND GET** and press **Return** to use the dBASE editor.

2. Type the following command file. (Don't type the explanatory remarks.)

<u>Remarks</u>

```
* GET.PRG -- Demonstrates use of the GET statement.
CLEAR                        && Clears the screen.
SET TALK OFF                 && Turns off dBASE dialog.
@ 2,20 SAY 'Enter new member information'       && Displays text in quotes.
USE MEMBERS                  && Puts MEMBERS database file in use.
SET CONFIRM ON               && Requires <cr> to move cursor to next field during data entry.
DO WHILE .T.                 && Continues operation while true.
   @ 3,0 CLEAR               && Clears the screen from row 3, column 0.
   APPEND BLANK              && Adds blank record to bottom of database.
   GO BOTTOM                 && Positions record pointer to last record in database.
   @  4,1 SAY REPLICATE (CHR(205),72)        && Draws double line across screen.
   @  5,5 SAY        'Name          ' GET NAME
   @  ROW()+1,5 SAY 'Address        ' GET ADR
   @  ROW()+1,5 SAY 'City, State & Zip ' GET CSZ
   @  ROW()+1,5 SAY 'Affiliation    ' GET AFFIL
   @  ROW()+1,5 SAY 'Date Joined    ' GET JOINED
   @  ROW()+1,5 SAY 'Age           ' GET AGE
   @  ROW()+1,5 SAY 'Paid          ' GET PAID PICTURE 'L'
   @  ROW()+1,1 SAY REPLICATE (CHR(205),72)  && Draws double line across screen.
   READ                      && Reads GET fields into current database record.
   WAIT 'Press "Q" to quit, any another key to continue ' TO STOP     && Pauses operation
   *                                                             with prompt.
   IF UPPER(STOP)='Q'        && Checks STOP for Q; UPPER() accepts lower or upper case.
      EXIT                   && Exits DO WHILE loop.
   ENDIF                     && Completes IF statement; passes control to next line.
ENDDO                        && Completes DO WHILE statement.
SET CONFIRM OFF              && Restores confirm status to default condition.
SET TALK ON                 && Turns dBASE dialog back on.
CLEAR ALL                    && Closes database and releases memory variable.
CLEAR                        && Clears the screen.
CANCEL                       && Cancels operation and returns to dBASE dot prompt.
```

3. Press **Ctrl-W** to write the command file to disk.

4. Run the command file by typing **DO GET** and pressing **Return**. Compare your screen to the following:

```
                        Enter New Member Information


        Name
        Address
        City, State & Zip
        Affiliation
        Date Joined            / /
        Age
        Paid              T
```

5. Fill in the data entry mask as shown; press **Return** after entering the information in each field.

```
                    Enter New Member Information


        Name              Johns, Bill G.
        Address           3435 Mesa Gulch
        City, State & Zip Tripoli, OK 80975
        Affiliation       Billings, Inc.
        Date Joined       05/25/85
        Age               41
        Paid              Y
```

Press "Q" to quit, any other key to add another... _   (Type Q)

Do cancelled

6. After experimenting with the command file, delete it by typing **ERASE GET.PRG** and pressing **Return**.

7. Turn to Module 30 to continue the learning sequence.

Module 38
GO, GOTO, GO BOTTOM, GO TOP, SKIP

DESCRIPTION

This module describes commands used to move the record pointer to a specific record within a database file. Like all commands, you must place a database in use before a record positioning command operates. Once the database is open, you can position the record pointer to records within the database using the GO and SKIP commands. A summary of each of these commands is included in the following list.

1. . GO n, GOTO n, or n   Moves the record pointer to record n. Notice that GO, GOTO, and simply typing a number all position the record pointer to the specified record number (n). To save keystrokes, you may prefer to use "n" or GO n.

2. . GO BOTTOM   Positions the record pointer to the last record of the database in use.

3. . GO TOP   Positions the record pointer to the first record of the database in use.

4. . SKIP   Moves the record pointer to the following record.

5. . SKIP n   Moves the record pointer n records below the present record position.

6. . SKIP −n   Moves the record pointer n records above the present record position.

Most of the entries in the preceding list are self explanatory. An example of each is provided to ensure that you understand their use. To set up the example, assume you're using a database file named INVTORY that contains 10 records.

```
. USE INVTORY          && Puts INVTORY database in use.
. GO BOTTOM            && Moves record pointer to last record in database.
. ? RECNO()           && Display record number (expressed as an integer).
        10            && dBASE dialogue displays last record number.
. 3                   && Moves record pointer to record 3.
. SKIP 3              && Moves record pointer to record 6.
. SKIP -2             && Moves record pointer to record 4.
. GOTO 7              && Moves record pointer to record 7.
. STORE RECNO() TO X  && Stores record number to memory variable X.
         7            && dBASE dialogue displays stored value.
. GO TOP              && Moves record pointer to record 1.
. GO X                && Moves record pointer to record 7, the value of X.
```

APPLICATIONS

As you can see, it's easy to move the record pointer to any record within a database. The GO TOP and GO BOTTOM commands are often used in command files. A popular combination is to APPEND BLANK, which adds a blank record to the bottom of a database (see Module 5), and then move the record pointer to the bottom of the database with GO BOTTOM to enter field contents from the keyboard in response to displayed prompts.

The GO TOP and SKIP commands are also commonly used from both the dot prompt and within command files. By using the DO WHILE command (Module 31), you can go to the top of a database file, display the current record, SKIP to the next record, display it, and so on until the end of the file is reached. The records can be printed simultaneously using SET PRINT ON. These commands are used in the Typical Operation section of this module to demonstrate their use.

TYPICAL OPERATION

In this illustration the GO TOP and SKIP commands are used to display certain fields of each record in the MEMBERS database, modified in Module 47. Begin at the dBASE dot prompt.

1. Type **MODIFY COMMAND SHOW** and press **Return** to use the dBASE editor.

2. Type the following command file. (Don't type the explanatory remarks.)

```
                                    Remarks
* SHOW.PRG  Lists names and membership dates  && Comment line.
CLEAR                        && Clears screen.
SET TALK OFF                 && Turns off dBASE dialog.
USE MEMBERS                  && Puts MEMBERS database in use.
GO TOP                       && Positions record pointer to top of database.
SET PRINT ON                 && Prints and displays data simultaneously.
DO WHILE .NOT. EOF()         && Causes continuous operation until end-of-file encountered.
   DISPLAY NAME, JOINED OFF  && Displays NAME and JOINED fields; record numbers are omitted.
   SKIP                      && Position record pointer to next record.
ENDDO                        && Ends DO loop; passes control to next statement if one exists.
SET PRINT OFF                && Turns simultaneous printing off.
WAIT                         && Pauses operation; displays "Press any key..." prompt.
USE                          && Closes database.
CLEAR                        && Clears screen.
CANCEL                       && Returns control to dBASE dot prompt.
```

3. Press **Ctrl-W** to write the command file to disk.

4. Prepare your printer for operation. When ready, type **DO SHOW** and press **Return**.

5. Notice that the following information is displayed and printed simultaneously.

```
name                    joined
Williams, David         11/15/80
name                    joined
Phillips, George W.     06/01/81
name                    joined
Galvin, Theodore A.     02/15/83
Press any key to return to dBASE III
```

NOTE

The "name" and "joined" displays are suppressed by adding the line SET HEADING OFF at the beginning of the program.

6. Press any key to return to the dBASE dot prompt when printing is finished.

7. Turn to Module 42 to continue the learning sequence.

Module 39
HELP

DESCRIPTION

The HELP command is used to display on-screen help information about the various dBASE commands. The HELP command is entered at the dBASE dot prompt by pressing the **F1** key or by typing:

    . HELP

and pressing **Return**. The following HELP menu is displayed.

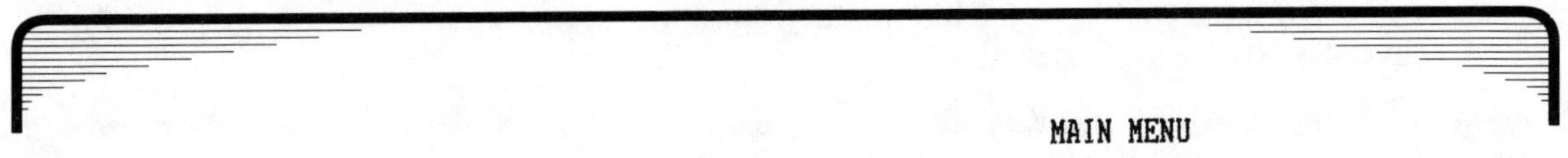

At this point you can make a selection by moving your cursor down or up with your arrow keys to highlight the selection of your choice. Once highlighted, press **Return**. You can also type the selection number (1 through 6) and press **Return**. The selected HELP screen is displayed. For example, if you wish to see the "What Is a . . ." screen, type **2** and press **Return**. The following screen is displayed.

```
                        What Is a ...
                        ════════════

                        0 - Command
                        1 - Expression
                        2 - Field List
                        3 - File
                        4 - Key Field
                        5 - Memory Variable
                        6 - Operator
                        7 - Record
                        8 - Scope
                        9 - Skeleton
```

Now you can see what a command is by typing **1** and pressing **Return**. Another screen is displayed. It's easy to move around in dBASE's HELP facility. To return to the previous menu, press the **PgUp** key. To leave the HELP facility, press **Esc**.

You can also display HELP information about a specific command by typing **HELP command** from the dBASE dot prompt, where *command* is any legitimate dBASE command. For example, typing **HELP USE** displays:

```
                                                              USE

                        USE
                        ══

Syntax       : USE [<database file>/?] [INDEX <index file list>]
                   [ALIAS <alias name>]

Description : Opens a database file and, optionally, any
               named index files.  USE also simultaneously closes
               any active database file in the currently SELECTed work area.
               USE without options closes the active database file.  USE
               optionally establishes alias names for open files.  Use ?
               to list the cataloged database files.

See also     : CLOSE, SET INDEX, REINDEX
```

Similarly, typing **HELP CREATE** displays:

```
                                                              CREATE


                                CREATE
                                ======


        Syntax      :   CREATE <new file> [FROM <structure extended file>]

        Description :   Create defines the structure for a new database (.dbf)
                        file and adds the file to the directory.
                        The FROM option forms a new database (.dbf) file in
                        which the structure is determined by the contents of
                        a file created with COPY STRUCTURE EXTENDED.
```

APPLICATIONS

The ability to display quick reference information on the screen is convenient if you forget which command performs a certain task. You can start by displaying HELP information, rather than referring to printed matter every time you get stuck or want to refresh your memory.

TYPICAL OPERATION

In this illustration the HELP command is used to display information about dBASE's SET PATH TO command. Begin at the dBASE dot prompt.

1. Press **F1**; the following information is displayed.

```
                                                            MAIN MENU


                         dBASE III Plus Main Menu
                         ========================


                     1 - Getting Started
                     2 - What Is a ...
                     3 - How Do I ...
                     4 - Creating a Database
                     5 - Using an Existing Database
                     6 - Commands and Functions
```

2. Type **6** and press **Return** for "Commands and Functions." Notice the following:

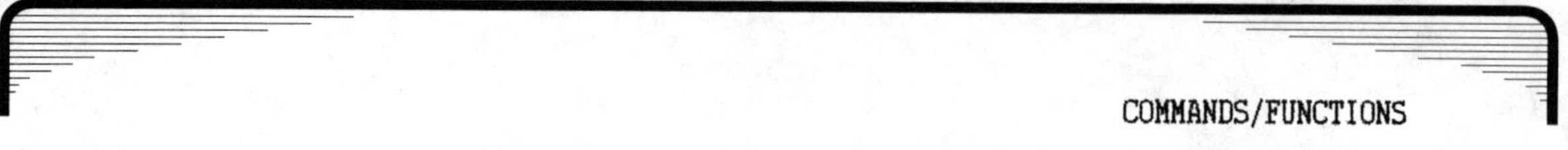


```
dBASE III PLUS Commands and Functions


    1 - Commands (Starter Set)
    2 - Commands (Advanced Set)
    3 - Functions
    4 - SET TO Commands
    5 - SET ON/OFF Commands
```

3. Select "SET TO Commands" by typing **4** and pressing **Return**. Compare your screen to the following:

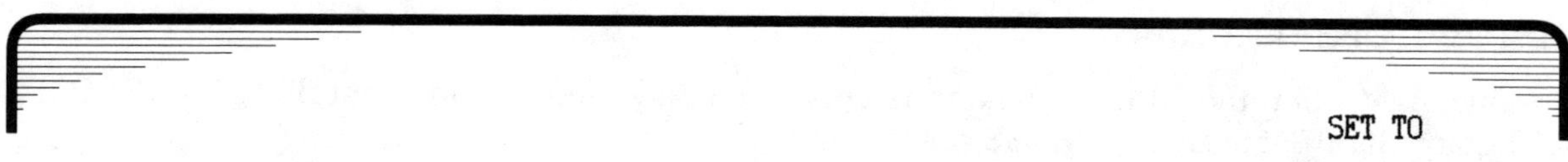


```
                        SET TO Commands


    1 - SET ALTERNATE      9 - SET FIELDS      17 - SET MESSAGE
    2 - SET CATALOG       10 - SET FILTER      18 - SET ORDER
    3 - SET COLOR         11 - SET FUNCTION    19 - SET PATH
    4 - SET DATE          12 - SET FORMAT      20 - SET PRINT
    5 - SET DECIMALS      13 - SET HISTORY     21 - SET PROCEDURE
    6 - SET DEFAULT       14 - SET INDEX       22 - SET RELATION
    7 - SET DELIMITERS    15 - SET MARGIN      23 - SET TYPEAHEAD
    8 - SET DEVICE        16 - SET MEMOWIDTH   24 - SET VIEW
```

4. Type **19**, for "SET PATH," and press **Return**. Check the following:

```
                                                              SET PATH


                        SET PATH
                        ════════


        Syntax      :  SET PATH TO [<path list>]

        Description :  Specifies additional file searching paths.
                       Commas (,) or semicolons (;) separate path names.
                       Directory names in path names are separated by
                       backslashes (\).
                       SET PATH TO limits the search path to the
                       current directory.
```

5. Press **Esc** to exit the HELP facility.

6. Turn to Module 18 to continue the learning sequence.

Module 40
IF, ELSE, ENDIF

DESCRIPTION

The IF, ELSE, and ENDIF commands form a complete branching statement. The entire set of commands is called the *IF statement*. It is similar in operation to the DO CASE, OTHERWISE, ENDCASE commands which form the CASE statement described in Module 30. However, the IF statement is better than CASE for checking the presence of a single condition. Look at the following IF statement.

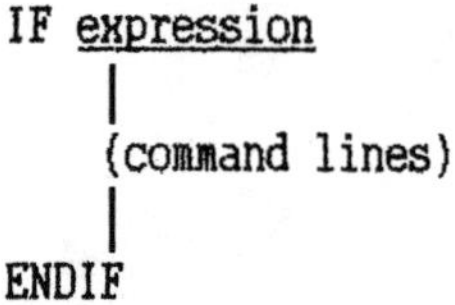

The IF statement checks to see if the expression is true. If the expression is true, the command lines within the IF statement are used. If the expression is false, control passes to the command line following the ENDIF statement.

The ELSE statement is an optional command that adds *branching* to the IF statement. For example, if you drink your coffee black unless real cream is available, you can use the following statements.

```
If real cream is available
    I'll take my coffee with cream.
Else
    I'll drink my coffee black
End if (or the decision) process.
```

Here's the command form in "computerese":

```
IF expression
    |
    (command lines)
    |
ELSE
    |
    (command lines)
    |
ENDIF
```

When the IF statement is used within a DO WHILE statement, ENDIF must occur before ENDDO (see Module 31). This is illustrated in the following diagram.

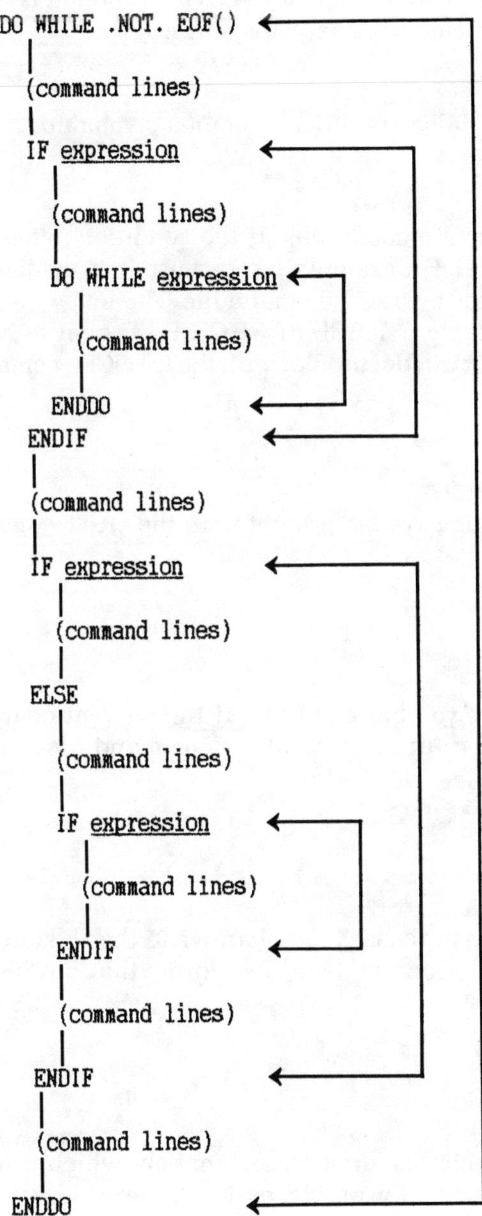

Notice how you can nest IF and DO WHILE statements within IF statements. Although it's not shown, you can also nest CASE statements within IF statements, so you have a large amount of flexibility in command file design.

You should also be aware of the IIF( ) function, described in Appendix B. This function is a one-line substitute for the complete IF-ELSE-ENDIF statement. It uses the form:

IIF(condition,command1,command2)

where a true condition executes the *command1*; a false condition executes *command2*.

APPLICATIONS

The IF command is a good tool to use for testing certain conditions. If the condition is true, the commands within the IF statement become operational. For example, you can use IF in conjunction with a set of commands that terminate operation of the current command file. The following three lines use IF to check the value of the memory variable CHOICE. If CHOICE is equal to X, you can exit the current command file and return to the dBASE dot prompt with the CANCEL command.

```
IF CHOICE='X'
    CANCEL
ENDIF
```

You can exit the current command file to the operating system prompt with the QUIT command with:

```
IF CHOICE='X'
    QUIT
ENDIF
```

where QUIT terminates dBASE operation and takes you back to DOS. If the current command file was called from another command file, you can return to the calling command file with the RETURN command in the form:

```
IF CHOICE='X'
    RETURN
ENDIF
```

In all three of these examples, IF is testing for an uppercase X. You can write the IF statement so that either an uppercase or lowercase X are accepted as true. Two forms that do this are:

```
IF CHOICE='X' .OR. IF CHOICE ='x'
```

or

```
IF UPPER(CHOICE)='X'
```

The logical OR expression is used in the first example. The uppercase function, which converts lowercase characters to uppercase, is used in the second example, and is preferred because it is shorter.

The IF statement is sometimes used in situations where multiple conditions are checked. Look at the following example.

```
IF CHOICE='1'
    DO ADD
ENDIF
IF CHOICE='2'
    DO CHANGE
ENDIF
IF CHOICE='3'
    DO DELETE
ENDIF
    |
```

The CASE statement is preferred to the IF statement for checking multiple choices.

One more practical example is presented. You can use IF to determine whether or not to print displayed text with the following command lines.

```
WAIT 'Type "P" to print, any other key to display ' TO PRT
IF UPPER(PRT) = 'P'
    SET PRINT ON
ENDIF
    |
(command lines)
    |
SET PRINT OFF
    |
RETURN
```

TYPICAL OPERATION

In this illustration a small database is created that contains expense information. The IF statement is used in a command file that displays expense information according to the date. Begin at the dBASE dot prompt.

1. Type **CREATE EXPENSE** and press **Return**; create the database structure as shown.

```
    field name    type       width   dec
  1 ITEM          Character     15
  2 DATE          Date           8
  3 AMOUNT        Numeric        6    2
  4 TAX           Numeric        5    2
  5 TOTAL         Numeric        6    2
  6 <cr>
```

2. Enter the following information into the database. Press **Return** in the TOTAL field to leave it blank.

RECORD	ITEM	DATE	AMOUNT	TAX	TOTAL
1	FILE CABINET	01/15/85	99.95	5.00	< cr >
2	FOLDERS	01/18/85	6.95	0.35	< cr >
3	DESK	02/14/85	350.00	17.50	< cr >
4	PAPER	04/02/85	22.50	4.13	< cr >
5	RIBBONS	06/16/85	59.00	2.95	< cr >
6	PRINTER CABLE	07/11/85	56.00	2.80	< cr >
7	FORMS TRACTOR	08/23/85	249.00	12.45	< cr >
8	SHEET FEEDER	10/21/85	899.95	45.00	< cr >
9	< cr >				

3. Let dBASE calculate the TOTAL field for you by typing **REPLACE ALL TOTAL WITH AMOUNT + TAX** and pressing **Return**.

4. Now create your command file by typing **MODIFY COMMAND IFCMD** and pressing **Return** to use the dBASE editor.

5. Type the following command file. (Don't type the explanatory remarks.)

```
                                            Remarks
* IFCMD.PRG -- Demonstrates some uses of the IF command.
SET TALK OFF              && Turns off dBASE dialog.
USE EXPENSE              && Puts EXPENSE database in use.
DO WHILE .T.             && Continues operation while true.
   CLEAR                 && Clears the screen.
   TEXT                  && Displays text until ENDTEXT is encountered.
           TYPE A NUMBER TO DISPLAY EXPENSE INFORMATION
                  Period                Press
              January - March             1
              April   - June              2
              July    - September         3
              October - December          4
              Exit to dBASE               X
ENDTEXT
WAIT ' ' TO CHOICE       && Pauses operation; stores keyed character to memory
*                           variable CHOICE.
CLEAR                    && Clears the screen.
IF UPPER(CHOICE)='X'     && If CHOICE equals X, the following statements are used.
   USE                   && Closes EXPENSE database file.
   SET TALK ON           && Turns dBASE dialog back on.
   CANCEL                && Returns control to dBASE dot prompt.
ENDIF                    && Passes control to following statement.
```

```
IF CHOICE='1'            && If CHOICE equals 1, the following statement is used to display
*                             the first quarter expenses.
   DISPLAY FOR DTOC(DATE) >= '01/01/'.AND. DTOC(DATE) < '04/01/'
ENDIF
IF CHOICE='2'            && If CHOICE equals 2, the following statement is used to display
*                             the second quarter expenses.
   DISPLAY FOR DTOC(DATE) > '03/31/' .AND. DTOC(DATE) < '07/01/'
ENDIF
IF CHOICE='3'            && If CHOICE equals 3, the following statement is used to display
*                             the third quarter expenses.
   DISPLAY FOR DTOC(DATE) > '06/30/'.AND. DTOC(DATE) < '10/01/'
ENDIF
IF CHOICE='4'            && If CHOICE equals 4, the following statement is used to display
*                             the fourth quarter expenses.
   DISPLAY FOR DTOC(DATE) > '09/30/'
ENDIF
WAIT                     && Pauses operation until a key is pressed.
LOOP                     && Loops control back to line following DO WHILE command.
ENDDO                    && Completes DO WHILE statement.
```

NOTE

The CASE statement may be preferred to the IF statements. However, this command file demonstrates two possible uses of the IF statement.

6. Press **Ctrl-W** to write the command file to disk.

7. Run the command file by typing **DO IFCMD** and pressing **Return**. Compare your screen to the following:

```
TYPE A NUMBER TO DISPLAY EXPENSE INFORMATION
          Period                 Press
     January - March               1
     April   - June                2
     July    - September           3
     October - December            4
     Exit to dBASE                 X
```

8. Type **1** to display January through March expenses. Check the following screen.

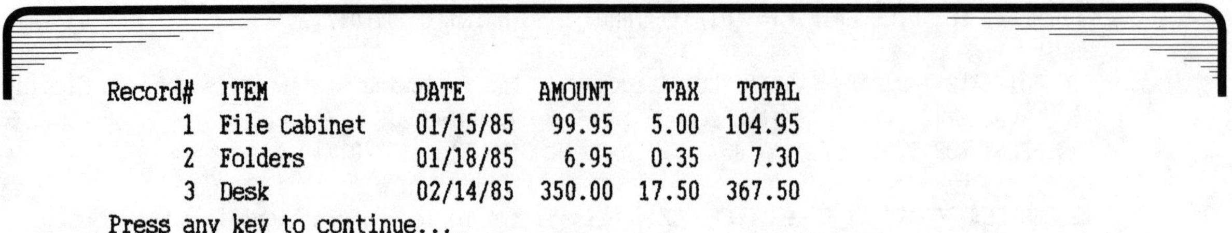

9. Press any key to return to the menu. After you've tested each display option in the menu, type **X** to exit to the dBASE dot prompt.

10 Delete the command file by typing **ERASE IFCMD.PRG** and pressing **Return**.

11. Turn to Module 31 to continue the learning sequence.

Module 41
INDEX, REINDEX

DESCRIPTION

The INDEX command lets you resequence database records in alphanumeric order. In this respect, INDEX is similar to SORT. The resulting index file has the extension .NDX and is associated with the database from which it was created. Changes to records within an index file are reflected in the database file because they are the same records. The index file simply lets you look at a database in an indexed, or different order. However, if you change the database file itself, REINDEX is used to update corresponding index files.

The INDEX command lets you use one or more *key* fields, where key fields are those used to control the indexing sequence. For example, you may want to index a customer database on the CITY and STATE fields. These fields, then, become your key fields. If you want to view the records within a database by state and cities within the state, your INDEX command is:

    . INDEX ON STATE+CITY TO *index name*

where *index name* is a descriptive index filename of your choice. This command tells dBASE to put states in alphabetical order and arrange the cities in alphabetical order within each state. Indexing is done in ascending order on either character-, numeric-, or date-type fields. Memo and logical fields can't be indexed.

USING AN INDEX FILE dBASE directs commands to the last index file created automatically. However, if you have just opened a database file containing index files, you can put the index file of your choice in use. For example, to use the index file SORTDEX, the name of the database file from which the index file was created is specified with the USE command. If the database file from which the SORTDEX file was created is named STATS, open the SORTDEX index file with:

    . USE STATS INDEX SORTDEX

You can think of this statement as saying, "Use the STATS database index file named SORTDEX."

INDEX COMMAND FORMS A few forms of the INDEX command were described in the preceding paragraphs. However, for your convenience they are collected in the following list with explanations of each.

1.   INDEX ON *fieldname* TO *filename*   Indexes database structure and contents, indexed on the named field in alphanumeric (ascending) order, to the named file.

    . INDEX ON NAME TO TEMPFILE

2. INDEX ON *field1 + field2*. . . TO *filename*   Indexes database on the named fields to the named index file.

    . INDEX ON ZIP+NAME TO TEMPFILE

When changes are made to existing database records, the index files are updated automatically. However, when new records are added to a database with the APPEND, BROWSE, or EDIT commands, they are not added to the index files unless you type:

    . SET INDEX TO *filename1,filename2*. . .

where *filename* is the name of one or more index files associated with the database in use. Once this command is in effect, changes to the database are reflected in the index files automatically.

REINDEX   The REINDEX command is available for updating existing index files. This is usually faster than using the SET INDEX TO command. Once you've made changes to a database, simply open the index file and type REINDEX. You'll see the message:

```
Rebuilding index - B:filename.ndx
n records indexed
```

This process takes only a matter of seconds. Once done, the index file is ready for use, reflecting the latest database changes.

MOVING THE RECORD POINTER IN AN INDEXED FILE   When you use an indexed file, you'll notice that the record numbers aren't in sequential order. If you GO BOTTOM or GO TOP, you're not at the bottom or top of the database, you're at the bottom or top of the index file. This is different. You can address records by record number, so if you store a record number in a memory variable, you can move to it in the indexed file. The following few command lines demonstrate the technique for storing a record number to a memory variable and then finding the record in an indexed file.

```
                               Remarks
. USE STATS                && Puts STATS database in use.
. GO BOTTOM                && Positions record pointer to last record in database.
. STORE RECNO() TO NBR     && Store record number to memory variable NBR.
. INDEX ON STATE+CITY TO NEWDEX  && Indexes on STATE and CITY fields to the index
                                    file NEWDEX.
. USE STATS INDEX NEWDEX   && Puts NEWDEX index file in use.
. GOTO NBR                 && Positions record pointer to record number saved in NBR.
```

The FIND and SEEK commands, described in Module 36, are powerful tools that are used to find the first record containing a specified expression. FIND locates character strings, while SEEK locates character strings enclosed in single or double quotes or brackets, numbers, or memory variable values. Like several of dBASE's commands, remember that FIND and SEEK are used only with indexed database files.

APPLICATIONS

There are several major advantages offered by the INDEX command. First, it lets you work with a single database file that may be indexed in a variety of ways. Second, indexing is quick. It also lets you take advantage of the FIND and SEEK commands (described in Module 36) which is an extremely fast way to find a specified value within a database record. When you begin reorganizing information within a database on a regular basis, you'll find yourself making frequent use of the INDEX command.

TYPICAL OPERATION

In this illustration the ABC database created in Module 10 is expanded with a DATE and AGE field. Next, the INDEX command is used to reorganize the database in date sequence. Finally, a new record is appended and the REINDEX command is used to update the index file. Begin at the dBASE dot prompt.

1. Type **USE ABC** and press **Return**.

2. Type **MODIFY STRUCTURE** and press **Return**. Add the following fields:

   ```
   DATE   Date      8
   AGE    Numeric   2
   ```

3. Press **Ctrl-W** and then press **Return** to return to the dBASE dot prompt.

4. Type **EDIT 1**, press **Return**, and update the database as shown.

   ```
   Record#  NAME              PHONE MAIL DATE      AGE
         1  Sergio, Vincent   4596  2084 10/21/82  29
         2  Bishop, Sam       2234  430  11/10/81  34
         3  Collins, Arthur   4554  323  06/12/83  43
         4  Harris, Robert    4353  2230 01/31/85  38
   ```

5. Type **INDEX ON DATE TO DSORT** and press **Return**.

6. Type **LIST** and press **Return**. Notice that the display is indexed in date order:

   ```
   . LIST
   Record#  NAME              PHONE MAIL DATE      AGE
         2  Bishop, Sam       2234  430  11/10/81  34
         1  Sergio, Vincent   4596  2084 10/21/82  29
         3  Collins, Arthur   4554  323  06/12/83  43
         4  Harris, Robert    4353  2230 01/31/85  38
   ```

7. Type **APPEND**, press **Return**, and add the following record.

```
NAME     Johns, Bill T.
PHONE    2332
MAIL     4544
DATE     09/15/85
AGE      24
```

Press **Return** to redisplay the dot prompt.

8. Type **CLEAR ALL** and press **Return** to close the database file.

9. Type **USE ABC** and press **Return** to reopen the database file.

10. Type **USE ABC INDEX DSORT** and press **Return**.

11. Type **LIST** and press **Return**; notice that the last record is not in the indexed file.

```
. LIST
Record#  NAME              PHONE MAIL DATE      AGE
      2  Bishop, Sam       2234  430  11/10/81  34
      1  Sergio, Vincent   4596  2084 10/21/82  29
      3  Collins, Arthur   4554  323  06/12/83  43
      4  Harris, Robert    4353  2230 01/31/85  38
```

12. Type **REINDEX** and press **Return**; notice the following:

```
. REINDEX
Rebuilding index - B:dsort.ndx
      5 records indexed
```

13. Type **LIST** and notice that the last record is now in the index file.

```
. LIST
Record#  NAME              PHONE MAIL DATE      AGE
      2  Bishop, Sam       2234  430  11/10/81  34
      1  Sergio, Vincent   4596  2084 10/21/82  29
      3  Collins, Arthur   4554  323  06/12/83  43
      4  Harris, Robert    4353  2230 01/31/85  38
      5  Johns, Bill T.    2332  4544 09/15/85  24
```

14. Type **CLEAR ALL** to close all files.

15. Type **ERASE DSORT.NDX** and press **Return** to recover disk space used by the practice index file.

16. Turn to Module 45 to continue the learning sequence.

Module 42
INSERT

DESCRIPTION

This module describes the INSERT command, which is used to insert new records within the interior of a database. The INSERT command is similar to the APPEND command, which is described in Module 5. While APPEND adds a new record to the end of a database, INSERT adds a record at a specified location within the database.

To insert a record, the record pointer is positioned to the desired record. You can use the GO command to move to a specific record number. The LOCATE command is sometimes used to position the record pointer to a record that contains a certain value within a field. The desired form of the INSERT command is used, and the contents of the inserted record are entered from the keyboard. All following record numbers are incremented by one. For example, if you have ten records in a database and you insert a new record following record number 5, the inserted record becomes record 6. Records 6 through 10 are renumbered 7 through 11.

Before the INSERT command is used, a database file is opened with the USE command. Once open, the record pointer is positioned and one of the following forms of the INSERT command is used.

1. . INSERT — Inserts a record after the current record. Then displays a record entry mask, like the one displayed by the EDIT or APPEND command, to let you type the contents of each field.

2. . INSERT BEFORE — This command is the same as INSERT except it inserts a record before the current record.

3. . INSERT BLANK — Inserts a blank record following the current record.

Most of the entries in the above list are self explanatory. An example of each is provided. To set up the example, a hypothetical database file named PARTS is used.

```
. USE PARTS        && Puts PARTS database in use (pointer at first record).
. INSERT BEFORE    && Displays a record entry mask for entering new
                      record 1. Type in field contents and press Ctrl-W
                      to save information.
. GO BOTTOM        && Moves record pointer to last record in database.
. INSERT BLANK     && Inserts a BLANK record following the last record in
                      the database.
. GO 12            && Moves the record pointer to record 12.
. INSERT           && Displays a record entry mask for entering new record
                      13. Press Ctrl-Q to quit without saving.
. CLEAR ALL        && Closes PARTS database.
```

To enter text into a Memo field, position the cursor to the memo field and press **Ctrl-Home**. This puts you in dBASE's full-screen editor. Type your text and press **Ctrl-End** to save it and return to the data entry mask.

APPLICATIONS

There are four dBASE commands that let you add records to a database. These are CREATE, APPEND, INSERT, and BROWSE. The various forms of the INSERT command allow you to add records at any location.

From the dBASE dot prompt (the interactive mode), you can use INSERT to add a record following the position of the record pointer, or INSERT BEFORE to add a record at the record pointer position. The INSERT BLANK command is used in the interactive mode or within a command file.

Perhaps the most common form used within command files is INSERT BLANK, which is similar to APPEND BLANK (Module 5). The ability to write a command file that inserts a blank record and then prompts the user to type in the contents is handy in a wide range of applications.

TYPICAL OPERATION

In this illustration INSERT BEFORE is used in a command file that allows an inexperienced user to type in the contents of a record. The MEMBERS database, modified in Module 47 is used. Begin at the dBASE dot prompt.

1. Type **USE MEMBERS** and press **Return**.

2. Type **MODIFY COMMAND INSREC** and press **Return** to use the dBASE editor.

3. Type the following command file. (Don't type the explanatory remarks.)

```
                                        Remarks
* INSREC.PRG              && Allows user to insert a new record.
CLEAR                     && Clears screen.
SET TALK OFF              && Turns off dBASE dialog.
USE MEMBERS               && Puts MEMBERS database in use.
WAIT                      && Pauses operation; displays prompt until key is pressed.
CLEAR                     && Clears screen.
GO TOP                    && Positions record pointer to first record.
INSERT BEFORE             && Inserts a blank record prior to record 1 and
*                            displays record entry mask.
WAIT                      && Pauses operation; displays prompt until key is pressed.
CLEAR                     && Clears screen.
SET TALK ON               && Turns dBASE dialog back on.
CANCEL                    && Returns control to dBASE dot prompt.
```

4. Press **Ctrl-W** to write the command file to disk.

5. When ready, type **DO INSREC** and press **Return**.

6. The following prompt is displayed; respond by pressing **Return**.

```
        Press any key to continue...
```

7. After pressing **Return**, the following entry mask is displayed.

```
        Record No.       1
        NAME          _
        ADR
        CSZ
        AFFIL
        JOINED        /  /
        AGE
        PAID       ?
        INFO       memo
```

8. Type in the following information. Press **Return** in the INFO field to complete data entry. Notice that the "Press any key . . ." prompt is displayed.

```
        Record No.     1
        NAME       Thompson, Bill G.
        ADR        4540 Garden Parkway
        CSZ        Bergenfield, NJ 07640
        AFFIL      Wilson Plastics
        JOINED     11/16/83
        AGE        28
        PAID       T
        INFO       memo

        Press any key to continue...
```

9. Press any key to save the record and return to the dBASE dot prompt.

10. Turn to Module 26 to continue the learning sequence.

Module 43
INTERACTIVE MODE (?), RECNO( )

DESCRIPTION

You've already entered several commands at the dBASE dot prompt. Although you may not have realized it at the time, you were operating in the interactive mode. The interactive mode, sometimes called "immediate mode," lets you enter a command at the dBASE dot prompt to obtain an immediate response. To further your skills in interactive dBASE operations, this module describes the use of the question mark (?), which is a shorthand form of the DISPLAY OFF command.

This module also introduces the RECNO( ) function, where RECNO stands for *record number*.

To begin, let's explore the RECNO( ) function. Here's a series of commands used to display the last record in a database.

```
. USE WAREHOUS
. GO BOTTOM
. ? RECNO( )
      325
```

This list of commands puts a database named WAREHOUS in use, positions the record pointer to the last (or bottom) record, and displays the record number. dBASE responds by displaying the record number, which appears as 325 in this simple example.

The ? RECNO() combination displays an integer value equivalent to the current record number (the record at which the record pointer is located). By converting the record number to an integer value (or whole number), you can store the record number value to a memory variable for future use. Memory variables are discussed in detail in Module 62. Here, they are used for illustration purposes.

```
. STORE RECNO( ) TO NBR
  325
```

At this point, you can check the contents of memory variable NBR with the ? command. This is done as follows:

```
. ? NBR
  325
```

What this command line really says is, "What is the value of memory variable NBR?" The response is printed by dBASE on the next line.

In addition to using the question mark as a DISPLAY command, you can also use it as a print statement. For example, a question mark by itself in a command file is the same as saying DISPLAY BLANK. This causes a blank line to be displayed. A question mark followed by text within either single or double quotation marks or brackets displays the text. This is handy for user prompts. A more detailed explanation is provided in Module 51.

The interactive mode is used in many ways. The following list shows a few examples of interactive dialog.

```
1.   . USE EMPLRECD          && Puts EMPLRECD database in use.
     . GO BOTTOM             && Positions record pointer to last record in database.
     . ? RECNO( )            && What's the number of the current record?
       325

2.   . ? 25 * 12             && What's the product of 25 times 12?
       300

3.   . ? 5(12 - 7)           && What's the product of 5 times quantity 12 minus 7?
       25

4.   . STORE 'CODE' TO X     && Stores the character string CODE to memory variable X.
       CODE
     . ? X                   && What's the value of memory variable X?
       CODE

5.   . ? DATE( )             && What's the current system date?
       08/12/84

6.   . ? CHR(7)              && What's the value of CHR(7)?

       "BEEP"                && CHR(7) causes system speaker to sound (ASCII 7).

7.   . ? '$10.00' + CHR(13) + '    _'  && CHR(13) is a carriage return; this underscores the '00'
                                          in $10.00 when printed.

8.   . STORE 8 TO Y          && Stores 8 to memory variable Y.
       8
     . STORE 9 TO Z          && Stores 9 to memory variable Z.

       9
     . ? Y * Z               && What's the product of Y times Z?
       72n

9.   . USE WAREHOUS          && Puts WAREHOUS database in use.
     . GO BOTTOM             && Positions record pointer to last record.
     . ? PART_NO             && What's the contents of the PART:NO field?
       MT-0912
```

When in the interactive mode, a double question mark (**??**) causes the display to appear on the same line. This is sometimes confusing, because the response is often run in with the command.

APPLICATIONS

There are many applications for using the question mark in the interactive mode. It lets you use dBASE like a calculator. You can enter the question mark followed by mathematical expressions to get quick answers. If you need a "calculator tape," you can type the SET PRINT ON command before you start your calculations. This causes displayed information to be printed simultaneously. Once the printer is active, you can enter your calculations from the keyboard.

The question mark is also used to display the contents of memory variables and database fields. This application is shown in entries 1 and 9 in the previous list of examples.

The ability to convert a record number to an integer is also an extremely useful tool. Without this capability, it would be difficult to enter a command that stores a record number to a memory variable automatically. By saving the record number, the record pointer can be returned to the same record later in the command sequence.

TYPICAL OPERATION

In this illustration the ? is used in the interactive mode to perform some calculations. Then you prepare a short command file that uses the record number function to save the record number value to a memory variable. Begin at the dBASE dot prompt.

1. Type the following calculations and press **Return** after each.

```
. STORE 7.50 TO RATE
  7.50
. STORE 40 TO HRS
  40
. ? RATE*HRS
          300.00
*"? 52*(RATE*HRS)"
        15600.00
. ? 15600/12
  1300
```

2. Type **MODIFY COMMAND SHOWLAST** and press **Return** to use the dBASE editor.

3. Type the following command file. (Don't type the explanatory remarks.)

```
                                            Remarks
* SHOWLAST.PRG            && Saves and displays number of last record in database.
CLEAR                     && Clears screen.
SET TALK OFF             && Turns off dBASE dialog.
?                        && Displays a blank line.
? '        THIS PROGRAM SHOWS YOU THE LAST RECORD NUMBER'     && Displays text.
?
? '        IN A DATABASE. ENTER A DATABASE NAME AND'
?
ACCEPT '        PRESS RETURN TO CONTINUE.' TO DB   && Accepts keyboard entry
*                                                    to memory variable DB.
CLEAR                     && Clears screen.
USE &DB                   && Substitutes value of memory variable DB as database name.
GO BOTTOM                 && Positions record pointer to last record.
STORE RECNO() TO REC      && Stores integer value of record number to memory variable REC.
?                         && Displays blank lines, text, and value of memory variables.
? '        THE LAST RECORD IN',DB,'IS',STR(REC,3,0)   && STR function displays numbers
?                           flush left. 3 characters and 0 decimal places are specified.
WAIT                      && Pauses operation until a key is pressed.
CLEAR                     && Clears screen.
USE                       && Closes database file.
CANCEL                    && Returns to dBASE dot prompt.
```

NOTE

The macro substitution function '&', which was used as &DB, is used to substitute the value of a string memory variable in place of the variable name itself. This is necessary when the value is needed outside of a DISPLAY or ? command. The number-to-string function (STR) is described in Appendix E.

4. Press **Ctrl-W** to write the command file to disk.

5. Type **DO SHOWLAST** and press **Return**.

6. The following prompt is displayed; respond by typing a database file name, such as **MEMBERS**, and pressing **Return**.

```
    THIS PROGRAM SHOWS YOU THE LAST RECORD NUMBER

    IN A DATABASE. ENTER A DATABASE NAME AND

    PRESS RETURN TO CONTINUE.
```

7. The following information is displayed on the screen.

```
        THE LAST RECORD IN MEMBERS IS  3

    Press any key to continue..._
```

8. Press any key to return to the dBASE dot prompt.

9. Turn to Module 38 to continue the learning sequence.

Module 44
JOIN

DESCRIPTION

If information about the same item, like a part number or person's name, is in two databases, you can use the JOIN command to create a third database with selected fields from each of the two existing databases. Before using the JOIN command, the two databases must be in use.

Two available forms of the JOIN command are:

JOIN WITH *alias* TO *filename* FOR *expression*
JOIN WITH *alias* TO *filename* FOR *condition* FIELDS *field list*

The *alias* expression, which is an optional alias name assigned to a selected database file, is described in Module 59.

Here's an example of the first form. Assume that you want to join information from a BLDG database and a LAND database into a third database named BOTH. The structure of the databases, (created and used in Module 59) are:

```
Structure for database :   Bldg.dbf
Field  Field name  Type       Width    Dec
    1  DES         Character     15
    2  PRICE       Numeric        9      2
    3  ACCDEP      Numeric        9      2
    4  BOOKVAL     Numeric        9      2

Structure for database :   Land.dbf
Field  Field name  Type       Width    Dec
    1  DES         Character     15
    2  PURCH       Numeric        9      2
    3  ACCAPP      Numeric        9      2
    4  MKTVAL      Numeric        9      2
```

Further, assume that the two databases contain the following information:

```
Bldg.dbf:
Record#  DES              PRICE     ACCDEP    BOOKVAL
      1  Plant         350000.00  90210.00 259790.00
      2  Sales Office  750225.00 235550.00 514675.00
      3  Warehouse     210000.00  20110.00 189890.00
```

```
Land.dbf:
Record#  DES              PURCH     ACCAPP     MKTVAL
      1  Plant         120000.00  50000.00 170000.00
      2  Sales Office   90000.00  22000.00 112000.00
      3  Warehouse     180000.00  30000.00 210000.00
```

To put the two databases in work areas, use the SELECT command (Module 59).

```
. SELECT 1
. USE BLDG
. SELECT 2
. USE LAND
```

With the two databases in work areas, you're ready to use JOIN. You can join the two databases to see all values associated with buildings and land having matching names in the DES field. Note that the LAND database was the last database selected, so it is presently active. The command:

```
. JOIN WITH BLDG TO BOTH FOR DES = BLDG->DES
```

joins the information into a new database. (Recall the *"Alias – > field name"* syntax from Module 59.) Now you can place the joined database, named BOTH, in use and check the contents with the LIST or BROWSE commands. This is done with:

```
. USE BOTH
. LIST OFF

DES              PURCH     ACCAPP     MKTVAL      PRICE     ACCDEP    BOOKVAL
Plant         120000.00  50000.00 170000.00  750225.00  235550.00 514675.00
Sales Office   90000.00  22000.00 112000.00  210000.00   20110.00 189890.00
Warehouse     180000.00  30000.00 210000.00  350000.00   90210.00 259790.00
```

This new database contains all building and land values associated with each piece of property in the BLDG and LAND databases.

You can also specify a field list in your JOIN command. Look at the following command line.

```
JOIN WITH BLDG TO BOTH FOR DES = BLDG->DES FIELDS DES, MKTVAL, BOOKVAL
```

The resulting database is displayed as follows:

```
. USE BOTH
. LIST OFF

DES              MKTVAL   BOOKVAL
Plant            170000.00 514675.00
Sales Office     112000.00 189890.00
Warehouse        210000.00 259790.00
```

The FOR expression can contain a statement like "FOR AMOUNT > = 100." This form of the command lets you select individual records.

APPLICATIONS

As you can see, the JOIN command is quite powerful. It provides an easy way to create a new database file from existing databases. Not only are the contents of each field transferred to the new database file, but the structure of each field is also transferred. This lets you create new database structures from existing ones. Once created, you can delete the contents with the ZAP command and add new data.

You can also use the JOIN command to collect information into one database from several database files. If you have information spread across several databases, you can collect it into a single database file. To achieve this, begin by joining two. Then take the resulting file and JOIN it with a third. You can continue this process until you've picked information from all of the databases containing the information you need. Remember, however, that you can use only a maximum of 128 fields in a single database.

TYPICAL OPERATION

In this illustration the JOIN command is used to collect information from the BLDG and LAND databases into the BOTH database, as described in the preceding examples. Begin at the dBASE dot prompt.

1. Create the two databases used in the preceding examples and enter the data as shown.

```
Structure for database :   Bldg.dbf
Field  Field name  Type       Width   Dec
    1  DES         Character     15
    2  PRICE       Numeric        9     2
    3  ACCDEP      Numeric        9     2
    4  BOOKVAL     Numeric        9     2
```

```
Contents of Bldg.dbf:
Record#  DES             PRICE    ACCDEP    BOOKVAL
      1  Plant          350000.00  90210.00 259790.00
      2  Sales Office   750225.00 235550.00 514675.00
      3  Warehouse      210000.00  20110.00 189890.00


Structure for database :   Land.dbf
Field  Field name  Type        Width    Dec
   1   DES         Character     15
   2   PURCH       Numeric        9       2
   3   ACCAPP      Numeric        9       2
   4   MKTVAL      Numeric        9       2


Contents of Land.dbf:
Record#  DES             PURCH    ACCAPP    MKTVAL
      1  Plant          120000.00  50000.00 170000.00
      2  Sales Office    90000.00  22000.00 112000.00
      3  Warehouse      180000.00  30000.00 210000.00
```

2. Put the two databases in use by typing the following four commands:

```
. SELECT 1
. USE BLDG
. SELECT 2
. USE LAND
```

3. Join the DES, MKTVAL, and BOOKVAL fields into a BOTH database by typing: **JOIN WITH BLDG TO BOTH FOR DES=BLDG– |DES FIELDS DES, MKTVAL, BOOKVAL**

4. Type **USE BOTH** and press **Return**; then type **LIST OFF** and press **Return** to view the joined database.

```
. USE BOTH
. LIST OFF
DES             MKTVAL    BOOKVAL
Plant          170000.00 259790.00
Sales Office   112000.00 514675.00
Warehouse      210000.00 189890.00
```

5. Modify the structure of the BOTH database by typing **MODIFY STRUCTURE** and pressing **Return**.

6. Add a TOTAL field as shown.

```
Structure for database :   Bldg.dbf
Field  Field name  Type        Width    Dec
    1  DES         Character      15
    2  BOOKVAL     Numeric         9      2
    3  MKTVAL      Numeric         9      2
    4  TOTAL       Numeric         9      2
```

7. Type **REPLACE ALL TOTAL WITH BOOKVAL + MKTVAL** and press **Return** to derive the TOTAL values:

8. Type **LIST OFF** and press **Return** to check the TOTAL values.

```
. LIST OFF
DES             MKTVAL    BOOKVAL     TOTAL
Plant         170000.00 259790.00 429790.00
Sales Office  112000.00 514675.00 626675.00
Warehouse     210000.00 189890.00 399890.00
```

9. If you wish to save space on your disk, type **CLOSE ALL** and delete the databases from your disk with the commands:

ERASE BLDG.DBF

ERASE LAND.DBF

ERASE BOTH.DBF

10. Turn to Module 66 to continue the learning sequence.

Module 45
LOCATE, CONTINUE

DESCRIPTION

The LOCATE command lets you find records within a database that match one or more specified string, numeric, or logical expressions. The location process begins with the first record in the active database and moves down in a top-to-bottom sequence. When a matching record is located, the record can be displayed, altered, deleted, or you may wish to extract information from one or more fields. If there are several records within the database that match the LOCATE parameters, you can move down to the next matching record using the CONTINUE command.

The general form of the LOCATE command is:

    LOCATE FOR *fieldname* = *expression*

Once a match is found, dBASE displays the record number in the form, "Record = n," where n is the record number. To find the next match, type **CONTINUE** and press **Return**. If the bottom of the file is encountered before another match is found, the message "End of LOCATE scope" is displayed.

Examples of the LOCATE and CONTINUE commands are provided in the following list.

1. LOCATE FOR *fieldname* = *expression*   Positions the record pointer to the first record where the named field contains the expression.

    . LOCATE FOR NAME = 'Jo'

    Locates first record containing a value that matches 'Jo', such as Jones and Johnson, where NAME is a character-type field that must match upper and lowercase.

    Record = 27   Located record number is displayed unless the SET TALK OFF command is in effect.

    . LOCATE FOR ZIP = 07632

    Locates first record containing 07632 in the ZIP field, where ZIP is a numeric-type field.

    . DISPLAY NAME, ZIP

    Displays NAME and ZIP fields of current record.

    . LOCATE FOR PAID

    Locates first record containing a logical true value in the PAID field, where PAID is a logical-type field.

```
. LOCATE FOR .NOT. PAID
```

        Locates first record containing a logical false value in the PAID field.

2. CONTINUE   Continues searching for next matching record beginning at the current record position. The CONTINUE command *continues* to find matching records until an end-of-file condition is encountered.

```
. CONTINUE
```

3. LOCATE FOR *field1* = *expression* .AND. *field2* = *expression*   Positions the record pointer to the first record having fields that match the expressions. Two or more fields can be specified; the .OR. statement can also be used.

```
. LOCATE FOR SUBSTR(DTOC(DATE),1,8) = '03/15/85'.AND. ZIP = 65450
. LOCATE FOR SUBSTR(DTOC(DATE),1,8) = '12/25/85'.OR. NAME = 'Santa Claus'
```

        Here, the substring and date-to-character functions are used to convert a date expression into a character expression.

4. LOCATE FOR *expression* $ *fieldname*   Locates the record containing a partial match within the named field. For example, if you're trying to find "Smithsonian" in the NAME field, your expression could be:

```
. LOCATE FOR 'Smith' $ NAME
```

5. LOCATE FOR *fieldname* = *memory variable*   Positions the record pointer to the first record wherein the field contents match the value of the named memory variable. The following example illustrates the use of a memory variable.

```
. STORE 'Smith' TO MNAME
. LOCATE FOR NAME = MNAME
```

6. LOCATE *scope* FOR *fieldname* = *expression*   This form of the LOCATE command lets you specify a scope, or range, in your instruction. The following example looks for a match in the "next 10" records.

```
. LOCATE NEXT 10 FOR ZIP = '75080'
```

The LOCATE command is a good way to identify records within a database that match certain parameters. The operation speed of LOCATE is slightly slower when a database is indexed.

The FIND and SEEK commands are other dBASE commands that let you find specific records within a database. However, FIND and SEEK operate only on key fields within an indexed database, and they find only the first record in a database that matches the specified parameter. If you need to find multiple records, FIND and SEEK are not the commands to use. The FIND and SEEK commands are described in Module 36. INDEX is described in Module 41.

APPLICATIONS

Because of its ease of use, the LOCATE-CONTINUE commands are excellent for quickly finding all records within a database containing a specified expression within one or more fields. The LOCATE and CONTINUE commands are frequently used within DO WHILE loops within command files. Here, records within an active database can be found, displayed, or altered automatically. The Typical Operation section of this module illustrates such a procedure.

TYPICAL OPERATION

In this illustration the LOCATE and CONTINUE commands are used in a command file to display selected records within the ABC database last modified in Module 41. Begin at the dBASE dot prompt.

1. Type **MODIFY COMMAND SEARCH** and press **Return** to use the dBASE editor.

2. Type the SEARCH.PRG command file. (Don't type the explanatory remarks.)

```
                                        Remarks
* SEARCH.PRG                && A command file that locates a record for viewing.
SET TALK OFF                && Turns off dBASE dialog.
SET HEADING OFF             && Turns off display of field names.
DO WHILE .T.               && Puts command file in DO WHILE loop.
  CLEAR                     && Clears screen.
  ? '          ENTER THE NAME IN THE RECORD YOU WANT TO SEE'   && Displays prompt.
  ?                                                            && Displays blank line.
  ACCEPT '          OR PRESS Q AND RETURN TO QUIT ' TO MNAME   && Displays prompt.
  CLEAR                     && Clears screen.
  IF UPPER(MNAME) = 'Q'     && Looks for condition where MNAME equals 'Q'.
    CLEAR ALL               && If MNAME equals 'Q', closes files and memory variables.
    EXIT                    && Exits DO WHILE loop.
  ENDIF                     && Passes control to next command line.
  USE ABC                   && Puts ABC database in use.
  LOCATE FOR UPPER(NAME) = UPPER(MNAME)  && Locates record with MNAME in NAME field.
  *                         Converts contents to upper case to assure a match.
  *                         The following IF statement looks for end-of-file
  *                         condition. Lines between IF and ENDIF are acted
  *                         upon only if end-of-file condition is encountered.
  IF EOF()                  && Looks for end-of-file condition.
    ? "          CAN'T FIND",MNAME  && Displays text and contents of MNAME.
    WAIT                    && Pauses operation until a key is pressed.
    LOOP                    && Returns execution to line following DO WHILE statement.
  ENDIF                     && Passes control to next command line.
  DO WHILE .NOT. EOF()      && Continues operation while not end of file.
```

```
      DISPLAY NAME,PHONE,MAIL OFF  && Displays named fields.
        CONTINUE                && Locates next matching record.
      ENDDO                     && Ends DO WHILE .NOT. EOF() statement.
       WAIT                     && Pauses operation until a key is pressed.
    ENDDO                       && Ends DO WHILE process when command file is exited.
    USE                         && Closes database file.
    SET HEADING ON              && Turns field heading display back on.
    SET TALK ON                 && Turns dBASE dialog back on.
    CLEAR                       && Clears screen.
    RETURN                      && Returns to display of dBASE dot prompt.
```

3. Press **Ctrl-W** to save the command file.

4. Run the command file by typing **DO SEARCH** and pressing **Return**.

5. Respond to the following screen prompt by typing a name, such as Bishop, and pressing **Return**, or type **Q** and press **Return** to quit.

```
ENTER THE NAME IN THE RECORD YOU WANT TO SEE

OR PRESS Q AND RETURN TO QUIT
```

6. Notice that the record containing the name, or the first few characters of the name you typed, is displayed. If a match is not located, the following prompt is displayed.

```
CAN'T FIND expression
Press any key to continue...
```

7. Notice that matches are displayed in a form similar to the following:

```
Harris, Robert      4335 2230
Press any key to continue...
```

8. Press any key, enter another name to locate, and press **Return**, or type **Q** and press **Return** to quit and return to the dBASE dot prompt.

9. Turn to Module 36 to continue the learning sequence.

Module 46
MODIFY COMMAND

(Developing Command Files)

DESCRIPTION

If you are working your way through this book using the learning sequence, you have used MODIFY COMMAND in previous modules. It was used to create new command files or to view existing ones.

The general form of this command is:

. MODIFY COMMAND *filename*

The MODIFY COMMAND command starts the built-in dBASE full-screen editor. This editor creates ASCII text files. Although you can create any kind of document, its intended use is for creating dBASE command (or program) files.

FILENAME EXTENSIONS If no extension is included with the filename, it is assigned the extension .PRG. If you specify the filename and extension, such as REPT.FRM for a report form file or LETTER.TXT for a text file, an editing screen is displayed for text entry. If the file already exists, the named file is displayed, ready to edit or view.

EDITING COMMANDS Once the full-screen editor is in operation, you can use the control sequences displayed in the help window at the top of the screen and listed in Appendix D. These sequences are used to move the cursor, insert, delete, and so on. If you want to suppress the help window, press **F1**.

When the file is typed, you can save it by pressing **Ctrl-W** for write. If you display a file, make changes, and then decide not to save the changes, you can abort without saving by pressing **Esc** (or **Ctrl-Q** for Quit).

This is about all there is to using the dBASE full-screen editor. You might type **MODIFY COMMAND SAMPLE** to create a new file. Enter several lines of text and experiment with the control keys. When you're satisfied that you know how they all work, you can either save the document for future practice with **Ctrl-W** or quit without saving with **Ctrl-Q**.

DEVELOPING COMMAND FILES The mechanics of creating a command file are easier if you plan ahead. Once you block out the general structure of your database and the necessary command files, you can begin writing and testing command files one at a time. To help you with the file creation process, some tips are given in the following few pages.

When you're ready to design an application, there are several things to consider. These are included in the following applications design steps.

1. **Database file structure**—The structure of your database is the first consideration in application design. Jot down a list on paper that includes the following information.

   a. What kind of information must you store and maintain (field names)?

   b. How many characters are needed for each piece (field) of information?

   c. What type is each information element (character, numeric, date, logical, or memo)? If numeric, how many decimal places are needed?

   When you've determined all the fields you'll need, their names, and their types and sizes, go ahead and create your database structure. Don't enter all of the data. Limit entry to one or two records for testing.

2. **Data manipulation**—Next, decide what you'll do with the information once you've captured it in a database file. Will you:

   a. Add records?

   b. Change records?

   c. Delete records?

3. **Reports**—Once you've decided how you'll maintain the information, decide upon the kinds of printed or displayed output you'll need. Will you want to:

   a. List information to the screen (all or selective)?

   b. List information to your printer (all or selective)?

   c. List information with the date?

   Your reports, labels, data entry and display screens can be designed using the appropriate dBASE development utilities described in Modules 20 through 24. They can also be developed from scratch by using the commands that display and print information.

4. **Application structure**—Once you have an idea of what you want to do with the information, you can block out the structure of the command files that make up your application. It's a good idea to use a modular structure, where separate command files perform different tasks. For example, you may want to write a command file for adding records, one for changing records and still another for deleting records. You can also write separate command files for each report type you want. This approach lets you develop several small, relatively simple command files instead of putting everything into one large command file that may take forever to debug. The diagram contained in Figure 46-1 illustrates a series of command files.

5. **Individual command file design**—With the main structure blocked out, you can begin the design of individual command files. If you wish, you can do this directly on your computer using MODIFY COMMAND, with a word processor, or with a pop-up utility like Borland's Sidekick.

   Begin with a MAIN MENU command file. Call it MENU. From the dBASE prompt, type **MODIFY COMMAND MENU** and press **Return** to access the dBASE full-screen editor. Begin typing a command file skeleton made up of comment lines that begin with an asterisk. These lines are there for reference only and have no effect on command file operation.

```
* MENU.PRG -A command file for displaying the address book menu.
* Use a DO WHILE loop to sustain operation.
* Display selection list.
* Use WAIT TO to display prompt and store selection.
* Use series of CASE statements to run the selected command file,
*   exit to the dBASE prompt, or exit to the operating system.
```

Save the MENU command file by pressing **Ctrl-W**.

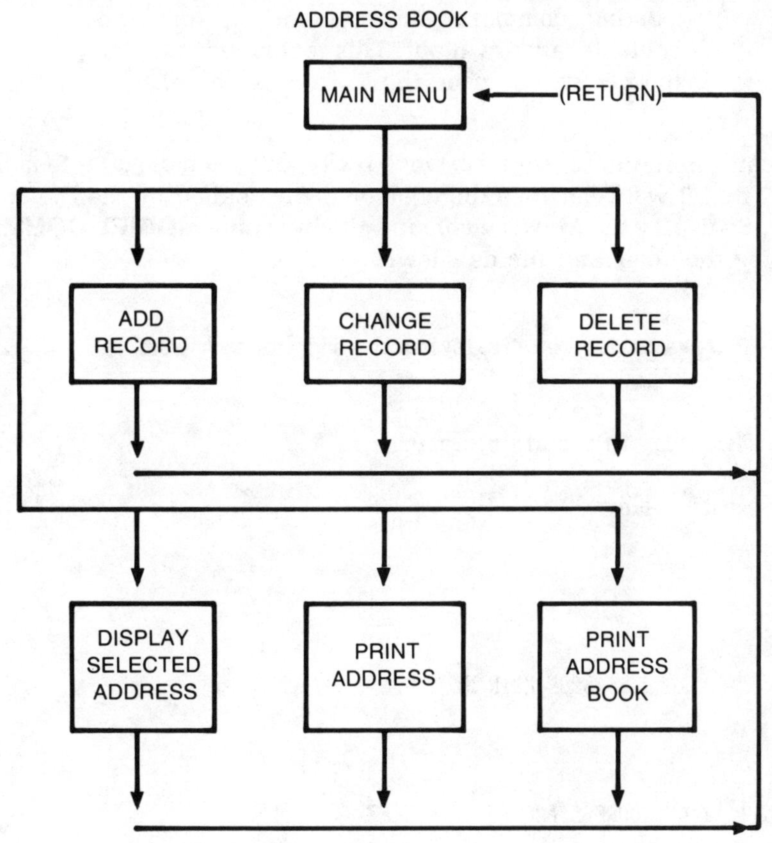

6. **Typing the command file**—Now that your MENU command file is outlined, you can type the command lines under each block. It's a good idea to leave your comment lines in place to show you what each section of the command file, or program, does. You should know that spaces within command files are ignored during operation, but they are counted as part of the 254 allowable characters on a command line.

If a command line exceeds the width of your screen, you can use a semicolon at the end of the line and press **Return**. The semicolon combines multiple lines into a single statement. Remember, when the command file is run, each line is executed in a top-to-bottom order. Therefore, be careful to organize your commands in the proper sequence.

NOTE

When command files use a series of the same or similar commands, you can make a copy of an existing command file, rename it, edit the contents, and try it out. This technique is faster than retyping everything from scratch.

Type the MENU command file for practice. Once it's typed, you can run it to make sure it works. Only selections 7 and 8 work because the command files called by the DO commands haven't been created yet. Redisplay the MENU command file by typing **MODIFY COMMAND MENU** and press **Return**. Type the command file as shown.

```
* MENU.PRG -A command file for displaying the address book menu.
CLEAR
SET TALK OFF
* Use a DO WHILE loop to sustain operation.
DO WHILE .T.
* Display selection list.
```

```
                    ADDRESS BOOK MAIN MENU'


                                              PRESS'
                                                '

        DISPLAY AN ADDRESS AND PHONE NUMBER      1'

        ADD A NEW ADDRESS AND PHONE NUMBER       2'
```

```
        CHANGE AN ADDRESS OR PHONE NUMBER          3'

        DELETE AN ADDRESS AND PHONE NUMBER         4'

        PRINT AN ADDRESS AND PHONE NUMBER          5'

        PRINT AN ADDRESS AND PHONE LIST            6'

        EXIT TO dBASE DOT PROMPT                   7'

        EXIT TO THE OPERATING SYSTEM               8'


    * Use WAIT TO to display prompt and store selection.

    WAIT 'Enter your selection: ' TO NUMBER

    * Use series of CASE statements to run the selected command file,
    *   exit to the dBASE prompt, or exit to the operating system.

        DO CASE
    CASE NUMBER ='1'
      DO DISP
    CASE NUMBER ='2'
      DO ADD
    CASE NUMBER ='3'
      DO CHANGE
    CASE NUMBER ='4'
      DO DELETE
    CASE NUMBER ='5'
      DO PRINT
    CASE NUMBER ='6'
      DO LIST
    CASE NUMBER ='7'
      CLEAR
      CLEAR ALL
      SET TALK ON
      CANCEL
    CASE NUMBER ='8'
      CLEAR
      QUIT
    ENDCASE
  ENDDO
```

Save the command file by pressing **Ctrl-W**.

7. **Testing the command file**—Now that your first command file is finished, you can test it. If you're using the SET TALK OFF command, you may wish to place an asterisk at the beginning of that line so you can see the dBASE dialog during test runs.

If the first command file runs without any hitches, you're ready to build the second one. If you encounter problems, you may wish to take advantage of the SET DOHISTORY ON to capture each command in a history file. You can type LIST HISTORY and press **Return** to display the commands for a blow-by-blow report of what's happening during program operation. Do not leave DOHISTORY on during normal operation, as it slows down program operation.

The SET STEP ON command lets you step the program through its paces a line at a time. The command file pauses at every step and waits for you to type **Y** to go on to the next step. It also gives you the option of typing **N** to continue or **Esc** to exit.

Once the first command file is operational, you can move on to the next one, writing and testing each command file as it is developed. It's like "eating an elephant;" you've got to do it one bite at a time.

When the MENU command file, prepared above, is run by typing **DO MENU**, the following display screen is displayed (if everything is typed in right).

```
                         ADDRESS BOOK MAIN MENU


                                                      PRESS

            DISPLAY AN ADDRESS AND PHONE NUMBER         1

            ADD A NEW ADDRESS AND PHONE NUMBER          2

            CHANGE AN ADDRESS OR PHONE NUMBER           3

            DELETE AN ADDRESS AND PHONE NUMBER          4

            PRINT AN ADDRESS AND PHONE NUMBER           5

            PRINT AN ADDRESS AND PHONE LIST             6

            EXIT TO dBASE DOT PROMPT                    7

            EXIT TO THE OPERATING SYSTEM                8


        Enter your selection: _
```

Type **7** to return to the dBASE dot prompt.

NOTE

You can draw rules and boxes with the @ row,col
and @ SAY REPLICATE commands described in
Modules 8 and 58.

APPLICATIONS

The MODIFY COMMAND *filename* is generally used to create or edit command files, but is also used to create or edit almost any kind of document. In this respect, dBASE's full-screen editor can be used as a word processor, capable of creating or changing almost any kind of file containing standard ASCII text characters.

TYPICAL OPERATION

In this illustration an Address Book database structure is designed. Then MODIFY COMMAND is used to write the ADD command file that works in conjunction with the Address Book Main Menu file created in the Description section of this module. Begin at the dBASE dot prompt.

1. Type **CREATE ADRBOOK** and press **Return**. Create the database structure shown in the following example.

```
       field name   type      width  dec            Remarks

   1   NAME         Character    25
   2   ST_ADR       Character    25
   3   CSZ          Character    25
   4   HPHONE       Character    14
   5   WPHONE       Character    14
   6   NOTES        Character    40
   7   <cr>


   Input data records now? (Y/N)? N         Type N to stop.
```

2. Type **MODIFY COMMAND ADD** and press **Return** to use the dBASE editor.

3. Type the following command file skeleton.

```
   * ADD.PRG -- Adds records to the Address Book application.
   * Erase screen and display introductory information.
   * Insert escape path to Main Menu.
   * Display data entry instructions.
   * Append new records for data entry.
   * Clear screen and display instructions to return to Main Menu.
   * Erase screen and return to Main Menu.
```

4. Fill in the command file skeleton by typing the ADD command file.

```
* ADD.PRG -- Adds records to the Address Book application.
* Erase screen and display introductory information.
CLEAR
                        PRESS RETURN TO ADD NEW RECORDS'

* Insert escape path to Main Menu.
                          OR TYPE "Q" TO QUIT'
WAIT ' ' TO CHOICE
CLEAR
IF UPPER(CHOICE)='Q'
    RETURN
ENDIF
* Display data entry instructions.
        TO STOP DATA ENTRY, PRESS RETURN AT THE BEGINNING OF A NEW RECORD.'

WAIT        PRESS ANY KEY TO START DATA ENTRY...'
* Append new records for data entry.
USE ADRBOOK
APPEND
* Clear screen and display instructions to return to Main Menu.
CLEAR
WAIT '      PRESS ANY KEY TO RETURN TO MAIN MENU...'
* Erase screen and return to Main Menu.
CLEAR
RETURN
```

5. Press **Ctrl-W** to write the command file to disk.

6. Type **DO MENU** and press **Return** to run the address book application from the MENU program.

7. Type **2** to run the ADD command file. Respond to the displayed prompts, type one record, and notice that the Main Menu is redisplayed upon completion.

```
              PRESS RETURN TO ADD NEW RECORDS

                OR TYPE "Q" TO QUIT

    TO STOP DATA ENTRY, PRESS RETURN AT THE BEGINNING OF A NEW RECORD.

    PRESS ANY KEY TO START DATA ENTRY...
```

```
Record No. 1          (Type a name, address, and phone information.)
Record No. 2          (Press Return at beginning of first field to stop data entry.)

   PRESS ANY KEY TO RETURN TO MAIN MENU...
```

8. Type **7** to return to the dBASE dot prompt.

9. When you finish experimenting with this operation, you can erase the practice command files and database from your disk using the ERASE command. Their filenames are:

   ADRBOOK.DBF
   MENU.PRG
   ADD.PRG

10. Turn to Module 29 to continue the learning sequence.

Module 47
MODIFY STRUCTURE

DESCRIPTION

There are times when you find that the structure of a database requires a change to fit an unexpected need. For example, you may need to add an additional field or change the length of a field. The MODIFY STRUCTURE command lets you insert, delete, add, and change fields within your database structure.

To modify the structure of a database, put it in use with the USE *filename* command. Then type:

    . MODIFY STRUCTURE

and press **Return**. The database creation mask is displayed showing field names, types, widths, and decimal places. You can move the cursor to the desired field and change the field information. You can also insert new fields at the cursor position by pressing **Ctrl-N**. Fields are deleted by pressing **Ctrl-U**.

Be careful not to modify field lengths or types that might affect important data. For example, if you make a field length shorter than the information contained within it, the data will be "trimmed" due to the shorter field length. If you change a character field that contains alpha text strings to a numeric field, you will lose the text, and the field will contain a value of zero.

APPLICATIONS

The MODIFY STRUCTURE command is used to change field names, lengths, types and to change the number of decimal places in a numeric-type field. It is also used to insert and add new fields or to delete unnecessary fields.

There is another use for the MODIFY STRUCTURE command. It is used to intentionally delete the contents of one or more fields within a database. This is accomplished by first deleting the desired fields using **Ctrl-U**. Then return to the dBASE dot prompt. Finally, use MODIFY STRUCTURE again to insert the field back into the database structure.

You can also use the REPLACE command to delete the contents of a single field. For example, if you wish to delete the contents of a character field named ZIP, use the command:

    . REPLACE zip WITH ' ' ALL

A blank space is inserted in the ZIP field of all records.

The contents of numeric fields are similarly replaced with:

    . REPLACE number WITH 0 ALL

TYPICAL OPERATION

In this illustration the structure of the MEMBERS database created in Module 18 is modified. The ST_ADR field is renamed to ADR, the C_S_Z field is renamed to CSZ, and the PAID_UP field is renamed to PAID. Begin at the dBASE dot prompt.

1. Type **USE MEMBERS** and press **Return**.

2. Type **MODIFY STRUCTURE** and press **Return**. (You could also type **MODI STRU** to save time as the first four characters of dBASE commands are all that are required.)

3. Notice the following display:

```
      field name   type       width  dec

1     NAME         Character     25
2     ST_ADR       Character     25
3     C_S_Z        Character     25
4     AFFIL        Character     25
5     JOINED       Date           8
6     AGE          Numeric        2    0
7     PAID_UP      Logical        1
8     INFO         Memo          10
```

4. Move the cursor to the "S" in the ST_ADR field name and delete "ST_" by pressing **Del** (or **Ctrl-G**) three times.

5. Move the cursor to the C_S_Z field name and delete each underline character with the **Del** key.

6. Move the cursor to the PAID_UP field name and delete "_UP" by positioning the cursor at the underline and pressing **Del**. Your structure should now resemble the following:

```
      field name   type       width  dec

1     NAME         Character     25
2     ADR          Character     25
3     CSZ          Character     25
4     AFFIL        Character     25
5     JOINED       Date           8
6     AGE          Numeric        2    0
7     PAID         Logical        1
8     INFO         Memo          10
```

7. Press **Ctrl-W** and press **Return** to save the modified structure.

8. Type **LIST STRU** to examine the changed database structure. Notice the following:

```
. LIST STRU
Structure for database :   Members.dbf
Number of data records :       3
Date of last update    : 11/24/88
Field  Field name  Type      Width    Dec
    1  NAME        Character    25
    2  ADR         Character    25
    3  CSZ         Character    25
    4  AFFIL       Character    25
    5  JOINED      Date          8
    6  AGE         Numeric       2      0
    7  PAID        Logical       1
    8  INFO        Memo         10
** Total **                    122
```

9. Type **CLEAR ALL** to close all files.

10. Turn to Module 69 to continue the learning sequence.

Module 48
NOTE, *, &&

DESCRIPTION

The asterisk character (*) is used in all of the command files in this book to insert comment lines. These lines are used to display the name of the command file or to annotate command files with descriptive comments about the purpose of following command lines. The NOTE command does precisely the same thing as the asterisk (*) character, and is used interchangeably.

The double ampersand (&&) is another comment designator that is used to insert comments on the same line as a command. The dBASE command interpreter ignores the && and following text.

Forms of *, NOTE, and && are shown in the following lines.

```
NOTE This comment line is for information purposes only.
* This comment line is exactly like the one above.
WAIT  && Pauses operation and displays "Press any key to continue. . ."
```

APPLICATIONS

It's a good idea to annotate your command files with comment lines. Following are some suggestions for comment line use.

1. Place the name of the command file at the beginning.

```
* ADD.PRG -- Adds a record to the Address Book application.
```

2. Enter a version number to the command file for *configuration control*.

```
* ADD program VERSION 2.1, January 6, 1988
```

3. Insert comments that describe the function of different sections of the command file.

```
* Locate NAME field that matches the memory variable MNAME.
WAIT ' ' && Pause operation without a following display.
```

4. Write yourself reminders about future changes that are needed in a command file.

```
* Don't forget to modify the DELETE program to display
* the record before it's deleted.
```

TYPICAL OPERATION

In this illustration comment lines are used in a sample command file to demonstrate the use of NOTE (or *) and &&. The sample command file works in conjunction with the MEMBERS database created in Module 17. Begin at the dBASE dot prompt.

1. Type **MODIFY COMMAND SAMPLE** and press **Return** to use the dBASE editor.

2. Type the following command file. Notice the use of comment lines.

> **NOTE**
>
> The use of comment lines are overdone here. Excessive comment lines begin to slow the speed of command file operation. However, because our sample command file and database are quite short, you won't notice any problem with operational speed.

```
* SAMPLE.PRG -- Makes use of comment lines.
* Version 1.00 December 7, 1988
CLEAR                       && Clear the screen
USE MEMBERS                 && Use members database.
NOTE            Use ACCEPT to get a name from the keyboard.
ACCEPT 'Enter the Name you want to look up ' TO MNAME
NOTE            Locate name; convert to upper case to assure match.
LOCATE FOR UPPER(NAME)=UPPER(MNAME)
CLEAR                       && Clear the screen.
DISPLAY NAME,ADR,CSZ OFF && Display the record.
WAIT                        && Pause operation; display prompt.
CLEAR                       && Clear the screen.
USE                         && Close the database.
CANCEL                      && End operation.
```

3. Press **Ctrl-W** to write the command file to disk.

4. Type **DO SAMPLE** and press **Return** to run the command file; prompts and responses are shown in the following example.

```
Enter the Name you want to look up Phil


    NAME                    ADR                 CSZ
    Phillips, George W.     11205 Dawn Drive    Lago Vista, TX 78641
    Press any key to continue...
```

5. When you finish experimenting with the command file, erase the sample file from your disk by typing **ERASE SAMPLE.PRG** and pressing **Return**.

6. Turn to Module 65 to continue the learning sequence.

Module 49
ON ERROR, ON ESC, ON KEY
with
INKEY( ) AND READKEY( )

DESCRIPTION

The ON ERROR, ON ESC, and ON KEY commands are used to intercept the occurance of a specified condition during dBASE operation. ON ERROR looks for an error condition; ON ESC looks for the **Esc** key; and finally, ON KEY looks for a specified key press.

The INKEY( ) function returns a number that corresponds to the most recent key pressed. Each of these commands and functions are described in the following paragraphs.

The READKEY( ) function returns a number that corresponds to a key code when one of the dBASE editing commands are used. The value of the key code designates whether or not the edited record was updated.

COMMAND PRECEDENCE The three ON command forms have an order of precedence. The order is:

1. ON ERROR

2. ON ESCAPE

3. ON KEY

This means that if both ON ESCAPE and ON KEY are in effect, the ON ESCAPE is honored in preference to the ON KEY command.

When ON ERROR, ON ESC, or ON KEY is used, it remains in effect until you cancel it using the ON command form without a following condition or expression.

ON ERROR The ON ERROR command looks for a dBASE execution or syntax error. By following it with a DO procedure or program filename or a message, you can trap and respond to potential errors in a predetermined, controlled way. Look at the following example.

```
SET PROCEDURE TO ERR_MSG
ON ERROR DO ERR_MSG

PROCEDURE ERR_MSG
? 'An error condition was encountered'
WAIT
ON ERROR    && Turns off ON ERROR condition.
CANCEL
```

The SET PROCEDURE TO ERR_MSG directs procedure calls to the ERR_MSG procedure file. If a program error is encountered, the ON ERROR DO ERR_MSG line runs the ERR_MSG procedure.

ON ESCAPE The ON ESCAPE command monitors your keyboard activity for the **Esc** key. The command line:

    ON ESCAPE ? " "

achieves the same result as entering SET ESCAPE OFF. If you press **Esc**, the expression following the ON ESCAPE command is executed. The following line displays the following text.

    ON ESCAPE ? "You just pressed the Escape key."

Look at the following command file with the name ON.PRG.

```
* ON.PRG--Test ON commands.
CLEAR
ON ESCAPE ? "You pressed the Escape key."
WAIT "Type a letter, number, or punctuation mark. " to mvar
? 'The ASCII code for the key you typed is '+ltrim(str(ASC('&mvar')))+'.'
WAIT
RETURN
```

When run, this command file first arms the ON ESCAPE condition and then displays the WAIT prompt, "Type a letter, number, or punctuation mark." Typing **Z** results in a screen that looks like this.

```
    Type a letter, number, or punctuation mark. Z
    The ASCII code for the key you typed is 90.
    Press any key to continue...
```

Pressing **Esc** results in a screen that displays the ON ESCAPE message, like the following one.

```
    Type a letter, number, or punctuation mark.
    You pressed the Escape key.
    The ASCII code for the key you typed is 0.
    Press any key to continue...
```

ON KEY   The ON KEY command monitors your keyboard activity. If you type a key other than the **Esc** key, the ON KEY command executes after the current command is completed.

The ON KEY value should always be removed from the type-ahead buffer. This is accomplished by using the INKEY( ) or READ commands, and prevents continuous looping, as if in a DO WHILE loop.

In the example contained in the Typical Operation section of this module, pay particular attention to how the INKEY( ) command is used in a procedure file. Also notice how the SET PROCEDURE TO and ON KEY commands are used.

INKEY( )   The number returned by the INKEY( ) function is an integer between 0 and 255. The integer value corresponds to the ASCII code value of the key that is pressed on the keyboard.

If no key is pressed, INKEY( ) returns a zero (0). INKEY( ) returns a value that corresponds to the first key in your *type-ahead buffer* when several characters are buffered. A list of special keys and corresponding INKEY( ) values are contained in the following table.

Key	Alternate	Value	Key	Alternate	Value
Right Arrow	Ctrl-D	4	Home	Ctrl-A	1
Left Arrow	Ctrl-S	19	Home	Ctrl-]	29
Up Arrow	Ctrl_E	5	End	Ctrl-F	6
Down Arrow	Ctrl-X	24	End	Ctrl-W	23
Ctrl-Right Arrow	Ctrl-B	2	PgUp	Ctrl-R	18
Ctrl-Left Arrow	Ctrl-Z	26	PgDn	Ctrl-C	3
Ins	Ctrl-V	22	Ctrl-PgUp	Ctrl- -	31
Del	Ctrl-G	7	Ctrl-PgDn	Ctrl- ^	30

The **Ctrl-S** sequence is used to pause screen scrolling. You can disarm this effect by entering SET ESCAPE OFF.

Use the INKEY( ) in the following two example command files.

```
* TIME.PRG -- Display the system time.
CLEAR                                   && Clear the screen.
DO WHILE INKEY() = 0                     && Establish DO WHILE loop until keypress.
   @ 00,72 SAY TIME()                    && Display the time at row,col position.
   @ 24,30 SAY 'Press a key to stop...'&& Display the text as a prompt.
ENDDO                                    && Complete DO WHILE statement.
CLEAR                                    && Clear the screen.
RETURN                                   && Return control to dBASE dot prompt.
```

This example uses the INKEY( ) function to branch to your menu selection.

```
* SELECT.PRG -- Displays a menu and used INKEY() to capture keypress.
SET TALK OFF                          && Turn dBASE dialog off.
CLEAR                                 && Clear the screen.
DO WHILE .T.                          && Establish DO WHILE loop.
TEXT                                  && Display typed text.
<1>  General Ledger
<2>  Accounts Receivables
<3>  Accounts Payables
<4>  Payroll
<5>  Quit
ENDTEXT                               && Ends text command.
MKEY=0                                && Store 0 to memory variable MKEY.
DO WHILE MKEY = 0                     && Establish interior DO WHILE loop while MKEY = 0.
    @ 1,72 SAY TIME()                 && Display system time on screen.
    MKEY = INKEY()                    && INKEY() set to value of MKEY.
    @ 7,30 SAY 'Make a selection: '&& Displays prompt.
ENDDO                                 && Complete interior DO WHILE statement.
DO CASE                               && Begin DO CASE statement.
  CASE CHR(MKEY) $ '1'                && Run next line if MKEY char code is 1.
    @ 20,30 say 'You selected General Ledger'
  CASE CHR(MKEY) $ '2'                && Run next line if MKEY char code is 2.
    @ 20,30 say 'You selected Accounts Receivable'
  CASE CHR(MKEY) $ '3'                && Run next line if MKEY char code is 3.
    @ 20,30 say 'You selected Accounts Payable'
  CASE CHR(MKEY) $ '4'                && Run next line if MKEY char code is 4.
    @ 20,30 say 'You selected Payroll'
  CASE CHR(MKEY) $ '5Qq'              && Run next line if MKEY char code is 5, Q, or q.
    exit
  OTHERWISE                           && Run next line if key is not recognized.
    @ 20,20 say 'Unrecognized selection--please try again.'
ENDCASE                               && Complete the DO CASE statement.
WAIT                                  && Pause operation and display "Press any key..." prompt.
CLEAR                                 && Clear the screen prior to redisplaying menu.
ENDDO                                 && Complete DO WHILE statement.
CLEAR                                 && Clear the screen prior to exiting the program.
RETURN                                && Return control to dBASE dot prompt.
```

READKEY( )   The READKEY( ) function returns an integer value representing the key pressed
to exit a full-screen editing command, such as APPEND, BROWSE, CHANGE, CREATE, EDIT,
INSERT, MODIFY, and READ. Each key pressed returns one of two possible values, depending

upon whether or not data is changed. If no data is changed, the values are 0 through 36 and 256. The integer 256 added to the corresponding value 1 through 36 is returned if a data change, or update, occurs. Look at the following chart of keys and READKEY( ) codes:

Key Pressed	Base Code	Update Code	Key Pressed	Base Code	Update Code
Ctrl-H,-S,Backspace	0	256	Ctrl-N	11	267
Ctrl-D,-L,Rt Arrow	1	257	Ctrl-Q,Esc	12	268
Ctrl-A,Home	2	258	Not Used	13	269
Ctrl-F,End	3	259	Ctrl-W,-End	14	270
Ctrl-E,-K,Up Arrow	4	260	Ctrl-M,Return	15	271
Ctrl-X,-R,Dn Arrow	5	261	Return past end	16	272 (1)
Ctrl-R,PgUp	6	262	Return at start	16	272 (2)
Ctrl-C,PgDn	7	263	Ctrl-],-Home	33	289
Ctrl-Z,-Lf Arrow	8	264	Ctrl- -,PgUp	34	290
Ctrl-B,-Rt Arrow	9	265	Ctrl- ^ ,-PgDn	35	291
Ctrl-U	10	266	F1	36	292 (3)

(1) APPEND
(2) MODIFY STRUCTURE/REPORT
(3) HELP function key

Look at the following simple example.

```
. ? READKEY( )
271
```

The value 271 (or 256 + 15) tells you that the Return key was pressed past the end of the line. An update occured. To try a quick experiment with the READKEY( ), perform the next two steps from the dot prompt.

1. Type **? readkey( )**, press **Down Arrow**, and then press **Return**.

2. Notice that 15 is displayed. This tells you that no update occurred.

```
. ? READKEY( )
15
```

The following command file excerpt shows an IF statement that updates the DATE field within an open database. The update occurs if **Ctrl-W** or **Ctrl-End** was used to save a file.

```
IF READKEY( ) = 270
    REPLACE DATE WITH DATE( )
ENDIF
```

APPLICATIONS

The ON ERROR, ON ESCAPE, and ON KEY commands provide convenient ways to trap dBASE syntax errors and keyboard input. You can establish appropriate responses to a variety of conditions, as shown in the preceding examples.

The INKEY( ) function lets you use nonprintable keys within command files to control branching operations.

The READKEY( ) function lets you design a way to control program operation based upon whether or not the computer operator updates the active database. The integer value returned by the operator's keypress is often stored to a memory variable, letting you work with a variable name rather than a numeric value. For example, if you want to let RC_UPDATE = 256 and RC_WRITE = 14, the command line:

```
IF READKEY( ) = 270
```

is rewritten

```
IF READKEY( ) = RC_UPDATE + RC_WRITE
```

This is equal to 256 (Back Space) + 14 (Ctrl-W or Ctrl-End), which tells you that the database has been updated.

TYPICAL OPERATION

In this illustration the ON KEY command and INKEY( ) functions are used in a command file and a related procedure file. The procedure file, PROC.PRG, contains a procedure named "WHOA." This procedure file is designated with the command line, "SET PROCEDURE TO PROC." The procedure WHOA is called from the "ON KEY DO WHOA" command line. Begin at the dBASE dot prompt.

1. Type **MODIFY COMMAND SHOW** and press **Return** to use the dBASE editor.

2. Type the following command file. (Don't type the explanatory remarks.)

```
                                            Remarks
* SHOW.PRG -- Display each record. Pause if a key is pressed.
SET TALK OFF                && Turns of dBASE III Plus dialog.
USE MEMBERS                 && Places MEMBERS database file.
SET PROCEDURE TO PROC       && Opens PROC procedure file.
CLEAR                       && Clears the screen.
ON KEY DO WHOA              && Executes the whoa procedure upon key press.
USE ADDRESS                 && Places the address database in use.
DO WHILE .NOT. EOF()        && Operate while not end of file.
    ? NAME,CITY             && Display NAME and CITY fields.
    SKIP                    && Moves record pointer to next record.
ENDDO                       && Ends do while statement.
WAIT                        && Pauses operation.
CLOSE ALL                   && Closes all open files.
```

```
CLEAR                           && Clears screen.
RETURN                          && Returns to dot prompt or calling program.
```

3. Press **Ctrl-W** to save the file.

4. Type **MODI COMM PROC** and press **Return** again, and prepare the following command file.

```
* PROC.PRG -- Procedure file
PROCEDURE WHOA                  && Name of procedure.
I = INKEY()                     && Intercept keypress.
WAIT "Press 'Q' to Quit, any other key to continue..." TO X
IF X $ 'Qq'                     && Check for X = 'Q' or 'q' value.
    CANCEL                      && Cancel program if X = Q or q.
ELSE                            && Branch if X is not Q or q.
    RETURN                      && Return to calling program.
ENDIF                           && End if statement.
```

5. Press **Ctrl-W** to save the file.

6. Type **CREATE ADDRESS** to prepare the following database structure; then enter the records as shown.

```
Structure for database:    Address.dbf
Field  Field Name  Type        Width   Dec
    1  NAME        Character      20
    2  ADDRESS     Character      20
    3  CITY        Character      15
    4  STATE       Character       2
    5  ZIP         Character       5
    6  JOINED      Date            8
    7  AGE         Numeric         3
** Total **                       74
```

```
#  NAME            ADDRESS              CITY           STATE ZIP    JOINED   AGE
1  John Billings   2320 Hawthorne Ave.  Trenton        NJ    03565  05/12/81  36
2  Mary Tremore    56 Park Lane         Culver City    CA    95065  11/01/83  27
3  Fred Franklin   3900 Brookside Road  Hobbs          NM    85676  09/18/79  43
4  Chuck Williams  56 Walmart Plaza     Jasper         TX    75611  07/11/80  39
```

7. Type **DO SHOW** and press **Return** to run the program. Experiment with the operation by pressing a key during the listing process. You will have to be quick to stop listing before it is complete. If you wish, you can insert a delay loop above the SKIP command line.

8. Use ERASE to eliminate the SHOW.PRG and PROC.PRG files from your disk. Save the ADDRESS database for later use.

9. Turn to Module 22 to continue the learning sequence.

Module 50
PARAMETERS

DESCRIPTION

The PARAMETERS statement is used to establish one or more data items (or values) in a command file. Once parameters are defined, the parameters command file is available as a standard *subroutine*, or program module. This parameter file is available to command files or is used from the dBASE dot prompt.

The command used to call stored parameters uses a WITH statement that lists the known values of the data items in the PARAMETERS list. An unknown value uses the data item (or memory variable) name. The general form of the PARAMETERS statement is:

> PARAMETERS *data item list*

The form of the calling command, typically used within command files containing the PARAMETERS statement, is:

> DO *command filename* WITH value1, value2, . . .

Still confused? Perhaps an example will help to clarify. Here is an example of how the PARAMETERS command is used in a command file called GASCALC.

```
                                          Remarks
* GASCALC.PRG -- Calculates gasoline mileage.
PARAMETERS MILES, GALS, MPG       && Identifies variables.
MPG=MILES/GALS                    && Establishes variable relationships.
RETURN                            && Closes file; returns to dot prompt.
```

To use the GASCALC command file, the following lines are entered at the dBASE dot prompt.

```
. MPG=0                           && Establishes value of variable MPG.
0                                 && dBASE dialog displays value.
. DO GASCALC WITH 328,18.6,MPG    && Runs command file with parameter values.
        17.63
```

The PARAMETERS statement is always the first executable command line within a command file. The command that calls the PARAMETER command file must contain a list of values and variables that match the number of parameters in the command file. For example, there are three parameters in the sample GASCALC command file. The DO GASCALC statement specifies three variables that match MILES, GALS, and MPG. Notice that the memory variable MPG is established before the command file is run. The value of MPG is unimportant at this point, because the command file evaluates MPG using MILES and GALS. The purpose of the MPG = 0 entry is strictly to establish MPG as a memory variable.

APPLICATIONS

As you can see, the PARAMETERS statement is a good way to create and store commonly used mathematical relationships. If you find yourself performing the same mathematical calculations over and over, you can use the PARAMETERS statement in a command file to take the drudgery out of your work.

You can also take a large set of standard calculation algorithms (or formulas) and put them into small command files that contain the PARAMETERS statement. For example, a cost estimator might want to store a series of estimating relationships in small command files that are called from other command files when needed. Be sure to use meaningful command file names to make it easy to remember which files perform what calculations.

TYPICAL OPERATION

In this illustration the PARAMETERS and DO WITH statements shown in the Description section of this module are used. Begin at the dBASE dot prompt.

1. Type **MODI COMM GASCALC** and press **Return** to use the dBASE editor.

2. Type the following command file. (Don't type the explanatory remarks.)

```
                                            Remarks
* GASCALC.PRG -- Calculates gasoline mileage.
PARAMETERS MILES, GALS, MPG    && Identifies variables.
MPG=MILES/GALS                 && Establishes variable relationships.
RETURN                         && Closes file; returns to dot prompt.
```

3. Press **Ctrl-W** to write the command file to disk.

4. Type **MPG=0** and press **Return**.

5. Type **DO GASCALC WITH 456,28.3,MPG** and press **Return**. Notice the following:

```
. MPG=0
0
. DO GASCALC WITH 456,28.3,MPG
         16.11
```

6. After you have experimented with the GASCALC command file, delete it by typing **ERASE GASCALC.PRG** and pressing **Return**.

7. Type **RELEASE ALL** to clear all memory variables.

8. Turn to Module 53 to continue the learning sequence.

Module 51

PRINT STATEMENT (?)

DESCRIPTION

Use of the question mark as an interactive mode operator was described in Module 43. In this module, the question mark is described in its role as a print statement. If you're familiar with the BASIC programming language, you know that when the command lines

```
10 PRINT "A space follows this line."
20 PRINT
30 PRINT "This is another line."
```

are run, the following lines are displayed.

```
    A blankline follows this line.

    This is another line.
```

Notice that PRINT without following text displays a blank line. You can think of the question mark as being equivalent to the BASIC PRINT statement. The statements required to produce the above display in dBASE are:

```
? 'A blank line follows this line.'
?
? 'This is another line.'
```

Displayed text is enclosed in either single or double quote marks or square brackets. If the text includes a single quote within it, surround your text using double quotes. On the other hand, text that includes a double quote should be enclosed in single quotes. The following lines demonstrate these principles.

```
? 'Press "Q" to quit'
?
? "Don't press the Esc key"
? [When it's done, press "X" to exit.]
```

To see additional examples of the print statement, review the MENU command file example in Module 46.

The TEXT and ENDTEXT commands, described in Module 65, also display text. Because these statements display every character exactly as typed, they can't be used to display field contents or memory variables.

In contrast, the print statement is used in conjunction with both field contents and memory variables. For example, you can display the value of a field or memory variable following a descriptive caption. As mentioned in Module 43, the question mark is similar to the DISPLAY OFF command. It is used to display the contents of database fields, memory variables, or following text. Check the following examples. Assume the DESCRIP, AMOUNT, and TAX are field names, and MVAR is a memory variable.

```
? 'The cost of',TRIM(DESCRIP),'is $'-LTRIM(STR(AMOUNT+TAX,6,2))


? 'The value of the memory variable is',MVAR


? 'A double vertical bar looks like ',CHR(186)
```

NOTE

In the first example the TRIM statement is used to eliminate trailing blanks; the LTRIM-STR statement converts the numeric value of AMOUNT+TAX to a character string. Once converted, the LTRIM string function trims leading blanks to eliminate unwanted spaces.

APPLICATIONS

The print statement is easy to use for displaying menus and prompts. The ability to follow the print statement with the contents of fields and memory variables makes its use in command files convenient. The print statement is also used with the CHR() function, described in Module 6, to combine graphic characters and text. The following command lines demonstrates this application.

```
                                    Remarks
* BOX.PRG -- Displays a box
SET TALK OFF                && Turns off dBASE dialog.
STORE CHR(201) TO A         && Stores upper left-hand corner graphic to A.
STORE CHR(187) TO B         && Stores upper right-hand corner graphic to B.
STORE CHR(200) TO C         && Stores lower left-hand corner graphic to C.
STORE CHR(188) TO D         && Stores lower right-hand corner graphic to D.
STORE CHR(205)+CHR(205) TO H  && Stores two horizontal lines to H.
STORE CHR(186) TO V         && Stores vertical bar to V.
CLEAR                       && Clears the screen.
?
? '       ',A+H+H+H+H+H+H+H+H+H+H+H+H+H+H+H+H+H+H+H+H+H+H+H+H+H+H+H+H+H+B
? '       ',V,'                                                      ',V
? '       ',V,'                                                      ',V
? '       ',V,'                                                      ',V
? '       ',C+H+H+H+H+H+H+H+H+H+H+H+H+H+H+H+H+H+H+H+H+H+H+H+H+H+H+H+H+H+D
?
WAIT
CLEAR
RETURN
```

This command file displays the following information and block characters on most personal computers when you type **DO BOX** and press **Return**.

Press any key to continue. . .

You should know that the same box can be created with the following command line:

@ 3,9 TO 7,66 DOUBLE

A horizontal rule is displayed with a command like:

@ 3,9 TO 3,66   or   @ 3,9 SAY REPLICATE(chr(205),57)

TYPICAL OPERATION

In this illustration the print statement is used in a command file to display information in the MEMBERS database. Print statements are used in the command file to display a menu, prompts, memory variables, and field values. If necessary, turn to Module 47, create the MEMBERS database structure, and add the records shown in Module 18. Then perform the following steps, beginning at the dBASE dot prompt.

1.   Type **MODIFY COMMAND PRINT1** and press **Return** to use the dBASE editor.

2.   Type the following command file. (Don't type the explanatory remarks.)

```
                                       Remarks
* PRINT1.PRG               && Demonstrates use of the Print Statement.
SET TALK OFF               && Turns off dBASE dialog.
DO WHILE .T.               && Begins DO WHILE loop; operates until CHOICE = 4.
* Display a menu:
CLEAR                      && Clears screen. Following text in quotes is displayed.
? '                          MEMBERSHIP MAINTENANCE'
?
? '                                                  Press'
?
? '                       Add a new member          [1]'
? '                       Change member information  [2]'
? '                       Delete a member record     [3]'
? '                       Exit membership maintenance [4]'
@ 2,17 to 2,59               && Draws underline beneath "Press."
@ 4,54 to 4,58               && Draws horizontal rule under menu title.
@ 0,16 to 9,60 double        && Draws frame around menu.
?
```

```
WAIT 'MAKE YOUR SELECTION ' TO CHOICE && Pauses operation; displays prompt in quotes.
USE MEMBERS                     && Puts MEMBERS database in use.
CLEAR                           && Clears screen.
DO CASE                         && Starts CASE statement.
   * Add a record:
   CASE CHOICE='1'              && If CHOICE = 1, uses following command line.
      APPEND                    && Adds (appends) record to bottom of database.
   * Change a record:
   CASE CHOICE='2'              && If CHOICE = 2, uses following command lines.
      ? "  To make a change, type the member's last name"
      ? '  and press RETURN.'
      ACCEPT '  ==============>' TO MNAME  && Accepts keyboard input to memory variable MNAME.
      CLEAR                     && Clears screen.
      LOCATE FOR UPPER(NAME)=UPPER(MNAME)  && Searches for NAME = memory variable MNAME.
      * If the name isn't found:
      IF EOF()                  && If end of file encountered, executes IF statement.
         CLEAR                  && Clears screen.
         ? "          Can't find",MNAME
         WAIT                   && Pauses operation; displays "Press any key..." prompt.
         LOOP                   && Returns control to line following DO WHILE command.
      ENDIF                     && Ends current IF statement (if end of file).
      * If the name is found, display the record:
      DO WHILE .T.              && Begins interior DO WHILE loop.
         ? NAME,CSZ,AFFIL       && Displays NAME, CSZ, and AFFIL fields.
         ?                      && Following text within quotes is displayed.
         ? '     Press              To'
         ? '       C              Change'
         ? '       N              Find Next',MNAME
         ? '       R              Return to the Menu'
         WAIT ' 'TO OPTION      && Pauses operation; stores keyed character to OPTION.
         CLEAR                  && Clears screen.
         * Return to the menu:
         IF UPPER(OPTION)='R'   && If upper or lowercase OPTION = R, executes IF statement.
            EXIT                && Exits interior DO WHILE loop.
         ENDIF                  && Ends current IF statement (OPTION = R).
         * Edit the record:
         IF UPPER(OPTION)='C'   && If upper or lowercase OPTION = C, executes IF statement.
            EDIT RECNO()        && Edits current record.
            EXIT                && Exits interior DO WHILE loop.
         ENDIF                  && Ends current IF statement (OPTION = C).
         * Find the next record containing the same name:
         IF UPPER(OPTION)='N'   && If upper or lowercase OPTION = N, executes IF statement.
            CONTINUE            && Searches for next record with MNAME in the NAME field.
```

```
    * If the name isn't found:
    IF EOF()              && If end-of-file encountered, executes following statements.
      CLEAR               && Clears screen.
      ? "            Can't find another",MNAME  && Displays prompt in quotes.
      WAIT                && Pauses operation; displays "Press any key..." prompt.
      EXIT                && Exits interior DO WHILE loop.
    ENDIF                 && Ends current IF statement (If end of file).
  ENDIF                   && Ends parent IF statement (OPTION = N).
ENDDO                     && Ends current DO WHILE statement.
* Delete a record:
CASE CHOICE='3'           && If CHOICE = 3, uses following command lines.
  ? "  To Delete a record, type the member's last name"
  ? '  and press RETURN.'
  ACCEPT '  ===============>' TO MNAME  && Accepts keyboard input to variable MNAME.
  CLEAR                               && Clears screen.
  LOCATE FOR UPPER(NAME)=UPPER(MNAME)   && Searches for NAME = memory variable MNAME.
  * If the name isn't found:
  IF EOF()                            && If end of file, executes following statements.
    CLEAR                             && Clears screen.
    ? "           Can't find",MNAME    && Text in quotes displayed.
    WAIT                && Pauses operation; displays "Press any key..." prompt.
    LOOP                && Returns control to line following DO WHILE statement.
  ENDIF                 && Ends current IF statement.
  * If the name is found:
  DO WHILE .T.          && Begins interior DO WHILE loop.
    ? NAME,CSZ,AFFIL    && Displays NAME, CSZ, and AFFIL fields.
    ?                   && Following text within quotes is displayed.
    ? '      Press              To'
    ? '        D               Delete'
    ? '        N               Find Next',MNAME
    ? '        R               Return to the Menu'
    WAIT ' ' TO OPTION  && Pauses operation; stores keyed character to OPTION.
    CLEAR               && Clears screen.
    * Return to the menu:
    IF UPPER(OPTION)='R' && If upper or lowercase OPTION = R, executes IF statement.
      EXIT              && Exits interior DO WHILE loop.
    ENDIF               && Ends current IF statement (OPTION = R).
    * Delete the record:
    IF UPPER(OPTION)='D' && If upper or lowercase OPTION = D, executes IF statement.
      DELETE            && Marks current record for deletion.
      PACK              && Deletes marked record.
      EXIT              && Exits interior DO WHILE loop.
    ENDIF               && Ends current IF statement (OPTION = D).
```

```
   * Find the next record containing the same name:
   IF UPPER(OPTION)='N'   && If upper or lowercase OPTION = N, executes IF statement.
      CONTINUE               && Continues LOCATE search from current record down.
   * If the name isn't found"
      IF EOF()              && If end of file encountered, executes IF statement.
         CLEAR              && Clears screen.
         ? "            Can't find another",MNAME  && Displays text in quotes followed
         *                                          by contents of variable MNAME.
         WAIT              && Pauses operation; displays "Press any key..." prompt.
         EXIT              && Exits interior DO WHILE loop.
      ENDIF                && Ends current IF statement.
   ENDIF                   && Ends parent IF statement (OPTION = N)
  ENDDO                    && Completes interior DO WHILE loop.
   * Return to dBASE:
  CASE CHOICE='4'          && If CHOICE = 4, uses following command lines.
     SET TALK ON           && Turns dBASE dialog back on.
     CANCEL                && Cancels command file operation; returns to dot prompt.
   ENDCASE                 && Ends CASE statement.
ENDDO                      && Ends exterior (initial) DO WHILE loop.
```

3. Press **Ctrl-W** to write the command file to disk.

4. Run the PRINT1 command file by typing **DO PRINT1** and pressing **Return**. The following menu and prompts are displayed. Try your own variations to test the program. (You may want to use this file as a model for your own command file.)

```
               MEMBERSHIP MAINTENANCE

                                     Press

         Add a new member            [1]
         Change member information   [2]
         Delete a member record      [3]
         Exit membership maintenance [4]


Make your selection _              (Type 1)


Record No.      3                  (Add a record with the name Jones.)
```

```
                MEMBERSHIP MAINTENANCE


                                          Press

          Add a new member              [1]
          Change member information      [2]
          Delete a member record         [3]
          Exit membership maintenance    [4]

Make your selection _                    (Type 2)



  To make a change, type the member's last name
  and press RETURN.
  ===============>:Phillips

Phillips, George W.        Lago Vista, TX 78641      Austin Medical Center

      Press              To
        C                Change
        N                Find Next Phillips
        R                Return to the Menu
  _                           (Type R to return to menu.)

                MEMBERSHIP MAINTENANCE


                                          Press
                                          -----
          Add a new member              [1]
          Change member information      [2]
          Delete a member record         [3]
          Exit membership maintenance    [4]

Make your selection _                    (Type 3)

  To Delete a record, type the member's last name
  and press RETURN.
  ===============>:Brown


Can't find Brown
Press any key to continue...
```

```
          MEMBERSHIP MAINTENANCE

                                      Press

          Add a new member              [1]
          Change member information     [2]
          Delete a member record        [3]
          Exit membership maintenance   [4]


Make your selection _                    (Type 4)

Do cancelled
```

5. When you have finished experimenting with this command file, type **ERASE PRINT1.PRG** and press **Return** to remove the command file from your disk.

6. Turn to Module 8 to continue the learning sequence.

Module 52
PRIVATE, PUBLIC

DESCRIPTION

The PRIVATE and PUBLIC commands are used with memory variables. A memory variable created from the dBASE dot prompt is "public," i.e., available until released with CLEAR ALL or RELEASE (Modules 14 and 62). Memory variables created within command files are retained until the command file ends operation.

If you want to prevent the memory variable from being released when a command file ends operation, you can declare the memory variable as being *public* when it is created. This is accomplished with the PUBLIC command. The PUBLIC command form is:

```
PUBLIC MVAR
MVAR=125.5
```

You can declare several memory variables as public by typing a list, such as:

```
PUBLIC A,B,C
STORE 'Hello' TO A
STORE 'GOODBY' TO B
STORE 33.333 TO C
```

In this example, the memory variables A, B, and C remain active until you intentionally release them.

"Private" memory variables are ones that are declared private during the operation of a *called* command file. A called command file is one that is called from another, higher level command file. This process is illustrated in the Typical Operation section of this module.

When operation of a called command file ends, private memory variables are released. This prevents them from interfering with other "public," or higher level memory variables, having the same name. Some forms of the PRIVATE command are:

```
PRIVATE X,Y,Z
X = 173.33
Y = 52
Z = 12

PRIVATE ALL

PRIVATE ALL EXCEPT A,B,C

PRIVATE ALL LIKE M??
```

APPLICATIONS

The PRIVATE and PUBLIC commands are handy tools for those who make heavy use of memory variables. These commands let you control the application of memory variables from one dBASE command file to another. You may find yourself creating memory variables in one command file that have use in other command files. If this is the case, they should be declared public. There may be times when you may wish to use an existing memory variable name in a lower level command file. Here, you can declare the memory variable private to keep it from conflicting with previously established memory variables.

TYPICAL OPERATION

In this illustration both the PUBLIC and PRIVATE commands are used in sample command files. Three short command files are created to demonstrate how one command file can call another. The RETURN command, which is described in Module 12, is used to move from a called command file back to the one from which it was called. In other words, it *returns* to the previous command file at the point from which it was called. Begin at the dBASE dot prompt.

1.   Type **MODI COMM TEST0** and press **Return**.

2.   Type the following command file. (Don't type the explanatory remarks.)

```
                                        Remarks
* TEST0.PRG -- The first command file in a series of three.
?' This program calls test1'  && Text within quotes is displayed on the screen.
SET TALK OFF                  && Turns off dBASE dialog.
WAIT                          && Pauses operation
DO TEST1                      && Calls TEST1 command file.
CANCEL                        && Ends operation; returns control to dBASE dot prompt.
```

3.   Press **Ctrl-W** to save the command file.

4.   Type **MODI COMM TEST1** and press **Return**.

5.   Type the following command file. (Don't type the explanatory remarks.)

```
                                        Remarks
* TEST1.PRG - Called from TEST0; calls TEST2
STORE 1 TO x                  && Stores 1 to memory variable X.
STORE 2 TO y                  && Stores 2 to memory variable Y
STORE 3 TO z
?' The value of x is',x       && Displays value of x.
?' The value of y is',y       && Displays value of y.
?' The value of z is',z       && Displays value of z.
WAIT                          && Pauses operation.
DO TEST2                      && Calls TEST2 command file.
?' The value of w is',w       && Displays value of w, which is public.
```

```
?' The value of x is',x        && Displays original value of x.
?' The value of y is',y        && Displays original value of y.
?' The value of z is',z        && Displays changed value of z.
WAIT                           && Pauses operation.
CLEAR ALL                      && Clears all memory variables.
RETURN                         && Returns to calling command file (TEST0).
```

6. Press **Ctrl-W** to save this command file.

7. Type **MODI COMM TEST2** and press **Return**.

8. Type the following command file. (Don't type the explanatory remarks.)

Remarks

```
* TEST2.PRG - Uses private and public commands
PRIVATE X,Y                    && Sets X and Y as private memory variables.
PUBLIC W                       && Sets W as a public memory variable.
W=10                           && Gives W a value of 10.
X=11                           && Gives X a value of 11.
Y=12                           && Gives Y a value of 12.
Z=13                           && Gives Z a value of 13.
?' The value of W is      ',W  && Displays the value of W.
?' The value of X is now ',X   && Displays the value of X.
?' The value of Y is now ',Y   && Displays the value of Y.
?' The value of Z is now ',Z   && Displays the value of Z.
WAIT                           && Pauses operation.
LIST MEMO                      && Lists active memory variables.
RETURN                         && Returns to calling command file (TEST1).
```

9. Press **Ctrl-W** to write the command file to disk.

10. Run the series of command files as described in the following sub-steps. Notice how information is displayed by the three command files. Be sure to study how memory variable values are affected by PRIVATE and PUBLIC,

    a. Type **DO TEST0** and press **Return**.

```
. DO TEST0                                    Remarks
This program calls test1
Press any key to continue...
```

b. Press a key and check the values of x, y, and z.

```
The value of x is          1  ⎫
The value of y is          2  ⎬   Original values of TEST1.
The value of z is          3  ⎭
Press any key to continue...
```

c. Press a key and check the values of w, x, y, and z; then review the status of the memory variables and the program files from which they were called.

```
The value of w is              10  ⎫
The value of x is now          11  ⎬  Values established in TEST2.
The value of y is now          12  ⎪
The value of z is now          13  ⎭
X          priv  (hidden)  N              1  (        1.00000000)C:test1.prg
Y          priv  (hidden)  N              2  (        2.00000000)C:test1.prg
Z          priv  N            13  (      13.00000000)        C:test1.prg
W          pub   N            10  (      10.00000000)
X          priv  N            11  (      11.00000000)        C:test2.prg
Y          priv  N            12  (      12.00000000)        C:test2.prg
     6 variables defined,       54 bytes used
   250 variables available,   5946 bytes available
Press any key to continue...
```

d. Press a key and check the values of w, x, y, and z.

```
The value of w is          10       W is public; still available.
The value of x is           1       Original value of x.
The value of y is           2       Original value of y.
The value of z is          13       Changed value of z.
Press any key to continue...
```

e. Press a key to return to the dot prompt.

11. Delete the test files by typing **RUN DEL TEST?.PRG** and pressing **Return**.

12. Turn to Module 17 to continue the learning sequence.

Module 53
PROCEDURE

DESCRIPTION

A procedure is a series of command lines within a command file that perform some operation. This collection of command lines is given a procedure name, and called by the PROCEDURE statement. If you are a Pascal programmer, you should be familiar with the use of procedures.

The first line within a dBASE procedure contains the procedure name in the form:

PROCEDURE *name*

where a procedure name must begin with an alpha character and can have from 1 to 8 characters consisting of letters, numbers, and underscores. The body of the procedure contains standard dBASE commands for performing some operation. The last line in a procedure contains the RETURN command. RETURN completes the procedure and returns control to the line following the command line from which the procedure was called. If called from the dBASE dot prompt, control is returned to the prompt.

The following example is a simple procedure file containing three independent procedures.

```
* HRLY.PRG - a procedure file that converts hourly wage rates

PROCEDURE hr_wk
    INPUT 'Enter the hourly rate ' to BASE
    CLEAR
    ? 'The weekly income is $',STR(BASE*40,7,2)
RETURN

PROCEDURE hr_mo
    INPUT 'Enter the hourly rate ' to BASE
    CLEAR
    ? 'The monthly income is $',STR(BASE*173.333,8,2)
RETURN

PROCEDURE hr_yr
    INPUT 'Enter the hourly rate ' to BASE
    CLEAR
    ? 'The annual income is $',STR(BASE*2080,9,2)
RETURN
```

To use a procedure file, the SET PROCEDURE TO *filename* command is entered. In our example, you would type **SET PROCEDURE TO HRLY** and press **Return**. This tells dBASE where to find the specified procedure. To use the hour-to-week conversion procedure (hr_wk) shown in the preceding example, you type:

```
. SET PROCEDURE TO HRLY<cr>
. DO HR_WK<cr>
```

In response, you see:

```
    Enter the hourly rate _
```

Type an hourly rate, like 7.50 and press **Return**. The hr_yr procedure file displays:

```
    The annual income is $  15600.00
```

To close the procedure file, type **SET PROCEDURE TO** and press **Return**.

APPLICATIONS

Procedure files are useful for repetitive tasks. For example, if you wish to display the same information many times or perform a recurring computation, you can build a procedure file that responds like a calculation tool box. This saves disk space that would otherwise be used by writing these procedures into every command file requiring common calculations.

A major advantage to procedure files is that they can be called from any active command file or from the dBASE dot prompt. Once stored, you can use them whenever you like. Remember to use a meaningful name for both your procedure files and procedures to make them easy to remember.

TYPICAL OPERATION

In this illustration the procedure file contained in the above example is used to demonstrate the use of procedures and how they are called. Begin at the dBASE dot prompt.

1. Type **MODI COMM HRLY** and press **Return** to use the dBASE editor.

2. Type the following command file. (Don't type the explanatory remarks.)

Remarks

```
* HRLY.PRG -- A procedure file that converts hourly wage rates

PROCEDURE hr_wk                          && Procedure name.
   INPUT 'Enter the hourly rate ' to BASE && Stores typed rate to memory variable BASE.
   CLEAR                                 && Clears the screen.
   ? 'The weekly income is $',STR(BASE*40,7,2) && Displays hourly rate as a character string.
RETURN                                   && Returns control to calling point.

PROCEDURE hr_mo
   INPUT 'Enter the hourly rate ' to BASE
   CLEAR
   ? 'The monthly income is $',STR(BASE*173.333,8,2)
RETURN

PROCEDURE hr_yr
   INPUT 'Enter the hourly rate ' to BASE
   CLEAR
   ? 'The annual income is $',STR(BASE*2080,9,2)
RETURN
```

3. Press **Ctrl-W** to save the procedure command file.

4. Type **SET PROC TO HRLY** and press **Return**.

5. Type **DO HR_YR** and press **Return**; respond to the rate prompt by typing an hourly rate, such as 8.25.

6. Notice that the annual rate is displayed.

7. Continue experimenting with the procedure file by using HR_WK and HR_MO.

8. When finished, type **SET PROC** and press **Return** to close the procedure file.

9. Type **ERASE HRLY.PRG** to delete the procedure file from your working disk.

10. Turn to Module 48 to continue the learning sequence.

Module 54
QUIT

DESCRIPTION

The QUIT command is one that you should become familiar with right away. It is used to "quit" dBASE and return to the operating system prompt. QUIT closes all files in use, clears all memory variables, and ends the dBASE session.

You should never end a dBASE session without either typing QUIT at the dot prompt or including QUIT in a command file as the last statement. (Command files are a list of dBASE commands that execute in the order entered. These are described in more detail as you progress through this book.) If you turn off your computer without using QUIT, you may damage open files.

Before starting dBASE, be sure that you have the proper configuration file (named CONFIG.SYS) and the DOS files on your system disk. This file takes effect when you turn on your computer's power. The CONFIG.SYS file is described in Module 2 and Appendix A, and contains the following lines:

```
FILES=20
BUFFERS=15
```

There is also a CONFIG.DB file (not to be confused with the CONFIG.SYS file) used to set dBASE default conditions when it is started. You can delete the CONFIG.DB file from your system disk if you are using a hard disk system. If you are using a two-floppy-drive system, delete the "STATUS = ON" and "COMMAND = ASSIST" lines from the CONFIG.DB file and add the line "DEFAULT = B:."

If you are using a floppy-drive system and added CONFIG.SYS and DOS to SYSTEM DISK #1 (described in Module 2), place it in drive A and turn on your computer. If you are using a hard disk version of dBASE, go to the dBASE III Plus subdirectory, type **DBASE**, and press **Return**. Remember to always respond to the date and time prompts to ensure that your files are marked with the current date and time.

A preliminary information screen is displayed followed by the dBASE dot prompt. At this point dBASE is waiting for your instructions. You can create files, edit them, print reports, and so on. If a menu screen containing windows is displayed, press **Esc** to display the dot prompt.

Once you are finished with your dBASE work, it is necessary to quit dBASE. This is done by typing **QUIT** and pressing **Return**.

The QUIT command returns you to the operating system prompt after displaying the following message.

```
*** END RUN    dBASE III Plus
```

APPLICATIONS

The QUIT command is used every time you end a dBASE session. It closes all files and returns you to the operating system prompt. The QUIT command is either typed at the dot prompt or included in a command file. (More about command files later.) In either case, the QUIT command is always used to exit dBASE.

Although the QUIT command is usually used to return to the operating system prompt, it may return you to a calling program, such as WordStar, if you entered dBASE from the application environment.

TYPICAL OPERATION

In this illustration dBASE is started and then the QUIT command is used to return to the operating system prompt.

1. With the dBASE program located in the default drive, type **DBASE** and press **Return**.

2. From the dBASE dot prompt type **QUIT** and press **Return**.

3. Notice the following display, assuming that the logged disk drive is C. The information below "Remarks" is not displayed.

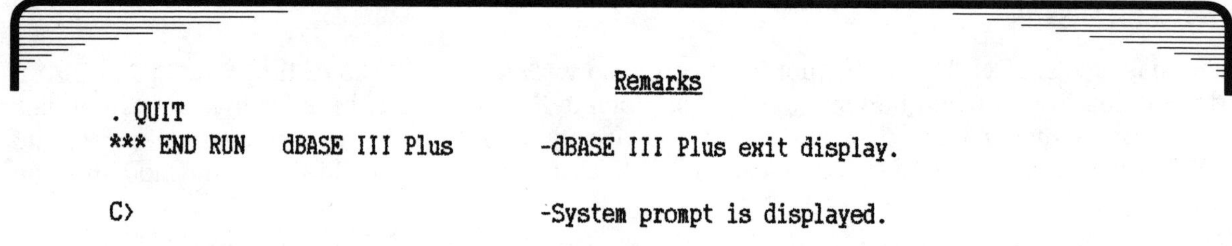

```
                                        Remarks
 . QUIT
 *** END RUN   dBASE III Plus        -dBASE III Plus exit display.

   C>                                -System prompt is displayed.
```

4. Turn to Module 27 to continue the learning sequence.

Module 55
RENAME

DESCRIPTION

The RENAME command is used to change the name of a file. The general form of the RENAME command is:

> RENAME *oldname* to *newname*

Some examples of the RENAME command are shown in the following list. Notice that you can rename files on any disk drive by placing the disk drive designator in front of the filename. Open files can not be renamed. If you wish to rename a file, you can close it with the CLOSE ALL command and then use the RENAME command.

1. RENAME *oldname* TO *newname*   Changes the original filename to the filename following the TO statement on the default disk drive. If no extension name is given, dBASE assumes the file is a database and automatically assigns a .DBF extension.

    . RENAME MEMBERS TO MBRS

2. RENAME B:*oldname* TO B:*newname*   Changes the original filename to the filename following the TO statement on disk drive B. Without extensions, database files are assumed.

    . RENAME B:MEMBERS TO B:MBRS

3. RENAME *oldname.ext* TO *newname.ext*   Changes the original filename and extension to the filename and extension following the TO statement.

    . RENAME B:LIST.TXT TO B:LETTER.TXT

APPLICATIONS

The RENAME command is used to maintain your files just as with the DOS REN command. If you decide to change your file naming scheme, you can use RENAME to assign a new name to the file of your choice.

TYPICAL OPERATION

In this illustration the RENAME command is used to change the name of a small practice file. Next, the ERASE command is used to remove the temporary practice file from your disk. Begin at the dBASE dot prompt.

1. Type **MODIFY COMMAND TEMP** and press **Return** to use the dBASE editor.

2. Type **This is a practice file** and press **Ctrl-W** to write the file to disk.

3. Type **DIR *.PRG** and press **Return**. Notice that a TEMP.PRG program is displayed in the directory listing.

4. Type **RENAME TEMP.PRG TO TEMP1.TXT** and press **Return**.

5. Type **DIR *.TXT** and press **Return**. Notice that the renamed file is displayed as TEMP1.TXT.

6. Type **ERASE TEMP1.TXT** and press **Return**. Notice the following:

```
. ERASE TEMP1.TXT
File has been deleted
```

7. Turn to Module 39 to continue the learning sequence.

Module 56
REPLACE

DESCRIPTION

The REPLACE command is used to REPLACE the contents of one or more specified fields within either the current record or all records, depending on the form of the command. You can also restrict replacements to certain records by using the "FOR *expression*" clause. Forms of the REPLACE command are shown in the following list.

1. REPLACE *field name* WITH *string*   Replaces the contents of the named field in the current record with the string, which can be character, numeric, or logical. After the replace command is used, the record pointer is repositioned to the last record. Therefore, be sure you know where the record pointer is before using the REPLACE command.

    ```
    . REPLACE PART_NO WITH '250987-01'
         1 record replaced
    ```

2. REPLACE *field1* WITH *string*, *field2* WITH *string*, . . .   Replaces the contents of the named fields in the current record with the corresponding strings.

    ```
    . REPLACE QTY WITH 125, PART_NO WITH '250987-01'
         1 record replaced
    ```

3. REPLACE *range field name* WITH *string*   Replaces the contents of the named field(s) with the corresponding string(s) for a range of records, such as "all" or "next 5."

    ```
    . REPLACE ALL PRICE WITH PRICE*1.05
        128 record replaced
    ```

    ```
    . REPLACE NEXT 3 PRICE WITH PRICE*1.05
         3 record replaced
    ```

4. REPLACE *field name* WITH *string* FOR *expression*   Replaces the contents of the named field(s) with the corresponding string(s) for all records that match the FOR expression.

    ```
    . REPLACE COST WITH COST*1.1 FOR DESCRIP='Tire'
    ```

> REPLACE *fieldname* WITH *memory variable*   Replaces the contents of the named field with the named memory variable.

```
. REPLACE DATE WITH MDATE
```

> REPLACE *date field name* WITH CTOD('MM/DD/YY')   Replaces the contents of a date field with the MM/DD/YY string expression.

```
. REPLACE DATE WITH CTOD('11/12/88')
```

You may wish to display the active database file with the LIST command so you can see which records require changing. You can move the record pointer to the first record requiring replacement by typing the record number and pressing **Return**. Then type the REPLACE command to make the needed changes. If every record requiring a replacement has a common expression, you can use the expression in your command to fix all records with one entry.

APPLICATIONS

The REPLACE command is commonly used to change the contents of the fields within a database in the interactive mode. In addition, the REPLACE command is often used in command files to replace the value of a field with a memory variable. The following three command lines create a memory variable with the name MZIP, open a database named PLACES, and then replace the contents of the ZIP field with 75074 in all records having a ZIP value of 75089.

```
MZIP = '75074'
USE PLACES
REPLACE ZIP WITH MZIP FOR ZIP = '75089'
```

Inclusion of the ALL, NEXT, and FOR *expression* statements let you make replacements on a *global* basis, that is, for all records in a database file that meet a specified condition or contain a common expression.

TYPICAL OPERATION

In this illustration the REPLACE command is used with the ABC database created in Module 10 to replace the MAIL fields containing "84" with "2084." Begin a the dBASE dot prompt.

1.   Type **USE ABC** and press **Return**.

2. Type **LIST** and press **Return**. Compare your screen to the following:

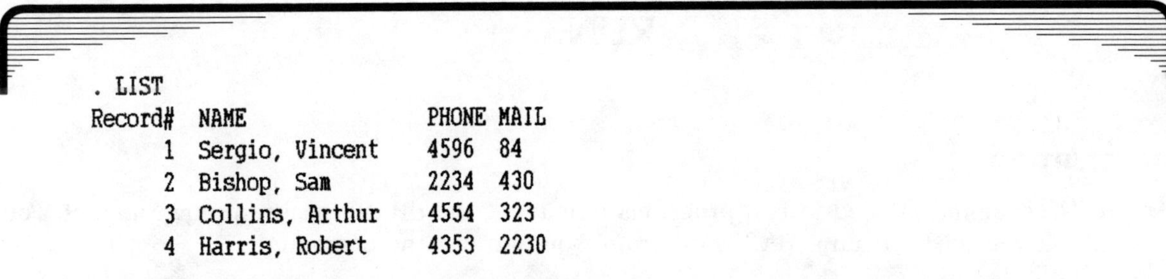

3. Type **REPLACE MAIL WITH '2084' FOR MAIL = '84'** and press **Return**.

4. Type **LIST** and press **Return**. Notice that "84" has been replaced with "2084."

5. Type **CLEAR ALL** and press **Return** to close all files.

6. Turn to Module 16 to continue the learning sequence.

Module 57
RUN, !

DESCRIPTION

The RUN command is used to run programs outside of the dBASE program environment. For example, if you wish to run a BASIC program, you can use the command:

    . RUN BASIC *filename*

You can substitute the exclamation mark (!) in place of the word "RUN" as an alternate command form. In this module, RUN is used.

If your computer has sufficient memory (more than 256K), the program executes. If it doesn't have enough memory, the message "Insufficient memory" is displayed.

You can also run common DOS commands, such as DIR and DEL with RUN. When the program or DOS command finishes operation, control is returned to dBASE.

APPLICATIONS

There are a number of DOS utilities that are useful from within dBASE. For example, the ability to delete multiple files having the extension BAK is accomplished with **RUN DEL TEMP?.***, which takes advantage of the DOS wildcard (*) and literal (?) features.

It is also possible to execute external programs, which provides a degree of interactive capability between dBASE and other programs. The Typical Operation section shows how you can write and run a basic program and then return to the dBASE dot prompt.

TYPICAL OPERATION

In this illustration you use RUN to execute a DOS directory command and then to run your computer's BASIC program. If you don't have BASIC on your system, you can omit that portion of this session. Begin at the dBASE dot prompt.

1. Type **RUN DIR** and press **Return**. Notice that a DOS file directory is displayed; then the dBASE dot prompt is redisplayed.

2. Type **RUN BASIC** and press **Return**. If you have an IBM PC, your screen should resemble the following. (Use **GWBASIC** if you have a PC compatible.)

```
The IBM Personal Computer Basic
Version D2.10 Copyright IBM Corp. 1981, 1982, 1983
60891 Bytes free

Ok
```

3. Type the following BASIC program lines, pressing **Return** after each.

```
10 FOR I = 1 TO 5
20 PRINT I
30 NEXT I
```

4. Type **RUN** and press **Return**; check your display.

```
10 FOR I = 1 TO 5
20 PRINT I
30 NEXT I
RUN
1
2
3
4
5
Ok
```

5. Type **SYSTEM** and press **Return** to return to the dBASE dot prompt.

6. Turn to Module 12 to continue the learning sequence.

Module 58
SAY, SAY GET, SAY PICTURE, CLEAR GETS, READ

DESCRIPTION

This module deals with a set of dBASE statements used to display text and accept keyboard entries into database fields and memory variables. The information in this module is directed at forms of the SAY statement. Because the SAY statement is often used in conjunction with the GET and @ row,col statements, information about these statements is also included. For more information about @ row,col and GET, see Modules 8 and 37.

@ row,col SAY "..."   Some forms of the @ row,col SAY statement are described in the following list.

1.   @ row,col SAY 'displayed text'   The text enclosed in quotes or square brackets is displayed beginning at the row,col coordinates.

     @ 5,20 SAY 'Read the information and press any key

2.   @ row,col SAY *fieldname*   The content of the named field is displayed beginning at the row,col coordinates. The named field in the current record is used.

     @ 7,15 SAY CITY

3.   @ row,col SAY *memory variable*   The content of the named memory variable is displayed beginning at the row,col coordinates.

     STORE 25 TO AMOUNT
     @ 12,35 SAY AMOUNT

4.   @ row,col SAY 'displayed text' + *memory variable*   Displays text and contents of specified memory variable as a single expression.

     @ 3,1 SAY 'The value of the memory variable is ' + MVAR

5.   @ row1,col1 TO row2,col2   Displays a single line window. The upper-left corner is at row1,col1; the lower-right corner is at row2,col2. Adding "DOUBLE" uses a double line.

     @ 4,4 TO 18,75
     @ 5,6 TO 17,74 DOUBLE

When SET DEVICE TO PRINT is active, the displayed output is directed to your printer instead of to your screen. To bring it back to your screen, you can enter SET DEVICE TO SCREEN. This is dBASE's default (normal) mode.

As with other print statements, you can use single or double quotes or square brackets around displayed text.

When output is sent to your printer, it's essential to organize your row-column positions sequentially, from top to bottom, left to right. This is critical when information is printed, because your printer can't move backwards; it prints a row and a column at a time. Some examples of this form of the SAY statement follow.

```
@ 10,15 SAY "Press any key to continue..."
@ 11,15 SAY 'Press Q to Quit, C to Continue'
```

THE ROW( ), COL( ), PROW( ), AND PCOL( ) FUNCTIONS   The ROW( ) and COL( ) functions return the current row and column position of the cursor. This is where text is displayed. Similarly, the PROW( ) and PCOL( ) functions return the current row and column position, as an integer, of printed output. If the cursor is presently at row 3, column 12, the expression:

```
@ ROW( )+1,COL( ) SAY TRIM(CITY) + STATE + ZIP
```

positions the contents of the CITY, STATE, and ZIP fields to row 4, column 12. These functions let you output information in a location relative to the current cursor or printer position, rather than having to compute absolute row and column position values.

You may wish to try the ROW( ) and COL( ) functions from the dBASE dot prompt. Type the following two lines and press **Return** to see the positions.

```
. ? ROW( ). ? COL( )
```

@ row,col SAY "...", GET *fieldname*   The SAY statement can incorporate the GET statement to display text and designated field contents. Because GET is used to display or display and modify field contents, it's not used for printing. If one or more <u>SAY GET</u> statements are followed by a command line containing the CLEAR GETS statement, the field contents are only displayed. However, if followed by the READ statement, the cursor is positioned in the displayed field. The READ statement lets you enter information directly into the displayed field from your keyboard. Some examples of this form of the SAY statement follow.

```
USE MEMBERS
@ 5,15 SAY "             Member's Name ", GET NAME
@ 6,15 SAY '             Street Address ', GET ADR
@ 7,15 SAY '        City, State, and Zip Code', GET CSZ
CLEAR GETS
@ 8,15 SAY "Is this member's dues paid (T/F)?", GET PAID
READ
```

The NAME, ADR, and CSZ fields are only displayed in rows 5, 6, and 7; the CLEAR GETS statement prevents the field contents from being modified. However, the cursor is positioned at the PAID field to allow modification. This is done by positioning the READ statement on a line following the last @ row,col GET statement.

@ row,col SAY *fieldname* PICTURE *expression*   The PICTURE clause lets you control the format of displayed or printed information. For example, if you wish to display all text in uppercase form, you can use:

```
@ 10,12 SAY NAME PICTURE '@!'
```

Notice that the ! sign is the uppercase control character. The @ sign tells dBASE that the following character is a control character. If @ is omitted, the control character is taken literally and displayed.

@ row,col GET *fieldname* PICTURE *expression*   This command form also lets you control the format of information from displayed fields. But more importantly, it lets you control the way that information is entered into a database. This is particularly helpful when consistency of data entry is important. For example, you might want all names in the name field of your database to be in uppercase. The statement used to force uppercase entry is:

```
@ 10,12 GET NAME PICTURE '!!!!!!!!!!!!!!!!!!!!'
```

The two preceding examples deal only with uppercase conversion. Many more control characters are available within the PICTURE clause. Some are considered functions, where they are preceded by the @ sign to control the displayed data. Others are called "template characters," because they control the placement of characters within the data area. Any character can be used as a template character, but only those listed in Table 58-1 are considered control characters. Notice the F and T in the Type column. The F designates function control characters, while the T designates a template character. The ! and A characters are both function and template characters.

APPLICATIONS

The variations of the SAY statement have many applications. With the @ row,col position statement, SAY is used to display and print text and the contents of fields and memory variables at specific row and column positions. The ability to use SAY with GET lets you display or print field contents at any row-column position. The contents are only displayed when GET statements are followed by CLEAR GETS; they may be changed when GET statements are followed by READ.

Finally, the PICTURE clause is used to control the way field contents are displayed, and in some cases, the format in which they are entered. For example, you can display dollars and cents with dollar signs and decimals, large numbers with commas and decimal points, negative values within parentheses, credits and debits with CR and DB, and so on. One popular application of the PICTURE '$9999.99' clause is to print dollar signs on checks.

TYPICAL OPERATION

In this illustration several variations of @ row,col-SAY are used in a command file named SAY.PRG. The command file uses the MEMBERS database last modified in Module 47. Use the records shown in Module 18. Begin at the dBASE dot prompt.

1.   Type **MODIFY COMMAND SAY** and press **Return** to use the dBASE editor.

Table 58-1 Say Picture Expressions

Character	Type	Description
A	F,T	Allows only alphabetical characters.
	F	@ 12,20 GET TITLE PICTURE '@A'
	T	@ 12,20 GET TITLE PICTURE 'AAAAA'
B	F	Positions numeric data flush left.
		@ 12,20 SAY 'Amount Due :' GET AMOUNT PICTURE '@B'
C,X	F	C displays "CR" after positive numbers to designate credit; X displays "DB" after negative numbers to designate debit. Used only with SAY.
		@ 10,30 SAY TOTAL PICTURE '@C'
D	F	Displays American date format (MM/DD/YY). Used only with date type data.
		@ 5,0 SAY 'Date :' GET DATE PICTURE '@A'
E	F	Displays European date format (DD/MM/YY). Used only with date type data.
		@ 5,0 SAY 'Date :' GET DATE PICTURE '@E'
L	T	Allows only logical values.
		@ 12,20 GET PAID PICTURE 'L'
N	T	Allows letters and digits.
		@ 8,5 SAY CODE PICTURE 'NNNNNNNNNN'
R	F	Displays typed text, which is not part of the data.
S	F	Limits the field width to a set number of characters.
		@ 10,12 SAY CITY PICTURE '@S10'
X	T	Allows any character.
		@ 5,5 SAY "Part Number? " GET PN PICTURE 'XXXXXX-XX'
Z	F	Displays zeros as blanks.
		@ 6,5 SAY PRICE PICTURE '@F'
9	T	Allows only digits for character data, digits, and signs for numeric data.
		@ 5,5 SAY 'TIME? :' GET TIME PICTURE '99:99'
(	F	Displays negative values within parentheses. Used only with SAY.
		@ 10,20 SAY PROFIT PICTURE '@('
#	T	Allows digits, blanks, and signs.
		@ 8,5 SAY 'Amount? ' GET AMOUNT PICTURE '####.##'
!	F,T	Converts lowercase to uppercase.
	F	@ 5,5 SAY 'NAME ' GET NAME PICTURE '@! AAAAAAAAAA'
	T	@ 5,5 SAY 'NAME ' GET NAME PICTURE '!!!!!!!!!!'
$	T	Displays $ signs in place of leading zeros in numeric-type fields.
		@ 8,26 GET COST * 1.1 PICTURE '$$$$$$$$$.99'
*	T	Displays * in place of leading zeros in numeric-type fields.
		@ 8,6 SAY 'PRICE :' GET COST * 1.1 PICTURE '********.99'
.	T	Controls the position of a decimal point in numeric-type data.
		@ 10,5 SAY 'VALUE? ' GET VALUE PICTURE '999.99'
,	T	Inserts a comma when there are numbers to the left.
		@ 5,10 GET TOTAL PICTURE '999,999.99'

2. Type the following command file. (Don't type the explanatory remarks.)

<u>Remarks</u>

```
* SAY.PRG -- Uses variations of the SAY statement.
CLEAR                       && Clears the screen.
SET TALK OFF                && Turns off dBASE dialog.
SET INTENSITY OFF           && Turns off reverse video display.
@ 2,15 SAY 'THIS PROGRAM ALLOWS UPDATING OF MEMBERSHIP INFORMATION'  && @ SAY positions text.
WAIT 'Press "Q" to Quit, any other key to proceed ' TO CHECK  && Pauses operation; stores
*                     character pressed to memory variable CHECK.
IF UPPER(CHECK)='Q'         && Checks for CHECK = Q; UPPER() accepts lower- or uppercase Q.
   CLEAR                    && Clears screen if CHECK equals Q.
   CANCEL                   && Cancels command file operation if CHECK equals Q.
ENDIF                       && Completes IF statement; passes control to next line.
USE MEMBERS                 && Puts MEMBERS database file in use.
DO WHILE .NOT. EOF()        && Continues operation while not end of file.
   CLEAR
* The following @ row,col lines display text and field values.
   @ 5,10 SAY 'Name       ' GET NAME PICTURE '@!'
   @ 6,10 SAY 'Address    ' GET ADR
   @ ROW(),COL()+3 GET CSZ
   CLEAR GETS               && Prevents modification of field values in rows 5 and 6.
   @ 7,10 SAY 'Affiliation ' GET AFFIL
   @ 8,10 SAY 'Date Joined ' GET JOINED PICTURE '@E'
   @ 9,10 SAY 'Age        ' GET AGE
   @ ROW(),COL() + 3 SAY 'Paid (Y/N)? ' GET PAID PICTURE 'L'
   READ                     && Allows modification of field values on rows 7 through 9.
   WAIT 'Press "Q" to Quit, any other key to proceed ' TO CHECK  && Pauses operation; stores
*                     character pressed to memory variable CHECK.
   IF UPPER(CHECK)='Q'      && Checks for CHECK = RETURN (or blank).
      EXIT                  && Exits DO WHILE loop to end command file operation.
   ELSE                     && If CHECK is not "Q", uses following command lines.
      SKIP                  && Positions record pointer to following record.
   ENDIF                    && Completes IF statement; passes control to next line.
ENDDO                       && Completes DO WHILE statement.
USE                         && Closes the database file.
SET TALK ON                 && Turns dBASE dialog back on.
SET INTENSITY ON            && Turns reverse video back on.
CLEAR                       && Clears the screen.
CANCEL                      && Cancels command file operation.
```

3. Press **Ctrl-W** to write the command file to disk.

4. Run the command file by typing **DO SAY** and pressing **Return**. Compare your screen with the following, and respond to the prompts as indicated. Also notice how CLEAR GETS prevents data entry while READ lets you make changes.

```
          THIS PROGRAM ALLOWS UPDATING OF MEMBERSHIP INFORMATION
        Press "Q" to Quit, any other key to proceed _     (Press a key)


        Name          THOMPSON, BILL G.
        Address       4540 Garden Parkway    Bergenfield, NJ 07640
        Affiliation   Wilson Plastics
        Date Joined   16/11/83
        Age           28   Paid (Y/N)?  Y     (Press the Down Arrow 4 times)




        Press "Q" to Quit, any other key to proceed _     (Press a key)


        Name          PHILLIPS, GEORGE W.
        Address       11205 Dawn Drive       Lago Vista, TX 78641
        Affiliation   Austin Medical Center
        Date Joined   01/06/81
        Age           39   Paid (Y/N)?  Y     (Press the Down Arrow 4 times)




        Press "Q" to Quit, any other key to proceed _     (Type Q)

        Do Cancelled
          .
```

5. Continue experimenting with your command file by using alternate PICTURE clauses and rearranging the position of the displayed text.

6. When finished, type **ERASE SAY.PRG** and press **Return** to delete the command file from your disk.

7. Turn to Module 37 to continue the learning sequence.

Module 59
SELECT, SET RELATION TO

DESCRIPTION

The SELECT command lets you select any 1 of 10 possible database *work areas*. A work area contains a database, and if you like, corresponding database index files. Although work areas are normally called with numbers 1 through 10 or letters A through J, you can use *alias* names to associate a meaningful "handle" with each database file and index.

The SET RELATION function lets you establish a relationship between two databases based on a common field. For example, you may have two employee database files, each using a common NAME field. One may contain phone mail station information, while the other contains job code and salary information. The relation can be established on the NAME field. More information and an example is provided on the next few pages, once a more detailed description of the SELECT command and work areas is given.

SELECTING WORK AREAS   dBASE uses *work areas* in which database and index files are stored and from which they are called. The SELECT command is used to associate a database file with a work area. The general form of the SELECT command is:

```
SELECT 1
USE dbfile1
SELECT 2
USE dbfile2
```

Now that dbfile1 is associated with work area 1, you can call it with the command:

```
SELECT 1 or SELECT A
```

You can select work areas and name databases until you reach 10 (or J). However, it's necessary to use the CONFIG.SYS file that contains:

```
FILES=20
BUFFERS=15
```

in order to organize your computer's memory to support ten database files and the operation of corresponding index and command files.

You can assign an alias name to a database file using:

```
SELECT 1
USE dbfile1 ALIAS JOBFILE
```

Here, the alias JOBFILE is used to call dbfile1 into use. The command:

```
SELECT JOBFILE
```

does the trick. To bring a database and corresponding index files into work area 4, use:

    SELECT 4
    USE Members INDEX Namesort, Agesort ALIAS Namefile

This places the index files NAMESORT and AGESORT in use with the MEMBERS database file in work area 4. After being selected and put into use, you can call this combination of files back into use using the alias. Look at the two examples:

    SELECT NAMEFILE or SELECT 4

As you can see, when multiple databases are put into work areas, they are easy to access with the SELECT command.

RECORD POINTER CONTROL   The key to changing information within any database file is to position the record pointer at the desired location. The record pointer stays in place within each database until moved by some command. This is true for individual database operation as well as when you are using several databases in different work areas. Look at the following illustration.

Work Area	1	2	3
Database	Equip	Bldg	Land
Record No.	1 2 – pointer 3 4 5	1 2 3 4 – pointer 5	1 – pointer 2 3 4 5
Field Names	Des Price AccDep BookVal	Des Price Deprec BookVal	Des Price AccApp MktVal

The three databases (Equip, Bldg, and Land) are selected into work areas 1, 2, and 3 with the following commands:

    SELECT 1
    USE EQUIP
    SELECT 2
    USE BLDG
    SELECT 3
    USE LAND

To verify the active databases and their work areas, you can type **DISP STATUS** and press **Return** to see:

```
    Select area - 1, Database in use: B:equip.dbf    Alias - EQUIP

    Select area - 2, Database in use: B:bldg.dbf     Alias - BLDG

    Select area - 3, Database in use: B:land.dbf     Alias - LAND
```

Notice that the record pointer is positioned at a different record in the preceding diagram. Commands that affect field contents and structure operate only on the active database file. You can extract, exchange, or edit information within any of the pointed records, or within records that match some expression in the selected databases.

For example, if you want to add the BookVal and MktVal fields (these names stand for *book value* and *market value*) of the pointed records and store them to a memory variable named TOTVAL, you can use:

STORE EQUIP–>BOOKVAL + BLDG–>BOOKVAL + LAND–>MKTVAL TO TOTVAL

Notice that the –> symbol is used to establish the relationship between a database or alias name and field name. If you wish to find the value of all buildings, equipment, and land, position the record pointer to the first record in each database by selecting each with **SELECT ALIAS** and typing **GO TOP**. Then type:

SUM EQUIP–>BOOKVAL + BLDG–>BOOKVAL + LAND–>MKTVAL TO TOTVAL

You can display individual fields in any of the working databases by typing:

DISP *alias–>fieldname*

Commands that move the record pointer affect only the selected database. For example, you can append a blank record to one database with APPEND BLANK, and then position the record pointer to the blank record with GO BOTTOM. Next, you can SELECT a second database and find a record with the LOCATE command. Once at the desired record, you can use the REPLACE command to move field contents from the second database to first database with:

REPLACE *alias1–>fieldname* WITH *alias2–>fieldname*

You can also transfer the contents of memory variables to databases using aliases and field names. Look at the following example:

```
. MVAR = 12950              && Stores 12950 to memory variable MVAR.
. SELECT 2                  && Selects database in work area 2.
. REPLACE AMOUNT WITH MVAR  && Replaces the contents of the AMOUNT field
                               with the contents of MVAR (12950).
```

SET RELATION   The general form of the SET RELATION function is:

SET RELATION TO *fieldname* INTO *work area* or *alias*

Recalling the discussion at the beginning of this module, a relationship can be established between two databases using a common field. The field *must* be indexed in both databases, and both databases must be in selected work areas. An indexed field is referred to as a *key field*.

Restated, the SET RELATION TO *fieldname* INTO *work area* or *alias* establishes a relationship between the two databases that contain a common key field.

The database in the active work area is linked to a second database residing in the named work area. The record pointer is coordinated between the two databases by moving to records containing the key expression or a specified numeric value. Remember, the key expression *must* exist in an indexed field.

An example should help clarify. You may wish to follow along on your computer to see how the SELECT command and SET RELATION function operate.

1.   Use the ABC database used in Module 56. If necessary, recreate it and enter the data as shown.

```
. use abc
. list struc
Structure for database: abc.dbf
  Field  Field  Name      Type        Width   Dec
      1  Name             Character      20
      2  Phone            Character       4
      3  Mail             Character       4
** Total **                              29


. list
Record #    NAME              PHONE   MAIL
       1    Sergio, Vincent   4596    2084
       2    Bishop, Sam       2234    430
       3    Collins, Arthur   4554    323
       4    Harris, Robert    4335    2230
```

2.   Type **COPY FIELD NAME TO ABC1** and press **Return**.

3.   Type **INDEX ON NAME TO PBX** and press **Return**

```
00% indexed
100% indexed                  4 Records indexed
```

4. Type **USE ABC1** and press **Return**; then type **MODIFY STRUCTURE** and add fields 2 through 4 as shown.

```
Structure for database: abc1.dbf
Field  Field Name  Type       Width    Dec
    1  NAME        Character    20
    2  EMPL_DATE   Date          8
    3  JOB_CODE    Character     4
    4  RATE        Numeric       7      2
** Total **                     40
```

5. Edit the records, adding the information in the EMPLDATE, JOBCODE, and RATE fields as shown.

```
Record#  NAME              EMPL_DATE JOB_CODE    RATE
      1  Sergio, Vincent   05/16/86  2320     2150.00
      2  Bishop, Sam       08/01/76  3200     4300.00
      3  Collins, Arthur   01/16/85  2145     2350.00
      4  Harris, Robert    06/01/86  1150     2425.00
```

6. Type **INDEX ON NAME TO EMPL** and press **Return**.

```
    100% indexed              4 Records indexed
```

7. Type the following instructions from the dot prompt, ending each with **Return**.

```
. select 1
. use abc index pbx
. select 2
. use abc1 index empl
. set relation to name into A
. display status
```

```
Select area:  1, Database in Use: C:abc.dbf   Alias: ABC
    Master index file:  C:pbx.ndx  Key: name

Currently Selected Database:
Select area:  2, Database in Use: C:abc1.dbf   Alias: ABC1
    Master index file:  C:empl.ndx  Key: name
    Related into: ABC
    Relation: name
```

8. Type the following command line and notice the resulting display.

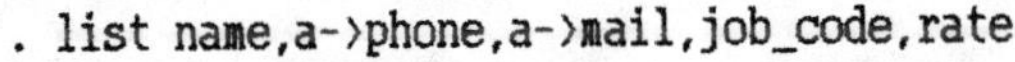

```
. list name,a->phone,a->mail,job_code,rate

Record#  name               a->phone a->mail job_code   rate
      2  Bishop, Sam          2234     430    3200    4300.00
      3  Collins, Arthur      4554     323    2145    2350.00
      4  Harris, Robert       4335    2230    1150    2425.00
      1  Sergio, Vincent      4596    2084    2320    2150.00
```

9. Notice how information from both databases is displayed simultaneously.

10. Type **CLOSE ALL** and press **Return**.

11. Use the following ERASE commands to restore disk space.

```
ERASE ABC1.DBF
ERASE PBX.NDX
ERASE EMPL.NDX
```

APPLICATIONS

Many applications require large amounts of data, such as accounting applications that combine sales order-entry, accounts receivable, and inventory. A residential real estate database can require close to 150 data elements when considering all information required in a multiple-listing agreement (ownership information, terms, legal descriptions, structural descriptions, land descriptions, room sizes, appliances, utilities, tax districts, and so on).

The ability to simultaneously use up to ten database files lets you ramble around in 1,280 fields instead of 128. By combining this amount of power with available memory variables, you can design extremely versatile applications.

TYPICAL OPERATION

In this illustration the SELECT command is used in a command file that addresses three databases. A blank record is appended to the bottom of one and data is transferred between the databases. Begin at the dBASE dot prompt.

1. Create 3 databases having the names and structures shown in the following lists.

```
Structure for database : Equip.dbf
Field  Field name  Type        Width    Dec
    1  DES         Character      15
    2  PRICE       Numeric         9      2
    3  ACCDEP      Numeric         9      2
    4  BOOKVAL     Numeric         9      2
```

```
Structure for database : Bldg.dbf
Field  Field name  Type       Width   Dec
    1  DES         Character     15
    2  PRICE       Numeric        9     2
    3  ACCDEP      Numeric        9     2
    4  BOOKVAL     Numeric        9     2

Structure for database : Consol.dbf
Field  Field name  Type       Width   Dec
    1  TEQUIP      Numeric        9     2
    2  TBLDG       Numeric        9     2
```

2. Enter the data in the EQUIP and BLDG databases as shown:

```
Contents of Equip.dbf:
Record#  DES              PRICE    ACCDEP    BOOKVAL
     1   Computer       4120.00   1248.00    2872.00
     2   Desk            795.00    265.00     530.00
     3   Printer        1895.00    425.00    1470.00

Contents of Bldg.dbf:
Record#  DES              PRICE    ACCDEP    BOOKVAL
     1   Warehouse    350000.00  90210.00  259790.00
     2   Plant        750225.00 235550.00  514675.00
     3   Sales Office 210000.00  20110.00  189890.00
```

3. From the dBASE dot prompt type **MODIFY COMMAND SELECT** and press **Return** to use the dBASE editor.

4. Type the SELECT command file. (Don't type the explanatory remarks.)

```
                                    Remarks
* SELECT.PRG            && Demonstrates uses of multiple databases with SELECT command.
CLEAR                   && Clears the screen.
SET TALK OFF            && Turns off dBASE dialog.
TEXT
         This utility consolidates all equipment and building
         values into a common database and displays the results.
ENDTEXT
?
WAIT
CLEAR                   && Clears screen.
SELECT 1                && Selects first database work area.
USE EQUIP               && Puts EQUIP database in use.
```

```
SELECT 2                      && Selects second database work area.
USE BLDG                      && Puts BLDG database in use.
SELECT 3                      && Selects third database work area.
USE CONSOL                    && Puts CONSOL database in use.
ZAP                           && Deletes all records in CONSOL database.
CLEAR                         && Clears the screen.
APPEND BLANK                  && Adds a blank record to the CONSOL database.
SELECT EQUIP                  && Selects EQUIP database.
SUM BOOKVAL TO MEQUIP         && Sums value of all equipment to the memory variable MEQUIP.
SELECT BLDG                   && Selects BLDG database.
SUM BOOKVAL TO MBLDG          && Sums value of all buildings to the memory variable MBLDG.
SELECT CONSOL                 && Selects the CONSOL database.
REPLACE TEQUIP WITH MEQUIP && Replaces contents of TEQUIP field with value of TBLDG.
REPLACE TBLDG WITH MBLDG   && Replaces contents of TBLDG field with value of MBLDG.
@ 10,20 SAY 'Total Equipment Value: ' get TEQUIP PICTURE '$9999999.99'
@ 12,20 SAY 'Total Building Value : ' get TBLDG PICTURE ' $9999999.99'
CLEAR GETS                    && Prevents changes to field values.
?                             && Displays a blank line.
WAIT                          && Pauses operation; displays "Press any key... " prompt.
CLEAR ALL                     && Closes all database files.
CLEAR                         && Clears the screen.
SET TALK ON                   && Turns dBASE dialog back on.
CANCEL                        && Cancels command file operation.
```

5. Press **Ctrl-W** to write the command file to disk.

6. Type **DO SELECT** and press **Return** to run the command file. Respond to the prompts as indicated.

```
           This utility consolidates all equipment and building
         values into a common database and displays the results.


    Press any key to continue...               (Press any key)


    Zap Consol.dbf? (Y/N) Yes                       (Type Y)


            Total Equipment Value:   $$$$4872.00


            Total Building Value :   $$964355.00


    Press any key to continue...               (Press any key)
    Do cancelled
```

7. After you have experimented with the command file, erase it and the CONSOL and EQUIP databases by typing:

   ERASE EQUIP.DBF
   ERASE CONSOL.DBF
   ERASE SELECT.PRG

8. Turn to Module 44 to continue the learning sequence.

Module 60
SET FUNCTIONS

DESCRIPTION

The dBASE program has a large repertoire of SET functions used to control the dBASE operating environment. For example, SET TALK OFF is a function you've used in command files to turn off the dBASE dialog. SET TALK ON turns the dialogue back on. SET PRINT ON directs displayed information to your printer. SET PRINT OFF turns simultaneous printing back off. These and many other SET functions are summarized in this module.

When you start dBASE, a number of pre-established SET values exist. These existing values are called *defaults*. You can change default values by entering the appropriate SET function in a command file or from the dot prompt.

For example, if you want to change the default drive to B, you can type **SET DEFAULT TO B**. If you want to turn off the dBASE dialog, which is normally on, you can type **SET TALK OFF**.

You can check the status of several SET functions by typing **LIST STATUS** and pressing **Return**. The following information is displayed by dBASE.

```
File search path:
Default disk drive: C:
Print destination:  PRN:
Margin =      0
Current work area =    1


ALTERNATE  - OFF   DELETED    - OFF   FIXED      - OFF   SAFETY     - ON
BELL       - ON    DELIMITERS - OFF   HEADING    - ON    SCOREBOARD - ON
CARRY      - OFF   DEVICE     - SCRN  HELP       - ON    STATUS     - OFF
CATALOG    - OFF   DOHISTORY  - OFF   HISTORY    - ON    STEP       - OFF
CENTURY    - OFF   ECHO       - OFF   INTENSITY  - ON    TALK       - ON
CONFIRM    - OFF   ESCAPE     - ON    MENU       - ON    TITLE      - ON
CONSOLE    - ON    EXACT      - OFF   PRINT      - OFF   UNIQUE     - OFF
DEBUG      - OFF   FIELDS     - OFF


Programmable function keys:
F2  - assist;
F3  - list;
F4  - dir;
F5  - display structure;
```

```
F6  - display status;
F7  - display memory;
F8  - display;
F9  - append;
F10 - edit;
```

Notice the list of function key assignments. You may want to use function keys in place of typing commands. For example, instead of typing **LIST** and pressing **Return**, you can press **F3**. The semicolon following the function key assignment represents the **Return** key.

You can change default parameters by typing the appropriate command from the dot prompt or by embedding the command within a command file. For instance, if you want to direct displayed output to your printer, you can type **SET DEVICE TO PRINT**. You can also type **SET** and press **Return** to use dBASE's built-in ASSIST function. Here, you can review and change SET parameters from a series of menus. The SET parameter menus include:

Options	Files
Screen	Margin
Keys	Decimals
Disk	

Typing **SET** and pressing **Return** displays the first menu window, which displays a series of SET options as shown in the following screen illustration.

```
   Options    Screen    Keys    Disk    Files    Margin    Decimals

   ┌─────────────────────┐
   │ Alternate   OFF     │
   │ Bell        ON      │
   │ Carry       OFF     │
   │ Catalog             │
   │ Century     OFF     │
   │ Confirm     OFF     │
   │ Deleted     OFF     │
   │ Delimiters  OFF     │
   │ Device      SCREEN  │
   │ Dohistory   OFF     │
   │ Escape      ON      │
   │ Exact       OFF     │
   │ Fields      OFF     │
   │ Fixed       OFF     │
   │ Heading     ON      │
   │ Help        ON      │
   │ History     ON      │
   │ Intensity   ON      │
   └─────────────────────┘
```

You can move through the options within a menu window with the down or up cursor key. Lateral movement across the menu bar is accompished with the right or left cursor key. The following illustrations show you the choices in each menu selection.

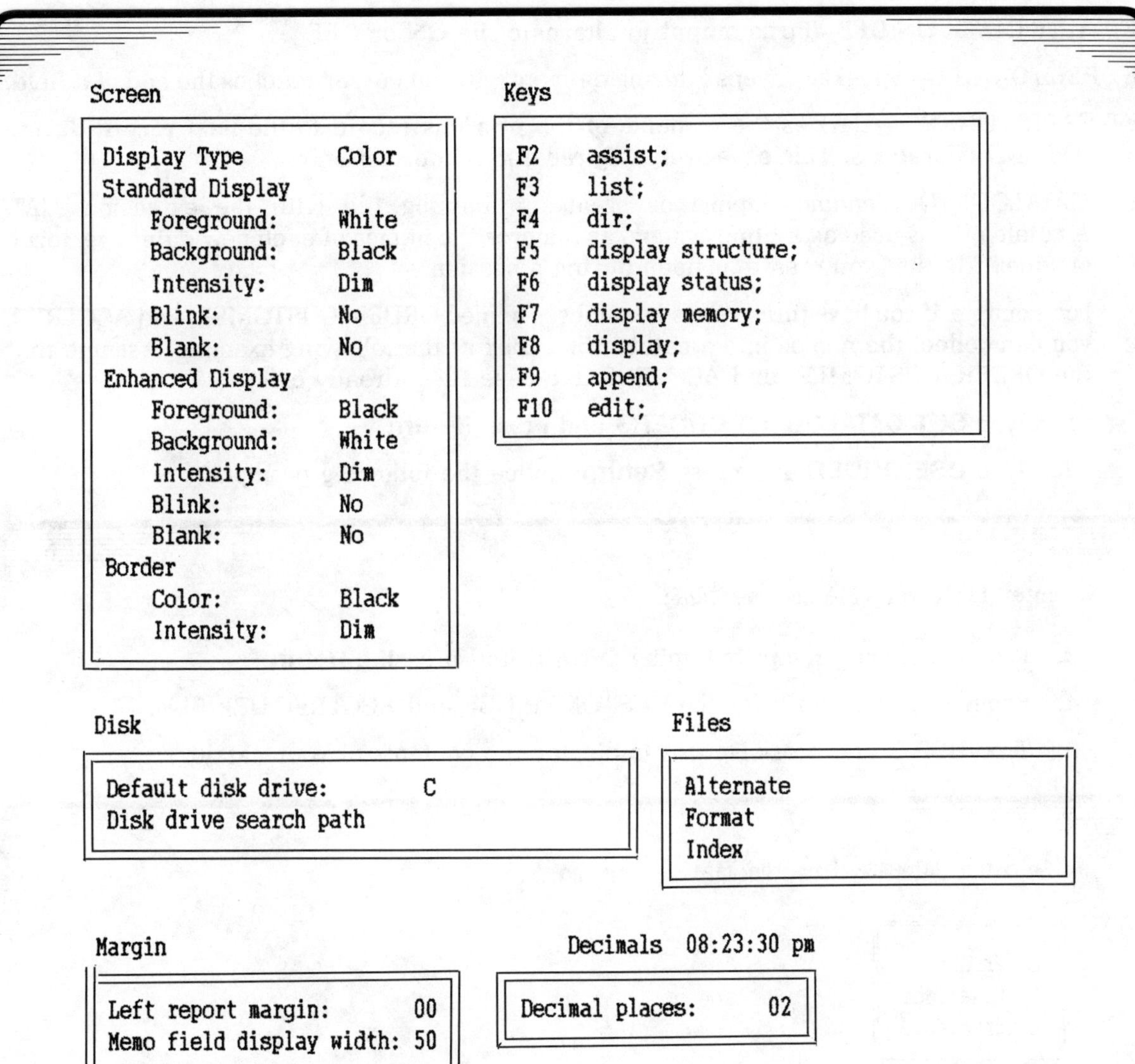

Each of the SET functions is described in the following list. The boldfaced parameter is the default value.

SET ALTERNATE TO *filename*—Directs displayed information to a file. The filename has the extension .TXT unless another is specified.

SET ALTERNATE ON/**OFF**—Turns output to alternate file ON or OFF.

SET BELL **ON**/OFF—Speaker "beeps" during data entry when cursor reaches the end of a field.

SET CARRY ON/**OFF**—Carries the contents of the previous record to the next record during APPEND operations. This saves retyping repetitive information.

SET CATALOG TO *filename*—Opens or creates a catalog file with the extension .CAT. A catalog file is used as a filing system, as it stores the names of each new database, form, or index file that you create or open during a session.

For example, if you have three related databases named ORDER, CUSTOMER, and ACCTREC, you can collect the names into a catalog file. Look at the following example. Assume that the ORDER, CUSTOMER, and ACCTREC database files already exist.

1. Type **SET CATALOG TO ORDERS** and press **Return**.

2. Type **USE ORDER** and press **Return**; notice the following prompt.

```
    Enter title for file customer.dbf:
```

3. Respond to the prompt by typing **ORDER** and pressing **Return**.

4. Repeat steps 2 and 3 for the CUSTOMER.DBF and ACCTREC.DBF files.

5. Type **USE ?** and press **Return** to display the contents of your catalog.

```
    Select a DATABASE from the list.        Ins

        order.dbf
        customer.dbf
        acctrec.dbf
```

```
order
```

This screen lets you select the desired database file with the **Up** or **Down Arrow** and **Return** keys.

If no catalog file is open or if you close the catalog file with **SET CATALOG TO** and **Return**, you can display the names of your catalog files with **SET CATALOG TO ?**.

SET CATALOG **ON**/OFF—The SET CATALOG command is normally ON, which lets you display and select existing catalogs from the dot prompt. If you wish to view your catalog names, use the SET CATALOG TO ? command.

You can discontinue the process of adding filenames to an open catalog file, but leave the catalog file open, with SET CATALOG OFF.

SET CENTURY ON/**OFF**—When ON, this SET command displays a four-digit year in the form 07/19/1988. The OFF setting displays the date in the form 07/19/88.

SET COLOR ON/OFF, SET COLOR TO—The SET COLOR command is used to set colors on a color monitor. If you have a monochrome monitor, the SET COLOR command is used to set text attributes, like bold, flashing, or underlined text. The SET COLOR command is controlled by the type of system you have, monochrome or color.

The general form of the SET COLOR command is:

SET COLOR TO *standard, enhanced, border, background*

where

standard is normal light-on-dark text.
enhanced is reversed dark-on-light text (inverse video).
border is the area around the edge of the screen.
background is the background color of the main screen area.

The color codes are:

Color	Code	Color	Code
Black	N	Red	R
Blue	B	Magenta	RB
Green	G	Brown	GR
Cyan	BG	White	W
Blank	X		

You can use * with a color code to designate blinking; use + with the color code for a high intensity (or bright) display.

Monochrome systems use U for underline, I for inverse video. Some monochrome systems have RGB color adapters, such as the Compaq and Eagle Spirit XL microcomputers. The U and I codes have no affect on these systems.

You can use the color codes with a *foreground/background* technique. For example, if you want bright white foreground text on a deep blue background, you can use:

. SET COLOR TO W+/B.

If you want bright yellow letters on a red background in your enhanced (inverse video) areas, add the second attribute:

. SET COLOR TO W+/B,GR+/R

Finally, if you want your border to match the blue background, use

. SET COLOR TO W+/B,GR+/R,B

To return to the default colors, type **SET COLOR TO** and press **Return**.

SET CONFIRM ON/**OFF**—A **Return** is required to complete data entry within a field when ON.

SET DATE *country*—This SET command configures the way the date is displayed. The following list shows the countries and corresponding date formats:

Country	Date Format
AMERICAN	mm/dd/yy
ANSI	yy.dd.yy
BRITISH, FRENCH, GERMAN	dd/mm/yy
ITALIAN	dd-mm-yy

where: mm = month, dd = day, yy = year

The default is in the American format, mm/dd/yy.

Check the following command example:

```
. ? date
07/19/87
. set date italian
. ? date()
19-07-86
.
```

SET DEBUG ON/**OFF**—Displayed output is sent to the printer when ON.

SET DECIMALS—This SET command controls the number of displayed decimal places. The general form of the command is:

. SET DECIMALS TO *n*

where n is a number corresponding to the number of decimal places you want to display. The following example demonstrates the SET DECIMALS TO command.

```
. x = 5.5
5.5
. ? sqrt(x)
        2.3
. set decimals to 6
. ? sqrt(x)
        2.345208
.
```

SET DEFAULT TO *drive*—Directs all commands and file searches to the designated disk drive.

SET DELETED ON/OFF—Commands like LIST and COPY ignore records marked for deletion when ON. The INDEX command does not ignore deleted records.

SET DELIMITER TO '/'—Specifies a character (/) to show field boundaries during data entry. SET DELIMITER ON is used to display the specified delimiter character. The default delimiter is a colon (:).

SET DELIMITER TO DEFAULT—Displays colons as the default delimiter character.

SET DELIMITER ON/OFF—Displays the delimiter characters when ON.

SET DEVICE TO SCREEN/PRINT—Displayed output is directed to your printer when SET DEVICE TO PRINT is used.

SET DOHISTORY ON/OFF—The SET DOHISTORY command controls whether the command lines within an executing command file are captured in the history buffer. The history buffer stores the last 20 command lines entered from the dot prompt or used in a command file, if SET DOHISTORY is ON. The SET DOHISTORY command is normally OFF, because ON slows program execution. The HISTORY file is a handy debugging tool, because it displays the last 20 command lines. If there is an error, you can enter LIST HISTORY to examine each command line for defective syntax. Experience the use of the SET DOHISTORY command as follows:

1. Create the following short command file named MENU1.PRG.

```
* MENU1.PRG -- Display menu window and pause operation.
CLEAR
@ 2,10 TO 15,70 DOUBLE
@ 3,12 TO 14,68
@ 5,13 TO 5,67
@ 4,40 SAY CHR(197)
@ 15,1 SAY ' '
WAIT
RETURN
```

2. Type **SET DOHISTORY ON**; then type **DO FRAME** and press **Return**.

3. Notice that a window is displayed and you are prompted to press any key.

4. Press **Return**, and then type **LIST HISTORY**. Notice that your command file was captured in the history buffer.

```
modi comm menu1
set dohistory on
do menu1
@ 2,10 TO 15,70 DOUBLE
@ 3,12 TO 14,68
@ 5,13 TO 5,67
@ 4,40 SAY CHR(197)
@ 15,1 SAY ' '
WAIT
RETURN
list history
```

5. Notice that the comment line in the command file is not included in the history buffer, because it is not executed.

TIP: If you want to capture the contents of your history buffer to a file, use the SET ALTERNATE TO *filename* and SET ALTERNATE ON commands. Then type **LIST HISTORY** and press **Return**. Next, close the alternate file with CLOSE ALTERNATE. To view the contents of the new file, use **TYPE** *filename* and press **Return** from the dot prompt.

SET ECHO ON/**OFF**—Echoes command lines to the screen during command file operation when ON. Used as a debugging tool.

SET ESCAPE ON/**OFF**—Pressing **Esc** halts program operation, unless you use the SET ESCAPE OFF command. SET ESCAPE is normally ON. When OFF, pressing **Esc** does not interrupt program operation.

SET FIELDS ON/**OFF**, SET FIELDS TO *field list*—The SET FIELDS commands are used in combination to designate which fields within a database are displayed or edited. For example, the following ADDRESS database has the following structure.

```
Field  Field Name  Type       Width  Dec
    1  NAME        Character     20
    2  ADDRESS     Character     20
    3  CITY        Character     15
    4  STATE       Character      2
    5  ZIP         Character      5
    6  JOINED      Date           8
    7  AGE         Numeric        3
** Total **                      74
```

The contents of the database are:

```
#  NAME            ADDRESS             CITY          STATE ZIP   JOINED   AGE
1  John Billings   2320 Hawthorne Ave. Trenton       NJ    03565 05/12/81 36
2  Mary Tremore    56 Park Lane        Culver City   CA    95065 11/01/83 27
3  Fred Franklin   3900 Brookside Road Hobbs         NM    85676 09/18/79 43
4  Chuck Williams  56 Walmart Plaza    Jasper        TX    75611 07/11/80 39
```

To restrict the display to the NAME, CITY, AND STATE fields, use:

. set fields to name, city, state

Now you can use SET FIELDS ON to make use of the SET FIELDS TO *field list* command. The LIST command gives you:

```
. use address
. set fields to name,city,state
. set fields on
. list
Record#  NAME                CITY            STATE
      1  John Billings       Trenton         NJ
      2  Mary Tremore        Culver City     CA
      3  Fred Franklin       Hobbs           NM
      4  Chuck Williams      Jasper          TX
```

When the SET FIELDS command is active, as in the example, displaying the database structure shows you which fields are selected.

```
. use address
. set fields to name, city, state
. set fields on
. display structure
Structure for database: C:address.dbf
Number of data records:        4
Date of last update   : 07/19/88
Field  Field Name  Type        Width    Dec
    1  >NAME       Character      20
    2  ADDRESS     Character      20
    3  >CITY       Character      15
    4  >STATE      Character       2
    5  ZIP         Character       5
    6  JOINED      Date            8
    7  AGE         Numeric         3
** Total **                      74
```

You can cancel the SET FIELD TO command (or filter) with SET FIELDS OFF or SET FIELDS TO ALL.

The SET FIELDS TO command does not establish the order of display. It only selects the fields within the open database file.
The SET FIELDS TO command is also used with CREATE VIEW FROM ENVIRONMENT to define the fields which make up the environment. You may wish to review the CREATE/MODIFY VIEW command as a quick refresher.

You can select fields in other work areas by preceding the field name with the filename's alias, in the form:

alias—>field2

The SET FIELDS TO command interacts with the following commands:

AVERAGE	COPY STRUCTURE	LIST	@...GET
BROWSE	DISPLAY	REPLACE	
CHANGE	EDIT	SUM	
COPY TO	JOIN	TOTAL	

The following commands ignore the SET FIELDS commands:

INDEX	SET FILTER
LOCATE	SET RELATION

SET EXACT ON/OFF—Requires an exact match when comparing data in a command like LOCATE FOR *fieldname = expression*. When OFF, partial matches suffice.

SET FILTER TO—The SET FILTER TO command is used to establish a condition, such as a "FOR expression," to restrict operation to the use of records within the active database file that match the established condition.

For example, SET FILTER TO ZIP > = '80000' restricts use to those records having a ZIP code number equal to or greater than 80000. Commands like BROWSE, EDIT, REPORT and so on comply with the SET FILTER condition.

You can also specify an existing query file, with the extension .QRY, to provide the filter condition. Using SET FILTER TO *filename* selects the named query file. Of course, the query file must have been created using the active database file. Refer to the CREATE/MODIFY QUERY command information if you need to refresh your memory.

If you have a catalog (see SET CATALOG TO), you can use **SET FILTER TO ?** to display a list of all query files, if any exist, associated with the active database file. Query (.QRY) files provide a filter condition to control which records are used in the active database file.

Finally, you can disengage the filter condition by typing **SET FILTER TO** and pressing **Return**.

You should be aware that the filter condition does not take effect until a command is used that causes the record pointer to change position.

SET FIXED ON/**OFF**—Determines whether the number of decimal places displayed as the result of calculations are set to the SET DECIMALS TO n value, or the default value of two places.

SET FORMAT TO *filename*—Uses the specified filename (a format file containing @ row,col SAY-GET commands) to display data entry masks with the APPEND, CHANGE, EDIT, and INSERT commands. The format file has a .FMT extension and is created with the dBASE III full-screen editor.

SET FUNCTION n TO *expression*—Lets you reprogram the function key (n) of your choice except for F1, which is not reprogrammable. Up to 30 characters can be used in the command string. The semicolon (;) is used to provide an automatic Return. Without the semicolon, Return must be pressed from the keyboard to enter the command string.

Example:

SET FUNCTION 2 TO BROWSE;

Pressing F2 enters BROWSE < cr.

SET HEADING **ON**/OFF—Field names are displayed above field contents when ON.

SET HELP **ON**/OFF—Controls the display of "Do you want some help? (Y/N)" when ran entry error is made.

SET HISTORY **ON**/OFF—The SET HISTORY command is normally ON. When it is ON, the last 20 commands entered from the dot prompt are kept in a history buffer. To view these commands, use LIST HISTORY. If SET DOHISTORY ON is active, the command lines in your dBASE III Plus program files are stored in the history buffer. You can turn your history buffer off with SET HISTORY OFF.

SET HISTORY TO n—Normally, the last 20 command lines are kept in the history buffer. The SET HISTORY TO command lets you provide a number between zero and 16,000 to change the size of the history buffer. For example, the command **SET HISTORY TO 100** stores the last 100 command lines in the history buffer.

SET INDEX TO *filename*—Opens the named index file.

SET INTENSITY **ON**/OFF—Turns reverse video on and off when @ row,col GET commands are used.

SET MARGIN TO n—Sets the left margin a specified number (n) of spaces from the left edge of the printed page. Does not effect displayed text.

Example:

SET MARGIN TO 10

Sets the left margin 10 spaces to the right.

SET MEMOWIDTH TO n—The SET MEMOWIDTH TO command controls the width of memo field output. The normal value is 50 characters, but there may be times when you want to change the width.

SET MENUS ON/OFF—Turns full-screen command menus on and off. When ON, user help information is displayed when commands like MODIFY STRUCTURE are used.

SET MESSAGE TO *text*—This command lets you display a line of text on the bottom line of your screen. To see the line, SET STATUS ON must be in effect. Look at the following example.

. SET MESSAGE TO 'Do not press Esc'

displays "Do not press Esc" on the bottom line of your screen. You can enclose the message in single or double quotes or square brackets.

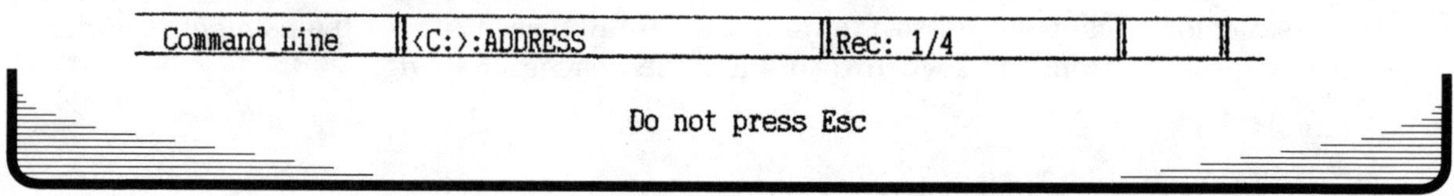

SET ORDER TO *n*—This command selects any one of up to seven open index files (numbered 1 through 7) as the controlling index file. That is, the controlling index file determines the order in which records are listed. The number 0 assigns control to the database file, using the unindexed order. For example, assume that you are working with a database file that has two indexes. The first index file uses the LastName field. The second index file uses the Salary field. The structure is:

```
    First Name
   *Last Name
    Address
    City
    State
    Zip
    Department
    Empl_Date
  **Salary
```

    * Designates key field for the first index file (1).
   ** Designates key field for the second index file (2).

If you want to list information by last name, you can use SET ORDER TO 1. If you want to list information in salary order, use SET ORDER TO 2. Finally, if you want to use the natural order of the unindexed database file, use SET ORDER TO 0.

The major advantage of the SET ORDER command is speed. It saves time because it doesn't have to open and close index files or move the record pointer.

SET PATH TO *path list*—Searches the specified drive(s) and pathname(s) to locate a specified filename.

SET PATH TO B:\DB\PRGS

Searches the current directory, then the \DB\PRGS subdirectory on disk drive B.

SET PRINT ON/OFF—Directs displayed text to your printer when ON. This includes text displayed with the print statement (?) and with @ row,col SAY commands.

SET PROCEDURE TO *filename*—Opens a procedure file containing from one to 32 utility programs (or procedures). These programs (or command file elements) are normally called from a command file.

<pre>
                              Remarks
SET PROCEDURE TO PROCFILE   && Opens PROCFILE file, which contains one or
*   more procedures.
DO PRNT   && Uses the PRNT utility within PROCFILE.
</pre>

SET RELATION TO *key expression* **INTO** *alias*—Establishes a relationship between two databases that contain a common key expression. The database in the active work area (see Module 51) is linked to a second database in a selected work area. The second database is called by its alias. The record pointer is coordinated between the two databases by moving to the record containing the key expression or a specified numeric value. The key expression must exist in an indexed (key) field.

<pre>
. SELECT 1   . SET RELATION TO PN INTO INVTORY FOR PN = 'ER-1500'
. USE INVTORY   . DISPLAY
. SELECT 2   Record# DES   PN   QTY   COST PRICE RESERVED
. USE INVPRICE INDEX PR   or   1 Battery   ER-1500   95   .47   1.05   0
. SELECT INVTORY   . SELECT 1
. SET RELATION TO PN INTO INVTORY   . DISPLAY
                                        Record# DES   PN   QTY   COST
                                            1 Battery   ER-1500   220   .47
</pre>

In the second example, the linkage is established by the part number. Notice that the record pointer is located at the appropriate records.

SET SAFETY ON/OFF—Displays the following user message when ON.

filename already exists, overwrite it? (Y/N)

SET STATUS ON/OFF—The SET STATUS command lets you display and suppress the display of a status bar at the bottom of the screen when you are working from the dot prompt. The status bar contains information about the active disk drive, database filename, and record pointer position. It is suppressed with SET STATUS OFF. It is turned on with SET STATUS ON.

SET TITLE **ON**/OFF—The SET TITLE command is used to display or suppress the display of the catalog file title prompt. When ON, you see a prompt similar to:

```
    Enter title for file address.dbf:
```

When OFF, you are not prompted to enter the file title. The file name is entered automatically. You must edit the title at a later time. The SET TITLE command is normally ON.

SET STEP ON/**OFF**—Halts command file operation after each command line. Lets you debug a program one step at a time.

SET TALK ON/**OFF**—Turns dBASE's user dialog on and off. Having the dialog on during command file operation displays extraneous text.

SET TYPEAHEAD TO *n*—The SET TYPEAHEAD command is used to control the size of the type-ahead buffer, which stores typed keystrokes while your computer is busy performing some task. The SET TYPEAHEAD command works only when SET ESCAPE ON is in effect. The normal type-ahead buffer size is 20. The maximum size of the type-ahead buffer is 32,000.

You can disable the type-ahead buffer with SET TYPEAHEAD TO 0, which disables the ON KEY command and the INKEY( ) function. The zero value setting is often used in conjunction with a command file using ON ERROR. This prevents buffering, giving control to the command lines designed to interact with error detection.

If you attempt to type beyond the limit of the type-ahead buffer, keystrokes are lost. If SET BELL is ON, your speaker alerts you when the buffer reaches its limit.

SET UNIQUE **ON**/OFF—Used with the INDEX command to transfer only one record containing the specified field.

```
SET UNIQUE ON
INDEX ON ZIP TO ZIPLIST
  193 Records indexed
```

There are 193 unique ZIP Codes in the active database.

SET VIEW TO *.vue filename*—The SET VIEW command is used to open a view file. The CREATE/MODIFY VIEW module describes the creation and use of view files, and guides you through the creation process.

In general, view files control the display of database information. View files list database and index files, their work areas, and the active work area; the relations between the database files; the active field list; the filter; and any open format (.FMT) files used.

As you can see, there are many helpful SET functions for controlling the way information is displayed, printed, and interpreted by dBASE. There are several SET functions that you'll rarely use, but there are others that you'll use in almost every command file you write, like SET TALK OFF/ON.

APPLICATIONS

SET functions are used in both the interactive mode and within command files. Some of the most frequently used SET functions are used to send displayed information to your printer (SET PRINT ON), to turn off half-intensity (or reverse video) display (SET INTENSITY OFF), and to turn off the dBASE message dialog.

During the development of this book, SET ALTERNATE TO *filename* and SET ALTERNATE ON were used to save typed and displayed information into text files, which were automatically assigned the extension .TXT. This enabled the capture of dBASE dialog, command file prompts, and database listings, which were then combined with descriptive text for use as examples. In fact, every command file in this book was written and run, and the resulting displays were sent to text files with the SET ALTERNATE TO function. This function is demonstrated in the Typical Operation section of this module.

TYPICAL OPERATION

In this illustration the SET ALTERNATE TO function is used with the PICNIC database, created in Module 63, to save displayed information to a text file. Then you view the text file using the dBASE editor. Begin at the dBASE dot prompt.

1. Type the indicated commands. Follow each by pressing **Return**.

    . SET ALTERNATE TO B:TEST. SET ALTERNATE ON. USE PICNIC

2. Type **LIST** and press **Return**. Compare your screen to the following:

```
. set alternate to test
. set alternate on
. use picnic
. list
Record#  NAME              GUESTS BRING      AMOUNT MEASURE
      1  Johns, Bill            3 Chips           5 Bags
      2  Collins, Ric           4 Dip             3 Cartons
      3  Miller, Gary           3 Hot Dogs        6 Packs
      4  Dickens, Charles       2 Mustard         1 Jar
      5  Crandal, Phil          4 Buns            5 Packs
      6  Johnson, J.D.          4 Chips           3 Bags
      7  Struthers, Susan       4 Pickles         1 Jar
      8  Cantwell, Julie        3 Beans           1 Pot
      9  Hicks, Ginger          3 Hot Dogs        3 Packs
     10  Tolliver, Greg         4 Buns            6 Packs
     11  Stevens, Jan           3 Chips           5 Packs
     12  Farris, Jody           3 Relish          1 Jar
     13  Jasper, Dave           2 Dip             2 Cartons
```

3. Type **CLOSE ALTERNATE** to close the **TEST.TXT** file created in step 1.

4. Type **MODIFY COMMAND TEST.TXT** and press **Return**. Notice that the typed commands and displayed listings contained in the previous steps are displayed.

```
. use picnic
. list
Record#  NAME                 GUESTS BRING        AMOUNT MEASURE
      1  Johns, Bill               3 Chips             5 Bags
      2  Collins, Ric              4 Dip               3 Cartons
      3  Miller, Gary              3 Hot Dogs          6 Packs
      4  Dickens, Charles          2 Mustard           1 Jar
      5  Crandal, Phil             4 Buns              5 Packs
      6  Johnson, J.D.             4 Chips             3 Bags
      7  Struthers, Susan          4 Pickles           1 Jar
      8  Cantwell, Julie           3 Beans             1 Pot
      9  Hicks, Ginger             3 Hot Dogs          3 Packs
     10  Tolliver, Greg            4 Buns              6 Packs
     11  Stevens, Jan              3 Chips             5 Packs
     12  Farris, Jody              3 Relish            1 Jar
     13  Jasper, Dave              2 Dip               2 Cartons
. close alternate
```

5. Press **Ctrl-Q** to abort. You're now back at the dBASE dot prompt.

6. If you want to conserve disk space, delete the TEST.TXT file by typing **ERASE TEST.TXT** and pressing **Return**.

7. Turn to Module 49 to continue the learning sequence.

Module 61
SORT

DESCRIPTION

The SORT command gives you the ability to copy the records and structure of a database to another database file arranged in either alphabetical, numerical, or alphanumeric order. The SORT is done on one or more named fields within the active database. You can also specify whether the SORT should be in ascending (A to Z or 0 to 9) or descending (Z to A or 9 to 0) order.

The following examples show forms of the SORT command accompanied by explanations of each. Before using SORT, place the desired database in use.

1. SORT ON *fieldname* TO *filename*   Copies database structure and contents, sorted on the named field in alphanumeric (ascending) order, to the named file.

    . SORT ON CITY TO NEWADR

2. SORT ON *fieldname* TO *filename* DESCENDING   Copies database structure and contents, sorted on the named field in descending order, to the named file.

    . SORT ON AGE/D TO TEMPFILE

3. SORT ON *field1, field2,* . . . TO *filename*   Copies the database to the specified filename organized on field1 and field2. This is called a *multiple-variable sort*. When entries in field1 are identical, field2 determines the order.

    . SORT ON AGE, NAME TO NEWFILE

4. SORT ON *field1* TO *filename* FOR *expression*   Sorts those records matching the expression to the designated file.

    . SORT ON NAME, AGE TO TENNIS35 FOR AGE $>=$ 35

As you can see, the SORT command is powerful. It resembles the COPY command (Module 16) except that you can organize your records in alphanumeric order. One limitation is that SORT doesn't let you use the SDF, DELIMITED, and TYPE clauses.

APPLICATIONS

The SORT command lets you enter data into a database in random order. Once the datab is entered, you can sort it in alphanumeric order. For example, you may wish to print a list of names contained in a database and use the list as a telephone directory. You'll probably want to sort them alphabetically before you print them. The SORT command is an excellent tool to use in the preparation of an address or telephone list. If you want to arrange an inventory database in part number order, you can use the SORT command for this too.

If you want to convert a database to standard data file format in sorted order, you can use a simple 2-step process. First sort the database; then use the target file and the appropriate COPY SDF or COPY DELIMITED WITH commands (Module 16) to convert the file to a .TXT file.

TYPICAL OPERATION

In this illustration the SORT command is used to rearrange the ABC database, last modified in Module 56, to a temporary database named ABCSORT. Then it is copied to a text file using the COPY SDF command. Begin at the dBASE dot prompt.

1. Type **USE ABC** and press **Return**.

2. Type **LIST** and press **Return**. Compare your screen to the following:

```
Record#  NAME              PHONE MAIL
      1  Sergio, Vincent   4596  2084
      2  Bishop, Sam       2234  430
      3  Collins, Arthur   4554  323
      4  Harris, Robert    4353  2230
```

3. Type **SORT ON NAME TO ABCSORT** and press **Return**.

4. Type **USE ABCSORT** and press **Return**; then type LIST and press **Return**. Check for the following display.

```
Record#  NAME              PHONE MAIL
      1  Bishop, Sam       2234  430
      2  Collins, Arthur   4554  323
      3  Harris, Robert    4353  2230
      4  Sergio, Vincent   4596  2084
```

5. Type **COPY TO TEXT DELIMITED WITH BLANK** and press **Return**.

6. Type **TYPE TEXT.TXT** and press **Return**. Check your display.

```
Bishop, Sam 2234 430
Collins, Arthur 4554 323
Harris, Robert 4353 2230
Sergio, Vincent 4596 2084
```

7. Type **USE** and press **Return** to close the database.

8. Type the following ERASE command lines and press **Return** after each to erase the practice files.

   ```
   ERASE ABCSORT.DBF
   ERASE TEXT.TXT
   ```

9. Turn to Module 41 to continue the learning sequence.

Module 62
STORE, RELEASE, SAVE, RESTORE

DESCRIPTION

Memory variables are nothing more than storage locations within your computer's main memory in which you can save character string, numeric, date, or logical values. You've used memory variables in some of the examples contained in previous modules, and until now, you've used them on "faith." This module should take the mystery out of these powerful little "pigeon holes" by describing the STORE, RELEASE, SAVE, and RESTORE commands, where:

STORE   Creates memory variables

RELEASE   Removes memory variables

SAVE   Writes memory variables to disk

RESTORE   Reads memory variables from disk back to memory.

Memory variables are created with the STORE, ACCEPT, INPUT, AVERAGE, and SUM commands. They are also created with an expression like:

```
. X = 'Hello'     or     . STORE 'Hello' to X
```

where the character string "Hello" is stored to the memory variable X.

Forms of the ACCEPT and INPUT commands are described in Module 4; the SUM and AVERAGE commands are described in Modules 63 and 9.

CHARACTERISTICS   You can have as many as 256 active memory variables at a time. However, all memory variables in combination cannot exceed 6,000 bytes (or characters).

A character memory variable can contain up to 254 characters. Numeric memory variables can contain more than 20 digits, but are only accurate to 15 significant digits.

Date memory variables contain eight characters, and are in the form mm/dd/yy (American notation) or dd/mm/yy (European notation). A date memory variable is created by storing it from a date field within a database or from the keyboard using the character-to-date function (CTOD), such as:

```
STORE CTOD('11/30/85') TO MDTE
```

The number of days between dates can be calculated by subtracting one memory variable date from another. You can also calculate a future date by adding a number to a date memory variable. For example, if you want to know the date 90 days from MDTE, which is 11/30/86, you can type:

```
? MDTE + 90
```

The response is 02/28/87.

Memory variable names are assigned when they are created. The name can have up to ten characters. It must begin with a letter, but may contain numbers and the underscore character. It's a good idea to make the name meaningful. If the memory variable contains the contents of a field, you might use the fieldname preceded with an M, like MNAME for the contents of a database NAME field.

STORE   Several forms of the STORE command exist. These are shown with examples in the following list.

STORE *expression* TO *memory variable*   Stores the expression to the memory variable, which can be up to ten characters in length.

```
. STORE 'Gov. Johnson' TO MGOV
      or
. MGOV = 'Gov. Johnson'
```

This command line stores a string expression to memory variable MGOV, dBase displays memory variable value following the command line.

```
. STORE .T. TO RUN
```

Stores the logical true value to memory variable RUN.

```
. STORE 144 TO MGROSS
```

Stores numeric value 144 to memory variable MGROSS.

```
. STORE 2*MGROSS TO M2GROSS
```

Stores the product of two times the value of MGROSS to memory variable M2GROSS.

```
. STORE MGOV+' elected.' TO MRESULT
```

Stores memory variable MGOV and the string "elected" to the memory variable MRESULT. "Gov. Johnson elected" is displayed when stored.

STORE *fieldname* TO *memory variable*   Stores contents of named field to memory variable. When this form of STORE is used, a database must be in use and the record pointer positioned to the desired record.

```
. STORE NAME TO MNAME
```

Stores contents of the NAME field to the memory variable MNAME.

STORE *field1* + *field2* + ... TO *memory variable*   Stores contents of named fields to memory variable. Trailing blanks are also stored when the plus sign is used.

```
. STORE NAME + ST_ADR TO MVAR
Miller, Gary        3270 Garden Brook
```

STORE *field1 - field2* + . . . TO *memory variable*   Stores contents of named fields to memory variable. Trailing blanks are omitted ("squashed") when the minus sign is used.

```
. STORE NAME - ST_ADR TO MVAR
Miller, Gary3270 Garden Brook
```

Alternate form to insert a single space between field values:

```
. STORE TRIM(NAME)-' '+ST_ADR TO MVAR
Miller, Gary 3270 Garden Brook
```

If you wish to see the memory variables in use, you can type **DISPLAY MEMORY** and press **Return** at the dBASE dot prompt. Information similar to the following is displayed.

```
. DISPLAY MEMORY
MGOV      pub   C   "Gov. Johnson"
RUN       pub   L   .T.
MGROSS    pub   N        144  (      144.00000000)
M2GROSS   pub   N        288  (      288.00000000)
MRESULTS  pub   C   "Gov. Johnson elected"
    5 variables defined,      56 bytes used
  251 variables available,  5944 bytes available
.
```

RELEASE   You can remove memory variables individually or in total with the RELEASE command. Forms of the RELEASE command are in the following list:

RELEASE *memory variable*   Removes named memory variable from use.

```
. RELEASE M2GROSS
```

RELEASE *memory variable1, memory variable2,* . . .   Removes named memory variables from use.

```
. RELEASE MGOV, MRESULTS
```

RELEASE ALL   Releases all memory variables from use.

RELEASE ALL LIKE M*   Releases all memory variables starting with M. The * is a "wild card" symbol representing all characters.

RELEASE ALL LIKE M?   Releases all two-character memory variables that begin with the letter M.

RELEASE ALL EXCEPT M?   Releases all memory variables except those two-character memory variables starting with the letter M.

Other commands that clear all memory variables from use are CLEAR ALL and QUIT.

SAVE and RESTORE   There are times when you'd like to SAVE your memory variables to disk for later use and then RESTORE them when you need them. That's precisely what the SAVE and RESTORE commands do. SAVE writes the named memory variables to a named disk file. You don't have to type a filename extension, as dBASE assigns .MEM as an extension automatically. The RESTORE command reads saved memory variables from disk back to your computer's memory. Forms of the SAVE and RESTORE commands are contained in the following examples.

SAVE TO *filename*   Saves all memory variables to the named file, which is automatically given a .MEM extension.

SAVE TO *filename* ALL LIKE *expression*   Saves all memory variables that match the expression. The * symbol is used as a "wild card," which is a substitute for one or more following characters. The ? symbol is used as a place-for-place substitute, and is used at the beginning or end of a memory variable name.

. SAVE TO MEMFILE ALL LIKE T???

. SAVE TO MEMFILE ALL LIKE ?NA*

. SAVE TO MEMFILE ALL LIKE M*

SAVE TO *filename* ALL EXCEPT *expression*   Saves all memory variables except those matching the expression. The * and ? symbols are used with the EXCEPT expression just as in other forms of the SAVE expression.

. SAVE TO MEMFILE ALL EXCEPT A*

. SAVE TO MEMFILE ALL EXCEPT A??

. SAVE TO MEMFILE ALL EXCEPT ?01

RESTORE FROM *filename*   Reads all memory variables previously saved to the named file. This command replaces all active memory variables with the restored memory variables.

. RESTORE FROM MEMFILE

RESTORE FROM *filename* ADDITIVE   Reads all memory variables previously saved to the named file. The ADDITIVE clause adds the restored memory variables to those already in use instead of writing over them.

APPLICATIONS

The ability to STORE selected information to memory variables is important in managing the contents of a database files. When writing extensive applications, you'll find yourself using the STORE command to duplicate the contents of certain fields into memory variables. Once in a memory variable, you can move the record pointer around in the database and selectively replace field contents with the contents of memory variables.

Often, memory variables are used as "scratch pads," where mathematical results, like subtotals, are STORED for later use.

If you find yourself approaching the maximum memory variable limit, which is 256 memory variables or 6,000 characters, the RELEASE command is available to eliminate memory variables that are no longer needed.

The SAVE and RESTORE commands let you take active memory variables and save them to disk, like "putting them on the shelf" for future use. Once this is done, you can begin with a new set of memory variables. When you need the old ones back, you can SAVE the current ones to another disk file and retrieve the original set with the RESTORE command. Remember to use the "ADDITIVE" clause if you don't want to overwrite active memory variables.

TYPICAL OPERATION

In this illustration the STORE, RELEASE, and SAVE commands are used in a command file that interacts with the MEMBERS database. Begin at the dBASE dot prompt.

1. Recreate the MEMBERS database structure shown as shown in Module 47. Edit the database contents to correspond to the records in Module 8.

2. Type **MODIFY COMMAND STORE** and press **Return**. A blank screen is displayed and you're in the dBASE full-screen editor.

3. Type the following command file. (Don't type the explanatory remarks.)

```
                                    Remarks
* STORE.PRG               Demonstrates use of STORE, RELEASE, and SAVE.
CLEAR                     && Clears the screen.
SET TALK OFF             && Turns off dBASE dialog.
USE MEMBERS             && Puts MEMBERS database in use.
TOT_AGE=0              && Stores 0 to memory variable TOT_AGE.
DO WHILE .NOT. EOF()    && Causes continuous operation until end of file encountered.
  ? NAME+ADR+CSZ        && Displays the NAME, ADR, and CSZ fields.
  TOT_AGE=TOT_AGE+AGE   && Accumulates total of AGE fields; SUM could be used.
  SKIP                  && Positions record pointer to next record.
  IF EOF()             && Checks for end-of-file condition; commands between IF and ENDIF
*                         are skipped unless the end of file is reached.
    RECS=RECNO()-1      && Stores last record number to memory variable RECS.
    AVG_AGE=TOT_AGE/RECS && Divides total age by the number of records; stores
*                         results to memory variable AVG_AGE.
    ?                   && ? displays lines and text in quotes.
    ? '        THE AVERAGE MEMBER AGE IS', STR(AVG_AGE,2,0)  && STR is a string function;
*                         see Appendix E.
    ? '        OUT OF',LTRIM(STR(RECS,)),'MEMBERS.'  && LTRIM and STR are string functions.
SAVE TO AGES            && Saves active memory variables to AGES.MEM file.
    ?                   && Displays blank line.
```

```
    WAIT                    && Pauses operation until a key is pressed.
    USE                     && Takes MEMBERS database out of use.
    RELEASE ALL             && Releases all memory variables.
    CANCEL                  && Returns control to the dBASE dot prompt.
  ENDIF                     && Passes control to following command line.
* LOOP                      && Returns execution to command line following DO WHILE statement.
ENDDO                       && Ends DO loop; passes control to next statement if one exists.
CLEAR                       && Clears the screen.
CLEAR ALL                   && Closes all files and releases all memory variables.
RETURN                      && Redisplays dBASE dot prompt.
```

4. Press **Ctrl-W** to write the command file to disk.

5. Type **DO STORE** and press **Return** to run the command file. Compare your screen to the following:

```
    Williams, David         3456 Fresno Circle      Tampa, FL 32656
    Phillips, George W.     11205 Dawn Drive        Lago Vista, TX 78641
    Galvin, Theodore A.     5545 Gulch Road         Culver City, CA 96750


        THE AVERAGE MEMBER AGE IS 46
        OUT OF 3 MEMBERS.

    Press any key to continue...
```

6. Press any key to redisplay the dBASE dot prompt.

7. Verify that no memory variables are active by typing **LIST MEMORY** and pressing **Return**. Notice the following:

```
    . LIST MEMORY
        0 variables defined,        0 bytes used
      256 variables available,   6000 bytes available
```

8. Read the saved memory variables from disk by typing **RESTORE FROM STATUS** and pressing **Return**.

9. Verify that the memory variables have been read from disk by typing **LIST MEMORY** and pressing **Return**. Check for the following:

```
. RESTORE FROM STATUS
. LIST MEMORY
TOT_AGE     pub   N        137 (        137.00000000)
RECS        pub   N          3 (          3.00000000)
AVG_AGE     pub   N      45.67 (         45.66666667)
      3 variables defined,     27 bytes used
    253 variables available,  5973 bytes available
```

10. Delete the .MEM file from disk by typing **ERASE STATUS.MEM** and pressing **Return**.

11. Delete the STORE.PRG file from your disk by typing **ERASE STORE.PRG** and pressing **Return**.

12. Eliminate the memory variables by typing **RELEASE ALL** and pressing **Return**.

13. Turn to Module 63 to continue the learning sequence.

Module 63
SUM

DESCRIPTION

The SUM command is used to add one or more numeric fields of an active database file. The result can either be stored to a memory variable or displayed. Forms of the SUM command and corresponding examples are shown in the following list.

SUM *fieldname*   Sums the contents of the specified field name and displays the result below (with SET TALK ON).

```
. SUM QTY
      12 records summed
   qty
   168
```

SUM *field1,field2 . . .*   Sums specified field names and displays the results below.

```
. SUM QTY,COST,PRICE*1.05
        105 records summed
 qty  cost      price
2309 34523.48 74560.86
```

SUM *fieldname* TO *memory variable*   Sums specified field name to the named memory variable.

```
. SUM QTY TO MQTY
. SUM QTY,COST TO MQTY,MCOST
```

SUM *fieldname* TO *memory variable* FOR *expression*   Sums specified field name to named memory variable for those records that match the specified expression.

```
. SUM QTY TO MQTY FOR COST > .99
```

SUM *fieldname* TO *memory variable* WHILE *expression*   Sums field name to named memory variable while expression is valid. If expression becomes invalid, summing ceases.

```
. SUM QTY TO MQTY WHILE COST <= 100.00
```

APPLICATIONS

The SUM command is used to store the arithmetic total of one or more fields within a database file to a memory variable for later use, or to display an arithmetic total in response to a direct user inquiry. The SUM command is used both in command files and in the interactive mode.

TYPICAL OPERATION

In this illustration a new database is created. Then the SUM command is used to find the sums of various numeric fields. Begin at the dBASE dot prompt.

1. Type **CREATE PICNIC** and press **Return**.

2. Prepare the database structure and enter the records as shown.

```
    field name   type        width  dec          Remarks
    =========================================

1   NAME         Character    20
2   GUESTS       Numeric       2    0
3   BRING        Character    12
4   AMOUNT       Numeric       3    0
5   MEASURE      Character    10    0
6   <cr>                                   Press Return to stop data entry.


    Input data records now? (Y/N)? Y      Type Y to enter data.
```

```
Record No.      1                      Record No.      8
NAME       Johns, Bill                 NAME       Cantwell, Julie
GUESTS      3                          GUESTS      3
BRING      Chips                       BRING      Beans
AMOUNT      5                          AMOUNT      1
MEASURE    Bags                        MEASURE    Pot
--------------------------------       --------------------------------
Record No.      2                      Record No.      9
NAME       Collins, Ric                NAME       Hicks, Ginger
GUESTS      4                          GUESTS      3
BRING      Dip                         BRING      Hot Dogs
AMOUNT      3                          AMOUNT      3
MEASURE    Cartons                     MEASURE    Packs
--------------------------------       --------------------------------
Record No.      3                      Record No.     10
NAME       Miller, Gary                NAME       Tolliver, Greg
GUESTS      3                          GUESTS      4
BRING      Hot Dogs                    BRING      Buns
AMOUNT      6                          AMOUNT      6
MEASURE    Packs                       MEASURE    Packs
--------------------------------       --------------------------------
```

```
Record No.      4                    Record No.     11
NAME       Dickens, Charles          NAME       Stevens, Jan
GUESTS        2                      GUESTS        3
BRING      Mustard                   BRING      Chips
AMOUNT        1                      AMOUNT        5
MEASURE    Jar                       MEASURE    Bags
----------------------------------   ----------------------------------
Record No.      5                    Record No.     12
NAME       Crandal, Phil             NAME       Farris, Jody
GUESTS        4                      GUESTS        3
BRING      Buns                      BRING      Relish
AMOUNT        5                      AMOUNT        1
MEASURE    Packs                     MEASURE    Jar
----------------------------------   ----------------------------------
Record No.      6                    Record No.     13
NAME       Johnson, J.D.             NAME       Jasper, Dave
GUESTS        4                      GUESTS        2
BRING      Chips                     BRING      Dip
AMOUNT        3                      AMOUNT        2
MEASURE    Bags                      MEASURE    Cartons
----------------------------------   ----------------------------------
Record No.      7                    Record No.     14
NAME       Struthers, Susan          NAME       <cr>    Press Return to stop
GUESTS        4                      GUESTS              data entry.
BRING      Pickles                   BRING
AMOUNT        1                      AMOUNT
MEASURE    Jar                       MEASURE
----------------------------------   ----------------------------------
```

3. List the structure of the database by typing **LIST STRUCTURE** and pressing **Return**.

```
. LIST STRUCTURE
Structure for database: C:picnic.dbf
Number of data records:        13
Date of last update   : 08/15/88
Field  Field Name  Type        Width    Dec
    1  NAME        Cha racter     20
    2  GUESTS      Numeric         2
    3  BRING       Character      12
    4  AMOUNT      Numeric         3
    5  MEASURE     Character      10
** Total **                       48
```

4. List the database by typing **LIST** and pressing **Return**.

```
. LIST
Record#  NAME               GUESTS BRING        AMOUNT MEASURE
      1  Johns, Bill             3 Chips             5 Bags
      2  Collins, Ric            4 Dip               3 Cartons
      3  Miller, Gary            3 Hot Dogs          6 Packs
      4  Dickens, Charles        2 Mustard           1 Jar
      5  Crandal, Phil           4 Buns              5 Packs
      6  Johnson, J.D.           4 Chips             3 Bags
      7  Struthers, Susan        4 Pickles           1 Jar
      8  Cantwell, Julie         3 Beans             1 Pot
      9  Hicks, Ginger           3 Hot Dogs          3 Packs
     10  Tolliver, Greg          4 Buns              6 Packs
     11  Stevens, Jan            3 Chips             5 Bags
     12  Farris, Jody            3 Relish            1 Jar
     13  Jasper, Dave            2 Dip               2 Cartons
```

5. Determine how many people will be at the picnic by adding the number of records to the sum of the guests.

```
. GO BOTTOM
. STORE RECNO() TO RN
       13
. SUM GUESTS TO TOT_GUEST
   13 records summed
   GUESTS
       42
. ? RN + TOT_GUEST
       55
```

6. Type **SUM AMOUNT FOR BRING = 'Chips'** and press **Return** to determine how many bags of chips will be brought to the picnic.

```
. SUM AMOUNT FOR BRING = 'Chips'
    3 records summed
   AMOUNT
       13
```

7. Type **CLEAR ALL** to close all files.

8. Keep the PICNIC database as it is used in several other exercises.

9. Turn to Module 9 to continue the learning sequence.

Module 64

SUSPEND, RESUME

DESCRIPTION

This pair of commands lets you suspend the operation of a command file temporarily, and then resume it. You can suspend program operation in three ways. First, you can enter SUSPEND on a command line. When encountered, program operation ceases and dBASE displays the dot prompt. A second way is to press the **Esc** key during a program input-output operation. This pauses program operations and displays:

```
*** INTERRUPTED ***
Called from - C:temp.prg
Cancel, Ignore, or Suspend? (C, I, or S)
```

The dBASE program "remembers" the position of the last line used in the command file. Use the RESUME command to restart program operation where you left off.

If your command file is designed to display information, it is a good practice to clear your screen with the CLEAR command before resuming program operation. Otherwise, you may have confusing screen clutter.

A third way to stop operation is to enter an error in a command file. The error stops normal operation and displays an error message followed by the "Cancel, Ignore, or Suspend?" prompt. If you choose suspend, you are returned to the dot prompt. Here, you may be able to examine the problem. Once fixed, you can restart program operation with RESUME. The third option is not a graceful way to suspend operation and is not recommended.

APPLICATIONS

During program development and debugging, you may wish to insert the SUSPEND command to halt program operation. For example, you may wish to examine the value of memory variables and use RESUME to restart program operation.

TYPICAL OPERATION

In this illustration you place the SUSPEND command in a short command file and then use RESUME to complete operation. Begin at the dBASE dot prompt.

1. Type **MODIFY COMMAND SUSPEND** and press **Return** to use the dBASE editor.

2. Type and save the following command file. (Don't type the explanatory remarks.)

```
* SUSPEND.PRG -- Demonstrates use of the SUSPEND and RESUME commands.
CLEAR
? 'The next line suspends operation...'
SUSPEND
WAIT 'The screen is cleared to remove unnecessary clutter...'
CLEAR
?
WAIT 'This is the end of the command file; Press any key...'
CLEAR
RETURN
```

3. Type **DO SUSPEND** and press **Return** to run the program. Respond to the prompt by pressing any key.

```
          The SUSPEND command pauses operation. After suspending,
             type RESUME at the dot prompt to continue program operation.'
   Press any key to continue...
   Do suspended
```

4. Type **RESUME** to resume program operation.

```
   This is the end of the command file
   Press any key to continue...
```

5. Press any key to complete program operation.

6. Type **ERASE SUSPEND.PRG** and press **Return** to delete the practice command file.

7. Turn to Module 50 to continue the learning sequence.

Module 65
TEXT, ENDTEXT

DESCRIPTION

The TEXT and ENDTEXT commands are used to display or print text, depending upon the status of your printer. Both of these commands are used in command files, and should not be entered at the dot prompt.

The TEXT command lets you enter multiple lines of text. The TEXT command is terminated with the ENDTEXT statement. An example of how the TEXT and ENDTEXT commands are used within command files is illustrated below.

```
CLEAR
SET TALK OFF
TEXT
This program is used to enter customer information from invoices,
change customer information, or delete obsolete customer information.
Before starting, be sure you have all the latest customer paperwork
available.
ENDTEXT
WAIT
CLEAR
TEXT

              ===================================
                    Customer Information System
              -----------------------------------
              1   ENTER NEW CUSTOMER INFORMATION

              2   CHANGE CUSTOMER INFORMATION

              3   DELETE CUSTOMER FROM FILE

              4   QUIT THIS PROGRAM

              =========  Select One  ==========

ENDTEXT
WAIT ' ' TO CHOICE
        :
(more command lines)
        :
```

APPLICATIONS

The TEXT and ENDTEXT commands are convenient for displaying long passages of text, menus, and multi-line prompts on the screen. You can also route the text to your printer by using SET PRINT ON prior to displaying the information to your screen.

The TEXT-ENDTEXT command pair makes displaying text as easy as typing. You can display text at any coordinate on the screen by positioning the cursor to the line of your choice and using blank spaces to move from left to right. The print (?) and @ row,col commands are also used to display or print text. These commands are described in Modules 8 and 51.

TYPICAL OPERATION

In this illustration the TEXT and ENDTEXT commands are used in a command file to demonstrate their use. Begin at the dBASE dot prompt.

1. Type **MODIFY COMMAND TXETX** and press **Return** to use the dBASE editor.

2. Type the following command file. (Don't type the explanatory remarks.)

```
                              Remarks
* TXETX.PRG -- Demonstrates the TEXT and ENDTEXT commands.
CLEAR                   && Clears the screen.
TEXT                    && Begins text command, following lines are displayed.

        SOME TEXT DISPLAY COMMANDS ARE:

        1.  DISPLAY
        2.  ? '   '
        3.  @ row,col SAY '   '
        4.  TEXT and ENDTEXT

ENDTEXT                 && Ends the text statement.
WAIT                    && Pauses operation and displays prompt.
CLEAR                   && Clears the screen.
CANCEL                  && Returns control to dBASE dot prompt.
```

3. Press **Ctrl-W** to write the command file to disk.

4. Type **DO TXETX** and press **Return** to run the command file. Compare your screen to the following:

```
            SOME TEXT DISPLAY COMMANDS ARE:

            1.  DISPLAY
            2.  ? '    '
            3.  @ row,col SAY '    '
            4.  TEXT and ENDTEXT

       Press any key to continue...
```

5. When you finish experimenting with this example, type **ERASE TXETX.PRG** and press **Return** to delete the file from your disk.

6. Turn to Module 51 to continue the learning sequence.

Module 66
TOTAL

DESCRIPTION

The TOTAL command is used to transfer the sum of matching fields to a designated database file. Matching fields are consolidated and the designated fields, which must have been previously indexed or sorted, are summed.

Clearly, an example is in order. Imagine that you have an inventory database with multiple entries for the same part number. The part number field is a *key field* (one that was indexed or sorted). If you wish to determine the total quantity on hand for each part number, you can TOTAL ON the part number field to a database file, specifying the quantity field. This process is demonstrated in the Typical Operation section of this module. Forms of the TOTAL command and corresponding examples are contained in the following list.

TOTAL ON *fieldname* TO *filename*   Totals the numeric values for those records having the same contents in the designated field name. The database in use is copied to the specified filename. If the database already exists, the existing structure is used. If it is a new database, the structure of database in use is copied.

. TOTAL ON PART_NO TO LUMBER1

TOTAL ON *fieldname* TO *filename* FIELDS*field1,field2* . . .   Totals the numeric values for those records having the same contents in the designated field name. The FIELDS clause limits the totaling to only those fields listed in the command. Without the fields clause, all numeric fields are totaled.

. TOTAL ON PART_NO TO LUMBER1 FIELDS PART_NO, QTY, COST, PRICE

TOTAL ON *fieldname* TO *filename* FIELDS *field1 field2*. . . FOR *expression*   This is the same as the previous command except that the FOR clause selects only those records matching the expression.

. TOTAL ON PART_NO TO LUMBER1 FIELDS PART_NO, QTY, COST FOR QTY > 0

TOTAL ON *fieldname* TO filename WHILE *expression*   This command form operates as long as the expression is satisfied. If the expression becomes invalid, the totaling process terminates. In the following example, if a value that is greater than 10 is encountered in the QTY field, the totaling process stops.

. TOTAL ON PART_NO TO LUMBER1 WHILE QTY <= 10

APPLICATIONS

The TOTAL command not only provides arithmetic answers, but it creates a new database that eliminates records having the same value in a key field. This process is accomplished because common records are consolidated as they are copied to the target database file.

TYPICAL OPERATION

In this illustration the TOTAL command is used with the PICNIC database created in Module 63. Begin at the dBASE dot prompt.

1. Type **USE PICNIC** and press **Return**.

2. Examine the structure of the database by typing **LIST STRUCTURE** and pressing **Return**.

```
. LIST STRUCTURE

    Structure for database :   Picnic.dbf
    Number of data records :      13
    Date of last update    : 08/26/88
    Field  Field name  Type      Width  Dec
        1  NAME        Character    20
        2  GUESTS      Numeric       2
        3  BRING       Character    12
        4  AMOUNT      Numeric       3
        5  MEASURE     Character    10
    ** Total **                     48
```

3. List the database by typing **LIST** and pressing **Return**.

```
. LIST
Record#  NAME              GUESTS BRING        AMOUNT MEASURE
      1  Johns, Bill          3 Chips            5 Bags
      2  Collins, Ric         4 Dip              3 Cartons
      3  Miller, Gary         3 Hot Dogs         6 Packs
      4  Dickens, Charles     2 Mustard          1 Jar
      5  Crandal, Phil        4 Buns             5 Packs
      6  Johnson, J.D.        4 Chips            3 Bags
      7  Struthers, Susan     4 Pickles          1 Jar
      8  Cantwell, Julie      3 Beans            1 Pot
      9  Hicks, Ginger        3 Hot Dogs         3 Packs
     10  Tolliver, Greg       4 Buns             6 Packs
```

```
11   Stevens, Jan        3 Chips      5 Bags
12   Farris, Jody        3 Relish     1 Jar
13   Jasper, Dave        2 Dip        2 Cartons
```

4. Determine the quantities of each picnic supply that has been volunteered by indexing the file and then using the TOTAL command. Type the commands shown at each dot prompt.

a. Index the PICNIC database file.

```
. INDEX ON BRING TO TEMP
    13 records indexed
```

b. List the indexed database.

```
. LIST
Record#   NAME                 GUESTS BRING        AMOUNT MEASURE
      8   Cantwell, Julie      3 Beans             1 Pot
      5   Crandal, Phil        4 Buns              5 Packs
     10   Tolliver, Greg       4 Buns              6 Packs
      1   Johns, Bill          3 Chips             5 Bags
      6   Johnson, J.D.        4 Chips             3 Bags
     11   Stevens, Jan         3 Chips             5 Bags
      2   Collins, Ric         4 Dip               3 Cartons
     13   Jasper, Dave         2 Dip               2 Cartons
      3   Miller, Gary         3 Hot Dogs          6 Packs
      9   Hicks, Ginger        3 Hot Dogs          3 Packs
      4   Dickens, Charles     2 Mustard           1 Jar
      7   Struthers, Susan     4 Pickles           1 Jar
     12   Farris, Jody         3 Relish            1 Jar
```

c. Total the indexed database file on the BRING field, placing the resulting totals in the AMOUNT field of a new database named PICNIC1.

```
. TOTAL ON BRING TO PICNIC1 FIELD AMOUNT
13 Record(s) totalled
 8 Records generated
```

d. Place the PICNIC1 database in use and list the structure.

```
. USE PICNIC1
. LIST STRUCTURE
Structure for database :   Picnic1.dbf
Number of data records :       8
Date of last update    : 08/26/88
```

```
Field   Field name   Type       Width   Dec
  1     NAME         Character    20
  2     GUESTS       Numeric       2
  3     BRING        Character    12
  4     AMOUNT       Numeric       3
  5     MEASURE      Character    10
** Total **                      48
```

e. List the contents of the database. Notice the total amounts for each item in the BRING field is contained in the AMOUNT field.

```
. LIST
Record#  NAME                GUESTS BRING      AMOUNT MEASURE
   1     Cantwell, Julie        3 Beans          1 Pot
   2     Crandal, Phil          4 Buns          11 Packs
   3     Johns, Bill            3 Chips         13 Bags
   4     Collins, Ric           4 Dip            5 Cartons
   5     Miller, Gary           3 Hot Dogs       9 Packs
   6     Dickens, Charles       2 Mustard        1 Jar
   7     Struthers, Susan       4 Pickles        1 Jar
   8     Farris, Jody           3 Relish         1 Jar
```

5. Type **CLEAR ALL** to close all files.

6. Turn to Module 68 to continue the learning sequence.

Module 67
TYPE

DESCRIPTION

The TYPE command "types" the contents of a text-type (ASCII) file to the screen. The TYPE command is similar to DOS' TYPE command. It is used to display text files, like dBASE command files, to the screen so that you can view them. If you wish to see a command file named MENU, you can use the command:

```
. TYPE MENU.PRG
```

The file is displayed. To pause the display as it scrolls up the screen, press **Ctrl-S**. Press any key, like the **Spacebar**, to resume output to the screen.

APPLICATIONS

The TYPE command provides a quick way to view a text file, whether it is a command file with the extension .PRG or a text file with the extension .TXT.

TYPICAL OPERATION

In this illustration the TYPE command is used to display the contents of a text file. Begin the following activity at the dBASE dot prompt.

1. Type **MODI COMM TEST.TXT** and press **Return** to use the dBASE editor.

2. Type the following two lines of text.

    ```
    This is a sample file.
    It is displayed using TYPE.
    ```

3. Press **Ctrl-W** to save the file.

4. Type **TYPE TEST.TXT** and press **Return**.

5. Notice the file is displayed on the screen.

```
. type test.txt
This is a sample file.
It is displayed using TYPE.
```

6. Type **ERASE TEST.TXT** and press **Return** to delete the file.

7. Turn to Module 34 to continue the learning sequence.

Module 68
UPDATE

DESCRIPTION

UPDATE is another powerful dBASE command that lets you combine the contents of two databases. This command allows you to replace the contents of one or more fields in a database with the contents of one or more fields from another database. The updated database must be in the selected work area. The source database must also be in an active, but unselected work area. (For information about selecting work areas, see Module 58.)

The general form of the UPDATE command is:

UPDATE ON *key fieldname* FROM *alias->fieldname* WITH *expression*

If you wish to replace several fields, you can use the form:

UPDATE ON *key fieldname* FROM *alias->fieldname* WITH *expression*, *field2* WITH *expression*, *field3* WITH *expression* . . .

The key (or indexed) field must have the same field name in both the source and target databases. A key field is one that was used as a basis for sorting or indexing.

One final form of the UPDATE command uses the RANDOM statement. This statement permits you to use a source database that is arranged in random order. That is, the source database may be unsorted or unindexed. However, the target database must always be sorted or indexed for UPDATE to operate properly.

Here is an example of how the UPDATE command is used. Assume that you have two databases that contain inventory quantities. The first database, called WHSE (for *warehouse*), contains parts in your warehouse. The second database, called WIP (for "work-in-process.") If you wish to update the WHSE database to those parts presently counted in WIP, you can use the UPDATE command.

If the key field name in both databases is PART_NO, and the field containing the quantity is QTY, you can proceed as follows:

```
. SELECT 1
. USE WIP
. SELECT 2
. USE WHSE
. UPDATE ON PART_NO FROM WIP REPLACE QTY WITH QTY + WIP->QTY
```

This series of commands puts WIP and WHSE in work areas 1 and 2, leaving WHSE in the active work area. The UPDATE command adds the contents of the QTY (or *quantity*) fields and replaces the WHSE quantity values with their present value plus the quantity value in the WIP database. Look at the following list.

WHSE				WIP			WHSE (After Update)	
PART_NO	QTY	+	PART_NO	QTY	=	PART_NO	QTY
A-1230	5		A-1230	2		A-1230	7
B-1001	12		B-1001	6		B-1001	18
D-3561	7		D-3561	3		B-3561	10
D-3562	8		D-3562	2		D-3562	10
W-1210	4		W-1210	2		W-1210	6

APPLICATIONS

The UPDATE command is good for establishing a common database that monitors changes in multiple databases. As in the example, counts from several warehouse databases can be consolidated into a master database file. In this way, the total inventory status can be viewed. Inventory information usually includes quantity, cost, price, and sales volume data that changes by the minute. It is often convenient to create and use a transaction database for maintaining those items that change. From the transaction database, you can UPDATE other relevant databases periodically to ensure that you have the latest information.

TYPICAL OPERATION

In this illustration the UPDATE command is used to change information in an inventory database file named INVTORY from another file named INVPRICE. The exercise includes the creation and indexing of these databases so you can try the commands on your computer. Start at the dBASE dot prompt.

1. Create the INVTORY database structure and enter the data as shown:

```
Structure for database :   Invtory.dbf
Field  Field name  Type        Width    Dec
    1  DES         Character      10
    2  PN          Character       8
    3  QTY         Numeric         3
    4  COST        Numeric         6      2
** Total **                      28


Record#  DES        PN       QTY   COST
      1  Battery    ER-1500  125   0.47
      2  Cable      CC-1312   25  12.50
      3  Plug       AMP-232   12   3.49
      4  Antenna    IRC-1212   6   9.50
      5  FM Radio   PA-005     8  56.50
```

2. Type **INDEX ON PN TO INV** and press **Return** to index the INVTORY database on the PN field to an index file named INV. (This makes the PN field the key field.)

3. Display the indexed database by typing **LIST** and pressing **Return**. Check the contents, noting the cost of the plug and antenna.

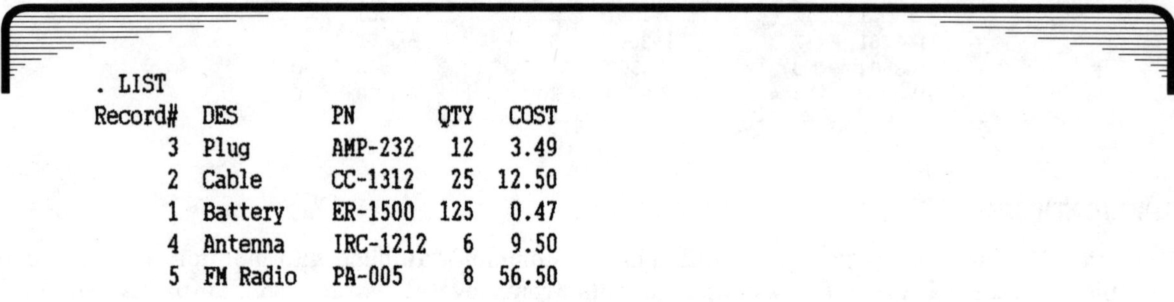

```
. LIST
Record#  DES         PN        QTY    COST
      3  Plug        AMP-232    12    3.49
      2  Cable       CC-1312    25   12.50
      1  Battery     ER-1500   125    0.47
      4  Antenna     IRC-1212    6    9.50
      5  FM Radio    PA-005      8   56.50
```

4. Now create another database named INVPRICE and enter the data as shown:

```
Structure for database :    Invprice.dbf
Field  Field name  Type        Width     Dec
    1  DES         Character     10
    2  PN          Character      8
    3  QTY         Numeric        3
    4  COST        Numeric        6        2
    5  PRICE       Numeric        6        2
    6  RESERVED    Numeric        3
```

```
Record#  DES        PN       QTY   COST  PRICE  RESERVED
      1  Battery    ER-1500   95   0.47   1.05         0
      2  Cable      CC-1312   20  11.90  22.95         0
      3  Plug       AMP-232   14   3.39   6.95         2
      4  Antenna    IRC-1212   2   9.05  18.95         1
      5  FM Radio   PA-005     7  54.00  96.00         1
```

5. Type **INDEX ON PN TO PR** to index the INVPRICE database on the PN field to an index file named PR.

6. Display the indexed database by typing **LIST** and pressing **Return**. Compare your screen to the following:

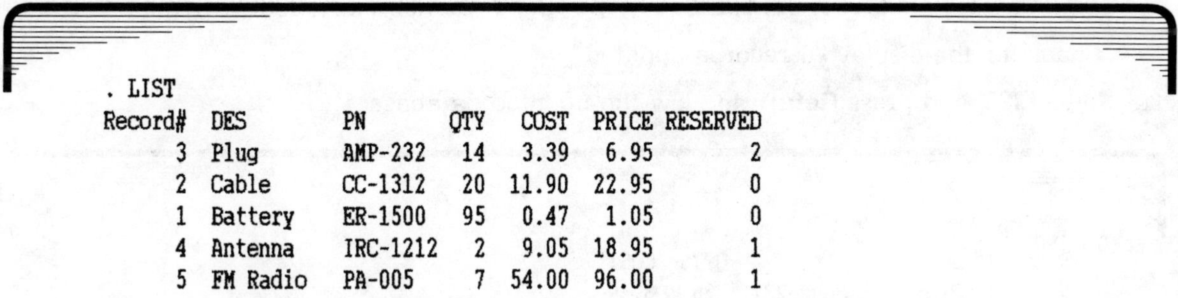

```
. LIST
Record#  DES        PN        QTY   COST   PRICE  RESERVED
     3   Plug       AMP-232   14    3.39   6.95      2
     2   Cable      CC-1312   20   11.90  22.95      0
     1   Battery    ER-1500   95    0.47   1.05      0
     4   Antenna    IRC-1212   2    9.05  18.95      1
     5   FM Radio   PA-005     7   54.00  96.00      1
```

7. List the INVTORY database using:

```
. USE INVTORY INDEX INV
. LIST
```

Compare the quantity and cost differences.

```
Invtory.dbf (index pr.ndx):

3  Plug       AMP-232    12   3.49  ◄──────── Cost difference
2  Cable      CC-1312    25  11.90
1  Battery    ER-1500   125   0.47
4  Antenna    IRC-1212    6   9.50  ◄──────── Cost difference
5  FM Radio   PA-005      8  54.00
```

All quantities are different, and the costs of the Plug and Antenna have increased. Assume that the quantity difference exists, because the INVPRICE database reflects inventory quantities at another storage location. You can update the costs in the INVTORY database and add the quantities to ensure it contains the total, up-to-date information with the UPDATE command using the following steps.

8. Put the two databases in work areas using the following sequence of commands:

```
. SELECT 1
. USE INVPRICE INDEX PR ALIAS SOURCE
. SELECT 2
. USE INVTORY INDEX INV ALIAS TARGET
```

Notice that the indexes are included with the databases by assigning alias names. Note that the aliases are called "SOURCE" and "TARGET."

9. Use the following command to update the INVTORY database. This command adds the quantities and changes the prices.

    ```
    . UPDATE ON PN FROM SOURCE REPLACE QTY WITH QTY + SOURCE-> QTY, COST WITH SOURCE-> COST
    ```

10. Check for the display "5 records updated."

11. Type **LIST** and press **Return** to view the updated database:

```
. LIST
Record#  DES        PN        QTY   COST
      3  Plug       AMP-232    26    3.49
      2  Cable      CC-1312    45   11.90
      1  Battery    ER-1500   220    0.47
      4  Antenna    IRC-1212    8    9.50
      5  FM Radio   PA-005     15   54.00
```

12. Check the COST and QTY fields. Note that the costs have been updated and the QTY fields added.

13. Type **CLEAR ALL** to close all files.

14. Use the ERASE command to delete the following files from your disk.

    ```
    INVTORY.DBF
    INV.NDX
    INVPRICE.DBF
    PR.NDX
    ```

15. Turn to Module 6 to continue the learning sequence.

Module 69
USE

DESCRIPTION

To use the information within a database, it must be open, or "in use." The USE command followed by a database filename and **Return** opens the named database file, or "puts it in use." Associated index and memo files, where memo files contain text and have the extension .DBT, are also opened with the USE command. Index files, which have the extension .NDX, are described in Module 33.

OPENING A DATABASE WITH USE If you try to enter a dBASE command that interacts with a database file without a database in use, the dBASE dialog displays the message "No database in USE, enter filename:_."

If this happens, no harm is done. Just type the database filename, such as **MEMBERS** for the MEMBERS database file, and press **Return**. It isn't necessary to include the database file extension .DBF when entering a database filename. The first portion of the filename suffices. This opens the database, or puts it in use.

The conventional way to put a database in use is to type the USE command followed by the database filename, like:

    . USE MEMBERS

If you want to direct your command to a disk other than the default disk, prefix the filename with the disk designator. For example, using the command **USE B:MEMBERS** opens the MEMBERS database on drive B.

If you are using drive B for your database files on a computer with two floppy drives, you should have entered the command **SET DEFAULT TO B:** from the dot prompt or entered **DEFAULT = B** in a CONFIG.DB file located on your dBASE program disk. (See Module 2 or Appendix A.)

If a database has associated index files, you can place the database and index files in use at the same time and assign an *alias* name to the entire group of files. For example, let's assume that the MEMBERS database has two index files named NAMELIST and JOINDATE. You can open the database and the two index files (up to seven index files are possible), and assign an alias name to the group with the command:

    . USE MEMBERS INDEX NAMELIST, JOINDATE ALIAS MBR

You can have as many as 10 databases in use at the same time. However, the CONFIG.SYS file (see Module 2 or Appendix A) must be in effect to have this many files open. Ensure that it is present on your DOS disk when you start your computer. The process for having multiple database files open is described in Module 59. For the time being, let's stick with opening and closing one database at a time.

CLOSING A DATABASE FILE WITH USE   If USE is typed without a database name, the active database file is closed. Databases are also closed with the QUIT, CLEAR ALL, CLOSE DATABASES, and CLOSE ALL commands.

There's another form of the USE command associated with index files. It is described in Module 41. To open an index file, use the command:

> . USE *database filename* INDEX *index filename*

APPLICATIONS

The USE command is used in dBASE's interactive mode (from the dBASE dot prompt) or within command files. In either case it is often one of the first commands issued when starting dBASE. Without issuing the USE command, the information within a database is unavailable, because the database file must be open to be read. When closed, the database contents can't be displayed, edited, sorted, indexed, or copied.

TYPICAL OPERATION

In this illustration the USE command is used to open the MEMBERS database file created in Module 18. If you have a two-floppy drive system, enter **SET DEFAULT TO B:** and press **Return**. Begin at the dBASE dot prompt.

1. Type **USE MEMBERS** and press **Return**. Notice that the dBASE dot prompt is redisplayed.

2. To check the database in use, type **DISPLAY STATUS** and press **Return**. Notice the following display.

```
Currently selected database:
Select area -  1, Database in use: B:members.dbf   Alias - MEMBERS

Press any key to continue...
```

3. Press **Esc** to interrupt the status display and return to the dBASE dot prompt.

4. Close the database file by typing **CLEAR ALL** and pressing **Return**.

5. Turn to Module 15 to continue the learning sequence.

Module 70
WAIT

DESCRIPTION

The WAIT command is used to pause command file operation until a key is pressed. When the WAIT command is used without following text, the prompt "Press any key to continue . . ." is displayed. Pressing a key continues command file operation. If you press **Esc**, command file operation is interrupted, and you can return to the dot prompt. Forms of the WAIT command are included in the following list. You can enter the command examples from the dBASE dot prompt if you wish to verify how they work.

WAIT   Pauses operation and displays "Press any key to continue. . . ."

WAIT

WAIT 'Prompt'   Pauses operation and displays prompt enclosed in quotes or square brackets.

WAIT 'Read the text and press a key to continue. . '

WAIT TO MVAR   Pauses operation, displays the "Press any key. . ." prompt, and stores pressed key to the specified memory variable.

WAIT TO CHOICE

WAIT 'Type a letter ' TO MVAR   Pauses operation, displays "Type a letter" as a prompt, and stores the first key pressed to the specified memory variable.

WAIT 'Type 0 - 9' TO CHOICE

WAIT ' ' TO MVAR   Pauses operation, suppresses display of a prompt, and stores value of pressed key to the specified memory variable.

WAIT TO CHOICE

If you entered these examples, you can see the results of the keys you typed by typing **DISP MEMO** and pressing **Return**. To release the memory variables, type **RELEASE ALL** and press **Return**.

Notice how the WAIT TO form of the command differs from WAIT as it stores the value of the pressed key to the designated memory variable. You may recall from Module 4 how the ACCEPT and INPUT commands are used to store either character or numeric strings to a named memory variable. In contrast, WAIT TO stores only a single character —the value of the first typed key.

APPLICATIONS

There are many applications for the various forms of the WAIT commands. WAIT is used to pause operation so you can read displayed information or prepare your printer or a disk drive for operation.

WAIT TO is used to store a menu selection (or a response to a prompt) to a memory variable. Once stored, you can use an IF or CASE statement to cause a resulting action, as demonstrated in the MENU program contained in Module 46.

The WAIT 'prompt' and WAIT 'prompt' TO forms of the command let you display user prompts in addition to performing the functions of WAIT and WAIT TO. If you want to suppress a prompt, use the form WAIT ' ' or WAIT ' ' TO *memory variable*.

Another advantage of the WAIT TO command form is that you don't have to follow your keyboard entry with **Return**. The typed character is stored to the memory variable without pressing **Return**. This sometimes helps new users, who are not aware of the requirement to press **Return** to complete a command.

TYPICAL OPERATION

In this illustration forms of the WAIT command are used in a command file. Begin at the dBASE dot prompt.

1. Type **MODIFY COMMAND WAITCMD** and press **Return** to use the dBASE editor.

2. Type the following command file. (Don't type the explanatory remarks.)

```
                                                  Remarks
* WAITCMD.PRG -- Demonstrates uses of the WAIT and WAIT TO commands.
CLEAR                    && Clears the screen.
?                        && ? displays following text.
? '     THIS COMMAND FILE DEMONSTRATES THE WAIT COMMANDS.'
?
WAIT                     && Pauses operation; displays "Press any key..." prompt.
DO WHILE .T.             && Continues operation while true.
   CLEAR                 && Clears the screen.
   ?                     && ? displays a blank line; text in quotes are displayed.
   ? '              PICK AN APPLICATION'
   ? '                            Press'
   ? '         Word Processing        1'
   ? '         Spread Sheets          2'
   ? '         Database Management  3'
   ? '         Exit to dBASE          4'
   ?
   WAIT ' ' TO CHOICE    && Pauses operation; stores keyed character to memory
   *                        variable CHOICE.
   CLEAR                 && Clears the screen.
```

```
DO CASE
  CASE CHOICE='4'        && If memory variable CHOICE equals 4, commands within
    *                       CASE statement operate.
   CANCEL                && Returns control to dBASE dot prompt.
   ? '-------------------------------------------------------------------'
  CASE CHOICE='1'        && If CHOICE = 1, following text lines are displayed.
    ? 'Word processing is used to prepare text files. Editing functions,'
    ? 'such as insert, delete, move, and copy, make word processing more'
    ? 'productive than conventional office typewriting.'
  CASE CHOICE='2'
    ? 'A spread sheet is a large planning form made up of rows and columns.'
    ? 'Text, numbers, and equations are entered at row-column intersections.'
    ? 'Different numerical values may be tried to test financial assumptions,'
    ? 'making the spread sheet a powerful financial analysis tool.'
  CASE CHOICE='3'
    ? 'Database managers are used to store and maintain frequently-used'
    ? 'information. Database contents can be edited, added to, deleted,'
    ? 'displayed, and printed. Calculations can also be made with database'
    ? 'management systems. dBASE III is a database management system.'
  ENDCASE                && Completes the DO CASE statement.
  ? '-------------------------------------------------------------------'
  WAIT                   && Pauses operation; displays "Press any key..." prompt.
ENDDO                    && Completes DO WHILE statement.
```

3. Press **Ctrl-W** to write the command file to disk.

4. Run the command file by typing **DO WAITCMD** and pressing **Return**. Compare your screen to the following and respond to the prompts as indicated.

```
    THIS COMMAND FILE DEMONSTRATES THE WAIT COMMANDS.

Press any key to continue..._


        PICK AN APPLICATION
                        Press
    Word Processing       1
    Spread Sheets         2
    Database Management   3
    Exit to dBASE         4


                    -Type 1
_
```

```
----------------------------------------------------------------
Word processing is used to prepare text files. Editing functions,
such as insert, delete, move, and copy, make word processing more
productive than conventional office typewriting.

Press any key to continue..._          -Press Return

            PICK AN APPLICATION
                        Press
        Word Processing      1
        Spread Sheets        2
        Database Management  3
        Exit to dBASE        4


    _                                 -Type 4
```

5. When you finish experimenting with the command file, delete it from your disk by typing **ERASE WAITCMD.PRG** and pressing **Return**.

6. Turn to Module 64 to continue the learning sequence.

Appendix A
FILE TYPES

INTRODUCTION

Several different types of files are created and used by dBASE III Plus. These include:

Backup files	.BAK
Catalog files	.CAT
dBASE configuration file	CONFIG.DB
System configuration file	CONFIG.SYS
Database files	.DBF
Database memo field file	.DBT
Report form files	.FRM
Label form files	.LBL
Memory variable files	.MEM
Database index files	.NDX
Command files	.PRG
Query files	.QRY
Screen files	.SCR
Standard data (or text) files	.TXT
View files	.VUE

When the files are created by dBASE, they are assigned different three-character extensions, like CUSTOMER.DBF. Other files, like text files and report form files are created by dBASE. Table A-1 contains a description and accompanying example for each file type listed.

Table A-1   dBASE File Types

File Type	Extension	Description
Backup	.BAK	Backup files are automatically created as a safety measure when an edited version of a text file is saved. For example, if you use the MODIFY COMMAND *FILENAME* statement to change a file, the previous version of the modified file is kept with a .BAK extension. This happens when you press **Ctrl-W** to save (write) your modified version.
Catalog	.CAT	A catalog of filenames, including databases, index files, form files, etc. is created as files are created or put into use. The catalog file is established with SET CATALOG TO *filename* before file.creation activity is started.

Table A-1   dBASE File Types (Continued)

File Type	Extension	Description
dBASE Config.	CONFIG.DB	This file is used by dBASE when it is started. It contains one or more commands that control dBASE operation. Normal defaults, including function key values and SET functions, are controlled by this file. It can also contain a command line that causes automatic execution of a command file. You can create this file using dBASE's full-screen editor, a word processor that produces ASCII files, EDLIN, or the DOS COPY command. Notice the following CONFIG.DB command lines. These serve as examples of what you can do with the CONFIG.DB file.
	DEFAULT = B:	Sets default to disk drive B. This is the same as entering SET DEFAULT TO B: from the dot prompt.
	F10 = 'GO TOP; DISPLAY;'	Arms function key F10 with the GO TOP and DISPLAY commands. The semicolons produce RETURN.
	COMMAND = DO INVOICE	Runs the INVOICE command file at startup.
System Config.	CONFIG.SYS	This file is used by DOS when you turn on your computer. It lets you have 20 files open at the same time, including 15 within dBASE III applications. It also creates 15 buffers, which speeds up dBASE III operation by letting it work in memory buffers rather than having to read and write information to your disk during sorting and listing. This file contains the following two lines:

```
FILES=20
BUFFERS=15
```

File Type	Extension	Description
Database	.DBF	A standard database file is created and saved using the CREATE command.

```
                                                    Remarks
. CREATE STOCK                          -Creates a new database named STOCK.
  field name  type      width  dec

1 NAME        Character 20            -Field name NAME, char type, 30 characters long.
2 AMOUNT      Numeric    6      2     -Field name AMOUNT, numeric, 6 digits with 2
                                        decimal places.
3 DATE        Date       8            -Field name DATE, date type, 8 characters long.
4 INFO        Memo      10            -Field name INFO, memo type, creates .MEM file
                                        type for text storage.
5 <cr>                                -Pressing <cr> in a blank field ends database
                                        preparation.
```

After the database structure is created and saved, the file appears as STOCK.DBF in the file directory.

Table A-1   dBASE File Types (Continued)

File Type	Extension	Description
Memo file	.DBT	When a database file contains memo (text) fields, an auxiliary file having the extension .DBT is created to contain the memo fields. Databases can contain as many as 128 memo fields. Each memo field can contain up to 5,000 characters. Although memo fields use a minimum of 512 bytes in the .DBT file, they only occupy 10 bytes in a database file. Memo files are accessed when a database is being edited with APPEND, BROWSE, CHANGE, or EDIT by pressing **Ctrl-Home** from the data entry mask. After typing text into a memo field, press **Ctrl-End** to return to the data entry mask.
Report form	.FRM	The CREATE/MODIFY REPORT command lets you create and save report format files that control the display and printing of data. The REPORT commands are described in Module 21.
Label form	.LBL	The CREATE/MODIFY LABEL command lets you create and save label formats files that control the display and printing of data. The LABEL commands are described in Module 20.
Memory variable	.MEM	Memory files are created when memory variables are written to disk using the SAVE command. The resulting file has the extension .MEM. This allows you to save memory variables to disk, and then clear memory to make room for more memory variables. The following example shows use of the SAVE command.

Remarks

```
. STORE 25 to MQTY          && Stores 25 to memory variable MQTY.
. STORE 'July' to MONTH      && Stores "July" to memory variable MONTH.
. SAVE TO MFILE              && Saves memory variables to disk file MFILE.MEM.
. CLEAR ALL                  && Clears memory variables; closes files.
. RESTORE FROM MFILE         && Reads memory variables from the disk
                                file MFILE.MEM into memory, which
                                restores MQTY and MONTH. .
```

File Type	Extension	Description
Index	.NDX	An index file is created from an existing database file. The records within an index file are sorted (rearranged alphabetically or numerically) on one or more specified fields, which are referred to as "key" fields. Records retain their original record number. Changes to the contents of index files change the database file.

Remarks

```
. USE STOCK                  && Puts STOCK database in use.
. INDEX ON PN TO INVTORY     && Indexes on PN field (which is the
                                key field) to a new index file named
                                INVTORY.NDX.
. USE STOCK INDEX INVTORY    && Puts the INVTORY index in use.
```

Table A-1   dBASE File Types (Continued)

File Type	Extension	Description
Procedure (or command file)	.PRG	A procedure or command file is created and saved using the dBASE full-screen editor or some other text editor. These are pure ASCII files and are transferrable (transportable) between different computer and operating systems. Command files are created and edited using the dBASE MODIFY COMMAND *filename* command.

Remarks

```
. MODIFY COMMAND PROCESS      && Starts the dBASE editor.
Ctrl-W                        && Writes (saves) the command file.
Ctrl-Q or Esc                 && Aborts without saving.
```

File Type	Extension	Description
Query	.QRY	A query file establishes a *filter* that restricts display to specific records that meet some established condition. The CREATE/MODIFY QUERY command is described in Module 22.
Screen	.SCR	A screen file is used to create or edit screen format files. The CREATE/MODIFY SCREEN command is described in Module 23.
Standard Data	.TXT	A standard data or text file is created by copying a database file with COPY TO *filename* SDF or DELIMITED. A .TXT file is also created when information is displayed when the SET ALTERNATE TO *filename* and SET ALTERNATE ON commands are in effect. The resulting file may be used by other programs, such as WordStar's MailMerge.

```
. COPY TO DATAFILE SDF           && Makes ASCII copy of the database.
. COPY TO DATAFILE DELIMITED
```

File Type	Extension	Description
View	.VUE	Contains the name of related database files and related index and format files, which list selected field names and relations. Used to call all related files with a single command. The CREATE/MODIFY VIEW command is described in Module 24.

Appendix B
dBASE COMMAND SUMMARY

INTRODUCTION

This appendix contains a list of dBASE commands and corresponding definitions. Where additional information or examples are found in modules, module numbers are included within parentheses following the definition. The terms and definitions are, for the most part, restricted to dBASE commands and functions, and those terms that are used in describing dBASE operations.

Although the table is by no means complete within itself, it does serve as a quick reference for dBASE commands and functions. Some of the entries include clarifying examples. Examples that begin with a period indicate that they are entered from the dBASE dot prompt. Examples that are not preceded with a period prompt imply that they are part of a command file.

COMMAND FORMS

You should know that dBASE commands operate with only the first four letters. This saves a lot of typing and minimizes potential typographical errors. For example, to save time, DISPLAY STRUCTURE is typed DISP STRU; SET ALTE ON does nicely for SET ALTERNATE ON, and so on.

Table B-1   dBASE Commands

Term	Definition

@ Print Function—The @ sign followed by a row and column number specifies the placement of text or data. The at function is accompanied by the SAY and/or GET statements. (Module 8)

```
@ 9,20 SAY 'PLEASE WAIT'
@ 7,12 GET AMOUNT
@ 5,15 SAY 'AMOUNT ' GET AMOUNT
@ 10,(80-(LEN(MVAR)/2)) SAY MVAR
```

&&—Used to enter in-line comments within command files. (Module 48)

```
CLEAR ALL        && Closes all files and memory variables.
```

ACCEPT—Used in conjunction with a text prompt for inputting string (or alphanumeric) memory variables. (Module 4)

```
ACCEPT 'Input your name ' TO MNAME
```

APPEND—Add one or more records or an entire file to the bottom of the database file in use. (Module 5)

```
. APPEND
. APPEND FROM OLDFILE
```

Table B-1   dBASE Commands (Continued)

Term	Definition

ASC('n')—Returns the ASCII code for the character n. (Module 6)

```
.? ASC('A')
65
```

ASSIST—Displays on-screen help menus to assist new users. (Module 7)

AT—The substring search function used to determine the position of a specified character within an expression.

```
. ? AT('lori','Florida')
    2
```

BOF( )—Returns the beginning of file status.

```
. ? BOF( )
```

BROWSE—A command used to view and/or edit a database in use. Typing BROWSE displays the active database. (Module 10)

CANCEL—Cancels command file (or procedure) operation and returns to the dBASE III command prompt. (Module 12)

CASE—One of several possible branches in a DO CASE routine. Terminated with an ENDCASE. (Module 30)

```
DO CASE
    CASE MVAR='1'
        STORE 'JAN' TO MONTH
    CASE MVAR='2'
        STORE 'FEB' TO MONTH
    OTHERWISE
        CLEAR
        CANCEL
ENDCASE
```

CDOW—Returns the day of the week in character form.

```
. ? CDOW(DATE( ))
Saturday
```

CHANGE—Lets you change data in one or more fields of each record that meets specified conditions. (Module 13)

```
. CHANGE FIELD PHONE FOR CITY ='NEW YORK'
```

Table B-1   dBASE Commands (Continued)

Term	Definition

CHR(nn)—Displays the character or symbol equivalent to the ASCII code nn. You may use this expression to store characters to memory variables. (Module 6)

```
. STORE CHR(186) TO V
. STORE CHR(205)+CHR(205) TO H
. ? V+H+V
```

CLEAR—Clears the display screen. When used with row and column coordinates, clears the screen to the right and below the coordinates. (Modules 8, 14)

```
. CLEAR
@ 3,40 CLEAR
```

CLEAR ALL—Clears all databases and memory variables in use. (Module 14)

```
. CLEAR ALL
```

CLEAR FIELDS—Clears SET FIELDS TO *field names* condition.

CLEAR GETS—Inserted in procedures immediately following displayed database fields to prevent the contents of the displayed fields from being modified. (Modules 37, 58)

```
@ 10,12 GET NAME
@ 12,12 GET ADDRESS
CLEAR GETS
```

CLEAR TYPEAHEAD—Clears the type-ahead buffer. (Module 14)

CLOSE—Used to close files by type. (Module 15)

```
. CLOSE DATABASES
. CLOSE PROCEDURE
. CLOSE ALL
```

CMONTH—Returns the month in character form.

```
. ? CMONTH(DATE( ))
April
```

COL( )—Returns the column position of the cursor.

```
X = COL( )+10
@ X,5 SAY 'Stop!'
```

CONTINUE—Used with the LOCATE command to continue searching a database for a specified expression. (Module 45)

```
LOCATE FOR NAME = 'Jones'
DO WHILE .NOT. EOF( )
    DISPLAY NAME,PHONE
    CONTINUE
ENDDO
```

Table B-1   dBASE Commands (Continued)

Term	Definition

COPY—Copies the structure and contents of one or more fields from one database to another. (Module 16)

```
. COPY TO NEWFILE FOR ZIP = '75074'
. COPY FIELD NAME,ADDRESS,PHONE TO NEWFILE
. COPY STRUCTURE TO ABC
. COPY STRUCTURE TO XYZ FIELDS PN, AMT
. COPY TO NEWFILE DELIMITED
. COPY TO NEWFILE TYPE WKS      && Copies in Lotus 1-2-3 format.
. COPY TO NEWFILE TYPE DIF      && Copies in VisiCalc format.
. COPY TO NEWFILE TYPE SYLK     && Copies in Multiplan format.
. COPY TO NEWFILE TYPE SDF      && Copies in ASCII (text) format.
```

COUNT—Counts the number of records that match a specified parameter. (Module 17)

```
. COUNT FOR ZIP = 78641
      8 records
```

CREATE—Used to create a new database. (Module 18)

```
. CREATE NEWFILE
```

CREATE FROM—Creates file structure from an existing database. (Module 19)

```
. CREATE NEWFILE FROM OLDFILE
```

CREATE/MODIFY LABEL—Creates/modifies a label file with the extension .LBL. (Module 20)

CREATE/MODIFY QUERY—Creates/modifies a query file with the extension .QRY. (Module 21)

CREATE/MODIFY REPORT—Creates a report format file with the extension .FMT. (Module 22)

CREATE/MODIFY SCREEN—Creates/modifies a screen file with the extension .SCR. (Module 23)

CREATE/MODIFY VIEW—Creates/modifies a view file with the extension .VUE. (Module 24)

CTOD—Converts a character type string to a date type variable.

```
. STORE CTOD('10/21/86') TO BIRTHDAY
```

DATE( )—Returns the system date. (Module 25)

```
. ? DATE( )              && Displays the present system date.
. STORE DATE( ) TO MDATE && Stores system date to the memory variable MDATE.
```

DAY—Returns the day of the month.

```
. ? DAY(DATE( ))
10
```

Table B-1   dBASE Commands (Continued)

Term	Definition

DELETE—Used to mark one or more records for deletion. (Module 26)

```
. DELETE
. DELETE ALL
. DELETE NEXT 8
. DELETE FOR NAME = 'Jones'
. DELETE FILE XYZ
. DELETE FILE B:ABC.FRM
```

DELETED( )—Returns deletion status of one or more records.

```
. ? DELETED( )
.F.
. DISPLAY FOR DELETED( )
```

DELIMITED Clause—Used to insert a comma delimiter between the fields of copied records. (Module 16)

```
. COPY TO NEWFILE DELIMITED
. COPY TO NEWFILE FIELDS NAME,ADDRESS SDF DELIMITED WITH #
```

DIR—Displays a file directory. (Module 27)

DISPLAY—Displays the current record, or a series of records meeting some parameter. (Module 28)

```
. DISPLAY
. DISPLAY FOR NAME = 'Jones, Bill'
. DISPLAY ALL
. DISPLAY TO PRINT
. DISPLAY HISTORY
```

DO *filename*—Executes the named command file. Execution is terminated with the CANCEL or RETURN command. (Module 29)

```
. DO MENU
```

DO CASE—See CASE.

DO WHILE—Sustains execution while a specified condition is true. When the condition becomes false or RETURN, CANCEL, or EXIT are encountered, control is transferred to the command line following ENDDO, which completes the DO WHILE statement. (Module 31)

```
USE PHONEBK
DO WHILE .NOT. EOF( )
      DISPLAY
      SKIP
ENDDO
CANCEL
```

Table B-1   dBASE Commands (Continued)

Term	Definition

DOW—Returns the day of the week as a numeric value.

```
. ? DOW(DATE( ))
6
```

DTOC—Converts a date-type string to a character-type string.

```
. STORE DTOC(DATE( )) TO MDATE
```

EDIT—Allows modification of record contents. (Module 20)

```
: EDIT 3
. EDIT FIELDS NAME,ADDRESS
. EDIT FOR NAME = 'University'
```

EJECT—Causes a printer form feed. (Module 33)

```
. EJECT
```

ELSE—See IF.

ENDCASE—See CASE.

ENDDO—See DO WHILE.

ENDIF—See IF.

EOF( )—End-of-file function; used to determine if the record pointer has reached the last record in a database. If it has, a logical true is returned. (Appendix G)

```
DO WHILE .NOT. EOF( )
     DISPLAY NAME, ADDRESS
     SKIP
ENDDO
IF EOF( )
     DISPLAY RECNO( )
ENDIF
```

ERASE—Used to erase files from disk. (Module 34)

```
. ERASE B:OLDFILE.DBF
```

ERROR( )—Used to detect an error condition. If such occurs, the ERROR( ) and ON ERROR functions are available to let you take an alternate path in your program execution. For example, upon error detection, you may branch to another menu option, delete an unnecessary file, or perhaps close a file. A small command file follows that incorporates the use of ERROR( ) and ON ERROR to return you to the dBASE dot prompt while suppressing the Cancel, Ignore, Suspend prompt. You may wish to type and save the QUICKOUT.PRG file. Then type, save, and run the ERREXIT.PRG to see how it works.

```
* QUICKOUT.PRG
PARAMETERS ERRNO

CLEAR
?' Encountered error:',STR(ERROR( ),4)
```

Table B-1   dBASE Commands (Continued)

Term	Definition

```
?'Error message text:',MESSAGE( )
?
WAIT
CLEAR
CANCEL

* ERREXIT.PRG—Suppresses Cancel, Ignore, Suspend dialog.
* Version 1.00
ON ERROR DO QUICKOUT WITH ERROR( )
COUNT=50
?'This program erroneously uses the reserved word "count." '
DO WHILE COUNT > 50
    COUNT=COUNT+1
ENDDO
RETURN
```

EXP—Returns the value of eX (natural exponent).

```
. ? EXP(1.000)
2.718
```

EXPORT/IMPORT—Used to transfer files between dBASE and PFS:FILE. (Module 35)

```
. USE ADDRESS
. IMPORT FROM ADR1 TYPE PFS
. EXPORT TO ADR2 TYPE PFS
```

FILE—Used as a clause to designate filenames with commands such as DELETE and LIST. (Modules 26, 28)

```
. ? FILE('PHONEBK.DBF')    && Checks for presence of PHONEBK database.
.T.                        && The file is present.
. LIST FILES ON B: LIKE *.FRM
```

FIND—Used to find the first record within an indexed database containing a specified character string. The find function only searches on the indexed (key) field. In the following example, the NAME field is indexed. (Module 36)

```
. USE PHONEBK
. INDEX ON NAME TO XYZ
. USE PHONEBK INDEX XYZ
. FIND Jones
. DISPLAY
. STORE 'Hood' TO NME
. FIND &NME
. DISPLAY
. SET EXACT ON          && Searches for an exact match.
. FIND Jones, H.P.
. DISPLAY NAME, CITY, PHONE
```

Table B-1   dBASE Commands (Continued)

Term	Definition

FOUND( )—The FOUND( ) function returns a logical true when the object of the FIND, SEEK, LOCATE, OR CONTINUE commands are found. If the object is not found, a logical false is returned. The structure and database shown below is used with the following command file, which uses the FOUND( ) function.

```
Structure for database:   Address.dbf
Field  Field Name  Type      Width    Dec
   1   NAME        Character    20
   2   ADDRESS     Character    20
   3   CITY        Character    15

Database Contents:
NAME                  ADDRESS               CITY
John Wilson           33 Main Street        Dallas
Sherry Tretorn        4544 Salamander Dr.   San Francisco
Bill Todd             6700 Lottie Way       New York
Stanley Blackwell     4533 Capital Avenue   Chicago
Trixie Johnston       5600 Lakeview Drive   Dallas

Command file:
* FIND.PRG--Check for a city in the address database.
SET TALK OFF
USE B:ADDRESS
DO WHILE .T.
CLEAR
ACCEPT 'Enter a city or Q to Quit and press RETURN: ' TO MCITY
IF UPPER(MCITY)='Q'
    EXIT
ENDIF
USE ADDRESS
LOCATE FOR '&MCITY' $ CITY
IF FOUND( )
    DO WHILE FOUND( )
        DISPLAY NAME,ADDRESS,CITY WHILE '&MCITY' $ CITY OFF
    ENDDO
ELSE
    ?'City name',mcity,'not found, retype a valid city name.'
ENDIF
?
WAIT
ENDDO
```

Table B-1 dBASE Commands (Continued)

Term	Definition

```
CLEAR
USE
RETURN
```

GET—Used with a screen position command to get or display the contents of a database field or memory variable. (Modules 37, 58)

```
USE RECORD
@ 7,35 GET NAME
CLEAR GETS
@ 9,30 GET DATE
READ
```

GO or **GOTO**—Positions record pointer to specified record number. (Module 38)

```
. GO 3
. GOTO 5
```

GO BOTTOM or **GO TOP**—Positions record pointer to the bottom or top (last or first) record within a database. (Module 38)

```
. GO BOTTOM
```

HELP—Displays dBASE Help menus and information about commands. (Module 39)

```
. HELP
. HELP DISPLAY
```

IF—Branches to execute a command if a condition is true. The ELSE statement is also used to branch to an alternate set of command lines if the first condition is false. (Module 40)

```
IF UPPER(MVAR) = 'Q'
    RETURN
ELSE
    EXIT
ENDIF
```

IIF( )—The IIF( ) function is used in place of an if,else,endif expression. It uses three expressions in the form:

```
IIF(exp,expT,expF)
```

The first expression is checked for a logical true or false. If it is true, the first expression, expT, is used. If it is false, the second expression, expF, is used. Notice the following example.

```
X='Yes'
Y='No'
IF EOF( )
    ? X          is the same as    X='Yes'
ELSE                               Y='No'
    ? Y                            ?IIF(EOF( ),X,Y)
ENDIF
```

You can use the IIF( ) function in a program or from the dot prompt.

Table B-1   dBASE Commands (Continued)

Term	Definition

IMPORT—See EXPORT.

INDEX—Indexes a database in alphabetical or numerical order on one or more specified fields. Indexing does not change record numbers, but redisplays information in alphanumeric sequence. (Module 41)

```
. USE PHONEBK
. INDEX ON NAME TO XYZ
. LIST
. INDEX ON CITY + ZIP TO FILE3
```

INKEY( )—Returns an integer corresponding to the last key pressed. (Module 49)

```
i = 0
DO WHILE i = 0
     TEXT
     [1]  Run
     [2]  Quit
     ENDTEXT
     i = INKEY( )
ENDDO
(More command lines)
```

INPUT—Used to input a numeric memory variable from the keyboard; usually accompanied by prompt text. (Module 4)

```
INPUT 'Enter your age ' TO MAGE
```

INSERT—Allows record insertion within a database following the current record pointer position. The BEFORE clause is added to cause insertion before the current record pointer position. The BLANK clause is used to insert a blank record. (Module 42)

```
. GO 3
. INSERT
Record No  4
. GO 5
. INSERT BEFORE
Record No  5
. GO 8
. INSERT BLANK
. GO 12
. INSERT BEFORE BLANK
```

INT—Converts numeric expressions to integers (whole numbers).

```
. STORE 9.345 TO X
. ? INT(X)
        9
```

Table B-1   dBASE Commands (Continued)

Term	Definition

JOIN—Joins two databases (a primary and secondary database) together to form a third database. The record pointer starts at the top of the primary database and creates records that contain field contents derived from both the primary and secondary databases. The example shows this process. (Module 44)

```
. SELECT 1
. USE BLDG
. SELECT 2
. USE LAND
. JOIN WITH BLDG TO NEWFILE FOR DES=BLDG->DES
. JOIN WITH BLDG TO NEWFILE FOR DES=BLDG->DES FIELDS DES,MKTVAL,BOOKVAL
```

LEN—Returns the length of a designated string.

```
STORE 'Summary Report' TO X
STORE LEN(X) TO Y          && Stores length of X to Y.
@ 2,((80-Y)/2) SAY X       && Centers 'Summary Report' on line.
```

LIST—Used to list the contents of a database to the screen. LIST is the same as DISPLAY ALL, except DISPLAY pauses output every 20 lines. Record numbers are omitted from the listing if the OFF clause is used. (Module 28)

```
. USE PHONEBK
. LIST OFF
. LIST TO PRINT
. LIST HISTORY
. LIST FOR ZIP > '75000'
```

LOCATE—Searches for an expression within a designated field. The CONTINUE command is used to find subsequent matches. (Module 45)

```
. USE ADDRESS
. LOCATE FOR STATE='CA'
Record =    3
. CONTINUE
Record =   12
. CONTINUE
End of locate scope
```

LOG—Returns the natural logarithm of a number.

```
. ? LOG(2.7128)
1.00000
```

Table B-1   dBASE Commands (Continued)

Term	Definition

LOOP—Causes execution control within a DO WHILE statement to return (loop back) to the command line following the DO WHILE command. (Module 31)

```
DO WHILE .T.
    ACCEPT 'Type a name: ' TO MNAME
    LOCATE FOR '&MNAME' $ NAME
    IF EOF( )
        LOOP
    ENDIF
    DISPLAY NAME, CITY, PHONE
    WAIT ' '
ENDDO
```

LOWER—Converts all text characters in an expression to lower case.

```
. STORE 'ABC' TO X
. ? LOWER(X)
abc
```

MESSAGE( )—This function returns an encountered error message. Look at the example used with the ERROR( ) function to see how you can use the MESSAGE( ) function.

Macro Substitution (&)—Substitutes memory variable value for memory variable name when preceded with &. Macro substitution is not recommended within DO WHILE loops. (Appendix E)

```
. STORE 'Jones' TO MN
. FIND &MN
```

MODIFY COMMAND—Used to create or edit a procedure or command file. (Module 46)

```
. MODIFY COMMAND MENU
. MODIFY COMMAND LETTER.TXT
```

MODIFY LABEL—See CREATE/MODIFY LABEL.

MODIFY QUERY—See CREATE/MODIFY QUERY.

MODIFY REPORT—See CREATE/MODIFY REPORT.

MODIFY SCREEN—See CREATE/MODIFY SCREEN.

MODIFY STRUCTURE—Allows modification of a database structure. (Module 47)

```
. USE PHONEBK
. MODIFY STRUCTURE      && Change structure; press Ctrl-W to save.
```

MODIFY VIEW—See CREATE/MODIFY VIEW.

MONTH—Returns the month of the year in numeric form.

```
. ? MONTH(DATE( ))
10
```

Table B-1   dBASE Commands (Continued)

Term	Definition

NOTE or *—Used to place comment lines in command files; placed at the beginning of a line. Notes are not displayed during command file operation. (Module 42)

    NOTE Last update on New Year's day

or

    * Last update on New Year's day

ON ERROR—Intercepts error condition and executes following command. (Module 49)

    ON ERROR DO ERR_PRG

ON ESCAPE—Intercepts Esc keypress and executes following command. (Module 49)

    ON ESCAPE ? "The Escape key was pressed."

ON KEY—Intercepts designated key press and executes corresponding commands. (Module 49)

    ON KEY DO PROC1

PACK—Used in conjunction with the DELETE command to purge all records marked for deletion. Record numbers are resequenced, or "packed," to eliminate gaps in record numbering. Once packed, a record can not be recovered. (Module 26)

    . USE PHONEBK
    . GOTO 7
    . DELETE
    . PACK

PARAMETERS—Defines one or more data items and corresponding values within a command file. Once defined, data items can be called by other command files. (Module 50)

    * RECT.PRG: Calculates area of a rectangle
    PARAMETERS S1, S2
    AREA = S1 * S2
    RETURN

PCOL( )—Returns the present printer column position.

    . ? PCOL( )
    15

PICTURE—Used with the GET and SAY commands to control format of input and output data. (Modules 37, 58)

    USE TARDY
    @ 5,10 SAY 'ENTER TIME ' GET TIME PICTURE '99:99'
    @ 5,11 SAY 'ENTER NAME ' GET NAME PICTURE '@!'

Print Statement ?—dBASE uses a question mark followed by characters and spaces within single or double quotes or brackets to display text. (Module 51)

    ? 'The State is'+ TRIM(STATE)+'.'

PRIVATE—Restricts memory variable use to the current command file. (Module 52)

    PRIVATE A,B
    A = 'Smith'
    B = 12

Table B-1   dBASE Commands (Continued)

Term	Definition

PROCEDURE—Identifies a series of command lines as a procedure that can be called from command files or the dBASE dot prompt. SET PROCEDURE TO *filename* is required for procedure operation. (Module 53)

```
. SET PROCEDURE TO PAYRATE

* PAYRATE.PRG:  Contains wage computation procedures
.PROCEDURE A                && Identifies procedure A.
   ANNUAL = 12 * MO         && Computes value of memory variable ANNUAL.
RETURN                      && Returns control to calling command file.
PROCEDURE B
   MO = 173.33 * HR
RETURN
```

PROW( )—Returns the present printer row position.

```
. ? PROW( )20
```

PUBLIC—Designates memory variables public; public memory variables are available to all command files. (Module 52)

```
PUBLIC F,G
F = .01
G = .T.
```

QUIT—Terminates dBASE operation and returns to operating system control. Clears all memory variables and closes all files. (Module 54)

```
. QUIT
```

READ—Inserted in procedures immediately following displayed database fields to allow data entry from the keyboard or to allow existing contents of the displayed fields to be modified. (Modules 37, 58)

```
USE PHONEBK
APPEND BLANK
@ 7,20 GET NAME
@ 9,20 GET ADDRESS
READ
```

READKEY( )—Returns the integer code of the last key pressed to exit from full-screen editing operations. The value of the code indicates whether data was changed. (Module 49)

```
IF READKEY( ) = 270
    RETURN
ENDIF
```

RECALL—Removes deletion mark from records designated for deletion with the DELETE command. (Module 26)

```
. USE PHONEBK
. GO 3
. DELETE NEXT 5
. RECALL 7
. RECALL ALL
```

Table B-1   dBASE Commands (Continued)

Term	Definition

RECNO( )—The record number function returns the position of the record pointer. (Module 43)

```
. GO 6
. ? RECNO( )
6
. SKIP
. ? RECNO( )
7
. STORE RECNO( ) TO X
```

REINDEX—Updates an existing index file to include all new database records. (Module 41)

```
. USE PHONEBK INDEX XYZ
. REINDEX
```

RELEASE—Releases (or deletes) specified memory variables. Often used to make room for new memory variables. (Module 62)

```
. RELEASE MNAME,X,Y
. RELEASE ALL
```

RENAME—Lets you to change the name of a file. (Module 55)

```
. RENAME TEMP.DBF TO PERM.DBF
```

REPLACE—Replaces the contents of one or more specified fields with new data. (Module 56)

```
REPLACE NAME WITH 'Jones, W.T.' .AND. STATE WITH 'NC'
REPLACE ALL PRICE WITH PRICE*1.05
```

REPORT FORM—Used to display and print database reports. (Module 21)

```
. USE MEMBERS
. REPORT FORM NAMES
. REPORT FORM NAMES PLAIN
. REPORT FORM NAMES TO PRINT
. REPORT FORM NAMES TO PRINT NO EJECT
. REPORT FORM NAMES TO FILE1
. REPORT FORM NAMES FOR STATE='TX'
. REPORT FORM NAMES HEADING 'UPDATED REPORT'
```

RESTORE—Reads a memory variable file from disk into memory. Memory variable files are saved with SAVE MEMORY TO *filename*. RESTORE deletes active memory variables unless the ADDITIVE clause is used. (Module 62)

```
. STORE 'ALPHA' TO A
. STORE 45 TO MNUM
. STORE .T. TO STATUS
. SAVE MEMORY TO MEMO
. RELEASE ALL
. (more command lines)
. RESTORE FROM MEMO
```

Table B-1   dBASE Commands

Term	Definition

RETURN—Returns control from the current command file to the command file from which it was called, or to the dot prompt if the current command file was executed directly from the dBASE dot prompt. (Module 12)

```
IF EOF( )
    CLEAR
    RETURN
ENDIF
```

ROUND—Rounds numbers to the designated number of decimal places.

```
. X = 1.125 * AMT
. ROUND(X,2)
```

ROW—Returns the row position of the cursor.

```
X = ROW( )+2
@ 3,X SAY 'Stop!'
```

SAVE—Saves active memory variables to specified file on disk. The saved variables are read back into memory using the RESTORE command. (Module 62)

```
. SAVE TO MEMO
. SAVE TO MEMO ALL LIKE T*
. SAVE TO MEMO ALL EXCEPT T?
. RESTORE FROM MEMO
. RESTORE FROM MEMO ADDITIVE
```

SAY—Used with @ row,col to display a screen message or the contents of a field. (Module 58)

```
@ 6,5 SAY 'ENTER DATE'
@ 8,5 SAY 'AMOUNT?' GET QTY
@ 9,5 SAY NAME
@ 10,12 SAY TOTAL PICTURE '999,999.99'
```

SDF—Designates the named file as a "system data format" file, which produces a text file with the extension .TXT. A text file can be read and edited with a word processor. A .TXT file can be appended to a database as long as it is properly organized (each field in the proper order with the proper separation [delimiter]). (Module 16)

```
. COPY TO NEWFILE SDF
```

SEEK—Positions the record pointer to the record containing a specified expression. (Module 36)

```
. SEEK 'Smith'
```

SELECT—Selects a work area for one of 10 possible database files. (Module 59)

```
. SELECT 1
. USE PHONEBK
. SELECT 2
. USE ADDRESS
. LIST
. SELECT 1
. LIST
```

Table B-1   dBASE Commands (Continued)

Term	Definition

SET—Used to change dBASE defaults, such as screen display, printer action, diskette activity, data entry, and keyboard entry. (Module 60)

```
. SET
```

SKIP—Causes record pointer to move forward or backward the specified number of records. SKIP used alone advances the record pointer one record. (Module 38)

```
. GO 5
. SKIP
. SKIP 3
. SKIP −2
```

SORT—Sorts the active database to another database in alphanumerical order on one or more specified fields. Sorting can be done in descending order (high to low) if the DESCENDING clause is used. (Module 61)

```
. SORT ON NAME TO TEMP
. SORT ON NAME TO TEMP1 DESCENDING
. SORT ON CITY, NAME TO TEMP2
```

SPACE( )—Returns a specified number of spaces.

```
. X = SPACE(10)
?'Totals: ', PRICE, SPACE(12), TAX, SPACE(5), PRICE+TAX
```

SQRT—Returns the square root of a numeric value.

```
. ? SQRT(64)
      8.00
```

STORE—Used to store a specified value to a memory variable. (Module 62)

```
. STORE 'HELLO' TO MWORD
. STORE 45 TO MNUM
. STORE .T. TO STATUS
? MNUM/9
5
```

STR—Converts a numeric value to a character string value.

```
. ? STR(AMT,6,2)
. Y = STR(AMT,6,2)
```

STRUCTURE—A statement used in conjunction with other commands to display, modify, or copy the structure of an active database. (Modules 16, 28, 47)

```
. USE STOCK
. DISPLAY STRUCTURE
. COPY STRUCTURE TO MYFILE
. USE MYFILE
. MODIFY STRUCTURE
```

SUBSTR( )—Returns a specified length of text beginning at a specified position.

```
. Y = 'PQRSTU'
. Z = SUBSTR(Y,3,2)
```

Table B-1   dBASE Commands (Continued)

Term	Definition

SUM—Sums contents of one or more specified fields and stores the result to a specified memory variable; may include conditional statements. (Module 63)

```
. SUM AMOUNT TO MVAL
. SUM AMOUNT TO MVAL FOR AMOUNT  >  10.00
. SUM (AMOUNT*2+6)/3
```

TEXT—Displays typed text until ENDTEXT command is encountered. (Module 65)

```
TEXT
One moment please. . .
The names are being sorted. .
ENDTEXT
```

TIME( )—Returns system time. (Module 25)

```
. ? TIME( )
11:12:21
```

TOTAL—Sums the numeric fields of the active database into a second database. The numeric fields in the target databae contain the totals for all records having the same key value of the original database. (Module 66)

```
. TOTAL ON COST TO FILE1
. TOTAL ON AMOUNT TO FILE2 FIELDS COST, PRICE
. TOTAL ON PRICE TO FILE3 FOR VENDOR  =  'AJAX'
```

TRIM—Eliminates trailing blanks from a character field or memory variable. (Appendix E)

```
. STORE TRIM(CITY) TO MCITY
. ? "City: ", TRIM(CITY)
```

TYPE *filename*—Lists the named file on the screen. A quick way to check the contents of an ASCII file, such as a command file. (Module 67)

```
. TYPE LISTING.PRG
```

TYPE( )—Displays the data type of a field or memory variable as N, C, L, M, or U for numeric, character, logical, memo, or undefined. (Appendix E)

```
. ? TYPE('ABC')
C
. ? TYPE(123)
N
. ? TYPE(.T.)
L
. ? TYPE(XY)
U
STORE 125 TO XY
. ? TYPE(XY)
N
```

Table B-1   dBASE Commands (Continued)

Term	Definition

UPDATE—Used to replace the contents of one or more fields in one database from another. The SELECT command is used to put the involved databases into active work areas. (Module 68)

```
. SELECT 1
. USE WIP
. SELECT 2
. USE WHSE
. UPDATE ON PART_NO FROM WIP REPLACE QTY WITH QTY + WIP->QTY
```

UPPER—Converts all text characters in an expression to upper case.

```
. STORE 'abc' TO X
. ? UPPER(X)
ABC
```

USE—Puts named database in use or closes active database. (Module 69)

```
. USE PHONEBK
. LIST NAME, PHONE
. USE
. USE MEMBERS INDEX NAMELIST
```

VAL( )—Converts a character string made up of numbers to an integer value to allow math operations. If the string is made up of alphabetical characters, a zero value is returned.

```
. STORE '12.95' TO Z
. ? VAL(Z)
        12
. X = 10 * VAL(Z)
        120
```

WAIT—Pauses the execution of a command file and displays either the prompt "Press any key to continue. . ." or a user-defined prompt. Also used to store a one-byte value to a memory variable. (Module 70)

```
WAIT
WAIT 'Press Esc to abort '
WAIT ' '
WAIT 'Type "Q" to Quit, any other key to continue. . .' TO OPT
```

YEAR—Returns the year as a numeric value.

```
. ? YEAR(DATE( ))
1988
```

ZAP—Deletes the contents of the active database. (Module 34)

```
. USE PHONEBK
. ZAP
```

Appendix C
dBASE OPERATORS

INTRODUCTION

The term *operator* is just another name for an arithmetic expression, like plus, minus, divide by, equal to, and so on. Instead of spelling out these operators, symbols are used to represent them. There are four types of dBASE operators: arithmetic, relational, logical, and string. Table C-1 contains a description and accompanying example of each operator.

Table C-1   dBASE Operators

Operator Symbol	Description
Arithmetic Operators	Arithmetic operators are used to achieve mathematical computations. They include addition, subtraction, multiplication, and division operators.

NOTE

In the following examples of operators, notice the dot prompt followed by a question mark. Typing a question mark and a space followed by the sample expressions lets you test operators.

Operator Symbol	Description
+	The plus sign is the addition operator.
. ? 37+144	
–	The minus sign (hyphen) is the subtraction operator.
. STORE 53 TO MNUM	
. ? MNUM-21	
*	The asterisk is the multiplication operator.
. ? 12*MNUM	
/	The slash sign is the division operator.
. ? 208/52	
( )	Parentheses are used for grouping.
. ? (27–(5+10)/3)*2	
∧ or **	The circumflex or double asterisk is the power or exponent operator.
. ? 12 ∧ 3	
EXP( )	This is the natural exponent (e) operator.
. ? EXP(12)	

Table C-1   dBASE Commands (Continued)

Operator Symbol	Description
LOG( )	This is the natural logarithm operator.
. ? LOG(10)	
SQRT( )	This is the square root operator.
. ? SQRT(162)	
Relational Operators	Relational operators are used to assign a relationship between two values. They include expressions like *greater than*, *less than*, *not equal*, and so on. There are many uses for relational operators, like finding all records in a database that contain a March transaction date or a dollar value relative to a specified value.
<	Less than operator.
. LIST FOR ZIP_CODE < 78000	
>	Greater than operator.
. SORT ON NAME TO NEWFILE FOR DATE > '01/01/83'	
=	Equal to operator.
. DELETE FOR AMOUNT = 0	
< > or #	Not equal to operator.
. DISPLAY FOR STATE < > 'CA'	
< =	Less than or equal to operator.
. REPLACE AMOUNT WITH AMOUNT*1.1 FOR QTY < = 10	
> =	Greater than or equal to operator.
. LIST OFF FOR DATE > = '01/01/84'	
Logical Operators	Logical operators produce true or false results or establish logical "rules" in a mathematical expression. For example, logical operators can require that only those records greater than one date and less than another be listed (see the .AND. example) or only those outside of a certain range be listed (see .OR. example).
.AND.	Joins two or more expressions to establish a value range. In the following example, the range is the full month of January.
. LIST FOR DTOC(DATE) > = '01/01' .AND. DTOC(DATE) < = '01/31'	
.OR.	Joins two or more expressions to exclude a value range or to offer alternative selections. In the first example, the range excludes the month of March. In the second example, three dates are selected for display. In the third example, records meeting a match in either the NAME or COMPANY fields are located.
. LIST FOR DTOC(DATE) < '03/01/' .OR. DTOC(DATE) > '03/31/' . LIST FOR DTOC(DATE) = '01/15/' .OR. DTOC(DATE) = '01/31/' .OR. DTOC(DATE) = '02/15/' . LOCATE FOR NAME = 'Johnson' .OR. COMPANY = 'Johnson'	

Table C-1   dBASE Commands (Continued)

Operator Symbol	Description
.NOT.	The "not true" operator is used to find conditions that are not true. For example, if you have a customer list and want to list all customer's records that haven't paid their bill, which could be indicated by the presence of a F, N, or blank in the logical PAID field of each record, you could use the following command.

```
. LIST FOR .NOT. PAID
```

;	The semicolon is used to continue a statement on the following line.
String Operators	String operators are used to control the spacing between adjoining fields when information is listed on the screen or printer.
,	The comma is a union operator which joins two database fields.

```
. LIST NAME,ADDRESS,CITY,STATE,ZIP
```

+	The plus symbol is used to concatenate (connect) two database fields when displayed or printed.

```
. LIST NAME+ADDRESS+CITY
```

–	The minus sign (hyphen) removes trailing blank spaces between adjoining fields. This operator is often referred to as a *blank squash*, because it "squashes" the space between adjacent fields. The space is actually moved to the end of the the last field, but the desired effect of eliminating extra spaces between fields is achieved.

```
. LIST NAME+CITY—', ',STATE
```

ASC( )	The character to ASCII function converts a character to its equivalent ASCII value.

```
. ? ASC('1')
49
. ? ASC('A')
65
```

CHR( )	The ASCII to character function converts an ASCII value to the equivalent character value.

```
. ? CHR(49)
1
. ? CHR(65)
A
```

MAX( )	The MAX( ) function returns the higher value of two numeric expressions.

```
. x=23
23
. y=14
14
. m=max(x,y)
        23
```

Table C-1   dBASE Commands (Continued)

Operator Symbol	Description
MIN( )	The MIN( ) function returns the lower value of two numeric expressions.

```
. x=23
23
. y=14
14
. m=min(x,y)
        14
```

MOD( )	The MOD( ) (or modulus) function returns the value of the remainder from a division problem. You can use the MOD( ) value to convert the remainder of a problem involving feet to inches. Look at the following command file to see how MOD( ) is used.

```
* DIF.PRG - - Compute difference between two lengths
SET TALK OFF
CLEAR
INPUT 'Enter longest length in inches: ' TO MLEN1
INPUT 'Enter shortest length in inches: ' to MLEN2
MDIF=MLIN1—MLEN2
MFEET=INT(MDIF/12)
MINCH—MOD(MDIF,12)
?'The difference is',ltrim(str(mfeet)), 'feet', 'and',ltrim(str(minch)), 'inches.'
WAIT
CLEAR ALL
RETURN
```

You can apply the same principle to calendar and clock times, miles, kilometers, or any other units of measure.

ROUND( )	This function rounds a number to a specified number of decimal places. The form of the expression is: ROUND(expression,n), where n is the number of decimal places.

```
. ? round(234.5678,1)
234.6000
```

Appendix D
dBASE CONTROL KEYS

INTRODUCTION

The control keys listed and described in Table D-1 are used for cursor control, text insertion and deletion, filing, and similar functions. Many of the control keys are used with the dBASE full-screen editor. They're similar to word processing control keys used in text entry and editing. Many are also used when browsing, editing, appending records, or when modifying the structure of a database.

Table D-1   dBASE Control Keys

Control Key	Description
Ctrl-A or Home	Moves cursor left one field (BROWSE mode) or left one word (dBASE editor).
Ctrl-B or Ctrl- →	Scrolls left (BROWSE mode).
Ctrl-C or PgDn	Moves to next record (EDIT and BROWSE modes); scrolls one-half screen up (dBASE editor).
Ctrl-D or →	Moves cursor right one character.
Ctrl-E or Up Arrow ↑	Moves cursor up one line.
Ctrl-F or End	Moves cursor right one field (BROWSE mode); moves cursor right one word (dBASE editor).
Ctrl-G or Del	Deletes the character at the cursor.
Ctrl-H or Backspace	Deletes the character to the left of the cursor.
Ctrl-I or Tab	Tabs cursor 5 characters to the right (dBASE editor).
Ctrl-KR *filename*	Read file from disk (dBASE editor).
Ctrl-KW *filename*	Write file to disk (dBASE editor).
Ctrl-M or Return	Enters command or ends line.
Ctrl-N	Inserts a line or field at cursor position.
Ctrl-P	Turns printing of displayed text on and off as it is written to the screen.
Ctrl-Q or Esc	Quits (abandons) editing without saving.
Ctrl-R or PgUp	Scrolls previous screen down (dBASE editor and BROWSE mode); moves to previous record (EDIT mode).
Ctrl-S or ←	Moves cursor left one character (EDIT, BROWSE, and dBASE editor); stops and resumes screen scrolling.
Ctrl-T	Delete next word (dBASE editor).
Ctrl-U	Turns on/off delete record mark (BROWSE and EDIT modes; deletes field definition (MODIFY REPORT mode and dBASE editor).
Ctrl-V or Ins	Toggles between insert/strikeover mode.
Ctrl-W or Ctrl-End	Saves (writes) file and ends editing; returns to edit mask from memo field.
Ctrl-X or Down Arrow ↓	Moves cursor down one line (MODIFY COMMAND mode); erases command line from dot prompt.
Ctrl-Y	Deletes current line.
Ctrl-Z or Ctrl- ←	Scrolls right (BROWSE mode only).
Shift-PrtSc	Prints displayed information on printer.
F1	Turns menus on/off during editing.
Ctrl-End	Returns from memo field text to edit mask.

Appendix E
dBASE STRING FUNCTIONS

INTRODUCTION

Remember the term *string*? A string is a series of characters and spaces. String types are either numeric (numbers), character (letters or a mixture of letters, numbers, punctuation marks, and spaces), or logical (yes or no, true of false). String functions are tools that let you control the way strings are stored or displayed, or that let you determine certain characteristics about them. There are string functions that let you convert numbers to characters, characters to numbers, decimal numbers to whole numbers (or *integers*), determine the number of characters in a string, and so on. The general form of a string function is the function's identifying command or symbol followed by the expression in parentheses.

Function(*expression*)

The expression is usually the value of a field or memory variable, but it can be a numeric or character string that's directly entered from the keyboard. Table E-1 describes string functions and provides examples.

Table E-1   dBASE String Functions

Function	Description
ABS( )	The absolute value function returns the difference between two numbers as a positive number. Store 12 to a and 21 to b. Then use ABS( ) to determine the absolute value of the difference between a and b.

```
. a=12
. b=21
. ? abs(a-b)
        9
```

Function	Description
ASC( )	The character to ASCII code function is used to display the ASCII character that is equivalent that is equivalent to the number used within the expression. The form of the character to ASCII function form is: ASC('X'), where X is a character

<u>Remarks</u>

```
. ? ASC('A')          && What is the ASCII code for A?
 65                   && The ASCII code for A is displayed.
. ? ASC('1')          && What is the ASCII code for 1?
 49                   && The ASCII code for 1 is displayed.
. STORE 2 TO X        && Store the value to to memory variable X.
. ? ASC('X')          && What is the ASCII code for the variable X?
 50                   && The ASCII code for 2 (variable X) is 50.
```

Table E-1   dBASE String Functions (Continued)

Function	Description
AT( )	The substring search function compares two character strings. It looks for the first string within the second string. In other words, where does string 1 start within string 2? If a match is found in the second string, an integer is returned equal to the starting position. If the string isn't found, a zero is returned. The form of the substring search function is: AT(string 1, string 2)

```
. ? at('rst','pqrstuv')
       3
```

Function	Description
CHR( )	The number to character function is similar to the BASIC chr$(x) function. The number to character function produces the ASCII character that is equivalent to the number within parentheses. The number to character function form is: CHR(X), where X is equal to an ASCII character code.

```
CHR(10)        && Line Feed.
CHR(13         && Return.
CHR(15)        && Commonly used to turns on compressed print.
```

Function	Description
INT( )	The integer function converts a decimal number to a whole number; fractional parts are discarded when a number is expressed as an integer. The integer function has the form: INT(numeric expression)

<u>Remarks</u>

```
. STORE 123.456 TO MNUM  && Stores 123.456 to MNUM.
  123.456                && Value displayed.
. ? INT(MNUM)            && What is the integer value of MNUM?
       123               && The integer value is displayed.
. STORE 0.06 TO MNUM
       0.06
. ? INT(MNUM)
       0
```

Function	Description
ISALPHA( )	The ISALPHA( ) function returns a logical true when the specified character expression begins with an alpha character. The standard form for ISALPHA( ) is: ISALPHA('expression')

```
. ? isalpha('duck')
.T.
. ? isalpha('789crt')
.F.
```

Function	Description
ISLOWER( )	The ISLOWER() function returns a logical true if the first character in the selected character expression is lower case.

```
. ? islower('hello')
.T.
```

Table E-1   dBASE String Functions (Continued)

Function	Description
ISUPPER( )	The ISUPPER( ) function returns a logical true if the first character in the selected character expression is upper case.

```
. ? isupper('Hello')
.T.
```

Function	Description
LEFT( )	The left function specifies the left-most number of characters to use the specified expression. The general form of the LEFT( ) function is: LEFT('expression',n), where the expression is a string and n specifies the left-most number of characters to use.

```
. ? left('Brigham',4)
Brig
```

Function	Description
LEN( )	The length function returns an integer value equal to the number of characters in the specified string. The form of the length function is: LEN(string)

Remarks

```
. STORE 'Smith' TO X      && Store Smith to X.
        Smith             && The value of X is displayed.
. ? LEN(X)                && How long is X?
        5                 && It is 5 characters long.
```

Function	Description
LOWER( )	The lower case function converts all upper case characters within a string to lower case. The form of the lower case function is: LOWER(string)

Remarks

```
. ? LOWER(AbcdE)          && Convert upper case to lower case.
        abcde             && Converted characters displayed.
```

Function	Description
LTRIM( )	The LTRIM( ) function trims any leading spaces from a character expression.

```
. ? ltrim('   spaces')
spaces
. ? ltrim(str(123.456,8,2))
123.46
```

Function	Description
Macro Substitution (&)	The macro substitution function makes use of the ampersand (&) symbol in front of a character-type memory variable name. When used, the contents of the memory variable are directly substituted for the &memory variable expression. If the substitution string precedes additional characters, it should be followed by a period. The form of the macro function is:

&memory variable or
&memory variable.characters

Remarks

```
. STORE "DISPLAY NAME" TO MDISP   && Stores text in quotes to MDISP.
. &MDISP                          && The contents of MDISP.
    DISPLAY NAME                  && DIPSLAY NAME command issued.
. STORE "GO BOTTOM" TO GB         && Stores text in quotes to GB.
. &GB                             && GO BOTTOM command issued.
```

Table E-1 *dBASE String Functions (Continued)*

Function	Description
. REPLICATE	Repeats the selected character a specified number of times. The expression:

. @ 10,01 SAY REPLICATE(chr(205),78)

gives you a double rule across the screen beginning at row 10, column 1. The next expression draws a series of twelve right brackets.

```
. x = ']'
. y = 12
. @ 10,20 say replicate(x,y)

    This is the same as:

. @ 10,20 say replicate(']',12)
```

| RIGHT( ) | The right function displays the right-most n characters of a string. The general form of the function is: RIGHT(string,n), where n is the number of characters to be displayed. |

```
. ? right(ABCDEFG,3)
EFG
. ? right(dtoc(date()),2)
86
```

| ROUND( ) | The round function rounds a numeric value to a specified number of decimal places. The form of this function is: ROUND(value,decimal places) |

<u>Remarks</u>

```
. ? ROUND(12.1478,2)        && Rounds the number to 2 decimal places.
  12.1400                   && Value rounded to 2 places.
```

| RTRIM( ) | This right trim function is identical to the TRIM( ) function. |

| SPACE( ) | The space function inserts a specified number of spaces on a line. The form of the space function is: SPACE(n), where n is the number of spaces. |

<u>Remarks</u>

```
. ? SPACE(5)+'X'+SPACE(5)+'X'  && Inserts 5 spaces, X, 5 spaces, X.
       X     X                 && Resulting display.
```

| STR( ) | The string function converts a number into a character. The string function makes provisions for character length and decimal places, and has the form: STR(number,length,decimals) |

<u>Remarks</u>

```
. STORE 678.0901 TO X      && Stores 678.0901 to X.
  678.0901                 && The value of X is displayed.
. STORE STR(X,6,2) TO Y    && Stores X as a six character string with
                              two decimals to Y.
  678.09                   && The value of Y is displayed.
```

Table E-1   dBASE String Functions (Continued)

Function	Description
STUFF( )	This function is used to modify part of a character string, by "stuffing" a new string into an existing one. The form of the STUFF( ) function is:

STUFF(expression, start, no. of characters, stuff string)

```
. mstr='There are two moons'
. ? stuff(mstr,11,3,'six')
There are six moons
. ? stuff(mstr,11,0,'sixty-')
There are sixty-two moons
```

| SUBSTR( ) | The substring function forms a character string from a portion of another character string. The value of the substring is specified by starting position and number of characters within the string from which it's being derived. The substring function has the form: SUBSTR(string,starting position,length) |

Remarks

```
. ? SUBSTR('ABCDEFG',2,4)      && Use substring starting at second
                                  character, four characters long.
        BCDE                   && The result is displayed.
. STORE 4 TO X
        4
. STORE 2 TO Y
        2
. ? SUBSTR('abcdefg',X,Y)
        de
```

| Substring Operator ($) | The substring logical operator is used to find a partial match within a field. The first example lists records containing New Hampshire, New Jersey, New Mexico, and New York in the STATE field. The general form of the substring operator is: |

List for 'partial expression' $ *field name*

Remarks

```
. LIST FOR 'New' $STATE
. ? 'lori' $ 'Florida'
        .T.
IF X = $ 'Aa1'      && IF is true if X equals A, a, or 1.
```

| TRANSFORM( ) | The transform function lets you assign PICTURE format attributes to character and numeric expressions without having to use the @ say command. See the PICTURE clause options in Table 58-1 of Module 58. |

```
. use order
. ? transform(sales,'$$99999.99')
$$$$$31.90
```

Table E-1   dBASE String Functions (Continued)

Function	Description
TRIM( )	The trim function eliminates trailing blanks from the contents of a character type field. For example, if you have a ten-character-length field that only has a four-character expression, use the trim function to eliminate the extra six spaces. Exercise caution when using the trim function with an indexed file, as the length of a key field is significant to the field value. The form of the trim function is:

TRIM(string)
or TRIM(field1-', ',TRIM(field2)

```
. STORE 'Jones     ' TO LN
. ? LEN(LN)
        10
. STORE TRIM(LN) TO X
. ? LEN(X)
         5
```

Function	Description
TYPE( )	The type function is used to identify the string type of the following string or memory variable. Types are either character (C), numeric (N), or logical (L). The type function form is:TYPE('string' or variable name)

```
. ? TYPE('123')
N
. STORE .T. TO LGC
.T.
. ? TYPE(LGC)
L
. STORE DATE() TO DTE
09/21/85
. ? TYPE(DTE)
D
. STORE 'ABC' TO TXT
ABC
. ? TYPE(TXT)
C
```

Table E-1   dBASE String Functions (Continued)

Function	Description

UPPER( ) — The upper case function converts all lower case characters within a string to upper case. The form of the upper case function is: UPPER(string).

```
. UPPER(AbcdE)
ABCDE
```

NOTE

The following four statements represent an excerpt from a command file.

```
WAIT 'Type Q to quit, any other key to continue...' TO X
IF UPPER(X)='Q'
    QUIT
ENDIF
```

VAL( ) — The character to number function function converts a series of (or String to Number) numbers that have been stored as characters to an integer value. The character string containing the numbers may have a sign and decimal point. The form of the string to number function is: VAL(character string)

<u>Remarks</u>

```
. STORE '123.321' TO MNUM   && Store string 123.321 to MNUM.
 123.321                    && The string is displayed.
. ? 2 * VAL(MNUM)           && Multiply the numeric string by 2.
 246                        && The answer is displayed.
```

dBASE DATE AND TIME FUNCTIONS

INTRODUCTION

Date and time functions are convenient for displaying or printing the current time and date on reports. dBASE offers a number of date and time functions. These are described with examples of each in Table 3-5.

Table F-1   dBASE Date and Time Functions (Continued)

Function	Description
CTOD( )	The character to date function converts the date expressed as a text string into a standard date type expression. The form of the year function is: CTOD(string) CTOD(date field) . STORE '09/21/88' TO ABC 09/21/88 . ? TYPE(ABC) C . STORE CTOD(ABC) TO DTE 09/21/88 . ? TYPE(DTE) D
DATE( )	The date function gives you access to the system date. You can use this function to store the system date to a memory variable or database field. The form of the date function is: DATE( ) . ? DATE( ) 09/21/88 . STORE DATE( ) TO DTE 09/21/88
DAY( )	The day of month function converts the date expression into the day of the month. The form of the day of month function is: DAY(date). . STORE DATE( ) TO DTE 09/21/88 . ? DAY(DTE) 21

Table F-1   dBASE Date and Time Functions (Continued)

Function	Description

DOW( ) — The day of week function converts the date expression into the day of the week expressed as a number. The form of the day of week function is: DOW(date).

```
. STORE DATE( ) TO DTE
09/21/88
. ? DOW(DTE)
6
```

CDOW( ) — The character day of week function converts the date expression into the day of the week expressed in text form, i.e. Sunday through Saturday. The form of the day of week function is: CDOW(date).

```
. STORE DATE( ) TO DTE
09/21/88
. ? CDOW(DTE)
Saturday
```

LUPDATE( ) — The last update function returns the date that a database file was last updated (or saved with changes). This is like looking at the DOS directory command to look at the file date. The form of the last update command is: LUPDATE( ).

```
. use address
. ? lupdate()
05/25/88
```

MONTH( ) — The month of year function converts the date expression into the month of the year expressed as a number. The form of the day of week function is: MONTH(date).

```
. STORE DATE( ) TO DTE
09/21/88
. ? MONTH(DTE)
9
```

CMONTH( ) — The character month of year function converts the date expression into the month of the year expressed as a name. The form of the day of week function is: CMONTH(date).

```
. STORE DATE( ) TO DTE
09/21/88
. ? CMONTH(DTE)
September
```

Table F-1   dBASE Date and Time Functions (Continued)

Function	Description
TIME( )	The time function gives you access to the system time. You can use this function to store the system time to a memory variable or database field. The form of the time function is: TIME( ).

```
. ? TIME( )
18:30:21.64
. STORE TIME( ) TO TME
18:31:05.11
```

Function	Description
YEAR( )	The year function converts the date expression into a year expression. The form of the year function is: YEAR(date).

```
. STORE DATE( ) TO DTE        -Stores the system date to memory variable DTE.
09/21/85                      -The stored date is displayed.
. ? YEAR(DTE)                 -What is the year?
1985                          -It is 1985.
```

Appendix G
dBASE RECORD POINTER AND STATUS FUNCTIONS

INTRODUCTION

These functions perform three tasks. First, they let you position the *record pointer* to different records within a database. Second, they provide information about a record or about the position of the record pointer. Finally, they provide information about files and the system environment. A descriptive list these important functions is contained in Table G-1.

Table G-1   dBASE Record Pointer and Status Functions

Function	Description
DBF( )	Lets you determine if a database file is in use. The following series of commands incorporates the use of DBF( ).

```
. use b:address
. ? dbf()
b:address.dbf
. use
. ? dbf()        && Blank line indicates that no database file is open.
```

You can store a database filename to a memory variable and then call it into use, using a macro substitution string, as follows:

```
. use b:address        && Open b:address.dbf
. file1 = dbf()        && Store the .dbf filename to file1
. close database       && Close all database files
. use &file1           && Reopen the b:address.dbf file
. ? dbf()              && Check to see if it worked
b:address.dbf          && It did.
```

Function	Description
DELETED( )	The DELETED( ) function returns the status of the current or specified records to determine whether or not they are marked for deletion when the PACK command is issued.

```
. USE MEMBERS
. LIST STRUCTURE

Field  Field name  Type       Width    Dec
    1  NAME        Character     25
    2  PHONE       Character     14
    3  PAID        Logical        1
** Total **                      41
```

Table G-1   dBASE Record Pointer and Status Functions (Continued)

Function	Description

```
. DELETE FOR .NOT. PAID
. GO TOP
. ? DELETED()
.F.                       && Indicates first record not deleted.
. LIST FOR DELETED()

Record#  NAME                      PHONE          PAID
       2 *William Butler           (512) 434-6787 .F.
       3 *Phillip Johnstone        (213) 323-5565 .F.


. RECALL ALL                && Recalls all records marked for deletion.
       2 records recalled
. USE
```

DISKSPACE( ) Commonly used with RECSIZE( ) and RECCOUNT( ) in applications that perform database backup operations. To check the space left on the logged disk drive, use:

```
. ? diskspace()
.   105472
```

RECCOUNT( ) counts the number of records in the selected database, while RECSIZE( ) returns the size of each record. Putting all of this together, you can keep from exceeding the capacity of your disk with a routine like the following one:

```
* CHKSPACE.PRG--Check the remaining disk space.
* Version 1.01
CLEAR
SET TALK OFF
USE ORDER
MSIZE = RECSIZE() * RECCOUNT()
IF DISKSPACE() > MSIZE
    SORT ON NAME TO NEWFILE.
ELSE
    @ 8,10 SAY 'Insufficient disk space...'
ENDIF
WAIT
RETURN
```

Table G-1   dBASE Record Pointer and Status Functions (Continued)

Function	Description

FIELD( )   The FIELD( ) function gives you the field name that corresponds to a numeric position within the selected file structure. The following example shows a database structure. Notice that the CITY field is third in line.

```
Field  Field Name  Type      Width   Dec
    1  NAME        Character   20
    2  ADDRESS     Character   20
    3  CITY        Character   15
    4  STATE       Character    2
    5  ZIP         Character    9
** Total **                    67
```

Now check the name of the third field as follows:

```
. ? field(3)
CITY
. ? field() = 'CITY'
.T.
```

FILE( )   The FILE( ) function is used to determine the presence of a specified file. It returns a true status if the file exists. If the named file is not found, false is returned. Assume the file ADDRESS.DBF. exists on the logged disk. The following query verifies its presence.

```
. ? file('address.dbf')
.T.
```

You can use the file( ) function to control program branching, as in the following programming example:

```
* FILECHK.PRG--Check for a file.
* Version 1.00
CLEAR
DO CASE
    CASE FILE('name.ndx')
        DO NAME
    CASE FILE('city.ndx')
        DO CITY
    OTHERWISE
        WAIT 'File not found, press any key to continue...'
        RETURN TO MASTER
ENDCASE
RETURN
```

Table G-1   dBASE Record Pointer and Status Functions (Continued)

Function	Description

You may wish to store a file name to a memory variable, as shown in the following example:

```
. MFNAME1 = 'B:NAME.NDX'
. ? FILE(MFNAME1)
.T.
```

FKLABEL( )   Used to determine or change a function key setting. Look at the following examples.

```
. ? FKLABEL(1)
F2
. ? FKLABEL(9)
F10
```

The following program file, which uses the FKMAX( ) function, prompts the user to type in new commands.

```
DO WHILE N <= FKMAX()
    ACCEPT "SET '+ " TO " TO STRING
    SET FUNCTION FKLABEL(N) TO STRING
    N = N+1
ENDDO
LIST STATUS
CANCEL
```

FKMAX( )   Returns the maximum function key number available on your computer. FKMAX( ) was used in the FKLABEL( ) example. The following example shows FKMAX( ) use from the dot prompt.

```
. ? FKMAX()
  9
```

GETENV( )   This function lets you check your operating system environment. Some typical queries are:

```
. ? GETENV('COMSPEC')
A:\COMMAND.COM
. ? GETENV('PATH')
\DOS
```

GO or GOTO   Positions record pointer to the top, bottom, or to a specified record number. You can also type the record number by itself to jump the record pointer.

```
. GO BOTTOM              && Moves record pointer to last record.
. GO TOP                 && Moves record pointer to first record.
. GO 6                   && Moves record pointer to record 6.
. 5                      && Moves record pointer to record 5.
```

Table G-1   dBASE Record Pointer and Status Functions (Continued)

Function	Description

ISCOLOR( )   This function returns a logical true value if you are using a color system and a logical false value if your system is monochrome. You can use the ISCOLOR() function to respond to your system configuration. The following routine is included within a command file to automatcially set your system parameters.

```
IF ISCOLOR()
    SET COLOR TO W+/B,B,BG
ELSE
    SET COLOR TO W+
ENDIF
```

See the SET COLOR ON/OFF command in Module 60 for color values.

NDX( )   This function is used to return the name of the active index file(s) in the selected work area. The following program is suggested.

```
* DEX.PRG--Displays open index files
CLEAR
i=1
NULL=""
DO WHILE NULL < NDX(i) .AND. i <= 7
    ? NDX(i)
    i=i+1
ENDDO
CLEAR ALL
WAIT
RETURN
```

Note that the numeric memory variable i must be between 1 and 7. If no index file is open, a "null" string is returned.

OS( )   The OS( ) function returns the operating system version in use.

```
. ? OS()
DOS 3.10
```

RECCOUNT( )   Counts the number of records in the selected database.

```
. USE ORDER
. ? RECCOUNT()
  118
```

RECNO( )   Returns the current record pointer position.

```
. GO TOP
. ? RECNO()
        1
```

Table G-1   dBASE Record Pointer and Status Functions (Continued)

Function	Description

RECSIZE( )   Checks the size of the records in the selected database.

```
. use order
. ? recsize()
  118
```

See DISKSPACE( ) for an example that uses both the RECCOUNT( ) and RECSIZE( ) functions.

SKIP   Moves the record pointer one or more records. Forms of the command are:

```
SKIP
SKIP 3          && Skips down 3 records.
SKIP -3         && Skips up 3 records.
```

```
. ? RECNO()
       1
. SKIP
Record no.      2
. SKIP 2
Record no.      4
. SKIP -1
Record no.      3
```

VERSION( )   The function returns the dBASE version in use. Check the following example.

```
. ? VERSION()
dBASE III PLUS  version 1.0
```

Appendix H
COMMON TERMS AND DEFINITIONS

INTRODUCTION

Several common terms and definitions encountered in this book are defined in this appendix. In addition to terminology specific to dBASE, many of the terms are common to computing.

Table H-1   Terms and Definitions

Term	Description
Alphanumeric	A combination of alphabetical and numeric characters used to form an expression, such as a part number. An example of an alphanumeric expression follows. PN A-10036-001 Notice that alphabetical, numeric, spaces, and punctuation characters may exist in an alphanumeric expression.
ASCII	American Standard Code for Information Interchange- -a standard data code used to represent alphabetical, numerical, and punctuation characters used in Electronic Data Processing systems.
Attribute	A special characteristic of a value or command.
Batch File	Often called command file or procedure, a batch file is a series of instructions, or commands, that can be used to perform a repetitive task. Following is an example of a batch file. (Module 46) USE FILENAME GO BOTTOM DISPLAY WAIT ERASE CANCEL
BIT	A single BInary digiT that has a value of either one or zero (on or off). Produced and used by digital computers to represent data characters and to control computer peripheral devices.
Byte	A single character, symbol, or control code used by a computer; made up of a unique pattern of eight bits, where the pattern specifies the character, symbol, or control code value.
Character	A letter, number, or punctuation mark.
Clause	A class of commands that have a specific objective; a clause may control the format of displayed or printed information or the structure of a database. Examples of clauses are: BLANK PICTURE DELIMITED SDF FOR STRUCTURE NEXT USING
Command File	See Batch File.

Table H-1 Terms and Definitions (Continued)

Term	Description
Delimiter	A separator, such as a comma, that designates the end of one field and the beginning of the next.
Error Message	A software-embedded message that is displayed when an illegal command or command form is attempted by the system user.
Extension	An optional one- to three-digit suffix which is part of a filename. Examples are:

PHONEBK.DBF	DBF designates a database file.
MENU.PRG	PRG designates a dBASE MS-DOS command file.
NAMELIST.FRM	FRM designates a dBASE report form file.

Term	Description
Field	An entry within a record, such as a name or address field within a customer record.
File	A document, database, program, or similar entity that has a filename, a beginning, and an end. Generally made up of discrete records having a length of from one to 1,000 characters (or bytes).
Filename	The name of a file, program, or document stored on magnetic media, such as tape or disk. Filenames are made up of from one to eight characters with an optional one- to three-character extension.
Interactive Mode	Used to enter commands directly from the the keyboard. This is the dBASE III default mode which displays a period as a prompt symbol. Besides using commands listed in this table, direct mathematical operations may be used. A few are listed as examples. (Module 43)

```
. ? 25+12              && The question mark and expression provides an
                          immediate answer.
37                     && dBASE on-screen response.
. GOTO BOTTOM          && Positions record pointer to last record.
. ? RECNO( )           && What is the current record number?
   29                  && The record number is 29.
. ? ((36+25)/10)*3     && A mathematical expression.
18.3                   && dBASE responds with the answer.
. ? MNUM*25            && Multiplies MNUM by 25.
125                    && dBASE respnds with the answer.
. ?? 10+MNUM           && The double question mark causes the answer to
                          print on the current screen line.
```

Term	Description
Memory Variable	A string, numeric, or logical value that is stored in and recalled from memory. (Module 62)

```
. STORE 25 TO MNUM        && The value 25 is saved to MNUM.
or
. MNUM = 25
```

Term	Description
Numeric Variable	A variable, such as X or MO, which contains a number value.

```
STORE 12 TO MO          && Stores 12 to memory variable MO.
```

Table H-1   Terms and Definitions (Continued)

Term	Description
Record	A collection of information, in one or more fields, about a specific item or person. dBASE records may contain up to 128 fields and 4000 characters. An entire dBASE database file may contain millions of records.
Record Pointer	Indicates the record number within a database that is presently being added, edited, displayed, or deleted. Record numbers indicate the sequential position of a record within a database.
String	A series of characters and spaces. String types are either numeric (numbers), character (letters or a mixture of letters, numbers, punctuation marks, and spaces) or logical (true or false, yes or no). Some examples of strings are:

```
"Bill Edwards" "February" "A-100.X"      Character strings.
"25" "456.05" "12345.67"                 Numeric strings.
"T" "F" "Y" "N"                          Logical strings.
```

Term	Description
String Function	String functions are tools that let you control the way strings are stored or displayed, or that let you determine certain characteristics about them. There are string functions that let you convert numbers to characters, characters to numbers, decimal numbers to whole numbers (called *integers*), determine the number of characters in a string, and so on. Appendix E describes string functions and provides examples.
String Variable	A unique variable, such as NAME or DATE, that is assigned a string value.

```
. STORE '10/21/84' TO MDATE
```

Term	Description
Syntax	The form, spelling, and/or organization of a command. If the syntax is incorrect, an error message is displayed and procedure execution is halted.
Variable	A value, usually the contents of a field within a database record or a memory variable. A variable may be a character string (made up of alphanumeric characters, spaces, and punctuation marks), a numeric value, a mathematical expression (equation), or a logical true or false, yes or no. (A blank in a logical field is the same as false or no.)

Appendix I
dBASE EXERCISES

1. About This Book
    a.   What are two other versions of the dBASE program?
    b.   How might you use examples in this book?
    c.   How many disk drives are needed with dBASE III Plus?
    d.   How much memory is required to operate dBASE III Plus?

2. dBASE III Plus Overview
    a.   Describe a database in your own words.
    b.   Define *record* and *field*.
    c.   Describe the field types used with dBASE III Plus.
    d.   List the following information:

    (1)   Maximum characters within a dBASE III record ________________
    (2)   Maximum fields within a record ________________________
    (3)   Maximum characters within a field ________________________
    (4)   Maximum records within a database ________________________

    e.   What is the CONFIG.SYS file.
    f.   Write a step-by-step procedure for starting the dBASE program.
    g.   How are dBASE commands entered?
    h.   What is a *command file*?
    i.   Prepare a list of the dBASE III Plus editing keys.
    j.   Describe two uses for the dBASE full-screen editor.

3. Recommended Learning Sequence
    a.   What is the advantage of following the *learning sequence*?
    b.   How should the learning sequence be used?
    c.   What is meant by an applications *model*?
    d.   What is the difference between a file saved on disk drive A and disk drive B?

4. ACCEPT, INPUT
    a.   What type of memory variable is created with the ACCEPT command?
    b.   What type of memory variable is created with the INPUT command?
    c.   What three characters are used to enclose displayed prompts?

5. APPEND
    a.   Define the term *APPEND*.
    b.   How is the APPEND function started?
    c.   How is the APPEND function stopped?
    d.   What is accomplished by APPEND BLANK?
    e.   Describe two uses for the APPEND FROM command.

6. ASC( ), CHR( )
    a.   What does the acronym ASCII stand for?
    b.   What does the ASC('n') function return?
    c.   How can the CHR( ) function be used to produce a "beep?"

7. ASSIST
   a. What is the purpose of the ASSIST command?
   b. What is the purpose of the Set Up menu?
   c. What is accomplished with the Create menu?
   d. Name three activities accomplished with the Update menu.
   e. What is the purpose of the Position menu?
   f. Name three activities accomplished with the Retrieve menu.
   g. What does Sort and Index do?

8. AT (@), Positioning Text and Data
   a. Write a working example of the @ row,col SAY command.
   b. What is the difference between @ row,col SAY and @ row,col GET?
   c. How can memory variables be used with the @ function?
   d. How are field and memory variable contents used with the @ row,col command?
   e. What does the SET INTENSITY command do?

9. AVERAGE
   a. What is the purpose of the AVERAGE command?
   b. Write the command to average all QTY fields within the active database.
   c. Write the command that stores the QTY field average to memory variable X.

10. BROWSE
    a. Name three uses of the BROWSE command?
    b. How are new records added to a database when BROWSE is active?
    c. What key sequences are used to move up or down a line (record) at a time?
    d. Write the key sequence used to achieve the following:

       (1) Delete a character ______________________________________
       (2) Insert one or more characters ______________________________
       (3) Mark a record for deletion ________________________________
       (4) Write changes to disk ____________________________________
       (5) Abort changes and return to the dBASE prompt ______________

    e. How can you limit the number of fields browsed?

11. CALL, LOAD
    a. What is the extension of a loaded and called file?
    b. Write the syntax used to load a file.
    c. Write the syntax used to call a file.

12. CANCEL, RETURN
    a. Describe a common function shared by the CANCEL and RETURN commands.
    b. Describe the difference between CANCEL and RETURN.
    c. What happens when neither CANCEL nor RETURN are present as the last line of a command file?
    d. How might RETURN or CANCEL be used within an IF statement?

13. CHANGE
    a. What is the purpose of the CHANGE command?
    b. Why would you use CHANGE instead of BROWSE or EDIT?
    c. Describe the display presentation associated with the CHANGE command.

14. CLEAR ALL, CLEAR TYPEAHEAD
    a. What is meant by *clear state*?
    b. Describe two situations where the CLEAR ALL command might be used.

    c.   What is cleared when CLEAR ALL is typed from the dot prompt?
    d.   What is a *type-ahead buffer*?
    e.   Write the command to set the type-ahead buffer to ten characters.

15.   CLOSE
    a.   When might you use CLOSE?
    b.   List five file types named with the CLOSE command.

16.   COPY
    a.   Define the term *delimiter*.
    b.   What does *SDF* mean and how is it used?
    c.   Write three forms of the COPY command and explain each.
    d.   What is a typical use for the SDF clause?
    e.   What extension is assigned to a file copied with the DELIMITED clause, and how can you view it?
    f.   What is the purpose of the command COPY TO *filename* TYPE WKS?

17.   COUNT
    a.   When COUNT is entered from the keyboard, what is displayed?
    b.   Write three forms of the COUNT command and explain each.
    c.   How might COUNT be used in a command file?

18.   CREATE
    a.   If you type **CREATE newfile** and press **Return**, what is displayed?
    b.   Write the rules that apply to field names.
    c.   Describe the five types of database fields.
    d.   In numeric-type fields, how many places should you include for two decimal characters? Why?
    e.   After the last field is entered, how do you stop the CREATE function? What are your options at this point?

19.   CREATE FROM
    a.   Write the general form of the CREATE FROM command.
    b.   What does an *extended structure* file contain?

20.   CREATE/MODIFY LABEL, LABEL FORM
    a.   What is the purpose of the CREATE or MODIFY LABEL command?
    b.   What is the extension of a label file?
    c.   What helpful guidance is provided?
    d.   How are standard label dimensions automatically displayed?
    e.   Write the LABEL command form to display label outlines.
    f.   Write the LABEL command form to write labels to a disk file.
    g.   Write the LABEL command form to print labels.

21.   CREATE/MODIFY QUERY
    a.   What is a query file?
    b.   What is the extension assigned a query file?
    c.   Describe what is meant by a *filter*?
    d.   How is a query file called into action?

22.   CREATE/MODIFY REPORT, REPORT FORM
    a.   What is the purpose of the CREATE and MODIFY REPORT commands?
    b.   What is the extension of a report file?
    c.   List the menu bar entries.
    d.   Describe the purpose of the Options menu.
    e.   How is a report printed?
    f.   Describe the use of the REPORT FORM command.
    g.   Write a REPORT FORM command that writes a report to a disk file.
    h.   What is the purpose of the PLAIN clause?
    i.   What is the purpose of the NO EJECT clause?

23. CREATE/MODIFY SCREEN
    a. What two file types are produced with the CREATE SCREEN command?
    b. What is contained in a screen file?
    c. What is contained in a format file?
    d. What is another term for *screen painter*?

24. CREATE/MODIFY VIEW
    a. Describe the purpose of a view file.
    b. How can you display a catalog of view files?
    c. What is a fast way to produce a view file once databases, index files, and relations are established?
    d. How is a view file called into use?

25. DATE( ), TIME( )
    a. Describe two uses for the DATE( ) function.
    b. What can you do with the TIME( ) function?
    c. How can you display the system date and time from the dBASE dot prompt?
    d. Write a command line that stores the system date to a memory variable.

26. DELETE, RECALL, PACK
    a. What does the DELETE command do when used with a database file?
    b. How can you verify which records are marked for deletion?
    c. Write four forms of the DELETE command and explain each.
    d. What does the PACK command do?
    e. Describe the use of the RECALL command.
    f. Write four forms of the RECALL command and explain each.
    g. Describe the purpose of the command LIST FOR DELETED( ).

27. DIR
    a. Describe the purpose of the DIR command.
    b. Write the DIR command that displays all database files.
    c. Write the DIR command that displays all .PRG files.

28. DISPLAY, LIST, CLEAR, TYPE, RECNO( )
    a. What is the difference between LIST and DISPLAY?
    b. Write six forms for the DISPLAY command and explain each.
    c. How is the DISPLAY command used to show a list of disk files?
    d. What does the command LIST STRUCTURE do?
    e. Describe the use of the CLEAR command.
    f. Write a command line that makes use of RECNO( ) and describe how it is used.

29. DO
    a. What is the purpose of the DO *filename* command?
    b. Name two places from which the DO command is used.

30. DO CASE, OTHERWISE, ENDCASE
    a. When might you use the DO CASE statement?
    b. Draw a diagram of the DO CASE statement that uses the OTHERWISE command.
    c. Under what circumstances does the OTHERWISE command take effect?

31. DO WHILE, EXIT, LOOP, ENDDO, EOF( )
    a. What is the purpose of a DO WHILE loop?
    b. Draw a diagram of the DO WHILE statement with an embedded IF statement.
    c. Describe the purpose of the LOOP command.
    d. Describe the purpose of the EXIT command.
    e. What is the consequences of a missing or misplaced ENDDO?
    f. What is a *delay loop*? When might you use one?
    g. How might EOF( ) be used with DO WHILE?

32. EDIT
    a. Describe the purpose of the EDIT command.
    b. Write the command lines necessary to edit record numbers 12 through 15 of a database file named STOCK.
    c. Write the EDIT command to restrict editing to the NAME and ADDRESS fields.
    d. Write a list of control keys used with the EDIT command. (**Tip:** Refer to Appendix D.)
    e. How do you abort EDIT without recording changes?
    f. How do you save changes and return to the dBASE dot prompt?

33. EJECT
    a. What does the EJECT command do when encountered in a command file?
    b. How many line feeds are in an inch?
    c. How many line feeds are in the standard 11-inch-long form?

34. ERASE, ZAP
    a. Write an ERASE command to erase a file named REPORT.BAK.
    b. What is an alternative to the ERASE command?
    c. What is the purpose of the ZAP command?
    d. What does dBASE do to prevent you from accidentally zapping a database file?
    e. Can you erase an open file? Explain.

35. EXPORT, IMPORT
    a. What type of files are used with EXPORT and IMPORT?
    b. Write the command form for:

       (1) EXPORT ____
       (2) IMPORT ____

36. FIND, SEEK
    a. What must be done to a database before the FIND or SEEK command is used?
    b. What is the difference between FIND and SEEK?
    c. What is meant by a *key field*?
    d. Describe the purpose of SET EXACT ON.
    e. Write a FIND command and explain what it does.
    f. Write a SEEK command and explain what it does.

37. GET, GET PICTURE, CLEAR GETS, READ
    a. What other statements are frequently used with GET?
    b. Write a command line that displays the contents of the NAME field beginning at row 7, column 20.
    c. If the field contents are to remain unchanged, what statement must follow the above command line.
    d. If the field contents are to be changed, what statement is used on the following command line?

38. GO, GOTO, GO BOTTOM, GO TOP, SKIP
    a. Describe the term *record pointer*.
    b. GO n and GOTO n both position the record pointer to record n. There's another alternative. Describe this third alternative and why you might prefer to use it.
    c. Write the command lines to move down one record, then back three.
    d. Write two command lines that position the record pointer to the last record in the open database and display the record number.
    e. Write three command forms that position the record pointer to the first record in a database.

39. HELP
    a. What is the purpose of the HELP command?
    b. What two ways can HELP information be displayed?
    c. What is the command form for displaying help information about the USE command?

40. **IF, ELSE, ENDIF**
    a. What other commands are similar to the IF, ELSE, ENDIF commands?
    b. Draw a diagram for the IF statement with an embedded ELSE.
    c. What is meant by nesting a statement within a statement? Give an example.
    d. If the expression following IF is false, what happens?
    e. Describe the purpose of the ENDIF statement.
    f. When might you use the ELSE statement?
    g. Describe two typical applications for the IF statement.
    h. What IF statement form does the IIF( ) function emulate?

41. **INDEX, REINDEX**
    a. What filename extension is assigned to an index file?
    b. Write two forms of the INDEX command and explain each.
    c. Describe the purpose of the REINDEX command.
    d. Explain the difference between GO BOTTOM in a database file and in an indexed file.

42. **INSERT, INSERT BEFORE, INSERT BLANK**
    a. Describe the similarity and difference between INSERT and APPEND.
    b. What is the difference between INSERT and INSERT BEFORE?
    c. What does the INSERT BLANK command do?
    d. What is the difference between INSERT and INSERT BLANK?

43. **INTERACTIVE MODE, RECNO( )**
    a. What is another name for *interactive mode*?
    b. Describe how the question mark is used with RECNO( ).
    c. Write the command lines to create a memory variable and then display its contents in the interactive mode?
    d. Write a command line to add the following numbers:

        (1)   25.60
        (2)   34.56
        (3)   -11.73

44. **JOIN**
    a. Describe the purpose of the JOIN command.
    b. Before the JOIN command is used, what is done to the involved databases?
    c. Write five command lines that use two hypothetical databases and JOIN them into a third database.
    d. Describe how the JOIN command is used to restrict combination to certain records within a new database? Write hypothetical command lines to demonstrate this function.

45. **LOCATE, CONTINUE**
    a. Contrast the LOCATE and FIND commands.
    b. What is the purpose of the CONTINUE command?
    c. Write a command line that locates a record containing Smith in the NAME field and Dallas in the CITY field.

46. **MODIFY COMMAND (Developing Command Files)**
    a. What other kinds of files are created with MODIFY COMMAND?
    b. What is assumed by dBASE if no extension name is specified with the MODIFY COMMAND *filename* statement?
    c. List ten control keys used in editing. (**TIP:**   See Appendix D.)
    d. Describe what is meant by *database file structure*.
    e. Describe the term *application structure*.
    f. Describe the use of NOTE lines within a command file.
    g. When a command exceeds the 80-column screen limitation, what can you do to continue the command on the next line?
    h. Describe a "short-cut" for creating a command file when it's similar to one that already exists.

    i.   What are two tools use to test a newly developed command file?

    j.   What does SET DOHISTORY ON to to command file speed?

47.   MODIFY STRUCTURE

    a.   What is the purpose of the MODIFY STRUCTURE command?

    b.   What key sequence is used to insert a new field? (**TIP**: See Appendix D.)

    c.   What key sequence is used to delete a field?

48.   NOTE, ∗, &&

    a.   Describe the purpose of NOTE or ∗ as used in a command file?

    b.   Describe three applications of NOTE or ∗.

    c.   How is && used on a command line?

49.   ON ERROR, ON ESCAPE, ON KEY, INKEY( ), READKEY( )

    a.   List the precedence of the three ON command forms.

    b.   Write a command line that prints 'Hello' when **Esc** is pressed.

    c.   What is the purpose of the ON ERROR command?

    d.   What is the purpose of the ON KEY command?

    e.   Describe the purpose of the INKEY( ) function.

    f.   How can you tell from a READKEY( ) function code whether a record has been updated or not?

50.   PARAMETERS

    a.   What is the purpose of the PARAMETERS command?

    b.   Write a sample command file containing the PARAMETERS command.

51.   Print Statement (?)

    a.   What is meant by the term *print statement*?

    b.   What characters surround displayed text?

    c.   Write the command line that would display the following prompt.

               Don't press the "ESC" key.

    d.   Write a hypothetical command line that displays text and the contents of the memory variable MX.

52.   PRIVATE, PUBLIC

    a.   Describe a PRIVATE memory variable.

    b.   Describe a PUBLIC memory variable.

    c.   Can a memory variable name be used more than once? Explain.

    d.   What happens to memory variables created within a command file when the command file is closed?

53.   PROCEDURE

    a.   What is a PROCEDURE command file?

    b.   What is in the first line of a PROCEDURE command file?

    c.   How is a PROCEDURE command file designated for use?

54.   QUIT

    a.   Describe the purpose of the QUIT command.

    b.   Describe two ways in which the QUIT command is entered.

55.   RENAME

    a.   Describe the purpose of the RENAME command.

    b.   Write a command line that renames STORE.DBF to WAREHOUS.DBF.

    c.   Write the command line to list all files on the disk in drive B.

56.   REPLACE

    a.   Describe the purpose of the REPLACE command.

    b.   Write three different forms of the REPLACE command and explain each.

57. RUN
 a. What is the purpose of the RUN command?
 b. What are some memory considerations before using RUN?
 c. Write the command line that runs the DOS DIR command.

58. SAY, SAY GET, SAY PICTURE, CLEAR GETS, READ
 a. What other statements are frequently used with SAY?
 b. Write a command line that uses the SAY statement to display a prompt beginning at row 5, column 10.
 c. Describe the purpose of the PICTURE clause.
 d. Write a command line that displays a seven-character, two-decimal place numeric field as dollars and cents.

59. SELECT, SET RELATION
 a. Describe the use of the SELECT command.
 b. How many work areas can be open at the same time?
 c. What is the purpose of the BUFFERS and FILES commands in the CONFIG.SYS file?
 d. What is an alias?
 e. When moving from one database to another, what happens to the position of the record pointers in the original database?
 f. How is a relation established between two databases?
 g. Describe the command LIST NAME, A->PAYCODE.

60. SET Functions
 a. In general, what do SET functions control?
 b. How can you determine the current status of SET functions?
 c. Describe the use of the following SET functions:

 (1) SET TALK OFF/ON
 (2) SET INTENSITY ON/OFF
 (3) SET ALTERNATE TO *filename*, SET ALTERNATE ON
 (4) SET DOHISTORY ON/OFF

61. SORT
 a. Write the command line for sorting a database in numerical order on the ZIP□CODE field.
 b. Write the command line for sorting a database in descending alphabetical order on the NAME field.
 c. Write the command form for sorting two fields at the same time.
 d. Write the command form for sorting on a specific set of records.

62. STORE, RELEASE, SAVE, RESTORE
 a. What is a memory variable and why might you use one?
 b. How many memory variables can be active at one time?
 c. How many characters (or bytes) are available for memory variables?
 d. How many characters can a string memory variable contain?
 e. How many significant digits are in a numeric memory variable?
 f. Write the command line that displays all active memory variables.
 g. Write the command line that deletes the memory variable MNUM.
 h. How may memory variables be saved to a disk file?
 i. How can memory variables be restored from the disk file to memory?
 j. What clause is used to prevent overwriting active memory variables when a memory variable file is restored from disk?

63. SUM
 a. Describe the function of the SUM command.
 b. Write four forms of the SUM command.

64. SUSPEND, RESUME
    a. What can you do with the SUSPEND and RESUME commands?
    b. What happens when you press **Esc** during command file operation?
    c. How can you restart the command file?
    d. Why might you use SUSPEND within a command file?

65. TEXT, ENDTEXT
    a. What is the purpose of the TEXT and ENDTEXT statements?
    b. Describe a common use of the TEXT and ENDTEXT statements.

66. TOTAL
    a. What does TOTAL doe with the sum of matching fields?
    b. Write three forms of the TOTAL command.
    c. What is done to involved databases before the TOTAL command is used?

67. TYPE
    a. What is the purpose of the TYPE command?
    b. What kind of files are displayed with TYPE?

68. UPDATE
    a. What is the purpose of the UPDATE command?
    b. What must be done before the UPDATE command can be used?
    c. Write three forms of the UPDATE command and explain each.

69. USE
    a. What is meant by opening and closing a database file?
    b. What happens if you issue a database command with no database in use?
    c. Write the command line for opening the MEMBERS database file.
    d. Describe four ways in which a database file is closed.
    e. Write a command line that assignes an alias name to the ADDRESS database.
    f. Write a command line that opens the ADDRESSS database and its index file having the filename CITIES.NDX.

70. WAIT
    a. What is the difference between WAIT and WAIT TO?
    b. What is displayed when either of these commands are encountered in a command file?
    c. Why might you want to pause command file operation?
    d. What happens if you press the **Esc** key in response to the "Press any key to continue. .." prompt?
    e. Describe a typical application for the WAIT TO command.
    f. Write the command form to suppress the display of a prompt.